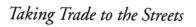

Taking Trade to the Streets

Taking Trade to the Streets

The Lost History of Public Efforts to Shape Globalization

Susan Ariel Aaronson

With Forewords by
Pat Choate *and* I. M. Destler

Ann Arbor

THE UNIVERSITY OF MICHIGAN PRESS

Copyright © by the University of Michigan 2001

All rights reserved

Published in the United States of America by

The University of Michigan Press

Manufactured in the United States of America

♾ Printed on acid-free paper

2004   2003   2002   2001   4   3   2   1

A CIP catalog record for this book is available from the British library.

Library of Congress Cataloging-in-Publication Data

Aaronson, Susan A.

    Taking trade to the streets : the lost history of public efforts to shape globalization /
Susan Ariel Aaronson ; with forewords by Pat Choate and I.M. Destler.

       p.   cm.

    Includes bibliographical references and index.

    ISBN 0-472-11212-0 (cloth : alk. paper)

    1. Free trade.   2. Foreign trade regulation.   3. Canada. Treaties, etc. 1992 Oct. 7.
4. General Agreement on Tariffs and Trade (Organization)   5. World Trade Organization.
6. Globalization.   7. Free Trade—United States.   8. United States—Commercial policy.
I. Title.

HF1713 .A15   2001

382—dc21   2001027049

382
A 113

Contents

Foreword

ONE OF THE IRONIES surrounding most contemporary policy debates is the reportage seems to concentrate more on personalities and tactics than on the substance of the issue. Consequently, the effects of any policy shifts increasingly seem to come as a surprise to the general public, and, when noticed, are too often viewed as isolated events rather than as part of larger structural change.

Certainly, the ongoing debates and changes in U.S. trade policy fit this description. For example, the fights to ratify the North American Free Trade Agreement (NAFTA) and the Uruguay GATT Agreement were largely portrayed at the time as a battle between the forces of good and bad. The forces of good were the free traders, led by newly elected President Bill Clinton. The bad were the protectionists, led by a coalition of national figures that included Ralph Nader, Patrick Buchanan, Jerry Brown, and Ross Perot—what White House spinners called the Halloween Coalition.

Of course, much can be lost in such radical simplification, and it was. Most important, the longer-term dimensions of the underlying structural shift—what has come to be known as globalization—tend to be unanalyzed with vital parts unnoticed. And often the result is costly indeed; for example, the $100 billion bailout of the Mexican economy in the mid-1990s, the ongoing loss of key sectors of the U.S. economy such as steel and textiles, and the recurring need for public bailouts of U.S. banks, to name only three.

Yet even where debate and discussion do occur, even between economists and scholars, epigrams and cliches dominate. In a perverse sense, those who study the topic the most seem trapped the deepest in the ideology and techniques they acquired in their early academic training. Perhaps this educated incapacity is normal. After all, the Marxist economists in the Soviet Union and East Germany were offering their orthodoxy even as those economies and societies were falling apart.

But for the interested lay person and public officials, this debate via epigrams produces more confusion than information. Most economists, for instance, argue that a large and growing portion of finance, commerce, and communication is increasingly unaffected by national borders. That is true. But the implication is that somehow the world is headed to a homogenized economy. That is not true. The differences between nations, their cultures, and their institutions are real and often so fundamental as to be insurmountable without a dangerous political revolution.

In the 1990s, a clever attempt was made to reconcile that paradox of economic globalization versus national differences. The resultant creation was the World Trade Organization (WTO)—a new international body that provides a forum for the negotiation of global trade rules, their administration, and their final judicial review. The creators of the WTO also endowed the organization with the authority to confront the domestic policies, practices, and regulations of member nations that might affect trade. With this, a new era of global regulation was born.

Brought into being in 1995 and located in Geneva, Switzerland, the WTO is at a nascent stage where its powers are only partially defined.

At a time when dozens of homeless transnational corporations with annual sales greater than the gross domestic products of all but a handful of nations are essentially unregulated, perhaps a strong, global regulatory body is necessary. The primary need for such a body may be more to ensure that these corporations act responsibly in their global activities than to protect the parochial economic interests of any single country. But that debate awaits.

In *Taking Trade to the Streets: The Lost History of Public Efforts to Shape Globalization*, Susan Aaronson provides a clear, cogent, thoughtful context for that discussion.

As she discusses in her early chapters, the political fight over terms of trade is as American as apple pie. It stretches from the Boston Tea Party—when American colonials dumped British tea into the harbor to protest English import taxes—to today's street demonstrations against the World Trade Organization.

Susan Aaronson tackles the clichéd nature of the current debate, using as a starting point the late Governor Adlai E. Stevenson's observation that trade policy is "one field where the greatest need is for fresh clichés." Then, she goes behind the labels of "free trade" and "protectionism" to describe the substantive, multilayered positions of the various participants; most notably those involved in the NAFTA and WTO ratification battles of the 1990s. It is a good history, presented in crisp writing that moves along, providing a factual overview that is understandable to the lay reader.

The publication of this book is timely, coming at the end of the Clinton administration and the beginning of George W. Bush's. The era of vast trade negotiations between nations that characterized the Clinton years may well be over. The WTO has been created to shepherd that process for the future. Those future negotiations are likely to be less seismic than what came during the 1990s.

Rather, the big changes that await are likely to be those of a regulatory nature, as the author points out. Already the power of nations to set their own rules is being challenged by the WTO. Further, the WTO may well have the mandate to regulate global business, something that none of its individual members seems able to do effectively. Inevitably, demands will be made on that body to perform that function. And if that road is taken, the world enters an entirely new and uncharted phase of globalization.

With *Taking Trade to the Streets*, Susan Aaronson makes a major contribution to the understanding of where the United States, indeed the world, is in this heretofore largely undocumented evolution.

Pat Choate
Economist and Author,
Director, Manufacturing Policy Project,
Washington, D.C.

Foreword

FOR TWO-THIRDS OF a century now, the United States has pursued a policy of reducing barriers to international trade. In the FDR years, we did so by negotiating bilateral deals with our principal trading partners. With the signing of the General Agreement on Tariffs and Trade (GATT) in the late 1940s, the means shifted to multilateral negotiations—first primarily with Europeans, but increasingly with nations around the globe. But the basic structure of bargaining remained—we sought reductions in foreign barriers to our products, and lowered our own trade barriers in exchange. Social issues—labor practices, environmental policies, human rights—were largely excluded from the discussion.

Trade negotiators and their business constituents came to regard this as the natural state of affairs. GATT talks were dominated by trade professionals, who sought concessions of the greatest commercial value to their nations' producers. And the negotiating efficacy of such a focus seemed undeniable: It resulted in the reduction of import barriers to a fraction of former levels and an explosion of global commerce. But as Susan Aaronson tells us, there has always been controversy about trade's social impact. With the rapid growth of that trade—not just in absolute terms, but as a share of the American economy—it is hardly surprising that social concerns should grow as well.

Moreover, today's debate over the impact of globalization parallels that over a nationalizing U.S. economy that became heated a century ago. Historians like my father[1] told how the excesses of late-nineteenth-century American capitalism gave rise to a robust reform movement, and how over the decades that movement led to a social compact that seeks to maintain the benefits of free markets while protecting other widely shared societal values.

---

[1]   See Chester McArthur Destler, *American Radicalism 1865–1901* (New London, Connecticut College, 1946; Quadrangle Books, 1966).

International trade affects these values. Its expansion seems, to many eyes, to undermine economic security and threaten the social compact. It is therefore substantively rational that critics seek international accords to protect and reinforce labor and environmental standards. It is politically rational that they seek the leverage of ongoing trade negotiations, under the auspices of the World Trade Organization, to advance this cause. The result, however, has been to throw the trade establishment into disarray, and to replace the longstanding American liberal-trade consensus with a political stalemate.

Because she is a historian, Susan Aaronson recognizes that these issues have ample precedent. And just as the business community had to accept New Deal regulation in the 1930s and the consumer and environmental legislation of the 1960s and 1970s, the trade community must help fashion constructive responses to today's social concerns. Aaronson's book helps us find ways to do so.

I. M. Destler
University of Maryland, College Park,
and the Institute for International Economics

Preface

AT FIRST GLANCE, the December 16, 1773, meeting in Old South Church in Boston and the November 26, 1999, teach-in in Seattle's Benaroya Symphony Hall have little in common. More than five thousand colonists, about a third of Boston's population, crowded into Old South Church. About half that number crowded into the twenty-five-hundred-seat Symphony Hall. The participants at both meetings focused on trade. The colonists wanted to shape the mother country's policies to increase trade, while most attendees at the teach-in focused on the costs of trade and globalization. The colonists learned of the December meeting through pamphlets, posters, and by word of mouth; the trade agreement critics who packed Symphony Hall learned about the meeting through the Internet, the press, E-mail, and by mailed invitations. Moreover, citizens around the wired world could watch the proceedings through the modern miracle of Web-casting.

The colonists argued over what to do about three ships carrying tea from the East Indies. They liked their tea—it had long been an important component of the Anglo-American diet. But in 1773, the British Parliament passed an act designed to save the East India Company from bankruptcy. The law required duties to be paid on the tea and returned to the company. It was one of a series of taxes that were placed on and then removed from the colonists. The colonists resented the tax as unfair as well as resented their lack of control over the home country's policies.

The colonists were deeply divided as to what to do about Britain's trade policies. While some colonists said that Governor Thomas Hutchinson should send the tea back to England, others worried about confronting the British. Still others in the back of the room hinted at a more aggressive strategy. They warned that sometime soon, the "Mohawks" (colonists disguised as Indians) would come and make Boston Harbor smell like, look like, and taste like a teapot. In their view, this violent strategy of harbor and street protests were necessary because Britain had undermined the colonists' democratic rights by empowering one corporation at the expense of the colonists.

The individuals who came to the December 1999 teach-in, in contrast, did not come from one city or nation. They came from India, Canada, Malaysia, Thailand, Chile, the Philippines, the United States, and even Great Britain. Almost all the speakers noted that globalization, which they described as "corporate-led" and directed, had hurt the planet, undermined democratically elected governments, and had a regressive effect on human rights and workers' rights. They condemned the policies of national governments and international organizations such as the World Trade Organization (WTO), the World Bank, and the International Monetary Fund. Most of the participants thought nonviolent street protests were an appropriate strategy to deal with such instruments of corporate-led globalization.

Although miles of distance, new technologies, and 226 years separated the two meetings, the participants in both meetings tackled the same topic—how trade and globalization affected other important policy goals—whether democracy, sovereignty, protecting the environment, promoting human rights, or encouraging equitable economic growth. I believe a review of the history of that debate may provide scholars with additional insights into how the public, in concert with policymakers, may best govern the global economy.

This book highlights the "lost" history of citizen attempts to influence how globalization is regulated—whether through trade agreements or other regulatory policies. This history is not really lost, but it seems to have been forgotten by policymakers and even the activists themselves. Thus, this book reminds us that this debate was central to the drafting of the U.S. Constitution, the development of a national economy in the late nineteenth century, and even the development of the global system of rules that govern trade and investment.

I will show that except for biotechnology, little that is new has emerged in the debate over globalization. *Globalization* can be defined as the growing social, political, and economic integration of the United States with other nations in the world. The United States is increasingly linked to other nations because of deliberate policy choices (such as trade and investment liberalization) and technological changes (whether satellites, the Internet, refrigeration, or supersonic jets) that bridge distance and time. Every day Americans see evidence of globalization, whether our headlines blare the spread of West Nile Virus (new to the North American continent) or the new German American multinational, the Daimler Chrysler company. I focus, in particular, on trade and describe how so many citizens have come to see trade agreements (and trade policy) as threatening national systems of social and environmental regulations—the so-called social compact. Using the United States as a case study, I examine the history of *trade agreement critics,* focusing particular attention on the North American Free Trade Agreement (NAFTA) between Canada, Mexico, and the United States and the Tokyo and Uruguay Rounds of trade liberalization under the General Agreement on Tariffs and Trade (GATT).

Trade agreements regulate how nations may trade and how they may protect their citizens, consumers and producers. They regulate tools of protection, such as tariffs or exchange controls. But beginning in 1974, with the Tokyo Round, they also began to regulate the use of nontariff barriers (NTBs) such as subsidies and national procurement and health and regulatory standards, which can also distort market conditions among domestic and foreign producers. This expanding purview of trade agreements has led critics to argue that trade agreements are deregulatory. But in their criticism, they also seem to be saying that trade agreements don't regulate effectively or don't regulate enough.

The colonists argued that the British Parliament was willing to tax its colonists to restore the British East India company to health. Many trade critics today argue that trade agreements such as the WTO have transferred power from the people to global corporations. Yet these same critics have devoted little attention to providing incentives and disincentives to ensure that global corporations behave responsibly as they produce goods and services around the world.

THIS BOOK MIGHT have taken 226 years if I did not have a patient family. I am so grateful to my husband, Doug Wham; my parents, Professors Shirley and Sheldon Aaronson; and my dear friend Professor Bill Becker, who helped me write and improve each draft. Many activists and scholars helped make this a better book: They include Atsuko Abe, Eugene Gholz, Steve Clemons, Ellen Frost, Dan Gardner, Tome Zeiler, Al Eckes, Mark Ritchie, Kimberly Ann Elliot, Steve Charnovitz, Bob Litan, Amy Porges, I. M. Destler, Debbie Lamb, Mira Wilkins, Ambassador Anthony Quainton, Ambassador J. Robert Schaetzel, Lori Wallach, Valerie Plompis, and my generous colleagues at the University of North Texas, George Mason University, the Brookings Institution, and the National Policy Association. I am grateful to Lance Lindblom, formerly of the Ford Foundation; Bernard Wasow, formerly of the Ford Foundation and now with the Century

Foundation; and Peter Weitz, formerly of the German Marshall Fund. Peter died as I revised this book; I miss him.

I am forever indebted to Pat Choate and Mac Destler—two men who have had a major impact on trade policy. Their views are much discussed in this book, and they both were kind to contribute forewords to this book.

Reporters Nancy Dunne, Paul Magnusson, and Alan Freedman provided valuable feedback on my conclusions. Greg Allen of National Public Radio helped me discover how to explain this lost history in ninety-second radio spots. I had the world's best editor, Ellen McCarthy, who was such a faithful believer in this book and a true friend. But I dedicate it to Allegra Ann Wham and Ethan Aaron Wham.

Susan Ariel Aaronson

Acronyms

AFL-CIO	American Federation of Labor and Congress of Industrial Organizations; the nation's largest labor organization
FTA	Canada/United States Free Trade Agreement
GAO	General Accounting Office
GATT	General Agreement on Tariffs and Trade
GPO	U.S. Government Printing Office
IATP	Institute for Agriculture and Trade Policy
ITC	International Trade Commission
MFN	most favored nation (normal trade privileges)
NGOs	nongovernmental organizations
NTBs	nontariff barriers such as procurement regulations and health and safety standards
RTAA	Reciprocal Trade Agreements Act of 1934
S&P	sanitary (relating to humans) and phytosanitary (relating to plants) regulations
TBT	Tokyo Round code relating to technical barriers to trade
USTR	U.S. Trade Representative
WTO	World Trade Organization

Glossary

comparative advantage   production of items in which a country's or company's relative efficiency is greatest compared with other countries or companies. A firm or country should concentrate production on items in which it has the greatest relative efficiency.

production standards   rules governing what is produced, affecting the design, physical characteristics, or safety of a product or service.

process standards   rules governing how goods are produced.

social compact   the norms that shape and constrain the domestic environment in which goods and services are produced.

unfair traders   countries that don't play by the shared rules governing trade.

CHAPTER I

How Trade Agreement Critics Redefined the Terms of Trade

ON NOVEMBER 30, 1999, some five thousand delegates from more than 135 nations traveled to Seattle, Washington. They met to discuss whether or not to launch a new round of trade talks under the aegis of the World Trade Organization (WTO). Despite the many pleasures of Seattle, most of the delegates did not enjoy their stay. The official talks were eclipsed by a week of street protests and sporadic violence, as vandals smashed the storefront windows of Nike, Starbucks, and McDonald's.[1]

In the United States and around the world, the protests became front page news. Reporters struggled to describe who these trade agreement critics were and why so many had taken to the streets. They found that the protesters came from all over the world and presented a wide range of political views. Nationalists such as Pat Buchanan of the United States and Maude Barlow of Canada argued that the WTO took power from democratically elected governments. Greens from around the world condemned the WTO for elevating trade objectives over environmental goals. Union leaders and human rights advocates criticized the WTO and other trade agreements for protecting property rights but ignoring worker rights.[2] Despite their diverse concerns, these trade agreement critics issued a common message—that globalization threatened national consumer, environmental, health, and worker regulations. Moreover, almost all the protesters argued that the WTO and other trade agreements were part of the problem, rather than central to the solution of regulating globalization. They condemned the WTO for transferring power from the people to global corporations.[3]

Most trade liberalization advocates were dismayed by the protests and unsure as to what to do about them. President William Jefferson Clinton said he shared the protesters' concerns about the WTO's lack of transparency and that he would continue to work to make the world trading system more equitable.[4] The director general of the WTO, Michael Moore, described the ministerial as a "disappointment."[5] The *Financial Times* characterized the Seattle Ministerial as a "disaster" and a "wake-up call."[6] But other observers took a less sanguine view; they described the protesters as "protectionists" who simply wanted to impede trade. Many economists, business leaders, and developing country officials alleged that trade agreement critics were using their concern for the environment or human rights as a smoke screen for their true intent, to protect domestic producers. After all, in their view, social and environmental issues are not "trade" issues, but rather national issues to be settled within WTO member nations.[7]

Policymakers, as well as many of the reporters and analysts covering the events in Seattle, forgot that the Seattle protests were not the first time that trade policy was made in the streets. In 1773, some sixty colonists, including five masons, eleven carpenters, twelve apprentices, and two doctors, traveled to Boston Harbor. Dressed as Indians, the colonists dumped British tea into the Boston harbor to protest British tea tariffs. But the Boston Tea Party did not improve trade relations between the colonists and the mother country. In 1774, Britain passed the Intolerable Acts, which provided for the quartering of troops in Boston, and closed the port. The colonists were so infuriated that delegates to the First Continental Congress voted not to trade with England until it changed its trade policies. Some thirty years later, abolitionists living in the newly independent United States and antislavery activists in Great Britain marched to protest the legal importation of slaves. These protests had a more positive impact. After several years of such protests, in 1807, the United States and Great Britain banned trade in slaves.[8]

Ironically, in recent years, the press has barely covered street protests against trade agreements such as the General Agreement on Tariffs and Trade (GATT) or the North American Free Trade Agreement (NAFTA). During the Uruguay Round, farmers protested in Geneva, headquarters of the GATT, as well as in Strasbourg, home of the European parliament. In 1992, while policymakers negotiated NAFTA, demonstrators protested the secret negotiating process.

Moreover, in May 1998 massive street protests in Geneva presaged the Seattle protests. Inside the grand palace housing the WTO, proponents of trade agreements celebrated fifty years of trade liberalization. Speakers from around the world argued that world trade has grown sixteenfold since 1950, because of the GATT's rules. They noted that the people of the world have benefited from that trade with more and cheaper goods as well as a better quality of life. Outside that grand palace, however, some ten thousand protesters disagreed. While some individuals quietly protested, others threw rocks and overturned cars.[9]

The 1773 protests in Boston Harbor, the 1998 protests in Geneva, and the 1999 protests in Seattle are part of a long-standing debate over what trade rules should cover and how such rules should affect other important national priorities such as protecting consumers or the environment. The public has long attempted to shape globalization—yet that history has not come to the fore. This book attempts to change that misperception by describing how so many individuals and non-governmental organizations have come to see trade agreements as threatening national systems of social and environmental regulations. Using the United States as a case study, I examine the history of trade agreement critics, focusing particular attention on NAFTA (the agreement between Canada, Mexico, and the United States) and the Tokyo and Uruguay Rounds of trade liberalization under the GATT. I also focus on whether such trade agreement critics are truly protectionist.

Trade agreements are internationally agreed upon regulations that govern the use of trade barriers. These agreements regulate how entities may trade and how nations may use protectionist tools.[10] Until the 1980s, most trade agreements regulated the use of traditional tools of protection—border measures such as tariffs and quotas. But policymakers recognized that domestic regulations, such as health and safety regulations, can, with or without intent, also distort trade.[11] Thus, they worked to include rules governing such regulations in the purview of the GATT and other trade agreements.

Trade agreement critics first began to focus on the threat of trade agreements to national systems of regulations in the 1980s, during an unusual confluence of events. The U.S. economy grew slowly during much of this period. Some citizens attributed America's slow growth to the nation's massive trade and budget deficits. The Reagan and Bush administrations reduced federal spending, including services to the working poor. They also attempted to deregulate key economic sectors and reduce the regulatory burden upon business. In 1991, the United States agreed to expand its free trade agreement with Canada to Mexico. Policymakers planned to create a continent-wide free trade area called NAFTA.[12] NAFTA was controversial because Mexico had very different social norms and systems of governance. Thus, while these policy developments were not part of a coordinated strategy to undermine the social compact, some individuals and groups concerned with the environment, human rights, and labor standards, for example, saw them as a deliberate challenge to U.S. norms.

Activists began to pay greater attention to other trade agreements in the 1990s. Their concerns grew as they looked at GATT in action, mediating trade disputes and serving as a forum for trade negotiations. Working with citizen activists in Canada, environmentalists and social activists in Public Citizen and other groups organized to preserve their influence over national systems of regulation. They also tried to hamper the progress of trade talks.[13]

This book also focuses on how trade agreement critics have built a fluid global movement to redefine the "terms" of trade agreements (the international system of rules governing trade) and to change how citizens talk about trade.[14] (The terms of trade is a relationship between the prices of exports and the prices of imports. This is a pun on how we talk about trade.) That movement, which has been growing since the 1980s, transcends borders as well as long-standing views about the role of government in the economy. While many trade agreement critics on the left say they want government policies to make markets more equitable, they are tactically allied with activists on the right who generally want to reduce the role of government in the economy.

This association of left and right is perhaps best illustrated by the working alliance among two key trade agreement critics in the United States, Ralph Nader (the noted consumer activist) and Pat Buchanan (the self-proclaimed "conservative of the heart").[15] Nader believes consumers must be citizen activists, always vigilant of business and government. Patrick J. Buchanan, in contrast, sees himself as a supporter of capitalism and a critic of big government. However, the two have found common ground in their belief that capitalism should serve the nation and not make the nation subservient to multinational corporations. Both men see the WTO as captured by such multinational business. They also agree as to how to remedy this problem. Both Nader and Buchanan want the United States to drop out of the WTO.[16]

Nader and Buchanan are not the only prominent American individuals or groups critical of trade agreements. The chorus of trade agreement critics includes the Rainbow Coalition, a nongovernmental organization concerned with racial equality issues; environmental groups such as the Sierra Club; and activist groups from the left (Greenpeace) and right (Phyllis Schlafly's Eagle Forum).[17] Prominent trade agreement opponents on the left include former California Governor Jerry Brown and former Texas Agriculture Commissioner Jim Hightower.[18] On the more rightward side of the spectrum, H. Ross

Perot (a data-processing billionaire) and Roger Milliken (a wealthy textile manufacturer and long-standing protectionist) have been willing to use their considerable wealth to educate their fellow Americans about the "costs" of trade and trade agreements.[19]

Such left-right coalitions are not new to the trade debate, nor unique to the United States.[20] In Great Britain, millionaire businessman Sir James Goldsmith worked with small farmers and environmentalists to argue for a return to more local and ecological trade.[21] In France and other parts of Europe, nationalists and farmers collaborated to form an anti-GATT movement.[22] In India, environmentalists, nationalists, and farmers joined to protest GATT rules on agriculture and intellectual property.[23]

Left-right coalitions, however, have not appeared in all democracies. For example, in Canada, concern about trade agreements has seemed exclusive to the left. This may be because many Canadians on the right see trade as a way to make Canada more like the United States—less interventionist.[24] In Australia, concerns about trade and immigration have been dominated by right-wing nationalists such as Pauline Hanson.[25]

While these left-right coalitions in the United States (and abroad) all sought to *hamper* trade agreements, they did not seek to *protect* the same interests. Buchanan and Milliken, as example, want to protect American jobs, American business, and American sovereignty. Nader, Brown, and Hightower of the United States and Barlow of Canada, in contrast, want to protect their ability to influence a democratically determined system of social regulation. Thus, while these trade agreement critics shared a strategy, they have not always shared objectives. They have different *goals and constituencies to protect.*

Trade Agreement Critics: 1996 Examples

In the U.S.
> Public Citizen
> Friends of the Earth
> U.S. Business and Industrial Council

In Canada
> Council on Canadians
> Canadian Environmental Law Association

In Europe
> Oxfam
> Friends of the Earth
> Transnational Institute

In Asia
  GATT Watchdog (New Zealand)
  Third World Network (Malaysia)

Source: Institute for Trade and Sustainable Development and
  www.onelist.com (anti-WTO list serve)

Some of these trade agreement critics proudly describe themselves as "new protectionists" in an attempt to differentiate their social and environmental objectives from the economic objectives of traditional protectionists. For example, many European Greens (an environmentalist political party) want capitalism to be as limited and as local as possible. They criticize global capitalism (and capitalism per se) because it has undermined the global commons in the interest of promoting economic growth.[26] In contrast, many other trade critics clearly state they do not want to impede trade, but rather to reconcile trade rules with national regulatory rules. They criticize capitalism at the margins.

Moreover, many of these trade agreement critics do not act like the protectionists in our history books who worked at the national level to ensure that policies redounded to the benefit of citizens or particular sectors. They have built an international coalition by relying on new technologies such as E-mail and the World Wide Web, and old techniques such as international meetings, teach-ins, and strategy sessions.[27] This internationalization does not mean that these individuals and groups are not protectionist. Nevertheless, until the 1980s it was unusual for protectionists to work internationally to protect national economic interests. According to Lori Wallach, who has been a key strategist and lobbyist for Public Citizen, the movement is composed of *internationalists/nationalists.* They work in tandem with foreign interest groups and governments to advance their positions (which may be in opposition to the official U.S. position) at home and abroad.[28] They have made common cause with citizens from other nations in the interest of battling the global free market. These activists agree that trade agreements can undermine democracy, government accountability, and important regulations. They disagree, however, about how to empower workers, communities, and activists around the world while encouraging economic growth, democratization, and technological change.

By transcending borders and by changing the content of the trade debate, these trade agreement critics of the left and right force us to rethink the free trade/protectionist paradigm for debating trade. For example, labor rights advocates want to grow the GATT/WTO system to include rules governing how workers are treated as they make goods and services.

In essence, these trade agreement critics want *to regulate (and enforce) the use of domestic regulations internationally through trade agreements.*

However, most trade agreement critics such as environmentalists and consumer advocates *want to ensure that trade agreements do not serve as barriers to domestic regulation* or make such regulation ineffective.[29] They fear that in today's integrated global economy, nations will compete to liberalize their markets by lowering their national regulatory standards or by inadequately enforcing these standards. They presume that stricter regulatory standards represent a source of competitive disadvantage. However, trade agreements may preserve or even raise national regulatory standards. According to political scientist David Vogel, "the impact of trade liberalization on regulatory standards is primarily dependent on the preferences of wealthy, powerful states, and the degree of economic integration among them and their trading partners. . . . Trade liberalization is most likely to strengthen consumer and environmental protection when a group of nations has agreed to reduce the role of regulations as trade barriers and the most powerful among them has influential domestic constituencies that support stronger regulatory standards."[30] Interestingly, many free traders fear that including domestic regulations in the world trading system could interfere with the efficiency of global markets and overload the current system of trade regulation. In essence, like the trade agreement critics, these free traders are arguing that including national standards within the trading system will lead to ineffective regulation.

Clearly, when we talk about trade today, we are talking about regulation. Regulations have important macroeconomic consequences; they can affect productivity, investment levels, prices, and other important economic factors. They can also change microeconomic conditions. Regulations may make some firms better off; others worse off. Many trade agreement critics call these differences in regulation "unfair." Yet nations trade because of their differences, whether those differences reflect government's role in the economy, natural resource allocation, or technological expertise. A free trade/protectionist paradigm does not accurately describe such trade issues. Why then, do so many observers label trade agreement critics protectionists?

WHAT IS PROTECTIONISM
AND WHO REALLY ARE PROTECTIONISTS?

Protectionism is difficult to describe because it is both an ideology and a government act. Protectionists generally believe that government should intervene to ensure that domestic producers dominate the domestic market. However, when government uses protectionist tools, it is changing market conditions. By sheltering domestic producers, these trade interventions distort the prices faced by domestic producers and consumers away from those arising in the world market.[31]

Freer traders, in contrast, believe markets work best without government interference. Under freer trade policies, governments do not use tax or regulatory policies to discriminate between foreign and domestic producers. They remain neutral in the market competition between foreign and domestic producers. However, most freer traders recognize that free trade policies are an ideal. There are many circumstances (such as an election) and reasons (such as to promote national security) why governments may want to protect certain sectors from foreign competition. If these governments determine they must protect certain sectors or workers, economists recommend that policymakers subsidize these sectors with tailored domestic policy tools. Economists also suggest that if policymakers must use trade policy to protect domestic constituents, they should use tariffs and limit the duration of such protection.

Almost all economists believe that freer trade policies are better economic policies than protectionist policies. Freer trade policies increase economic welfare to both producers and consumers (the general interest), although some interest groups may be hurt by foreign competition.[32] However, the general public does not always concur.

In 1996, the Kaiser Family Foundation, the *Washington Post,* and Harvard University cosponsored a study assessing differences in how the general public, untrained in economics, and those trained in economics see economic policy. One does not need formal training in economics to be a rational economic actor. But the study found that those untrained in economics see the world differently than do those trained in economics. Many Americans may characterize the different behavior of other nations as unfair, simply because it is different. Those trained in economics, in contrast, recognize nations have different political and economic cultures. Moreover, citizens untrained in economics tend to look at an event or trend in isolation, while those trained in economics can weigh economic costs and benefits to the economy as a whole, as well as to specific sectors. These differences in perspective have important implications both for how citizens view trade policy and for how policymakers act.[33]

One's views about trade influence how people talk about trade. Where economists almost always make the case for freer trade by arguing that it increases economic efficiency, they rarely make a case for

freer trade based on equity to the bulk of citizens. However, both protectionists and many of today's trade agreement critics almost always
make a case for protection based on equity arguments. These arguments may be easier for voters to relate to.

This mixed context of ideas and perceptions constrains policymakers. Policymakers must attempt to balance a wide range of policy
goals other than increasing economic welfare, including appeasing
important constituents or maintaining certain sectors of the economy.
Most policymakers recognize the benefits of freer trade ideas, but these
ideas may not always be politically palatable. At the same time, protection has certain attractions to policymakers. For example, policymakers
can use tariffs to assist certain sectors, without directly increasing the
costs to taxpayers.

In 1982, the Office of the United States Trade Representative
(USTR), which develops and negotiates U.S. trade agreements, wrote a
primer for the public on trade. *A Preface to Trade* defined protectionism
as "the setting of trade barriers high enough to discourage foreign
imports or to raise their prices sufficiently to enable relatively inefficient domestic producers to compete successfully with foreigners."[34]
These barriers "protect" domestic producers from lower-priced foreign
goods (although some domestic producers need imported components
to remain competitive). Under this definition, protectionism is an economic and political act. Protectionists tend to be individuals directly
concerned with protecting their economic interests: industries or communities hurt by imports.

This definition may help us understand why steel industry workers
may call for protection, but not why so many environmentalists,
human rights advocates, and church leaders criticize trade agreements.[35] It certainly cannot explain why so many people took to the
streets of Seattle and Geneva to protest trade agreements. Many of
these protesters do not appear to have a direct *economic* interest to protect, but they do have a direct *political* interest to protect. They want to
protect their ability to influence national regulations and norms.

Although the official definition is out of date, it is a definition
policymakers, the press, and the public share.[36] When we talk about
trade, most Americans still divide trade into a tug-of-war between two
camps: the freer traders and the protectionists. However, there are many
problems with talking about trade as if it is a dialectic. Although many
Americans have a particular mind-set about trade, their multiple roles in
society may make it difficult for them to be ideologically consistent. As
an example, most Americans are simultaneously consumers and pro-

ducers. From a consumer's perspective, freer trade can be good because it can yield a greater supply of goods at lower prices. However, freer trade also may endanger consumer welfare. For example, the United States bans the use of certain pesticides at home but allows U.S. manufacturers to sell some of these pesticides abroad. These banned pesticides may eventually show up in imported food, creating a "circle of poison." Concerned about their health, U.S. consumers may blame trade policy for this inconsistency. Finally, from a worker's perspective, trade may stimulate job creation. But foreign competition may reduce the market share of U.S. companies, and these companies may be forced to trim their staff or worker benefits to increase competitiveness. Thus, workers may blame trade for unemployment or economic uncertainty.

The protectionist/free trade dialectic also does not really help us understand the evolution of global trade policy. There is no single free trade or protectionist vision for trade policy. Freer traders today agree that trade should be regulated by a system of rules (trade agreements) governing how entities and individuals may trade and how nations may protect. But they disagree about what such trade agreements should include. Moreover, they disagree about the role of regional trade agreements and multilateral trade agreements in encouraging or discouraging trade. Protectionists also do not agree on what trade policies should do and what should be the turf of trade agreements. They also disagree on what actions constitute "unfair" trade.

The debate we heard in Seattle provides a good example of how the free trade/protectionist dialectic actually inhibits communication. In Seattle, some union representatives said that it was *unfair* for American workers to compete with workers in Mexico or Indonesia. They said such workers often have no power to bargain collectively and government officials, rather than markets, set wages and working conditions. Some developing country officials countered by labeling this perspective both "protectionist" and *unfair*. Former Mexican President Ernesto Zedillo of Mexico stressed "every case where a poor nation has significantly overcome poverty . . . has been achieved while engaging in production for export . . . that is, by participating in globalization." Such officials argue that the comparative advantage of many developing countries is their cheaper labor or lower regulatory standards. In this view, trade and globalization are the only ways for the poor of the world to escape poverty. Thus, it is *unfair* that the protesters deny these people their opportunity to participate in this process. Moreover, they argued that it was *unfair* that citizens of developed countries demand that developing countries immediately adopt high norms overseas. But many of the Seattle protesters alleged that Zedillo could not speak for the mass of Mexicans or other citizens of developing countries who spend each day struggling to survive. After all, he was in cahoots with multinationals. Moreover, the protesters argued that Mexico is not a democracy like Canada, the United States, or Japan where the people can throw out corrupt leaders.[37]

Finally, the free trade/protectionist dialectic doesn't describe economic or political reality. No government on Earth permits totally free trade. In every nation, protectionism ebbs and flows depending on many factors, such as the state of the economy, the political clout of those interest groups dependent on trade or protection, public awareness of trade, or the strength or weakness of protectionist ideas. American history provides a good example of how trade policy fluctuates.[38]

Protectionism in American History

The United States has always mixed freer trade and protectionist policies, despite our supposedly laissez-faire views. Thus, today the United States is the world's largest trading nation and leads global efforts to liberalize trade. However, the United States uses tariffs and quotas to protect and also uses protectionist tools to induce other nations to reduce their trade barriers.[39] Moreover, other nations allege the United States also practices a more covert form of protectionism by using extraterritorial application of its environmental laws to protect certain sectors such as its tuna and shrimp fishing industries.[40]

For most of U.S. history, protectionists were *economic nationalists.* The American version of economic nationalism evolved as a variant of mercantilism, which called for the accumulation of *national* wealth by exporting as much as possible and importing as little as possible. This economic strategy would make governments rich—but not necessarily their citizens.[41] Like their mercantilist counterparts in Europe, America's economic nationalists called for tariffs to impede trade and raise import costs.[42] But America's economic nationalists hoped that protection would make not only the new nation prosperous, but its people as well.[43] As a result, economic nationalists could argue that they were acting both in the national interest and in the individual citizen's interest.

Until the twentieth century, U.S. protectionism and economic nationalism could not be divorced because policymakers relied on the tariff to do two other important tasks: nurture the new nation's economic development and finance government. The public and policymakers believed that protectionists generally had the national interest in mind. But as the U.S. economy became increasingly intertwined with the world economy, freer trade ideas became ascendant. Freer trade became a tool to hamper the spread of communist regimes that threatened both American democracy and prosperity. Americans gradually became more supportive of economic internationalism from the 1940s to the 1980s. Yet the United States never fully abandoned protection for certain sectors. Many Americans continued to believe that trade could be unfair, that trade could threaten American sovereignty, and that freer trade policies could yield unemployment and inequity.[44]

Trade grew dramatically after the second world war. Policies and institutions such as the GATT, the World Bank, and the International Monetary Fund (IMF) made it easier for governments to adopt market-opening policies. Innovations in transportation, communications, and banking also facilitated trade and investment.[45] By the mid-1970s, the global village was a reality, but many Americans did not think they lived there. Although U.S. imports and exports were increasing, trade was still a relatively small percentage of gross domestic product.

In the 1980s, however, a confluence of problems made economic interdependence increasingly contentious in the United States and abroad.[46] For example, in both the United States and Europe, unemployment was relatively high, while growth was stagnant or slow. In 1985, U.S. unemployment was about 8.5 percent while growth was about 3 percent. In Europe, unemployment was over 11 percent while growth was about 2 percent. Policymakers as well as citizens found it easier to blame outsiders (trade, foreign investment, and immigrants) for these problems.[47]

Public support for economic internationalism was never great.[48] Some Americans became more receptive to protectionist tools and rhetoric, especially Japan-bashing.[49] Between 1980 and 1993, a growing number of Americans began to feel the economy was declining and out of control. Policymakers wrestled with many problems, including high interest rates, sluggish productivity growth, a low savings rate; inadequate job creation, and wage stagnation for many Americans.[50] They proposed a wide variety of reforms to address these problems. One of the most prominent new policy approaches was deregulation.

The Evolution of Regulatory Policy

Most industrialized nations developed their first regulations in the late 1880s, around the same time that nations became more interdependent.

These regulations served many different goals. Some of these regulations were designed to regulate specific sectors (such as railroad regulation) or other groups of economic actors (the Sherman Antitrust Act). Such economic regulation was often justified because the market failed to encourage competition. But social and environmental regulations are based on a different rationale—that the market can't always produce a pristine environment, a healthy workplace, or protect consumers from adulterated food.[51]

By the 1970s, Europe, Canada, and the United States had a complicated patchwork of rules protecting workers, consumers, shareholders, and the environment.[52] In the United States, these regulations included the 1962 Air Pollution Control Act, the 1963 Equal Pay Act (to eliminate differences in pay based on sex), and the 1974 Campaign Finance Amendments, which restricted amounts of political contributions.[53]

Each industrialized nation developed its own fluid system of regulation, reflecting its national economic, social, and political cultures.[54] These systems grew or shrunk over time based on a wide range of factors, including public support for regulation and the rise of new issues (e.g., civil or disability rights) to be regulated. These regulations, however, came with costs to economic efficiency as well as to democracy.[55] As Martha Derthick and Paul J. Quirk have written in their thoughtful study of deregulation, "the predominant view of both economists and political scientists was that regulation presented a case in which the benefits of government policy were concentrated in a few well-organized interests—the firms and unions that were protected from competition—whereas the costs were widely dispersed among consumers whose incentives to organize were insufficient to induce political action."[56] In this regard, sector-specific regulation was like sector-specific protection.

But during the Carter administration (1977–81), economists, activists, and others began to focus on the costs of regulation. Some condemned the regulatory process for its costs to economic efficiency, while others argued that America's sector-specific regulatory agencies had been captured by business.[57] Still others argued that policymakers had used regulatory tools and policies to do too many things, from redistributing income to promoting one sector of the economy at the expense of others.[58] As a result, an unusual left/right coalition in the 1980s called for sector-specific deregulation; among its prominent advocates was Ralph Nader, who would also become an important player in the trade debate.[59] Deregulation actually began during the Carter administration, but it seemed to gather force during the 1980s.

President Reagan thought the best way to rebuild America's economic and strategic might was to reduce the government's role in the economy.[60] During his tenure, America deregulated its banking and telephony sectors. This deregulation encouraged competition and reduced prices to banking consumers. But to some observers, including many on the left who had called for deregulation, its implementation seemed a sellout to business.[61]

Many Americans could not divorce Reagan's sector-specific deregulation from other Reagan administration policy. President Reagan also hoped to reduce government social safety nets and worker, consumer, and environmental regulation. These regulations are often called the *social compact*, but because they evolve over time, they cannot be characterized as a formal treaty or compact between citizens and their government. According to economist Dani Rodrik, the social compact consists of policies, regulations, and "norms that shape and constrain the domestic environment in which goods and services are produced."[62] The social compact includes policies designed to minimize the sometimes harmful side effects of economic activities such as pollution or soil erosion.

Social regulations confer benefits on the general public at the expense of a well-organized small public (usually business). Sector-specific regulations, in contrast, confer benefits on a few well-organized interests (usually business and/or workers). These social regulations were erected by groups and individuals who fought long and hard for these protections.[63] Such groups and individuals, whether friends of the earth, social activists, or consumer activists, would not give up these protections without a fight.

However, while deregulation gained the support of some Americans from the left, middle, and the right, the left found itself alone defending the social compact. In the 1980s, the social compact was difficult to defend, as many countries found many of their firms were becoming increasingly global. Trade liberalization from the Tokyo Round encouraged increased trade with developing countries. Many of these same countries removed restrictions on foreign investment, while privatizing important sectors from energy to telephony. Meanwhile, technological improvements in transportation and communications reduced the costs of doing business overseas. As their firms moved overseas, citizens and communities lost jobs, opportunities, and tax revenues. This was especially true in manufacturing regions such as Detroit or Pittsburgh, home to, respectively, America's once mighty auto and steel industries. With already huge budget deficits, Democratic and Republican policymakers did not want to increase taxes on citizens to make up for lost business taxes. This was ironic, because that same social compact was established to cushion citizens against the costs of capitalism (including global capitalism). In the face of massive budget deficits, some citizens began to question the costs of extensive pension, unemployment, and welfare benefits.[64] However, business leaders from both big and small firms were the most vocal about their costs to producers, consumers, and the economy as a whole.[65]

Deregulation also occurred in other industrialized nations. In many European nations, government retreated from providing specific services (e.g., telephone or transportation systems). Investment, including foreign investment, poured into sectors once solely the turf of national governments. Privatization also aroused controversy.[66] Thus, in many industrialized nations, deregulation and the erosion of the social welfare state occurred in tandem, at the same time that many industrialized nations became more reliant on global capital and more dependent on trade. Some policymakers and the public came to see this process as potentially infringing upon each nation's sovereignty.[67] Meanwhile, as the winds of globalization blew upon the United States and other economies, trade policies and tools were changing, too.

The Intersection of Trade Regulation and Social Regulation

Throughout history, when policymakers wanted to protect, they tended to use border measures. These measures, called *commercial policies*, include tariffs, quotas, and exchange restrictions, which can be applied at the border to control imports.[68] In 1947, most of the world's most important trading nations agreed to a set of common rules, the GATT, governing the use of such border measures.

GATT was simply a club, but it was a club with strong rules. The participating nations agreed to the idea that trade benefits are maximized if private entities (and not governments) decide to import or export. All the nations that adhered to the GATT followed three principles: most favored nation status, national treatment, and consensus. The most favored nation principle meant that a tariff rate applied to goods from one member of the GATT would be applied to such goods from all GATT members. The principle of national treatment meant that foreign firms would be subject to the same rules and regulations as a country's domestic firms. And finally, GATT made decisions only by unanimous agreement (not majority rule). Thus GATT moved slowly.[69]

However, because the rules of that club governed how entities may trade and how nations may protect, it limited how and when nations could use such border measures.

By binding governments to particular trade policy rules, GATT's disciplines helped create greater global and national economic efficiency. Over time, GATT not only helped nations reduce trade barriers but also helped to increase world and national income. A growing number of nations clamored to join the GATT system, from its eight original signatories in 1948 to over 137 as of this writing.[70] GATT regulated how and when nations could use commercial policies to protect, but it did not limit nations from devising and relying on other strategies for protection.

In the 1960s, policymakers became increasingly aware that some nontariff barriers (also called invisible tariffs) were being widely used as trade barriers.[71] These nontariff barriers (NTBs) included product regulations, health and safety regulations, certain subsidies, and procurement regulations. Standards and regulations are among the most important NTBs. Standards are voluntary, usually defined by an industry or nongovernmental organization, while regulations are legally binding and are usually imposed to safeguard citizens, consumers, and the environment.[72] Why did these standards and regulations seem to be proliferating? Was it because they had always existed but became more apparent as the GATT rules restricted use of border measures? Or were these NTBs proliferating because more countries were relying on them to protect more frequently and, as a result, such NTBs were distorting trade? By 1973, according to John Jackson, the noted legal scholar of GATT, GATT had catalogued some eight hundred NTBs used by its contracting parties.[73] These NTBs allowed policymakers to protect covertly. Economist Edward John Ray has written that by relying on domestic policies rather than commercial policies to protect, a government could "assist special interests without advertising the extent to which it is taking such action" for protectionist reasons.[74]

Policymakers have long been aware that national systems of regulation might distort trade between domestic and foreign producers.[75] During World War II, policymakers tried to find common rules to govern potential trade distortions of each nation's unique approach to capitalism by developing the International Trade Organization (ITO). The ITO's charter was comprehensive and truly revolutionary: it broke new ground by attempting to harmonize a wide swath of foreign and domestic policies that could affect trade flows. It had provisions governing the use of border measures as well as rules governing national employment, investment, and competition (antitrust) policies. But the

U.S. Congress never voted on the ITO and it was abandoned in 1950. However, the commercial policy provisions of the ITO were in the GATT, which did not require direct congressional approval. And by 1950, GATT was already successful in governing trade.[76]

However, the GATT did not effectively govern the use of NTBs such as standards and procurement policies. Moreover, although the GATT had a system of mediation of trade disputes, it had no mandate or tools to regulate the potential trade distortions of national regulatory systems.

During GATT's first three decades, economists, business leaders, and policymakers called on Congress to grow the GATT system by devising rules to govern such NTBs. Many members of Congress were sympathetic to such concerns, but they did not want trade negotiations to step onto the turf of domestic policy, affecting sovereignty. GATT had been deliberately designed not to force such changes. It was an agreement, not a treaty.[77] Its provisions were only binding insofar as they were not inconsistent with America's existing legislation.[78] Moreover, GATT negotiators did not initially succeed at developing a common approach to regulating the potential trade distortions of such NTBs. In 1967, they tried to negotiate international rules governing dumping (where imports are priced at less than their costs of protection), but Congress balked at this threat to its control of trade policy.[79] In 1974, in the hopes of stimulating trade and economic growth, Congress changed course and approved the negotiation of NTBs. During the Tokyo Round of trade negotiations under the GATT, policymakers attempted to negotiate common rules governing the trade distortions of some such regulations. Although they could not achieve a consensus on including such rules in the GATT system, they did devise a new strategy. Rules on some of these NTBs were contained in codes regulating subsidies, procurement policies, and standards. But not all GATT signatories signed on to these additional codes; their adherence to GATT's broader rules was essentially "à la carte."[80] Trade policymakers, economists, and business leaders gathered a wide range of evidence to show that GATT à la carte was not working. They noted that creative approaches to protection were proliferating and increasingly distorting trade.[81] However, many of these so-called invisible tariffs were not designed to protect producers from *foreign* competition. They were called for by citizens to make their *national* markets more equitable or more efficient.

The Reagan administration concluded that these national regulations would need to be governed by multilateral rules.[82] Representatives of some one hundred nations agreed to participate in a new round of trade discussions, which began in Uruguay in 1986. The negotiations took some seven years, but in 1993 the participants agreed to a more comprehensive approach to trade regulations, including rules regarding the trade implications of some domestic policies (such as health and safety standards) that could distort trade flows. They also created a new international organization, the WTO, to govern trade and subsume the GATT.[83]

But in this attempt to find common ground on trade negotiation and social regulation, some trade agreement critics alleged that the Reagan administration was attempting to use the GATT system to effectively deregulate through international agreement what it could not achieve nationally.[84] Their perspective, although a bit exaggerated and conspiratorial, is understandable. Many individuals on the left saw it as part and parcel of Reagan administration policies to reduce government's role in markets. They organized to protect their systems of regulatory protection, to defend their nation's unique social compact.

WHAT WOKE UP THE TRADE AGREEMENT CRITICS?

The allegations that GATT was less about trade than global deregulation resonated around the world, but they were especially effective in the United States. Protectionists have long argued that trade agreements were unconstitutional because Congress delegates its authority to regulate foreign commerce to the executive branch. Critics of trade agreements also alleged that trade agreements were not in the national interest.[85]

These arguments were not only historically consistent, they were effective. GATT had never been popular on Capitol Hill. In granting authority to negotiate trade agreements to the executive branch after 1948, Congress consistently authorized a GATT disclaimer. The disclaimer stressed that in approving participation in negotiations, Congress did not denote approval or disapproval of the GATT. The disclaimer signaled that Congress had effectively drawn a "line in the sand" beyond which it would not cede control over trade policy to the president or to the GATT.[86]

In the Trade Act of 1974, however, Congress did an abrupt turnaround both about the GATT and about delegating new authority to the executive branch. This law authorized negotiations of NTBs under the aegis of the GATT. And it developed a process—"fast-track"—by which Congress could only indirectly influence these negotiations. Congress required the president to consult on the scope and progress of these negotiations, as well as any potential changes to U.S. laws or regulations. Once such negotiations were complete, however, the law gave Congress authority only to vote up or down on bills detailing the negotiations and their implementation. Under fast-track, Congress could not amend such bills.[87] Beginning in the 1990s, this process increased congressional and public suspicions. This is ironic, because it was developed by Congress. To some groups concerned about health and safety standards, the fast-track process seemed complex, opaque, and unfair. It fueled their concerns about the direction of trade policy and the public's ability to shape it.[88]

One additional factor also fueled suspicion about trade policy-making and the GATT. Because the United States was (and is) the world's largest trading nation, it is frequently engaged in trade disputes. In the two decades before the Uruguay Round, these disputes increased in frequency. Some of these disputes were so contentious that the press, albeit incorrectly, referred to them as "trade wars." After the Tokyo Round, a growing number of these disputes centered on policies other than border measures, for example, environmental regulations.[89] GATT panels, which would weigh such disputes, almost always argued that public policies must not discriminate between foreign or domestic producers, however noble the policy goal.

In reviewing such decisions, environmental and consumer advocates feared that local preferences could be subordinated to international standards, elevating the views of experts over locally determined consumer and citizen preferences.[90] Their concern rose to a fever pitch when Mexico challenged the trade effects of the Marine Mammal Protection Act at the GATT.

GATTZILLA VERSUS FLIPPER

In 1972, as a key component of its efforts to protect and conserve the environment, the United States passed the Marine Mammal Protection Act (MMPA); it limited the number of dolphins that could be killed while fishing for tuna. The original MMPA was not intended to apply to foreign fishing fleets; instead the law was meant to regulate domestic fishing practices. However, the law was ineffective. Some U.S. fishers complied, while others reflagged their ships as foreign registry to elude the rules. In 1988, after a suit by the Earth Island Institute, an environmental organization, Congress inserted specific language into the act stating that all tuna to be sold in the United States had to be caught in ways that conserved dolphins.[91] Those nations wanting to export tuna to the United States could not exceed two times the U.S. rate of dolphin kill. Thus, the regulations both protected dolphins and did not discriminate or provide U.S. producers with a market advantage over foreign producers. But the 1988 regulations led to a ban on tuna imported from Columbia, Costa Rica, Italy, Japan, Mexico, Panama, and other nations that did not change their tuna fishing techniques. Angry Mexican fishermen claimed that the tuna import provisions of the act were in fact trade barriers and they took their case to the GATT.[92] Staff at Ralph Nader's Public Citizen and other environmental, consumer, and citizens groups began to closely watch this case, which they named "GATTzilla versus Flipper."

In 1991, a GATT panel composed of international trade law experts found that the tuna import embargo embodied in the law was "GATT illegal" because the MMPA did not simply ban a product (tuna) but banned the process used to make that product (killing dolphins along with the tuna). The panel found that the MMPA was an attempt to make U.S. environmental laws reach beyond U.S. borders.[93] The panel's decision, however, was nonbinding. As a trade agreement, the GATT had no power to force changes to U.S. law.

But the decision woke up a wide range of environmentalists around the world to the fact that environmental regulations could be challenged at the GATT as trade barriers. They organized to protest the panel's decision. They saw it as a signal that under the GATT, countries cannot limit importing products having production or harvest methods that may harm the environment. Given both the decision and its potential effects on environmental protection, some feared that democracy (which fostered the environmental movement) could be subverted by international trade law (which could undermine the environmental movement).[94] At the same time, policymakers, economists, and many trade agreements proponents saw the decision differently. They were concerned about this U.S. attempt to use unilateral trade measures (trade policy) to achieve changes to another nation's policies or to achieve social or environmental goals. Moreover, some developing country officials complained that the United States expected them to place environmentalism over their economic development.[95]

Some nations, such as Mexico, also saw this attempt to regulate tuna fishing as covert protectionism. There is some evidence that in passing the original legislation, Congress may have been motivated not solely by a desire to protect dolphins, but also by a desire to weaken the comparative advantage of the foreign fleet relative to U.S. tuna fishers.[96]

Nonetheless, it is hard to believe that environmentalists refused to change the MMPA out of protectionist intent. They did not want other nations or organizations to tell them how to regulate the environment. Thus, they demonized the GATT. However, they could have adopted a different strategy of promoting consumer awareness around the world of how tuna was caught and encouraging firms to produce and consumers to demand "dolphin-free tuna." Such a strategy would have been internationalist, nontrade distorting, and perhaps even more effective.

METHODOLOGY OF THIS BOOK

Governor and former presidential candidate Adlai E. Stevenson understood the essence of trade policy; he once described it as one field where the greatest need is for fresh clichés. This book proves his point. Citizen groups have long been involved in the trade debate. Although many of their concerns seem modern, human rights, consumer safety, and conservation are not new to the trade debate. In certain periods, social issues were central to the public debate over trade; in other periods, especially during the first thirty years of the GATT, they were off-stage.

As this book cannot focus on all the areas where trade affects domestic policy objectives, I have chosen three such issues: food safety, the environment, and labor standards. These three issues provide different windows into the trade debate and the concerns of modern trade agreement critics. But these three issues illuminate how trade policy becomes contentious when it appears to undermine democratically determined norms and regulation.

Food safety became a trade policy issue in the nineteenth century. Although nations have long traded commodities and crops, nineteenth-century advances in transportation and refrigeration led to increased trade in food products.[97] Today much of the food and vegetables eaten by Americans is imported from nations with different systems of food safety and pollution regulation.

During the Uruguay Round, participating nations revised the rules relating to food, plant, and animal health standards. Each nation retained the right to determine its own level of food safety protection so long as the resulting rules were necessary, based on scientific principles, and devised so they distorted trade as little as possible. To some food safety advocates, this approach elevated trade over consumer welfare. Many of those groups who care about food safety issues want to take food safety issues out of the purview of the WTO. When they call for changes to food safety rules, they are often called protectionist. But these groups are generally not motivated by a desire to distort trade so as to favor domestic producers.

The environment has also been the subject of trade debates since the nineteenth century. As noted earlier, conservationists have long recognized that for conservation measures to be effective, they would have to be multinational. However, no one organization or set of rules governs environmental practices.

Environmental issues have become more contentious in recent years. As nations and their citizens have become more affluent, people are more willing to pay (through taxes, consumption, or government expenditures) to protect the environment. Growing numbers of the world's peoples now recognize that they can reconcile growth and environmental protection by practicing sustainable development. Although they may support the idea of sustainable development, citizens and policymakers in developing countries are not as able to afford or to enforce stringent environmental and public health regulations. Moreover, they often see environmental policies in many developed countries as measures to thwart developing country exports. At the same time, however, many environmentalists have alleged that some multinational companies have threatened to move their operations to nations with lower environmental and public health standards. These individuals fear that increased trade will yield "a race to the bottom" among nations for such standards. Their concerns grew when they saw the GATT mediate the dolphin-tuna case. These concerns became front page news when the debate over NAFTA occurred in the United States, Canada, and Mexico (1992–93).[98] Environmentalists were determined to protect their system of environmental protection. But they disagreed as to whether such standards could be incorporated within the system of rules governing trade.

Until recently, the GATT system said little about protecting the environment. Article XX does allow nations to restrict imports when such protection is necessary to protect human, animal, or plant life or health. But this approach makes the legitimacy of environmental regulations turn on *what* is produced and not *on how* it is produced.[99] Many environmentalists resent this logic because it elevates trade/commercial concerns over other concerns, such as public health or conservation.[100]

Labor standards also have a long history as a trade policy issue. In the United States, the Founding Fathers wrestled with the implications of slavery upon the new nation. They also discussed whether to ban trade in slaves and whether to tax interstate commerce in slaves.

Since the nineteenth century, proponents and critics of trade agreements alike have worked to include labor standards in trade agreements. Although the GATT (and now the WTO) does ban trade in goods made by forced labor, the GATT/WTO system does not include a code on how workers are treated as they produce goods or services. The United States has pressed for such labor standards throughout the history of the GATT. However, officials from other nations, especially populous developing nations such as India, are strongly opposed. These nations fear such standards could impede their comparative advantage (in low wage labor). They (and some free traders) call those who advocate including labor standards in the GATT/WTO system "protectionists."

This book focuses not only on these issues, but also on the citizen activists and nongovernmental organizations (NGOs) in the trade debate. Many such NGOs criticize the GATT/WTO. One way to understand the growing political clout of trade agreement critics is to examine the commonalities and differences in their objectives and strategy. This may provide some insights into whether these individuals and groups are protectionists. First, many of these groups have dissimilar objectives. For example, advocates of labor standards want to enhance the international rules governing trade to include core labor standards. Many nutritional and consumer groups, in contrast, want to take food safety out of the GATT/WTO system, because they have concluded that this system is opaque, undemocratic, and thwarts national values and objectives. Ralph Nader's consumer group Public Citizen provides a good example. Although Nader helped build the modern regulatory state with his advocacy of federal health, safety, and environmental regulations, Public Citizen does not see government at the international level as an appropriate tool to regulate international business across borders. Nader fears that citizens will be unable to monitor international bureaucrats and hold these officials accountable.[101] He supports a protectionist outcome, although his motivation does not appear protectionist. Economic nationalists have a similar negative view of international institutions. Patrick J. Buchanan, for example, wants the United States to withdraw from the WTO, because it was "erected on ideas American patriots must reject." Yet even economic nationalists find common ground internationally, as Buchanan acknowledges: "If the French wish to subsidize farmers to preserve their countryside why shouldn't they?"[102] Finally, environmental groups are divided about trade agreements. Some want to include environmental rules, while others feel international attention would best be focused on creating an international environmental organization.[103]

Most of the trade agreement critics come from social activist groups on the left. However, when nationalists or traditional protectionists played an important role in the trade debate, this book will highlight their activities.

Despite their different objectives for reforming trade policies, trade agreement critics shared a three-pronged strategy. First, they have forged both formal and informal international alliances. These alliances work to warn citizens around the world about trade agreements. Thus, most of these trade agreement critics have fostered political alliances beyond borders. Second, relying on new communicative technologies, they rely on a global grassroots, rather than simply an "inside the Washington beltway," strategy. On the Internet and the airwaves, in the print media and on Capitol Hill, they used every forum available to warn their fellow Americans about the dangers of globalization, its impact on American democracy, and its costs for the American social compact. Third, they often used old-fashioned tactics (such as consumer boycotts) or 1960s tactics such as rallies and teach-ins. They also used 1990s tactics such as "outing" and shaming celebrities for their association with sweatshops.[104] These activists have worked hard to educate their fellow citizens in the United States and around the world about the costs of trade and global economic interdependence.

Most of these groups do not seem to receive funds from traditional protectionist, isolationist, or economic nationalist groups.[105] However, they have *structured* an alliance with isolationist, economic nationalist, and traditional protectionist interests to hamper trade liberalization.[106] This structure, as well as their reliance on a protectionist *strategy,* has led many trade experts and policymakers to assume that all the members of these groups are protectionists.

To summarize, some of these trade agreement critics have protectionist objectives; others do not. All have hampered trade liberalization. All agree with Ralph Nader that freer trade will undermine democratic systems of regulating national economies. Yet are these groups truly protectionist? Many are. They recognize that internationalization of standards may undermine the comparative advantage of some developing countries that do not enforce environmental or labor standards. Thus, they use these standards as a benchmark and a tool to keep imports out. Others such as H. Ross Perot and Pat Buchanan believe that national economic policies must be designed to increase the wealth and the power of the nation. Their nationalistic objectives are inherently protectionist.

However, some of these individuals and groups may be thwarting protectionism. Congressman Richard Gephardt, the minority leader in the House (1996–2000), has argued that nations and firms that engage or acquiesce in exploitative labor or environmental practices create an unfair competitive advantage. He notes that corporations can search the world to find the lowest standards (although this is only one factor as to where firms locate production). He believes this creates unfair competition, which puts downward pressure on labor and environmental standards in other countries. If the world trading system include rules governing the environment or workers, many citizens in industrialized countries would see the rules as made in their interest as well as in the corporate interest. Thus, he argues that by demanding that the world trading system include these issues, trade agreement critics are hampering protectionist sentiment in many industrialized nations.[107] Gephardt's motivation appears protectionist, but the outcome he wants may reduce protectionism.

Although these trade agreement critics represent an important movement in the United States and among international civil society, historians, economists, and political scientists have paid little attention to them until recently. Like policymakers, they presumed that trade policy would continue to be dominated by elites and experts in business labor, academia, and government.

When they write books about trade, economists, historians, and political scientists tend to focus on the tug-of-war between government officials, members of Congress, and representatives of special interests—groups of citizens organized to protect their economic and political interests. For example, I. M. Destler, the premier scholar of U.S. trade policy, states, "The main story in the politics of American trade . . . has been the development of . . . antiprotectionist counterweights."[108] However, policymakers and business leaders are paying attention to these groups. In a May 18, 1998, speech at the WTO, President Clinton "called on the WTO to become more open and accountable to increase public confidence in the WTO." He proposed that private citizens be able to present their views, but he did not clarify as to how.[109] Business leaders have found growing congressional opposition and concern about trade agreements. They attribute this opposition and concern to the actions of protectionists and trade critics. The president has not had new fast-track authority since 1993; thus, he can begin negotiations with other trading partners, but he cannot provide these trading partners with assurances that Congress will approve such negotiations without amendment. In April 1998, trade agreement critics stalled negotiations on a multilateral agreement on investment.[110] Clearly, trade agreement critics have had a major influence on trade policies.

Polls and news accounts reveal that greater numbers of citizens are paying attention. This is true in the United States as well as overseas—in Australia, India, Malaysia, Canada, and Europe. Trade agreement critics, as noted previously, have been adept at using new technologies to expand the public debate about trade. They have used faxes, radio talk shows, the Internet, and E-mail in service to that debate. Their actions contrast with that of the official trade community, which tends to disseminate press releases, appear on news shows, and essentially preach to the choir, rather than the public at large. The Internet provides a good example of this contrast. While trade agreement critics have used E-mail and the Internet to organize and educate citizens since the 1990s, USTR uses the Internet primarily as a dissemination device.[111]

To understand the impact of these trade agreement critics, I monitored a wide range of data and public opinion sources including archival data, government documents, editorials, magazines, journals, newspapers, talk show transcripts, interviews, Web sites, congressional testimony, and polls. This helped me better understand that we cannot divorce the debate over trade from the debate about what government should do in the face of globalization. Moreover, my respect for history led me to stress the continuity of public concerns about trade and globalization.

ORGANIZATION OF THIS BOOK

Context is everything in the debate over trade. Chapter 2 shows that in the nineteenth century, as in the twentieth century, a broad swath of Americans found much to criticize in U.S. trade policies. But because protection was the norm, protectionism was taken for granted. Instead the debate was about how much to protect. Nonetheless, social issues and trade often intersected. The tenor of the debate changed during the Great Depression. The Trade Agreements Act of 1934 transferred authority for trade policy to the executive branch, for a limited duration. Policymakers hoped that opening foreign markets, by reducing U.S. and foreign trade barriers, could create new markets and new jobs. This act was regularly renewed by Congress. During World War II, policymakers even tried to create an international organization, the ITO, to coordinate domestic and trade policies internationally. However, as discussed earlier, the ITO was never voted on by Congress.

The trade debate again changed after World War II when trade was linked to policies resisting the spread of communism. The world's leading trading nations acceded to the GATT. GATT's role was limited to governing traditional tools of protection. But as policymakers discovered that domestic policies could distort trade, they ever so gradually found ways to enlarge GATT's purview.

Chapter 3 describes the evolution of America's modern social compact and notes that its heyday occurred at the same time that business leaders, policymakers, and economists became concerned that such regulations increasingly distorted trade flows. This was not the only irony. In 1974, Congress authorized the president to negotiate rules governing NTBs, such as social regulations, at the very time Congress was weighing how to impeach President Richard Nixon. This act was also important because it set up the fast-track procedure. This law explicitly linked trade to human rights improvements (results) through the Jackson-Vanik amendment.

Chapter 4 discusses how protectionist views and tools evolved during the 1980s. The United States and other governments, responding to high budget deficits, footloose capital, and restive transnational companies, attempted to cut a wide range of government programs and reduce government's role in the economy. Moreover, many individuals of the left saw deregulation in the Reagan administration's trade policies. Ironically, although the Reagan administration succeeded at reducing the role of the federal government in the economy, it became more interventionist on trade. Competitiveness and managed trade became rubrics for protectionism.

Chapter 5 details how the U.S./Canada Free Trade Agreement (FTA) educated first Canadians and later Americans to the potential costs of trade agreements to their national system of social and environmental regulations. During the NAFTA debate, a wide range of consumer, civic, environmental, development, and labor rights groups worked with religious groups to criticize the NAFTA. They forged the first transnational movement to criticize trade liberalization.

But that movement became divided nearly as soon as it began. Some environmental groups accepted side agreements to the NAFTA. They saw these side agreements on the environment and labor as a positive, albeit incremental, approach to encouraging trade while protecting each nation's social compact. Moreover, these groups decided that by accepting an incremental approach and participating, they could achieve greater influence on the policy-making process in the United States.

Chapter 6 examines how some of these groups responded to the Uruguay Round. During the Reagan administration, Mark Ritchie, a family farm and food safety activist, sounded the alarm about how trade could affect achieving other policy goals. His concerns resonated with individuals active in the environment, social justice, and economic development in the United States and abroad. Ritchie and other family farm, development, consumer, and environmental activists worked to revise the Reagan, Bush, and later Clinton trade proposals. Many activists saw these reforms as deregulatory, rather than re-regulatory. Ultimately, they rejected incremental or reformist solutions. When the Uruguay Round was debated by Congress, most of these activists opposed it. Only Consumer Union publicly came out in strong support. These groups did not succeed in turning Congress against the revisions to trade proposed in the Uruguay Round, but to a great degree, these groups helped set the terms of the congressional debate. That is, they forced Congress to focus on how the Uruguay Round reforms might affect American sovereignty and its system of laws and regulations.

Chapter 7 offers some conclusions about these trade agreement critics and U.S. trade policy, focusing on the similarities and differences among traditional protectionists and trade agreement critics today. They make many of the same arguments about equity, social stability, and sovereignty. But as I will show, they have done little to ask how trade policy can be made more equitable. They have alleged that industrialized nations are abandoning key regulatory goals in the international interest of encouraging trade. They condemn policymakers for elevating trade over the achievement of other policy goals. But they have not asked whether hampering trade agreements really helps achieve important goals such as improving work conditions, food safety, or the environment. Moreover, the trade agreement critics have focused on government actions and not on corporations, the key agents of globalization. I note the irony of this strategy, given the roots of many activists in consumer activism.

As students of trade policy, we need to understand the influence of civil society as we attempt to understand how global economic interdependence is changing the United States and the world. The public has long attempted to shape globalization. As we observe and attempt to understand that process, we must accurately characterize citizens concerned about the environment, labor standards, human rights, food safety, and democracy. Some of these citizens groups may truly be trying to erect or maintain trade barriers; some may be trying to grow the GATT/WTO system; and others may be trying to ensure that trade policy does not trump the achievement of other important policy goals. Nonetheless, by their actions, they have forced a more honest and comprehensive debate about how to regulate the global economy.

CHAPTER 2

Same Arguments, Different Context

A Brief History of Protectionism from 1789 to the 1960s

WHEN BENJAMIN FRANKLIN wrote that "in this world nothing is certain but death and taxes," he was referring to tariffs.[1] Tariffs— duties applied at the border—were America's main tool for regulating trade. However, when Americans talked about tariffs, they weren't only talking about a tool to restrict trade. They were talking about a device that could nurture the new nation's economic growth as well as finance the U.S. government. Moreover, when Americans talked tariffs, they also were discussing the implications of government intervention in the economy. At times, social issues forced a debate about tariffs; at other times, U.S. trade policy inspired Americans to weigh the social ramifications of the nation's trade policy tools and objectives.

Tariffs were one of the few tools available to nineteenth-century policymakers to encourage economic growth.[2] Tariffs not only were effective tools, they also did not require any additional expenditures; that is, they were "off-budget."[3] Tariffs, the main source of federal revenue from 1789 until 1916, were an indirect tax; thus, many citizens did not link the costs of governance with the costs of protectionism. More- over, tariffs often provided government with a surplus.

The tariff walls erected by both Republicans and Democrats came with real costs to the American social compact. Tariffs were inherently inequitable. Although all consumers, rich or poor, had to absorb the costs of tariffs, the burden of tariffs fell heaviest on the poorest con- sumers, who had little disposable income. These men and women, whether they toiled the land or in factories, spent much of their earn- ings on purchasing the taxed goods.[4] America did not reduce its reliance on tariffs to finance government until 1916, when Congress passed an income tax. This income tax was designed to tax more heavily those Americans with higher earnings and tax less heavily those with lower incomes.

It was not until the Great Depression that policymakers began to dismantle America's tariff walls. In 1934, Congress passed the Reciprocal Trade Agreements Act, calling for bilateral negotiations to reduce trade barriers and expand market access for U.S. companies. This legislation was a radical change: It modernized as well as internationalized the process of trade policy-making. After World War II, U.S. policymakers used trade policy to cement a connection between trade liberalization and economic/political stability. From then on, the United States led global efforts to establish rules to govern trade.

Yet global leadership of efforts to liberalize trade did not stop policymakers from protecting certain sectors of the economy, such as textiles and agriculture, or from using new tools to protect, such as nontariff barriers (NTBs).[5] These NTBs included administrative regulations such as marks of origin, laws banning convict or forced labor products, and sanitary restrictions such as quarantines. Policymakers sometimes relied on these NTBs strictly to protect. Not surprisingly, sometimes national regulations such as worker or consumer protective measures distorted trade. But policymakers' reliance on such tools to protect was not always transparent. According to trade scholar Percy Bidwell, these NTBs attracted little attention in the press, were "rarely debated in Congress, and never the subject of discussion by women's clubs or businessmen's forums."[6]

This chapter describes how arguments for protection evolved as the American economy, economic institutions, and policies changed over time. The debate began when the colonists first took to the streets and harbors to protest taxation (the use of tariffs) without representation. Social issues such as how trade policy could promote human rights were often part of the debate. For example, the relationship of trade and slavery bedeviled the debate at the Constitutional Congress.

Members of nongovernmental organizations (NGOs) have had a long history of bringing social issues to the fore. They were also involved in the development of the postwar international organizations to regulate the global economy such as the United Nations, the International Trade Organization (ITO), the World Bank, and the GATT. Although such NGOs continued to shape domestic economic and social policies, the GATT did not cooperate with such groups; it worked with governments.

America's commitment to trade liberalization did not mitigate public support for relying on protectionist tools. The public had been weaned on protection. In 1789 as well as in 1959, citizens believed that protectionism preserved jobs, maintained social stability, and helped the economy flourish.[7]

GROWING THE NATION WITH TARIFFS

Citizen activism on trade has marked the United States since its first days as a British colony. The colonists were addicted to imports such as tea, conveniences, and small luxuries.[8] But with the end of the Seven Years War, in 1763, the British government consistently raised taxes on these goods. The colonists perceived these taxes as excessive and unjust. They set up groups to protest Britain's trade policies. In 1764, some of the colonists organized the nonimportation movement (America's first consumer movement) to boycott imported products. The organizers of the boycott hoped that it would inflict economic hardship upon English merchants and manufacturers, who would then pressure their politicians to alter these taxes. But the British responded schizophrenically to the boycott. They removed some taxes and then reinstated others.[9] In 1774 and 1775 the Continental Congress made the boycott a formal policy and pledged to boycott an assortment of British goods starting December 1, 1774. Americans of all social classes and regions participated. They shared a common argument: that the British system of taxation discriminated among British citizens. But the boycott caused hardship and did not change British tax policies. Growing numbers of colonists began to advocate a different strategy: independence, which they achieved after a difficult war.[10]

Independence forced the leaders of the new nation to find ways to reconcile conflicting policy objectives. On one hand, most of the men who sat down to write the Constitution for the new nation were concerned about human rights. On the other hand, the war had devastated the South, and its plantation owners demanded slaves to rebuild the Southern economy. In 1787, however, the report of the Committee of the Whole at the Constitutional Convention contained no reference to slavery or trade in slaves, an important human rights and foreign policy issue. It also did not clarify whether the new nation would ban interstate commerce in slaves and whether such commerce should be taxed. Taxing interstate commerce in slaves allowed the new nation to raise much needed revenue. Colonel George Mason of Virginia denounced the traffic in slaves as "infernal," while Elbridge Gerry of Massachusetts wished merely to refrain from sanctioning the slave trade. Others pointed out the inconsistency of condemning the slave trade and defending slavery. But most delegates agreed with Roger Sherman of Connecticut that "it was better to let the Southern States import slaves than to part with those States."[11]

Ultimately, delegates from the South pointed their way to a compromise. Article I, Section 9 of the Constitution did not prohibit the migration or importation of slaves prior to the year 1808. It also allowed the States to impose a tax or duty on such trade in slaves, not to exceed ten dollars for each person.[12] Thus, the Constitutional Convention allowed slavery, let the new nation raise revenue from slavery, and joined the South and North, two very different economies, together in political and economic union.

The pamphleteers of the times were well aware of the implications of this compromise for other policy objectives. *The Independent Gazetteer* wrote that this compromise was "especially scandalous and inconsistent in a people, who have asserted their own liberty by the sword, and which dangerously enfeebles the districts wherein the laborers are bondsmen." Noah Webster thought the compromise was "pitiful." But in *The Federalist* No. 41, James Madison wrote, that the compromise "ought to be considered as a great point gained in favor of humanity, that a period of twenty years may terminate forever . . . a traffic which has so long . . . upbraided the barbarism of modern policy."[13]

This was not the only compromise developed by the Founding Fathers. They recognized that the United States could not produce many of the goods its citizens needed; thus, the United States had to trade. But they also wanted to nurture a diversified economy, which meant they would have to provide infant industries with protection.[14] Thus, they adopted a bifurcated strategy: They used tariffs to develop the new nation and protect its infant manufacturing and iron industries, but they also signed treaties of navigation and commerce and encouraged a reciprocity policy on shipping. This mix of policies to encourage freer trade and policies to protect domestic producers has marked the United States ever since.[15]

The institutional structure of government probably encouraged this mix of policies. The Constitution gave the president responsibility for managing foreign affairs. However, Congress was "to regulate commerce with foreign nations" and to "lay and collect . . . duties." By definition, Congress was more receptive to local and often more protectionist concerns.[16] Despite the importance of trade to the new nation's economic growth, Americans focused their attention on developing America's vast and rich internal resources.[17] Trade historian John Dobson concluded that few Americans "showed much concern or even awareness of the . . . international consequences" of the tariff. James A. Field described the Federalists as individuals who "saw commerce from the view of the individual shipowner or merchant and national policy as individual interest writ large."[18]

America's leaders, however, initially thought of tariffs principally as a means of financing government. The first Congress passed the Tariff Act of 1789 to raise revenue. This act levied a 5 percent duty on imports, higher duties on luxury items, and a few specific duties on articles like coffee, tea, and molasses.[19] However, some Americans (notably Alexander Hamilton and eastern industrialists) began to see tariffs as a tool to stimulate U.S. economic development. Hamilton used an equity argument to make his case for protection. He argued that other nations used tariffs to protect their home market manufacturers and thus, "the principles of distributive justice" dictated that the United States pursue a similar policy to obtain "a reciprocity of advantages."[20] Hamilton preferred to promote manufacturing by having government subsidize manufacturers, but he recognized the young nation's fiscal constraints.[21] Unlike subsidies, tariffs did not require any on-budget authority.

The notion of using tariffs to protect America's infant industries gained ground as the country struggled to develop. By raising the price of imports, tariffs served as an incentive to buy U.S.-produced goods. Government officials liked the selective nature of tariffs, as well as the fact that the Treasury captured tariff revenue.[22]

Policymakers became more supportive of this approach after the War of 1812. The first protective tariff was designed to keep alive industries such as wool that had been hurt by the war. Whig Kentucky Congressman Henry Clay outlined his American system. He believed protection of America's manufacturing and textile industries would yield a great and strong market.[23] But the Democrats disagreed with such policies, which they saw as favoritism, and advocated a tariff "for revenue only." Clay, however, was able to argue that the Democratic approach was "free trade," which could only yield dependency and poverty: "The Democrats . . . would let your grain wither in your barns—they would let mechanics and manufacturers sink in an unequal contest with the pauper labor of Europe . . . rather than grant protection."[24] The point was clear to America's workers, many of whom came to view protectionist policies as furthering equity among Americans. That view would be hard to dislodge.

Clearly, the Democrats and Whigs had very different perspectives about government. The Jacksonian Democrats thought government intervention tended to benefit one class at the expense of another. They insisted that freer trade and destruction of economic privilege would speed up economic advancement for all Americans. Thus, Jacksonian Democrats opposed corporate welfare, such as the government's aid to the Collins Steamship Lines, or high levels of protection, "high protectionism," which they feared would encourage sluggishness among protected sectors.[25] However, the Whigs argued that tariffs would ensure that U.S.-produced capital would remain in the United States, benefiting all classes of Americans. Today's laborers could use these funds to transform themselves into tomorrow's capitalists, just like Andrew Carnegie, who used such capital to transform himself from a laborer to a capitalist.[26] Thus the Whigs seemed to believe that tariffs could actually promote equitable economic growth among Americans.

This perspective, that protectionism could promote equity among Americans, gained greater support in the 1850s. Although the United States relied on foreign capital and had a growing international trade, the federal government rarely intervened to encourage exports.[27] In the forty years prior to the Civil War, general tariff levels remained moderate, but tariff protection spread to many sectors. Legislators learned it was simpler to compensate those injured by tariffs by protecting them, too, rather than to reduce the protection given to the first party. Any one interest, once granted protection, tended to regard that level of protection as its prerogative. But America's growing recourse to tariffs was not universally supported; in fact the spread of tariffs stimulated heated and divisive debate.[28] Among the most important debates was the tug-of-war over using tariffs to nurture the North's economic growth.

HUMAN RIGHTS, EQUITY ISSUES, AND U.S. TARIFF POLICIES

In the two decades preceding the Civil War, the U.S. economy increasingly relied on cotton exports to fuel growth. While the immigration of people and capital encouraged growth, according to Nobel Prize–winning economic historian Douglass North, "Cotton . . . initiated the concomitant expansion in income, in the size of domestic markets, and . . . the movement of people out of self-sufficiency into the market economy."[29]

King Cotton tied the North and South together in many different ways. Many Northerners denounced the Southern dependence on slaves to produce cotton, but that same cotton helped finance the North's development and diversification and fueled the burgeoning textile mills. At the same time, tariffs gave Northern manufacturers a captive market among Southern farmers. Many Southern farmers resented these same tariffs, because they believed other nations would retaliate by protecting their home markets. These farmers also understood that these tariffs increased prices on the consumer or producer goods that they needed.

Such mutual dependence led to a tug-of-war over the direction of U.S. trade policy. For example, in 1860, the Buchanan administration negotiated a reciprocal trade agreement with Mexico, but the Senate turned down the treaty. Northern and Western manufacturers and farmers might have benefited from greater market access to Mexico. However, according to historian Alfred Eckes, "Many lawmakers feared that the Buchanan administration intended to expand the slave system [beyond U.S. borders]."[30] Their opposition to strengthening the slave system was greater than their interest in gaining new customers in Mexico (export policies). In this case, social issues forced a debate over trade policy.

Clearly, slavery was not only a domestic policy issue, it was also a trade policy issue. Americans of North and South struggled with the question of whether to ignore, permit, or ban the products made with slave labor. Before the Civil War, North and South achieved an uneasy compromise that limited the expansion of slavery. But this compromise could not erase the truth that, given regional economic interdependence, America's Northern and Western economies were indirectly dependent on the product of slave labor. Other nations also had to deal with this issue; for example, American cotton fueled Britain's mills.

In 1807, both the United States and Britain formally abolished the slave trade.[31] But ships carrying slaves still entered U.S. ports. In fact, Americans participated in the trade under the flags of other nations, such as Spain and Portugal. From 1810 to 1814, England signed treaties banning the slave trade with Portugal, Denmark, and Sweden. In 1833, after many years of antislavery protests, the British Parliament abolished slavery in the British West Indies. Given the stormy relationship between the two countries, Northerners and Southerners alike saw the British legislation as "an attempt to weaken the Southern economy." A congressman from South Carolina made it clear that he did not think the British had the moral authority to comment on the Southern slave system, given Scottish poverty and "enslaved subjects" in Ireland.[32] The congressman had a point. Britain had been actively involved in the slave trade since the sixteenth century.[33]

But some British officials and citizens thought that they could use trade policy to change U.S. human rights conditions, or at least ensure enforcement of the ban on the slave trade. In 1841, the *Enterprise,* a ship carrying slaves that was bound for the United States, was driven by rough weather to Bermuda (part of the British empire). As just noted, *trade* in slaves was banned by both nations, but this ban was not always effective or enforced. Because slavery was illegal in British soil, British Foreign Minister Palmeston ordered that the slaves on the *Enterprise* be set free. But some Americans saw this act as a slap in the face to U.S. sovereignty. In 1842, Daniel Webster negotiated a compromise guaranteeing the United States free navigation of all border waters. Each party agreed to police its own ships in an effort to stamp out the slave trade. Thus, the two nations had effectively concluded a trade agreement to regulate a social policy objective: to end trade in slaves.

Yet this use of trade policy could not change a basic fact. The United States still allowed slavery and produced many new slaves each year. Moreover, by the years 1845–60, the price of cotton began to rise, correlating with a growing global demand for cotton goods. Much of the Southern economy was devoted to producing both cotton and slaves. Not surprisingly, the demand and price of slaves also rose. To broaden supply, some Southerners called for a lifting of the ban on the sale of slaves.[34]

Throughout this period, antislavery activists in the United States and abroad stepped up their efforts. Politicians and religious leaders in Ireland and Britain wrote letters and pamphlets urging Americans to wipe out slavery.[35] In 1834, the American Antislavery Society sent petitions and propaganda to Congress and clergy throughout the South. In 1835, in response to Southern protests about these petitions, the House passed the gag rules, preventing the House from taking action on these petitions. But abolitionists denounced these gag rules as a violation of the Constitution. In their eyes, human rights and trade policies were clearly linked. But they would have to work to convince their fellow Americans.

Although most Americans resented the British (of all people!) commenting on their internal affairs, some Americans teamed up with British antislavery activists. They thought an international movement could be more effective in ending slavery. In 1839, they organized the first international NGO to influence official policy as well as civic group action in both nations.[36] According to political scientists Margaret E. Keck and Kathryn Sikkink, religious leaders, especially Quakers, Methodists, Presbyterians, and Unitarians in both nations, were the backbone of the antislavery movement. Its members "drew on a tradition of transatlantic networking and information exchange that had flourished . . . during the last decades before American independence." The antislavery groups borrowed tactics, organizational forms, research, and language from each other. The transnational movement used facts and personal testimony to motivate citizens in both nations to oppose slavery. They cosponsored two conferences in London (in 1840 and 1843).[37]

The binational antislavery movement was noteworthy on both sides of the pond. It was both an early illustration of how civil society can affect trade policy-making and one of the first international human rights movements. It inspired other reform movements such as temperance and women's rights.

In this period, new ideas were also transforming trade policies. In 1846, Britain repealed its Corn Laws, which had greatly taxed grain imports (increasing the cost of food). The Corn Laws hit hardest on the poorest consumers and the growing number of landless urban workers who could not feed themselves. These laws had also favored the land-owning aristocracy.[38] While peasants and farmers had been moving to the cities for new economic opportunities throughout the nineteenth century, when these trade laws were eased, the trickle became a flood. These workers provided an ample supply of labor for England's industrialists. As England's economy grew, the standard of living (although not the work conditions) of some of her citizens improved. Ever so gradually, other European nations eased their protectionist regimes as they too industrialized.[39] Although many workers toiled in horrible conditions, growing numbers entered the middling class. These workers had greater disposable income to purchase more food and manufactured goods, creating expanding demand. To some observers, industrialization and open markets were creating a virtuous circle of economic growth and a rising standard of living. To other observers, including many of the same workers, the circle was not quite so virtuous. Some of these workers would eventually demand changes to public policies to tame the costs of capitalism.[40]

While British policymakers were increasingly enthusiastic about the benefits of freer trade, American policymakers and citizens clung to tariffs as the principal tool for both protection and economic development. Workers and capitalists believed that the tariff nurtured industrialization, which could both stimulate economic growth and diversification and increase the demand for labor. As the demand for labor increased, they argued that workers' wages would rise as well. According to historian Eric Foner, workers thought that the tariff helped create the middling class to which they hoped to rise.[41]

But in reality, many Americans were never to join this virtuous circle because they were torn between "the lords of the loom and the lords of the lash"—the capitalists, wealthy landowners, and industrialists who held political and economic power in the United States.[42] Moreover, although labor was relatively more scarce and more expensive in the United States than in Europe, American workers did not feel empowered. Although the frontier provided alternative ways to make a living, opportunities varied by region. Jobs were not always plentiful for unskilled workers. Moreover, the economy was bedeviled by boom and bust cycles, which made workers feel less secure about job stability. Finally, although American real wages and purchasing power was rising, many skilled and nonskilled workers feared competition from new immigrants and slave labor. Many white workers understood that emancipation could be a considerable threat to their standard of living because emancipation would expand the pool of workers, bringing down the price of labor. Frederick Douglass noted that the workers in Baltimore feared that educating slaves to be mechanics might "give slave-masters power to dispense . . . with the services of the poor white man." These workers feared competition with both free blacks and skilled slaves.[43] Nonetheless, both workers and intellectuals dismissed the links between the wage-slaves that made the cloth and the slaves that produced the cotton, as well as the policies that encouraged industrialization and those that maintained slavery.[44]

Equity among Americans, however, would become an important trade policy issue. Southern and Western farmers felt triply burdened by tariffs. In general, their home markets were not protected by tariffs, and they paid higher prices for the goods they consumed. At the same time, because America's trading partners generally felt compelled to match America's tariff policies, U.S. farm exports were less competitive in foreign markets. Although U.S. manufacturers were becoming more efficient, consumers had to pay relatively high prices both for foreign and domestic goods, including many necessities such as food or clothing. Congress, however, was not yet ready to change U.S. tariff policy in response to the needs of farmers or consumers. It was not until 1865, when the Thirteenth Amendment was ratified, that slavery and the slave trade were fully abolished. In 1871, Congressman Banks introduced a bill to prohibit Americans from owning slaves in foreign countries.[45]

After the Civil War, Republicans led the nation, and protectionism spread to even more sectors. Historian Paul Wolman notes that America's burgeoning steel, oil, and processing industries were hungry for capital and "believed themselves most vulnerable to European competition." As before, policymakers nurtured these sectors with tariffs. In some cases legislators let the industries determine the level of protection they required as compensation for internal taxes levied on manufactured goods. Although protectionism was at its essence "corporate welfare," policymakers as well as the public believed such protection was effective. Workers thought that tariffs brought them higher wages; farmers thought that tariff walls protected them from foreign competition in the home market. However, low-tariff views persisted among most Democrats and especially in the Northeast, among merchants, traders, bankers, and Eastern industrialists.[46] By this period, economists, policymakers, and other experts began to propose other more tailored policy tools. Moreover, a growing number of Americans in farms, cities, academia, and government began to question the view that protectionism benefited all Americans and preserved the nation's relatively high standard of living.

Pressure for Change

In 1882, Congressman William M. Springer challenged his fellow Americans to rethink their views about the tariff: "No party in this country . . . proposes free trade. . . . The issue is between those who desire an immediate revision of the tariff . . . and . . . [those who desire] the removal of those burdens which are . . . depriving thousands of laborers all over the country of employment, producing strikes, lockouts, and low wages."[47]

Springer was reminding his fellow Americans that tariff policies might no longer be the best or only tool to serve so many policy goals. He was not alone in his evolving critique. As the American economy became more urban, industrialized, efficient, and diversified, a growing number of Americans criticized America's addiction to tariffs and called for a new role for government in mitigating such changes. Social issues were forcing a debate on tariffs at the same time that tariffs were forcing a debate on social issues.

Farmers provide a good example. As America's farmers adopted new seeds and farming techniques, their production grew dramatically, while prices declined. According to historian Lawrence Goodwyn, the dollar-a-bushel wheat of 1870 brought sixty cents in the 1890s; corn averaged forty-five cents a bushel in 1870, and by 1899 it was ten cents a bushel.[48] Producers attempted to prevent even further price deflation by exporting. However, new markets could not solve the farmers' problems of overproduction. Canadian, Russian, Argentinean, and Australian farmers also needed new markets, and they wanted reciprocal market access to the United States. After the panic of 1873, the situation for America's farmers grew more dire. Some farmers found they could not recoup their production costs with the prices they received for their production. During the last decades of the nineteenth century, duties on agricultural products increased, partly as compensation to farmers for the higher prices farmers paid for manufactured goods and partly to thwart imports. But tariff protectionism could not help farmers expand markets for their production; they needed trade agreements that would facilitate mutual tariff reduction. Many farmers began to rethink their attitudes about government's role in the economy. Some called for political change; others decided to help themselves by forming cooperatives; and still others created new political movements such as the Grangers and the Populists. These farmers were coming to understand that government could help them, just as it had helped some manufacturers.[49]

Other Americans were also reexamining their attitudes about government. As Robert Wiebe and other historians have noted, this period was a time of great labor and social unrest. To temper this unrest, economists, social workers, and other professionals called for rigorous and planned solutions to American problems of unemployment, booms and busts, income inequality, massive poverty and wealth, and labor unrest.[50] These progressive reformers began to demand federal regulation to temper the invisible hand of markets.

Some of these reformers criticized America's addiction to high tariffs. For example, some business executives recognized that they could capture foreign markets and achieve further economies of scale and scope if the United States offered the carrot of lower tariffs for reciprocal tariff reduction. At the same time, leaders of the new national union, the American Federation of Labor, were divided on trade policy. They had long supported tariff protection, but some members were no longer convinced that high duties protected high wages. Other union workers worked in exporting sectors that could benefit from reciprocal trade agreements. Finally, a growing number of union leaders (and even many workers) gradually recognized that tariffs kept the prices of many necessities (such as food and clothing) artificially high.[51]

Ironically, some progressive reformers who also wanted tariff reform argued that those same high tariffs had nurtured the big businesses now clamoring for reciprocal tariff reductions. They stressed that high tariffs were "the mother of trusts," helping America's ever bigger business to reap higher prices for their products and gain greater market power to use against their workers, consumers, and smaller competitors. A growing number of reformers came to question tariffs for a different reason; they were an inequitable approach to financing government. All consumers had to pay tariffs. But the poorest consumers had little discretionary income and no escape from tariffs on their necessities. As a result, these citizens had little or no funds to save or invest. Middle-class or wealthy citizens also paid tariffs but had enough disposable income to save or invest for their future needs.[52]

Still other business leaders blamed America's extensive system of tariffs for creating inequities in the market among producers. Some business leaders (especially those from small- and midsized businesses) believed that many of their larger competitors were using protectionist tariffs to hold domestic prices at an artificially high level. According to historian Paul Wolman, in the waning years of the century, the chairman of the tariff committee of the National Association of Manufacturers called on Congress to investigate if tariff schedules were "congressional permits to create trusts."[53]

The tariff reform movement transcended class and region. It included editorialists from the *New York Evening Post* and the *Louisville Courier Journal,* academics from Cornell and Yale University, Democrats and Republicans, farmers and business executives.[54] The reformers had diverse suggestions: Some wanted lower tariffs, others a tariff for revenue only. Still others wanted reciprocity agreements that would lower U.S. tariffs for reciprocal concessions.[55] None of these tariff reformers wanted to end protectionism, simply to reduce it or to control it.

However, this diverse reform movement was countered by an effective and equally broad-based defense of protectionism. According to Robert Wiebe, the Home Market Club of Boston, the Philadelphia Manufacturers' Club, the National Association of Wool Manufacturers, the American Iron and Steel Association, and the American Protective Tariff League guarded the nation's tariff wall.[56]

This lobby also devised effective protectionist arguments that resonate today. First, as before, the protectionists argued that tariffs protected high wages. In their view, the tariff let America absorb ever-increasing numbers of workers, yet gave them rising living standards.[57] Second, they exported the issue of equity. According to Congressman (later President) William McKinley of Ohio, "Free trade gives to the foreign producer equal privileges with us. . . . It invites the product of his cheaper labor to this market to destroy the domestic product representing our higher and better paid labor."[58] In this view, the tariff equalized competitive conditions between U.S. and foreign producers. By linking nativist and protectionist sentiment, these protectionists helped make small producers more afraid of imported goods than goods produced by American big business. Moreover, the tariff lobby alleged that protectionism preserved American social stability. They raised fears that lower tariffs would undermine industrial development, cause lower wages and unemployment, and destroy the farmers' home market.[59] According to historian David M. Pletcher, protectionists such as Horace Greeley defended tariffs as "an early form of social planning" benefiting workers and manufacturers alike. They even argued that protectionism would further U.S. trade. "Some argued that high tariffs also actually increased foreign trade in the long run by maturing American industries and enabling them to create a better product."[60]

Voters consistently responded to protectionist entreaties because they believed the tariff had succeeded in building America's economic might. Ever so gradually, economic, social, and technological change would motivate them to think differently about what government could and should do to encourage economic growth and discourage market failures.

How Changes in Economic and Social Conditions Affected U.S. Trade Policy

Technological and communication advances (railways, steamships, telephones) in the late nineteenth century brought nations of the world closer. Economist Dani Rodrik has argued that from 1890 to 1913, the world economy may have been more integrated than it is today, as capital and labor moved between nations. Millions of immigrants traveled from the Old World to the New, expanding the U.S. labor force by some 24 percent before World War I. But these immigrants did not always find the streets were paved with gold. Economist Jeffrey Williamson noted that in this period, "globalization . . . accounted for more than half of the rising inequality in rich labor-scarce countries (such as the United States and Australia) and for a little more than a quarter of the falling inequality in poor, labor-abundant Sweden and Ireland."[61]

Technological advances helped manufacturers and farmers become more efficient. As noted, prices fell throughout the last three decades of the nineteenth century. But in the years before World War I, the cost of living rose. Wages lagged behind the rising cost of living. According to trade scholar Cynthia Hody, advocates of tariff reform exploited the lag in wage increases relative to the cost of living to repudiate claims that high tariffs protected Americans' high standard of living. The economic downturn of 1907 "tarnished the myth equating protection with prosperity."[62]

The economic and political costs associated with economic interdependence scared producers as well as policymakers in the late nineteenth century.[63] Agriculture provides a good example. In the 1870s, Europe suffered years of bad crops and had to import to feed her people. But as European farmers recovered, they sought to protect their markets from U.S. competition. In 1895, the French government passed a new tariff allowing them to retaliate against countries charging high duties on French exports. Germany also began to sour on free trade as the nation was transformed from a food exporting country to a diversified manufacturing country and food importer. In June 1879, the Reichstag passed a new protective tariff.[64] These nations turned to protection because they were determined to be self-sufficient in producing their food.[65] Even in Great Britain, the world leader of efforts to promote free trade, some producers organized a Fair Trade League. The British did not, however, raise food tariffs, because the British people believed that freer trade rather than protection enabled consumers to obtain cheaper food.[66]

Economic interdependence was accompanied by increased economic intervention in the industrialized democracies. Policymakers took action to cushion the social, political, and economic costs of economic and technological change.[67] The rise of regulation paralleled the rise and complexity of big business. As government gained new responsibilities, and farmers and manufacturers sought new markets, regulations multiplied at the state and federal level. Among these responsibilities were railroad regulation, consumer regulation, and regulation of business practices (antitrust).[68] Some of these regulations were designed not only to protect consumers, but also to protect producers. Nonetheless, this was a new style of economic policy—"rule-making."

Regulations also multiplied at the international level. Treaties and agreements to protect workers, conserve the environment, and ensure food safety were among the most important international regulations.

Ironically, given its legacy of slavery, the United States was among the first nations to enact rules related to trade in goods made by forced labor. In the Tariff Act of 1890 (section 51), the United States banned goods manufactured by convict labor. Great Britain, Australia, and Canada also adopted similar bans. The Berne Convention of 1905 banned the production of matches made with phosphorus; Congress passed the ban in 1912. These national laws inspired international cooperation. In 1919, the Treaty of Versailles, signed after World War I, pledged nations to "endeavor to secure and maintain fair and humane conditions of labour . . . in all countries in which their commercial and industrial relations extend." It also formed an International Labor Organization (ILO) to establish rules and monitor these efforts.[69]

Policymakers did not ignore the global commons. In 1910, Congress made it unlawful to manufacture, import, export, or ship in interstate commerce any insecticide adulterated or misbranded insecticide. The Federal Seed Act of 1912 prohibited imports of adulterated grains and seeds.[70] Out of recognition that there needed to be an international law protecting sea mammals, the United States, Russia, Japan, and Great Britain signed the Fur Seal Treaty of 1911 to regulate hunting and importation of seals. In 1927, the League of Nations, created by the Versailles Treaty, convened a conference to deal with the growing frictions of world trade. The conferees recognized the importance of conservation and agreed to exempt measures taken to preserve animals or plants "from degeneration or extinction."[71]

Many of these international regulations were developed by citizen and professional groups such as conservationists, birders, and naturalists. These individuals worked with their overseas counterparts to pressure their governments at the national level. Ecologists were early on thinking globally and acting locally.[72] However, in the late nineteenth century, most regulations were developed at the state or provincial level, then at the national level. Sometimes exporters and importers found that national regulations distorted trade, leading to trade disputes. Other times, policymakers deliberately turned to such regulations to preserve domestic markets for local producers. The United States and several European nations sparred over such regulatory policies in the late nineteenth century.

In the 1870s, U.S. meat producers and packers became more efficient and began exporting to Europe. Despite transportation costs and tariffs, American pork and canned meats were about 40 percent cheaper than their European competition. By the 1880s, the United States exported about 60 percent of its production of such products to Europe. European producers were understandably concerned about these imports and called for protection. In 1879, Italy and later Hungary alleged American hog meat contained trichinae, and they prohibited pork imports. France and Germany issued similar bans in 1880. Americans alleged these bans were unnecessary and strictly protectionist. But they may also have been legitimate. In contrast with American pork consumers, many Europeans did not boil their pork and thus got trichinosis from uncooked meat. These regulations prevented others from getting this condition.[73] American hog producers and meat packers were up in arms over these national regulations, but they were not inspired to educate European consumers on how to prepare such pork. Nor did these U.S. producers press for changes in U.S. tariff walls. Instead, pork producers pressed for U.S. food safety regulation. On August 30, 1890, President William Henry Harrison signed a bill authorizing microscopic inspection of pork for export. It also gave him the ability to retaliate against foreign regulations that suppressed U.S. exports.[74] The Meat Inspection Act was designed to reassure the European governments that American meat was safe because it was microscopically inspected by U.S. government inspectors. Such domestic regulation would not only serve to reassure foreign consumers and governments, it could also help big producers gain even further market share in the United States. Small producers that did not export did not have to have inspections. Exporters, in contrast, could use such inspections as an incentive to lure U.S. consumers.

But countering European food safety regulation with U.S. food safety regulation did not provide an adequate solution for American pork exporters. Much of the European market remained closed. While Germany and Austria-Hungary removed their bans on American pork in 1891, the French continued to protect. The U.S. counsel found evidence that the French government directed its customs inspectors to find trichinae in some 25 percent of all American meat.[75] Although the French Academy of Medicine noted that American pork was as safe as any pork, the ban remained.[76] In an 1884 interview with a New York newspaper, Germany's Chancellor Bismarck admitted protectionist intent: "It is absolutely necessary for us people of Europe to protect ourselves against your competition."[77]

The pork trade dispute illuminates how national regulations can distort trade. In this example, while some European nations used regulatory policies to protect, the United States used regulatory policy to expand its exports. But the level and scope of tariffs stayed constant. A reduction in U.S. tariffs might have inspired a reduction in foreign protectionism. While government intervention to assist economic growth or prevent market failures increased ever so gradually, the tariff remained sacred. U.S. policymakers continued to rely on tariffs to protect, nurture economic growth, and raise revenue.

Tariff reformers did achieve some reforms to the tariff system before World War I.[78] In 1890, Congress and the executive branch negotiated a change to trade policy-making that would have significant implications not just for trade policy objectives, but to how trade policy was made in the United States. Reciprocity treaties gave the president new authority to conduct trade negotiations, while Congress got the right to impose penalty duties on free imports from countries producing certain tropical products such as sugar, coffee, or molasses that imposed unreasonable duties on U.S. exports. This strategy was supposed to persuade our trading partners to make concessions in response to concessions the United States had made. The Ways and Means Committee described this tactic as an "endeavor to apply the golden rule to commerce." However, this approach was repealed in 1894.[79]

Presidents Chester Arthur, William McKinley, Teddy Roosevelt, and William Howard Taft also sought congressional approval of reciprocity treaties.[80] However, Congress did not always concur with this new approach to tariff policy, and high protectionists often challenged this experiment. In 1894, Democrats noted, "We do not believe that Congress can rightly vest in the President of the United States any authority or power to impose or release taxes on our people."[81] In 1909, President Taft created a special advisory panel, the Tariff Board, to investigate how tariff rates affected trade. But the Democratically controlled Congress determined that this board was too partisan and killed it in 1912. In the years that followed, the American Federation of Labor, the United States Chamber of Commerce, and the presidents of Columbia and Stanford universities, among others, called for an independent tariff commission. In 1916, Congress approved legislation creating the Tariff Commission. The Commission used economics to analyze world trade and production and scientifically determine the appropriate level of tariffs.[82] This was a first step in modernizing and internationalizing trade policy. However, it did not end America's reliance on the tariff as a tool to protect and nurture economic growth.

TARIFF REFORM

Why was the tariff sacred? For much of U.S. history, policymakers saw trade policy as a domestic issue, not subject to international negotiations. According to the trade scholar William Kelly, the United States tariff "although negotiable in principle, had not been very negotiable in fact."[83] This was probably because the tariff served multiple economic and political goals.

True tariff reform came only after Woodrow Wilson and the Democratic Party captured the White House and Congress in 1913. The Underwood Tariff lowered duties substantially. In 1916, Congress passed an income tax, making fiscal policy less regressive and finally breaking the link between tariffs and revenue. Yet this important policy change did not destroy public perceptions that tariff walls could protect Americans from unemployment or economic change.

Many Americans still linked patriotism, economic nationalism, and protectionism. Europe was at war in 1914, and some protectionists argued that Europe would dump its cheap goods once the war ended. Thus, they opposed the plans of the reformers (mainly Democrats) to lower tariffs. According to Robert Wiebe, wool manufacturers accused the Democrats of placing "some other country first and America afterwards" in their tariff policies. Spokesmen for the chemical industry alluded to "alien influences among low-tariff congressmen."[84] Protectionists were not afraid to scapegoat internationalism.

But international economic developments would force American trade policy to change. Like most policy changes, the modernization and internationalization of U.S. trade policy moved one step forward, two steps back. In the interwar period, the industrialized world found it difficult to respond effectively to economic changes. Governments began to forgo international cooperation and pursued economic nationalistic and aggressive economic policies.[85]

The 1920s were a time of major economic dislocation for many farmers. In 1921, Congress imposed high duties on about forty agricultural products and added protection for manufacturers in 1923. In this period as well, according to economist Charles P. Kindleberger, there was a shift in the terms of trade between primary product exporters and manufactured goods exporters. The value of agriculture exports slumped and farmers around the world bought less. As demand contracted, the developed economies contracted credit and imposed trade restrictions. Agricultural nations went into a slump.[86] American exporters were deeply hurt by this drop in demand because they were dependent on foreign markets. By 1922, American companies held 16.9 percent of total world exports and 12.9 percent of total world imports, and American business increasingly relied on imports for raw materials.[87] Congress responded by passing increasingly protectionist tariff bills. But clearly trade barriers could not stimulate economic growth. By 1929, the stock market crashed, many banks failed, and credit for lending and investment shrunk.

The Tariff Act of 1930, the Smoot-Hawley Tariff, raised rates on many different types of manufactured and agricultural products, even products the United States did not produce. Moreover, the Tariff Act also increased administrative protection and NTBs. The Act included Section 307, an embargo on "products of forced labor and/or indentured labor under penal sanctions." According to Senator James G. Blaine, its sponsor, this provision was designed to protect American labor and to improve foreign labor provisions. "America shall not give . . . comfort to those employers and planters in foreign countries whose forced and indentured labor is brought to poverty. . . . American agriculture and the

American workers ... should not be placed in competition with forced and indentured labor." Despite its idealistic objectives, this strategy was clearly designed to preserve the jobs of Americans.[88]

Yet some Americans genuinely hoped to use these trade provisions to improve human rights overseas. Trade scholar Percy Bidwell reported that in 1931–32, some individuals claimed that in the Soviet Union, where the state was the sole employer, all Soviet exports "approximated forced labor." They called on Congress to ban Russian lumber imports.[89] They did not succeed but would inspire other human rights activists to see that trade incentives (such as access to America's huge market) and sanctions could be both a carrot and a stick for change.

Although it was a tariff act, the Smoot-Hawley Tariff Act also ordered an absolute embargo on all imports of fresh meat from countries where foot and mouth disease was known to exist. (Ironically, however, in 1932, when the disease broke out in California, interstate commerce continued.) The United States also required that its trade partners prove that their products had been free from foot and mouth disease, rinderpest, and several other animal diseases if they wanted to sell meat to the United States. From the perspective of America's trade partners, these consumer protective measures seemed protectionist. They were right. During the hearings on Smoot-Hawley, a witness from the Nebraska Stockgrowers' Association stressed that if these sanitary restrictions were removed, "it means the sunset of the American cattleman."[90]

The hearings on Smoot-Hawley were the last glory days of tariff protectionism. Farmers, workers, and manufacturers argued, "I believe in high tariffs. . . . Every American industry should be given adequate protection. . . . Importers . . . believe in the . . . protectionist theory of our government." Even those individuals and groups who questioned the spread of protection did not deviate from that model. Some argued, "We are in favor of protection but . . ." or "The protective principle is not questioned, but . . ." or "I am a protectionist, but . . ."[91]

As investment declined, unemployment rose, and economic stagnation spread throughout the world. Some academic, farm, labor, government, and business leaders began to think differently about what government could do to facilitate economic revival. But trade reformers did not repudiate protectionism. Instead they built bilateral trade liberalization on the tariff protectionism that had long been U.S. policy.

In 1933, President Franklin D. Roosevelt and a Democratic Congress began several years of policy experimentation. With 25 percent of the workforce unemployed, many Americans were less certain that protected markets could create jobs. They called on government to provide a solution.

The Roosevelt administration tried many different strategies to revive the economy, including loan programs and government work programs. In 1934, the Congress approved two unusual steps. First, by authorizing U.S. membership in the ILO, Congress acknowledged that international cooperation could be an effective strategy to raise labor standards around the world. However, Congress did not provide for trade sanctions to enforce such cooperation. Second, the Congress gave President Roosevelt limited authority to negotiate bilateral trade liberalization. The preamble of the Reciprocal Trade Agreements Act (RTAA) noted it was designed to "restore the nation's standard of living," create jobs, and increase the purchasing power of the American public. The RTAA also formalized a process by which the public could have input into trade policy-making. It created the Committee on Reciprocity Information to hold hearings on the views of interested parties.[92]

The RTAA was not a repudiation of protectionism; it passed as an amendment to the Smoot-Hawley Tariff Act. As before, tariffs could only be reduced selectively on a product-specific basis. Tariff concessions were granted in return for equivalent concessions by other nations and "only after exhaustive study shows that they will not result in material injury to any group of American producers." Thus, the RTAA built freer trade policies upon sector-specific protection. Policymakers could not use this act to make horizontal or economy-wide cuts in tariffs.[93]

The RTAA could do little to reduce protectionist use of NTBs. Like her sister trading nations, the United States had become increasingly dependent on NTBs to protect. These were domestic policies, and Congress would not subject such policies to international negotiations. In Senate testimony discussing trade agreements, Dr. Strong, the chief of the Federal Bureau of Entomology, denied any connection between trade agreements and health and safety regulations: "It has never been submitted to me by the State Department or any other department of this government as any reason why we should take any kind of action in quarantine. They have left the quarantine restrictions . . . entirely out of any trade agreement."[94] Executive branch policymakers essentially were saying to the Congress that America should lower tariffs in the interest of expanding world markets. But the executive branch also stressed that such trade agreements could not compel changes to U.S. norms or laws.

Although these agreements could not cover NTBs, the RTAA radically changed the trade policy-making process by changing the procedures and players involved in making trade policy. According to political scientist Stephen Haggard, by delegating this authority to the executive branch, Congress allowed new organizational interests and government officials to develop competence on trade issues. Such officials would be less likely to kowtow to special interests and might take a more internationalist approach to trade. Executive branch officials had to weigh tariff reductions from the standpoint of the national interest rather than from the perspective of those protected by specific tariffs.[95]

The RTAA not only modernized the trade policy process, it also internationalized its objectives. The act coupled freer trade and jobs. The RTAA also explicitly linked the health of the U.S. economy to the world economy in legislation, *a revolutionary concept in U.S. law*.[96] Congress finally acknowledged that it was in the national interest to weigh the international implications of U.S. trade policy.

Protectionists tried to meet the challenge of the legislation by making old wine in new bottles. They argued that the Trade Agreements Act of 1934 and its renewals were an unconstitutional delegation of power from the Congress to the executive branch. The Supreme Court disagreed.[97] But protectionists did effectively raise two constitutional questions that would return to halt all future renewals of the RTAA. They argued that trade agreements between the United States and other nations were not "executive agreements" but treaties requiring the advice and consent of the Senate. Protectionists also alleged that it was unconstitutional for Congress to delegate authority to the president to change tariff rates. However, Congress had simply delegated this authority for a limited amount of time. Congress could always decide not to renew its grant of authority.[98] But protectionists would continue to use these arguments to say that freer trade agreements were not only unconstitutional, they were undemocratic.

This experiment in executive branch trade policy-making, pressed by Roosevelt's secretary of state, Cordell Hull, did not get very far during the Great Depression. According to historian Robert M. Hathaway, "despite more legislation designed to open up channels of trade than in any previous period of American history," American exports and imports remained far below their 1929 levels. Firms continued to fail in record numbers and unemployment remained relatively high. These changes to trade policy did not yield many new jobs for those who bore the regressive costs of protectionism.[99]

The war years, however, were a major turning point in moving the United States toward greater efforts to liberalize trade.[100] This was also a time of government intervention and experimentation. Policymakers began to use policy tools (like budgetary policy, later monetary policy) to nurture specific sectors or the economy as a whole. Meanwhile, as the Allies fought the Axis, British and U.S. postwar planners developed a broad range of plans to encourage international trade and economic growth. These individuals acted with urgency because they thought that the postwar period would prove a good time to liberalize trade: U.S. unemployment was virtually nonexistent, and support for protection was relatively weak. American industry was less dependent on protection because of wartime demand and because the war cut off foreign competition. Moreover, the global economy would soon be adjusting to peacetime needs—and this should lead to increased demand. They decided that the United States could use the carrot of tariff reductions to facilitate access to its huge market, to induce other nations to relax their many barriers to trade.[101] To build a consensus among the Allies upon this strategy, the postwar planners used a flexible policy tool: lend-lease. Lend-lease supported the defense efforts of America's allies while tying these same nations to international security and economic cooperation after the war's end. While nations such as Britain and France resented using lend-lease as a tool to facilitate these economic objectives, their leaders complied because they needed American assistance to win the war against the Axis.[102]

LINKING TRADE AND THE SOCIAL COMPACT

The architects of the world trading system envisioned two mechanisms to govern world trade, the GATT and the ITO. The GATT was simply a temporary multilateral agreement designed to provide a framework of rules governing the use of border measures such as tariffs and quotas. It was built on the RTAA of 1934, and it allowed the executive branch to negotiate bilateral agreements that could then be generalized to other trading partners. The ITO, in contrast, set up a code of world trade principles as well as a formal international institution. The ITO's design reflected the understanding that domestic policies, with or without intent, could distort trade and favor domestic producers. The ITO broke new ground by attempting to harmonize a wide swath of foreign and domestic policies that can affect trade flows. Its charter was designed to "facilitate, through consultation and cooperation, the solution of problems relating to international trade, employment, economic development, commercial policy, business practices (antitrust), and commodity policy." Its architects truly hoped it would help make global markets more efficient and more equitable. Chapter II of the charter allowed nations to avoid unemployment by taking measures "appropriate to their political, economic and social institutions." Chapter II also obligated members to take appropriate action for eliminating unfair labor conditions, particularly in production for export. The charter had exemptions for protecting the health and safety of citizens or to conserve the environment. But the charter contained no way to enforce such social policies. For example, regarding unfair labor conditions it stated, "each Member should take whatever action may be appropriate and feasible to eliminate such conditions within its own territory."[103]

The ITO was the most comprehensive international agreement ever negotiated. It was redrafted several times from 1946 to 1948 by representatives of many nations who emerged from the war with damaged economies. These nations pushed for a wide range of exceptions and escapes, which essentially contravened the objective of freer trade. By 1947, some observers thought the ITO codified exceptions to the rules of trade, rather than codifying the rules of trade.[104]

The ITO was designed not only to be responsive to difficult market conditions but also to be sensitive to public opinion. The ITO had provisions for civil society to influence its deliberations, separate from governments. This was especially important to U.S. policymakers. Representatives from civil society served on the U.S. delegation in negotiating the ITO's final charter at Havana, Cuba.[105]

As the ITO evolved and was redrafted, the U.S. Congress hold several hearings on the ITO and the GATT. The business community was divided on the ITO, and many members of Congress did not understand it. In their view, the ITO did not fit the realities of a postwar world threatened by communism. Congress never voted on the ITO and signaled that it preferred the less comprehensive GATT. After 1950, the Truman administration abandoned the ITO and focused on the GATT.

The GATT was tailored to fit the limited grant of legislative authority to the executive under the 1945 extension of the RTAA. This grant empowered the president only to negotiate border measures such as tariffs or quotas. The GATT did not include most of the charter's provisions on NTBs, employment policies, and such. It did, however, include the ITO's Article XX permitting nations to restrict trade when necessary to protect human, animal, or plant life or health or to conserve human resources. Such exceptions were not allowed to be arbitrary or a disguised restriction on international trade.[106]

However, the GATT said almost nothing about the relationship of the effects of trade (whether trade degrades the environment or injures workers) and the conditions of trade (whether disparate systems of regulation, such as environmental or labor standards, allow for fair competition). In the 1940s to the 1970s, few policymakers would admit that their systems of regulations sometimes distorted trade. Such systems were the turf of domestic policymakers, not foreign policymakers.[107] The GATT also said little about domestic norms or regulations. In 1971, the GATT established a working party on environmental measures and international trade, but it did not meet until 1991, after much pressure from some European nations.[108] Clearly, regarding the nexus between trade and social, environmental, and consumer regulations, GATT was a work in progress that was progressing slowly.

To some degree, progress was impeded by the GATT's failure to consult national and international NGOs that also worked on issues that crossed borders. These groups included the World Wildlife Fund on conservation or the International Confederation of Free Trade Unions on labor rights. Although the architects of the ITO provided for a role for civil society, the GATT bureaucracy turned insular. The GATT made no connections to such groups in the interest of favoring the general interest over the specific interests of interest groups.[109] At the same time, civil society, with the exception of business, farm, and labor organizations that lobbied at the national level about trade, tended to ignore the GATT.

Labor standards provide a good example of the difficulty of accommodating international trade rules and national social norms. U.S. policymakers worked hard to get the GATT to include such labor standards. In 1953, the Eisenhower administration tried and failed to get the ITO's labor standards clause included in the GATT.[110] When the Kennedy administration presented the Trade Expansion Act, "the issue of fair labor standards in international trade was specifically recognized," according to the special trade representative (the White House's chief trade negotiator).[111] During the Johnson administration, officials debated how to encourage the ILO and the GATT to work together "in the development of reasonable international labor standards including multilateral enforcement of such standards for goods moving in international trade."[112] These officials recognized that many of America's trading partners would see such standards as protectionist trade barriers. They decided labor standards must be part of the GATT and enforced by the GATT, but they maintained that trade negotiators "must make absolutely clear that we do not intend to make labor standards a subterfuge for protectionism."[113]

Although these trade policymakers seemed eager to grow the GATT, Congress did not share their enthusiasm about this club of trading nations. Congress consistently authorized a GATT disclaimer in its extension of the RTAA, stressing that congressional approval of the act should not be construed as denoting approval or disapproval of the GATT.[114]

From 1948 to 1970, GATT sponsored six rounds of trade talks to reduce trade barriers. Despite its expanding aegis, the GATT was relatively weak in governing NTBs. According to a *New York Times* writer, "The lowering of tariffs has . . . been like draining a swamp. The lower water level has revealed all the . . . stumps of non-tariff barriers that still have to be cleared away."[115] These NTBs were proliferating. Economist Edward John Ray believes that by the 1970s, NTBs were used in a wide range of industries. He concluded that these tariff negotiations were more "effective in changing the form of protectionism than in changing the relative level of protectionism."[116] Thus, because its rules did not cover such measures, the GATT ironically inspired new strategies for protectionism.

Neither GATT's success nor its limitations inspired much public interest.[117] By the 1950s, the American public was neither widely enthusiastic about freer trade nor increasingly protectionist. Anticommunism was a stimulus for this new attitude. In the postwar era, economic internationalism seemed to be in the national interest. The United States survived the war with its production capability intact and its productivity high, in contrast with that of Europe or Asia. Many firms had to export, and many producers believed that such exports could ensure that the workforce (especially World War II veterans) remained employed. With the end of the war, Republican and Democratic policymakers, business leaders, and other elites began to see that economic internationalism could prevent economic rivalries and yield greater prosperity for the United States and its allies.[118] The linkage between national security, the domestic economy, and international political stability continued through the 1960s.[119] Republicans and Democrats alike concurred with this perspective. It seemed cheaper to help the world's nations through trade than by relying on expensive foreign aid programs to prevent the spread of communism. Moreover, Americans were relatively unchallenged as exporters, given higher labor and investment productivity. Americans often produced the best, most high-tech, cost-effective products.

However, multilateralism came with on-budget costs to the U.S. economy and other industrialized economies. As John Gerard Ruggie thoughtfully pointed out: "From the start, international liberalization was coupled with a domestic social compact. Governments asked their publics to embrace the change and dislocation that comes with liberalization in return for the promise of help in containing and socializing the adjustment costs."[120] In the United States, policymakers attempted to forestall protectionism by funding unemployment compensation. But such funding was relatively small and reached few workers. Not surprisingly, protectionism was never dormant. Some sectors, such as shoes, watches, and gloves, needed relief from injurious imports in the 1950s. Other sectors were co-opted by legislation, such as the escape clause, which provided for the withdrawal or modification of concessions (tariff bindings negotiated under the GATT) that caused or threatened to cause injury to a domestic industry.[121]

Although economic *internationalism* rather than economic *nationalism* was now seen as patriotic, many Americans continued to believe in protectionism as a preferred economic policy tool. After all, they believed that protectionism had helped make America strong. Moreover, many Americans believed economic policy should benefit Americans first. Finally, protectionists continued to root their arguments in the American economic tradition, in economic self-interest, and in American values. Echoing history, they argued that lower tariffs forced American workers to compete with slave or low-wage labor, undermining American democracy and lowering the nation's standard of living.[122] They also argued that freer trade was undemocratic and linked support for freer trade with support for communism.[123] But the context in which protectionists made their arguments had changed. Thus, they would now begin their case by stating, "I am a free trader but . . . my industry or community deserves protection."[124]

America's transition from protectionism to economic internationalism was never complete. Historian Alfred Eckes noted that in 1959, CIA director John McCone predicted "the problem of foreign competition with American business was . . . going to grow rapidly."[125] Moreover, multilateral trade liberalization was built on an inherent contradiction. Sector-specific protection was patched onto broader trade policies.[126] Thus, protectionism was never fully discredited.

In 1947, economist Jacob Viner, an adviser to the Department of State on postwar trade negotiations, wrote, "There are few free traders in the present-day world, no one pays attention to their views, and no person in authority anywhere advocates free trade."[127] Nonetheless, in the postwar era, protectionists were relatively quiet, but they would not remain quiet for long.

The debate over trade policy was never just about how to protect. Because tariffs had diverse functions, when Americans talked about trade they were also talking about what the federal government should do to encourage economic growth, how it should do it, and how it could be paid for. They were talking in addition about how trade policy affected the achievement of other important policy goals, such as promoting democracy or human rights. However, because tariffs seemed to do these functions well, economic nationalists held sway over the trade debate. Protectionism was the American way for much of U.S. history.

Trade policy was slowly internationalized as the United States became more economically interdependent. During the Great Depression, a growing number of Americans understood that expanded trade could create greater national economic growth. Such economic growth could be made more equitable with a global system of rules. Such rules were written in the ITO. But the ITO never came into existence. The GATT was initially limited to rules governing border measures. Trade policymakers did not focus on NTBs, believing that such regulations were the turf of domestic policy. But its proponents did not convince the public that the GATT could help regulate global markets (help make markets work equitably as well as efficiently). The GATT did not develop relationships with civil society. It kept the organized public—whether business or human rights activists—at arm's length and relied on governments to communicate the rationale for trade agreements.

In the 1960s, the federal and state governments gained new responsibilities for protecting the environment and citizens from harm. In this period, open markets began to stimulate greater public protest. As unemployment increased, producers often blamed trade. Although the United States continued to protect certain sectors and to exempt others from trade liberalization, the United States led global efforts to regulate protection. Meanwhile, some groups saw an opportunity to use trade policy to achieve other important policy goals, such as encouraging human rights overseas. In the 1970s, policymakers found it hard to reconcile national and international social policies with freer trade. This dilemma is examined in chapter 3.

CHAPTER 3

How the GATT Came to Intersect with the Regulatory Social Compact

IN 1965, ATTORNEY Ralph Nader loaded a slingshot and lobbed at General Motors, one of the world's largest corporations. In a grim, fact-laden book, *Unsafe at Any Speed,* Nader criticized the design, production, and marketing of an unsafe car, the Corvair.[1] With this volley, Nader helped modernize America's approach to social regulation, calling for government regulation of business as well as public monitoring of such regulation. Nader became a liberal icon, devoting "his life to defending the American public against corporate negligence and government indifference."[2]

In the United States and other industrialized nations, activists such as Ralph Nader demanded, obtained, defended, critiqued, and monitored a wide range of regulations to govern discrimination, the environment and public health, and the workplace.[3] These "social regulations" were designed to achieve functional objectives such as ensuring certain workplace conditions or providing labeling or content information to consumers. Moreover, these social regulations were economy wide rather than sector-specific.[4]

In the 1960s to 1980s, the number and scope of social regulation expanded dramatically. But these regulations were not written in stone; the regulatory system grew and shrunk as markets and public priorities for regulation changed over time. Nonetheless, there was often wide public support for such regulation, especially in the area of environmental protection.

Many business leaders, however, understandably saw these regulations as costs to the bottom line instead of investments in the general welfare of their stakeholders. Business executives did not respond uniformly. Some firms quietly accepted such increased regulation; others saw it as an opportunity to gain market share from their competitors because they could more quickly or more easily amortize the costs of regulation. However, most business leaders saw this trend as a major impediment, distracting business from responding to domestic and global market conditions.

These business leaders needed to be alert because market conditions were changing rapidly. The Kennedy Round, the sixth round of international tariff negotiations (1962–67), sponsored under the aegis of the GATT, had dramatically lowered tariffs, which helped Americans increase both their exports and their imports. Stores from Saks Fifth Avenue to Sears were bursting with goods from around the globe. The price and availability of these goods kept U.S. companies on their toes and helped dampen American inflation. But some Americans lost jobs as American firms lost market share due to foreign competition.

Trade's costs and benefits were simply not on the agenda of most Americans. However, a small, vocal, and growing minority of Americans joined economic nationalists in questioning the cost of trade and economic interdependence in the 1960s and 1970s. Their voices got louder in the 1970s, as European and Japanese firms captured growing shares of U.S. and global markets for industries as diverse as textiles and steel.

Members of Congress and some policymakers grew concerned about the fate of the workers and proprietors in these sectors, but the GATT limited their ability to use traditional protectionist tools such as tariffs. However, Washington is a town of ambitious creative individuals and ever so gradually, some sectors demanded and received other tools of protection such as voluntary restraint agreements or quota "arrangements." State and local policymakers were also "creative" in their approach to protection. For example, some states and cities passed ordinances requiring retailers to post signs noting, "Japanese Goods Sold Here," or "Communist (Soviet) Goods Sold Here."[5] Moreover, policymakers became more creative in their use of regulations—for example, procurement regulations—as a tool to discriminate among domestic and foreign producers. At the same time, business leaders began to understand that these regulations gave them a slight market edge over their foreign competitors. These executives had a home court advantage: They found it easier and cheaper to comply with domestic regulations than many of their foreign competitors.

The United States was not alone in its growing recourse to such NTBs in the 1960s and 1970s. Trade policymakers, economists, and business leaders around the world were very worried about the proliferation of these "invisible" barriers to trade. In 1939, economist Percy Bidwell wrote that the proliferation of these barriers stemmed from "the steady extension of government regulation of domestic business."[6] Yet not all NTBs are regulations (such as subsidies). Moreover, most regulations were not designed to distort trade. Why did these NTBs, especially regulations, seem to be proliferating? Nations were trading more at the same time that they were regulating more. But there was little international common ground on how to govern the trade distortions of these NTBs. During the Kennedy Round of trade negotiations, GATT signatories tried to negotiate common rules to govern NTBs. But in 1967, the U.S. Congress balked.

By the 1970s, however, Congress acknowledged that the United States would have to find international common ground on regulating NTBs. To do so, Congress would have to grant unprecedented authority to the executive branch at the very time that America was facing a constitutional crisis: an investigation of President Richard M. Nixon's abuse of presidential powers. As pressure grew on President Nixon to resign, Congress seized greater control over trade policy-making.

In 1974, Congress passed the Trade Act of 1974 (PL 93-618), which granted new authority to negotiate such NTBs. The act provided for strict congressional monitoring of the scope of the negotiations and spelled out a process for adjusting U.S. law if necessary. The law also set up a system of advisory committees designed to make trade policy-making more democratic. But the act was historic for other reasons. In the Jackson-Vanik amendment, Congress explicitly linked trade policy to Soviet willingness to improve its human rights record. By so doing, Congress made social results an acceptable objective for some trade agreements and made it easier for groups not concerned with the economic effects of trade (such as those concerned about protecting dolphins) to influence trade policies.

America in the Sixties and Seventies

Americans were doing well in the 1960s. From 1965 to 1973, U.S. real growth in gross domestic product rose 1.6 percent, and real wages per hour increased at an annual rate of 2.6 percent. America was the confident world economic leader, the world's leading exporter of goods, foreign investment, technology, and even culture. Although the United States was receptive to importing new products, people, and ideas from abroad, Americans may have taken their economic success for granted. Because of their enormous market share, shrewd management, and technological edge, many American executives, economists, and government officials may have assumed that the days of American economic dominance would never end.[7]

However, many of these same executives were laying the seeds for other producers and other economies to improve their productivity and standard of living. Many companies were expanding their overseas investment in people and technologies. At the same time, policymakers in other nations were doing everything they could to attract foreign investment by training their citizens to be productive workers and spending government funds on research and development. Global markets reflected these trends. American companies were losing market share in sectors where U.S. firms were long considered invulnerable, such as computers, aircraft, semiconductors, engines, steel, and automobiles. For example, in 1960, the United States had some 24 percent of the world's trade in manufactured goods, but by 1975, it had declined to some 18 percent, as other nations' share, such as Germany's and Japan's, increased. Moreover, America's trade surplus was slowly declining throughout the 1960s. U.S. companies and consumers increasingly depended on foreign producers for a wide range of goods from shoes to cameras. As a result, according to the President's Council on Competitiveness, by the 1970s, the United States was no longer "immune against the vicissitudes of other economies and the economic policies of their governments."[8]

America's slowly declining economic prowess, however, was not central to public concern. In the 1960s and 1970s, Americans were preoccupied with social and political issues such as civil rights, women's rights, the environment, poverty, and the escalating war in Vietnam. Some Americans took that debate directly to the public—door to door, marching in the streets, organizing sit-ins and teach-ins.[9] But many other Americans saw such actions as an assault on American values and authority figures. As Vice President Spiro Agnew said in 1969, "policy cannot be made in the streets."[10] However, these citizens took to the streets to ensure that official policies were made in the sunshine, by a cross section of the concerned public.

These activists had a great influence on public policy in the 1960s and 1970s. Ralph Nader provides a good example. Nader built on tactics learned in the civil rights and environmental movements: combining public education, peaceful confrontation, sound science, and shrewd public relations. These tactics would also characterize his response to trade policy in the decades that followed, when he would attempt to raise public concern about trade agreements in the United States and abroad.[11]

In the 1960s, however, Nader focused on the misdeeds of U.S. big business. His book, *Unsafe at Any Speed* struck a raw nerve. America was car country; Americans valued their car as an investment, as testimony to their standard of living, and as transportation. However, many Americans were shocked to learn about how unsafe some cars were. When General Motors tried to discredit the messenger, Nader gained even greater credibility as an advocate of consumer safety and business accountability. He sued General Motors and used his winnings to finance a new kind of public interest group designed to research and develop strategies as to what citizens could do to make government and corporations more accountable. (His affiliate, Public Citizen, would play a leading role in criticizing trade agreements fifteen years hence.) Public interest research groups and human rights, environmental, labor, and consumer groups, among others, demanded that government intervene in new ways and in different areas. In the next ten years, the United States began to regulate discrimination (a human rights and labor rights violation), the environment, human health, and the workplace. These regulations also gave consumers, citizens, and workers new legal rights to challenge business.[12]

Many of these regulations (such as environmental regulation) were very popular with the public.[13] Some opened up new opportunities for more Americans; others improved working conditions, the environment, and human rights. However, because these regulations came with costs to taxpayers and producers, they weren't very popular with executives. Business leaders often tried to pass on these costs to consumers.

The United States was not alone in this trend of using government to regulate the environment, the market, and the workplace.[14] Other nations such as Germany, Denmark, Canada, and Japan also took on new and expanded responsibilities to protect consumers, workers, and the environment. Most of these social regulations were not designed to distort trade, but sometimes without deliberate intent, they may have had a trade distorting effect. For example, the 1966 Fair Packaging and Labeling Act required producers to state what a package contains, how much it contains, and who made the product. Both foreign and domestic producers would have had to hire engineers to redesign the package to include such information, but foreign companies would also have to hire translators to write this information in English. By clearly stating where the product was made and by whom, consumers would find it easier to buy American, if they so chose. Thus, although such requirements would raise initial costs for all producers, these costs may have been higher for foreign producers. Moreover, domestic companies might be able to respond more quickly or more efficiently to such regulations and amortize these costs.

These social regulations were put in place at the same time that many nations, including the United States, were increasingly relying on NTBs to protect. Thus, without intent, these social regulations may have *appeared* protectionist in intent and in effect. Yet some of these regulations may have been designed with a secondary goal of protection. For example, the 1966 Traffic Safety Act, inspired by Ralph Nader, delineated safety standards for motor vehicles. Although it clearly had a consumer protective rationale, some foreign governments and producers perceived that it was written in such a way that U.S. car makers would find it easier to comply with.[15]

Such social regulations proliferated at a time when imports were rising and producers demanded protection. U.S. consumers were increasingly attracted to imports because they were often well made and cheaper than U.S.-made goods. In some instances, U.S. goods were more expensive due to inflation.

America's inflation problem was caused by poor macroeconomic management. Taxpayers supported President Lyndon Baines Johnson's Great Society Programs (such as Head Start, VISTA, Medicare, and the National Endowment for the Arts) as well the Vietnam War, and this massive spending led to inflationary pressures. After 1967, inflation made imports more attractive. By 1970, Americans had the pleasure of coping with stagflation: inflation coupled with recession. The U.S. trade balance (the surplus of dollars spent on exports over imports) was $6 billion in 1964; by 1971, it had turned negative, to −$1.3 billion. By 1979, the trade deficit was −$24 billion.[16] Not surprisingly, more Americans raised their voices in support of protectionism. They could argue that protectionist policies put Americans first and came at no direct cost to the taxpayer. This was certainly true when Americans asked for traditional modes of protection such as tariffs or quotas. But the GATT limited policymakers' ability to use traditional protectionist tools. U.S. policymakers began to recognize that NTBs such as health and safety standards might serve dual purposes: to regulate domestic markets and allow policymakers to covertly protect.

Many of the advocates of such social regulation did not envision these regulations as multipurpose tools. They paid little attention to trade policy, except to note how it benefited big business leaders. Moreover, trade policy was relatively closed to their involvement. Anyone, if they paid their way to Washington, could testify during congressional debates on trade or meet with administration policymakers. However, in this period, trade policy was developed by a small circle of elites in government, with advice from leaders from business, labor, academia, and agriculture. Environmentalists, consumer activists, and human rights activists were not part of that inner circle. Citizen activists did not foresee that some of the social regulations that they had just helped erect might be viewed not just as tools to correct market failures, but also as tools to distort trade.[17]

ON THE TRAIL OF NONTARIFF BARRIERS

As noted in chapter 2, the United States had long taken the position that nations should use overt border measures such as tariffs to protect. This was a key reason why the United States pushed for a comprehensive multilateral trade agreement to govern how nations used protectionist measures (the GATT). But the GATT did not regulate many types of NTBs. In 1956, the United States persuaded Japan to voluntarily restrain its exports of cotton textiles to the United States, and soon Great Britain announced a similar agreement with Hong Kong. These measures were gradually followed by an international quota arrangement on fibers (the Multi-fiber agreement), and special NTB protection for footwear, steel, and autos.[18]

Although U.S. trade policymakers pressed for rules to govern such NTBs, they also began to use them. U.S. trade with Canada provides a good example. In the 1960s, the two nations were each other's most important trading partners. In a 1963 study, the Canadian American Committee (a business/academic study group under the aegis of the National Planning Association) found that each nation had a panoply of regulations, administrative fiats, vague or unduly stringent standards for health and quarantines, and special protective devices that distorted trade. The authors of the study noted that the revival of vigorous overseas competition had led "high-tariff interests" to press policymakers to use NTBs to protect: "The restrictive potential of nontariff trading regulations makes them an appealing means of retreat from tariff commitments."[19] Some of these NTBs included social regulations.

Unelected policymakers in both countries were now using NTBs to protect, often without informing their citizens that they were using these measures as tools of protection. These same policymakers would have had to gain legislative approval to use tariffs or raise tariff levels.[20] Nor were these NTBs erected in a transparent manner. According to the Canadian American Committee, tariff changes are "major governmental undertakings, often attended by months of public hearings and discussion." But as "the system of administrative controls spreads its intricate network over the foreign trade of Canada and the United States, it attracts much less attention . . . is rarely debated in Congress or Parliament or discussed by women's clubs or businessmen's forums."[21] Policymakers could protect without appearing to be protectionist. While most citizen activists seemed unaware of this trend, it upset some executives.

Policymakers and business leaders were not just worried about the undemocratic use of these NTBs in the United States and Canada; they worried about their proliferation around the world.[22] During the Kennedy Round negotiations, many European governments asked the United States to negotiate NTBs. Congress, surprised by these negotiations, tried to curtail them. But in the interest of reaching an international agreement, U.S. negotiators pressed on. They signed an antidumping code and agreed to relinquish a system of special tariffs applied to certain imports of chemicals used to make dyes, plastics, perfumes, and other products.[23] When members of Congress found out about these agreements, they balked. On June 28, 1966, the Senate issued Concurrent Resolution 100 expressing the sense of Congress that "in connection with the negotiations to carry out the Trade Expansion Act of 1962 no agreement . . . should be entered into except in accordance with legislative authority delegated by the Congress."[24] Although Congress approved the results of the Kennedy Round and became a signatory of the antidumping code, it refused to change its laws related to dumping. Thus, U.S. adherence to the code was moot. Congressional intent was clear: Only Congress could authorize such NTB negotiations.

However, by the late 1960s, Congress was in a bind. Members recognized that important constituents (such as influential business leaders) believed that the use of NTBs must be regulated internationally by a common set of rules. But to achieve that goal, Congress would have to grant the president new authority to negotiate trade agreements. If these negotiations succeeded, Congress might have to change U.S. law and regulatory practices. Congress did not want to do that. Consequently, Congress could not come to a consensus as to what to do. President Lyndon Johnson, who had great success at pushing his social agenda through Congress, could not get trade negotiating authority in 1968; his trade bill was not even reported out of the House Ways and Means Committee. [25]

Cataloging Nontariff Trade Barriers

Nonetheless, some members of Congress understood that since trade policy was their bailiwick as well as the president's, they must find a solution to resolve the growing issue of NTB proliferation. If they wanted to negotiate the reduction of these NTBs, they must debate how to grant the president such new authority. Congressman Hale Boggs saw opportunity in this dilemma. In July 1967, his Subcommittee on Foreign Economic Policy of the Joint Economic Committee sponsored a series of hearings. They reviewed the Kennedy Round results and listened to government officials and business leaders from Italy, Great Britain, and the United States. Boggs seemed to be trying to prepare his colleagues for a much broader trade debate. "Trade policy touches many other policy issues, political as well as economic; it should not be dealt with as though it were entirely in a separate compartment."[26] Boggs understood that once national issues were now international issues, such as human rights, consumer safety, or antitrust policies.[27] But most of his counterparts did not share this larger perspective.

While Congress debated the Kennedy Round, Boggs's committee focused on what to do about NTB proliferation. The appendix to the 1967 Subcommittee on Foreign Economic Policy hearings included a forty-two page list of NTBs used by major U.S. trading partners. It also included a 1962 study by lawyer Noel Hemmendinger on U.S. NTBs. Hemmendinger showed that the United States was far from pure; it relied on quantitative restrictions, procurement laws (the Federal Buy American Act), labeling (country-of-origin marking), antidumping legislation, and customs practices.[28]

The committee did not take one lawyer's view as gospel but called on a wide range of experts to testify on the impact of these barriers. Joseph Greenwald of the State Department predicted "nontariff barriers are an important problem, and they will be more important as time goes on."[29] He and other government officials noted that how America handled its own NTBs would be a major test of American reliability and interest in trade liberalization. Only one man talked about how this process might affect America's system of social regulation. William Diebold of the Council on Foreign Relations warned that there are many barriers "in which the trade barrier effect is incidental to the pursuit of some other objective perhaps. Such a matter as health or safety. We are now seeing international discussions about the automobile safety arrangements which have to be adopted in this country, because they cause problems for foreign producers."[30] Diebold reminded Congress that it was more expensive for foreign producers to comply with America's increasingly diverse and complex system of regulation. Thus, he warned the Congress should not be surprised that America's trade partners saw many such regulations as covertly "protectionist." Mr. Kenneth Younger, director of Britain's Royal Institute of International Affairs, took a different point of view. He testified that the only way for the GATT to find common ground on NTB negotiations would be for the GATT's contracting parties to negotiate economic union.[31]

Clearly, the experts were divided as to what to do about the proliferation of NTBs as tools to protect. According to Mr. Greenwald, "When you come to nontariff barriers, you get involved in purely national legislation, tax systems, fiscal systems, and it gets extremely complicated. They are related to national economic policies that aren't adopted purely in terms of international trade."[32] To Greenwald, it was an issue of governance. But to economist Robert Baldwin, it was simply an issue of harmonizing regulations: "It is important to . . . establish clear-cut rules that do not discriminate against foreigners in cases where the national interest is not involved."[33] This issue would not be settled in the years that followed.

The 1967 hearings did not assuage the concerns of executives, government officials, and academics about the spread of NTBs. Thus, they sought to spearhead an international consensus about what to do. In 1969, the Committee on Economic Development (CED), a business-study group, coauthored a review of nontariff distortions of trade with its British, European, Australian, and Swedish counterparts. On health and safety standards, they noted, "Products may well be declared noxious in one country and perfectly safe in others. . . . The main issue in this field should therefore be an international harmonization of the regulations. . . . Governments should agree to investigate thoroughly existing foreign regulations before initiating new laws in the field of public health and safety."[34] Although this solution sounded logical, it ignored differences of culture, science, and politics among nations. Most governments and their citizens would not find it acceptable.

Trade officials thought that Congress might be pushed into action if its members had a better understanding of these NTBs. The Special Trade Representative compiled a short list from a survey of U.S. industry. In 1967, the GATT decided to draw up its own inventory, based on notifications submitted by its member governments. By 1971, the inventory consisted of eight hundred separate items. The Department of Commerce noted that the House Ways and Means Committee found such NTBs in sixty-nine nations as well as in the United States.

But knowing which nations used NTBs was not the same as knowing how to tackle them. As official William B. Kelly of the Department of State noted, "The Congress now enjoys the luxury of berating the Administration for not doing more to eliminate foreign NTBs without assuming the necessary responsibility for NTB negotiations."[35]

SOCIAL ISSUES AND TRADE:
LABOR AND HUMAN RIGHTS

The growing use of NTBs was not the only problem that could thwart future agreement on trade. Congress was also concerned about American workers and wanted trade agreements to reflect these worries. U.S. workers competed not only with less productive foreign counterparts but also with foreign workers who toiled in unfair working conditions. In 1967, the House Education and Labor Committee marked up a bill (H.R. 478) amending the Fair Labor Standards Act of 1938, giving the president permission to restrict imports if the secretary of labor found that imported goods from low-wage areas impaired or threatened to impair the standard of living of domestic workers or the economic welfare of communities. Congress passed the bill in 1967, but the legislation allowed the president to approve or reject its recommendations. It was without teeth, but as historian Alfred Eckes notes, it allowed Congress to show its dissatisfaction about America's growing reliance on imported goods.[36] Neither Johnson nor Richard M. Nixon, a Republican who became president on January 20, 1969, was likely to act on this bill. Although Nixon sponsored workplace safety and environmental legislation, he was less concerned about voter welfare than voter employment.[37] The bill never became law.

Congress's focus on labor rights may have encouraged a focus on human rights overseas.[38] Throughout the 1960s, Congress had debated the costs and benefits of improving trade relations with the Soviet bloc.[39] However, a growing number of Americans—Jews as well as gentiles—became increasingly concerned about human rights conditions in the Soviet Union and several of its satellite nations. The Soviets said that they denied their citizens emigration rights because they wanted to encourage assimilation among their national minorities. But in 1968, the Soviet Union began to permit some Jews to leave at a heady price: an education tax. In 1970, only a thousand were allowed out, but in 1971, almost thirteen thousand Jews were allowed to emigrate to Israel or other nations. This tax and the ambiguity of Soviet emigration policy infuriated some Americans. In 1970 and 1971, the Jewish Defense League (modeled after the Black Panthers) attempted to embarrass the American, Israeli, Soviet, and American Jewish establishments about the plight of these Jews. Some Jewish leaders talked about using trade policy as leverage to achieve human rights improvement in the Soviet bloc.[40]

In 1971, the National Center for Jewish Policy Studies developed legislation to tie Soviet concessions on emigration to U.S. trade privileges. This group was influenced by the work and tactics of Ralph Nader. Like Nader's affiliated organizations, it used both confrontational (protests) and traditional tactics to achieve its goals. This approach would gain the devoted leadership of two influential members of Congress, Senator Henry Jackson of Washington and Representative Charles A. Vanik of Ohio. This was not the first time human rights and trade were linked or the first time Jewish groups had tried to change trade policies with Russia; in 1912, Jewish pressure forced the abrogation of a commercial treaty with Russia.[41] But it was the first time that a special interest group trying to achieve social policy goals (emigration) linked with a special interest group widely perceived as protectionist (the AFL) to alter U.S. trade policy. This led some policymakers to see these human rights activists as protectionist, too.

By the early 1970s, Congress seemed increasingly receptive to protectionist rhetoric and demands. First, although trade was increasingly important to the health of the economy, imported goods were increasing faster than exports. In 1960, the United States imported $14 billion of goods and exported $19 billion; by 1970, imports were $39 billion (almost a threefold increase), while exports were $42 billion (an increase of 2 1/4). By 1979, the United States imported $212 billion worth of goods while exporting some $184 billion. Much of this increase can be accounted for by the increased inflation and higher price of oil after 1973.[42] Second, support for the cold war paradigm—that economic internationalism could thwart the spread of communist regimes overseas—was breaking down. Sector-specific protection designed for import-besieged sectors such as textiles, shoes, and watches did not provide permanent solutions to their problems, although they came at no cost to the taxpayer. A growing number of workers and the union officials that represented them were increasingly disappointed with the on-budget programs designed to cushion workers from the costs of trade liberalization.[43] Thus, they argued for protection. After all, legislators could provide such special assistance without directly alienating most taxpayers. Protection was generally off-budget.

Third, as economist Anne Krueger has noted, trade became more important to the U.S. economy at the same time that trade policymakers were increasingly susceptible to special interest pressures. For example, after the 1960s, the State Department, which took a broad international-ist perspective, played less of a role in making trade policy than other departments, such as the Department of Agriculture, that had large special interest constituencies. At the same time, members of Congress felt increasingly pressured to act on behalf of their constituents.[44] Not surprisingly, policymakers developed new rationales to justify their support for protection. For example, Republican/libertarian leader Barry Goldwater stressed that he believed in laissez-faire, but since other nations did not play by the rules of American capitalism, the United States was justified in protecting its weaker producers.[45] America's most famous libertarian was arguing that protectionism was essentially an appropriate response to unfair trade. Other members argued that because other nations did not really reduce their tariff barriers as much as the United States in the rounds of trade liberalization, the United States should not continue to dramatically reduce its barriers.[46] Senator Everett Dirksen of Illinois noted that "foreign-produced goods have prospered in our markets. But foreign markets have not reciprocally responded to our products of America's mines, farms, forests and industries." Thus, he was arguing the protectionism was justified because American producers had not obtained similar market share results overseas.[47]

Finally, protectionism was bolstered because it had become more creative. According to economist Robert Baldwin, tariff cuts achieved in the Kennedy Round (some 35 percent for Japan, the United States, the United Kingdom, and the European Community) "have revealed more clearly than before the host of other devices tending to reduce the benefits of international trade. . . . Consequently . . . many people . . . want governments to turn their attention to this neglected aspect." He was talking about NTBs.[48]

Procurement regulations provide a good example of how these rules could distort trade. For example, the United States had become an active user of "Buy America" provisions—laws or regulations requiring that certain categories of goods purchased by the government had to be produced domestically. The United States also relied on voluntary export restraints where the exporting nation voluntarily inhibited its exports instead of the importing nation applying a quota.[49] This was creative protectionism.

Creative protectionism, however, could not solve America's macro-economic problems. As noted earlier, in the second half of the 1960s, policymakers struggled to provide both guns and butter, and consequently Americans suffered through inflation. Logically, the real value of the dollar should have declined. But under the global monetary system, most of the world's currencies were linked to gold or the U.S. dollar. The dollar was not allowed to reach its real (lower) market value.[50] The high value of the dollar hurt American exports and American economic growth. As the elephant sneezed, many other nations suffered.

NIXON'S WILLIAMS COMMISSION
AND NEW APPROACHES TO TRADE

In 1970, President Nixon sought flexible economic policy solutions for trade. In a letter transmitting his trade legislation, he asked Congress for "a clear statement of Congressional intent" for negotiating NTBs. Nixon admitted he had no authority to negotiate these barriers and that his request could be perceived as a threat to democracy as well as the constitutional separation of powers (something he would soon be concerned with).[51] But as in 1969, he failed to get Congress to agree to a new round of trade negotiations.[52] So in the Washington manner, he called on a commission of experts to advise him on the direction of economic policy, to "take full account of the changes on the world economic scene." This commission, the Williams Commission, was chaired by a senior executive of IBM, one of America's largest multinational corporations. Although its purview touched on a wide range of regulations of concern to workers, environmentalists, and others, its membership did not include environmentalists, religious leaders, or community leaders. Instead it was composed of academics, business and labor leaders, and one farm leader, the same individuals and groups that had typically debated trade policy.[53]

The Williams Commission reported "a growing concern . . . that the United States has not received full value for the tariff concessions . . . because foreign countries have found other ways . . . of impeding our access to their market." According to the commission, Americans suffered from a "crisis of confidence," due to a decline in America's comparative advantage and technological lead.[54] As a result, the United States was relying on NTBs, although "a further proliferation of NTBs would be likely to weaken the . . . GATT."[55]

Commission members studied the diversity of NTBs used in the United States and around the world. They were especially concerned about health and safety regulations such as those recently enhanced in the United States. Commission members noted that regulations or standards might not be protectionist in intent but might be enforced in a manner that could distort trade. The commission cited, as an example, municipal building codes that effectively banned the use of imported steel in urban skyscrapers. Because foreign steel producers may not be aware of these standards, the steel they produce may not meet local codes, thwarting foreign sales in the United States.[56] The commission also noted that the United States and other nations had regulations affecting boilers and pressure vessels, plumbing, firefighting, and electrical equipment. The commission was so concerned about the use of such health and safety standards as NTBs that they delineated them in several pages of charts.[57]

The commission concluded that comprehensive trade negotiation could both encourage economic growth as well as reduce the trade distortions of NTBs. But the Williams Commission was unclear as to what these negotiations should achieve. For example, they did not determine whether international environmental regulations should be harmonized, given that they recognized that "setting the level of acceptable pollution is largely a domestic decision."[58] The commission seemed to be saying that many U.S. social regulations were a "comparative disadvantage"[59] to American exports; because they increased producer costs. But they also noted that such regulations impeded foreign exports to the United States. The message was contradictory; and it did not address whether trade barriers would make good environmental policies or whether proper environmental policies could raise welfare and expand trade.

Interestingly, although the Williams Commission gave a confusing message on the environment, it did call for nations to agree on a core set of labor standards. The Commission noted that international acceptance of core labor standards (such as the right to organize and collectively bargain) could increase political support for multilateral trade liberalization in the United States. The United States should support a multilateral effort to "gain international acceptance of a code of fair labor standards which would include . . . realistic means for enforcing the code."[60]

BURKE-HARTKE AND THE
TRADE REFORM ACT OF 1973

The Williams Commission could have given President Richard Nixon political cover to take bold international action, but Nixon ignored the Commission's recommendations. Nixon's economic advisers, however, would not let him ignore the international sources of some of America's economic problems. In 1971, some Americans saw economic decline when the United States had its first trade deficit since 1893. That year, Nixon allowed Treasury Secretary John Connolly to devalue the dollar, but this strategy did not ease inflationary pressures. Meanwhile, Nixon kept the lid on inflation through wage and price controls. When these controls were lifted, inflation took off. In March 1973, Treasury Secretary George Schultz effectively forced the rest of the world to accept floating exchange rates.[61]

Some members of Congress had more radical ideas about America's international economic policies. In 1972, Congressman James Burke (D-Massachusetts) and Senator Vance Hartke (D-Indiana) introduced the Foreign Trade and Investment Act (Burke-Hartke).[62] The bill was rooted in the idea that multinationals had shipped jobs overseas, and thereby eroded the U.S. industrial base. It called for quotas "for virtually all imports that competed with U.S. production." This approach was extremely controversial. It would have contravened both the GATT system and the long-standing capitalist belief that, in general, markets and not policymakers should decide how goods and services are provided.[63]

The bill reflected growing concern about America's growing dependence on imports as well as the impact of imports upon the health of American producers (see the following chart). For example, from the 1950s until the mid-1960s, unionized labor supported trade liberalization, in the belief that trade encouraged new jobs and economic growth and thwarted the spread of communism.[64] Workers and sectors that were injured by imports could demand and sometimes receive protection.

But as imports increased, and unemployment for blue-collar workers increased from 3.9 percent in 1969 to 6.3 percent in 1970, many workers and union leaders concluded that their jobs were going overseas (or down

Imports Share of the U.S. Market in 1970
U.S. Ratio of Imports to Consumption by Value (or by Volume [*])

Product	Percent
Textiles	12
Flatware	22
Leather gloves	30
Footwear (nonrubber)	30
Black and white TVs	52*
Radios	70*
35-mm still cameras	100*

Source: Peter G. Peterson, *The United States in the Changing World Economy,*
Vol. II. Background Material (Washington: GPO, 1971), Chart 26.

south to Mexico). Whether they were right or wrong, or whether trade or technological change was to blame for this job loss, union members and leaders recognized these arguments played well on Capitol Hill. Moreover, they understood that Congress would never appropriate enough money to help unemployed workers. So they called for the federal government to provide the time-tested, off-budget remedy, protection.[65]

Although Burke-Hartke did not pass the Congress, it marked a turning point in how Americans conceived and talked about trade agreements. During the discussion of the bill, it again became acceptable for policymakers to divide trade into two categories, fair and unfair. Certain nations were consistently described as unfair traders; they included Japan, other Asian economies, and of course the Soviet Union and its satellites.[66] Burke-Hartke was also noteworthy because it was the first time Congress tried to regulate the behavior of multinational corporations across borders. Thus, the bill aroused U.S. multinationals from their passivity; their executives worked harder to defend trade liberalization with words as well as dollars.[67] Finally, the bill helped set the tone for and raised the visibility of future trade debates. As trade grew more important to the American economy, a wide range of interest groups came to understand that they had something at stake in the debate over trade policy.

CONTEXT IS EVERYTHING

As members of Congress debated what approach to take on foreign economic policy, domestic economic conditions got worse. In late 1973, the OPEC (the Organization of Petroleum Exporting Countries) oil embargo and rising oil prices led to massive layoffs in the automobile industry and then in other sectors as well. Companies found it hard to adjust to rising energy prices. According to economist David Calleo, rising food and petroleum prices led to a collapse in demand— and eventually recession and unemployment. The American public was also finding this inflation difficult to live with. In 1973, the Consumer Price Index (a government measure of inflation) rose by some 8.4 percent. By the first quarter of 1974, it had spurted to 12.3 percent. Not surprisingly, 62 percent of those polled by Gallup in 1973 thought inflation was the most important problem facing the country.[68]

President Nixon hoped that inflation could be conquered by reducing government spending. He proposed a budget to starve the welfare state by terminating price supports as well as programs (such as Head Start, VISTA, Medicare, and the National Endowments for the

Arts and Humanities). Congress did not concur and moved to reenact appropriations that the president had pocket vetoed or impounded.[69] Nixon's budget-cutting threats were mainly rhetorical, but he had sent a message: He was willing to reduce government's role in the economy.

Nixon also wanted a big foreign policy coup to distract the public from economic problems: a trade agreement with the Soviet Union to cement his program of détente (cooperation with the Soviets). Nixon had helped gain farm support for closer ties by encouraging massive food sales to Russia, and he foresaw an important market in China, too.[70] He could not achieve these goals without congressional approval. On behalf of President Nixon, Democratic Ways and Means Chair Wilbur Mills introduced H.R. 6767 on April 10, 1973. This bill called for much more than normal trade relations with America's cold war nemesis. Nixon again wanted congressional permission to negotiate NTBs. If these negotiations were successful, they might require changes in U.S. regulations or legislation. Understandably, Nixon's request was controversial. In a written statement, his chief trade negotiator, Special Trade Representative William Eberle noted, "The Administration attaches a great deal of importance to the reduction of trade barriers other than tariffs." The administration needed flexibility because "there is no single negotiating approach for seeking multilateral solutions."[71]

However, in the case of legislation, timing is everything and the president's timing for this bill was terrible. On April 8, John Dean, the president's White House counsel, met with federal prosecutors and revealed what he knew about White House involvement in the burglary of Democratic national headquarters at the Watergate apartment complex in June 1972, and its subsequent cover-up. (This burglary was also an undercover attempt to install bugging devices in the telephones of Democrats.) As the cover-up continued and then cracked, America plunged into a major constitutional crisis. In the months that followed, television and radio recorded the deliberations of the House Judiciary Committee as it weighed the impeachment of the president.[72] Thus the president's request for new authority must be viewed in the context of his attempt to dismantle many government programs and the constitutional crisis. It occurred in a climate of growing distrust of government and dismay that government could not solve America's economic problems. It also came at a moment when Americans increasingly questioned the benefits of trade agreements.[73] Finally, it came at a scary time in the world. On October 6, 1973, the Yom Kippur war broke out; Israel was at war with most of the Middle Eastern nations. The United

States was Israel's most important ally while the Soviets were the most important suppliers and allies to many of Israel's enemies. As Secretary of State Henry Kissinger attempted to broker a peace deal, he argued that a trade agreement with the Russians should be clean. If the Congress linked trade benefits to emigration, it could undercut his efforts to gain Soviet support for a cease-fire.[74]

But some members of the House saw these problems as a bargaining chip to achieve their policy goals. They argued that if Nixon wanted to totally change the paradigm for foreign policy (détente) at a time of such flux, members of Congress wanted the model for trade to change as well. They did not want to repeat past mistakes, when, as Congressman Collier noted, "we gave the executive a blank check. . . . Congress . . . extricated itself from maintaining any relationship with what we were negotiating."[75] That was a mistake that Congress would not longer perpetuate. But the members did not agree on how to grant the president greater authority to negotiate the panoply of tariff and NTB barriers to trade while maintaining traditional control over the legislative process.

The House hearings on the president's bill were rancorous, detailed, and focused on this new grant of authority. The president's men made their case in conciliatory tones. According to Ambassador William R. Pearce, deputy special representative for trade negotiations, "we can't ask you for an advance grant of authority to do away with NTBs; in most cases they are linked in very subtle ways to all sorts of domestic legislation. . . . Even if you are willing to give us that authority, it is doubtful that it would be constitutional." Thus the executive branch seemed to believe that its request for NTB negotiating authority was moderate and limited in scope.[76]

But members of Congress did not concur. They were concerned not only about granting such authority but about its broader implications for the American polity. While Congressman Al Ullman worried about the constitutionality of the request, Congressman Charles Vanik worried about federalism and asked whether trade agreements and implementing legislation can override state laws constituting NTBs.[77] Congressman Robert F. Drinan worried the proposed bill did not set "a rule, a measuring stick by which it can be determined whether the President is or is not complying with congressional policy." Congressman Peter Frelinghuysen also expressed grave worries about negotiations on "the elusive realm of nontariff barriers. . . . These impediments to trade are so inextricably intertwined in a web of domestic social, economic and political considerations that Congress would benefit by knowing what the executive branch has in mind before they enter into negotiations." Congressman James F.

Burke stressed that "we are giving the president powers he never had before . . . at a time when the climate in this country is such that the public are questioning us on whether or not we should give the president any further powers. . . . Let's hope we are not around here locking the door after they steal the horse."[78] Interestingly, supporters of multilateral trade liberalization such as the American Importers Association and the Committee for National Trade Policy echoed these concerns.[79]

Members were particularly interested in how granting such authority might affect health and safety standards at the federal, state, and local levels.[80] Congressman Corman wondered whether Oregon's law prohibiting the importation of beverages in nonreturnable containers could be negotiated away by the president. Secretary of Commerce Fred Dent surmised that the president could, in effect, negotiate away such a provision. Congressman Corman also worried that "Buy American" laws could be negotiated away.[81] Congressman Charles Vanik asked the General Accounting Office (GAO) how a grant of such authority might affect environmental protection laws such as those protecting endangered species. The GAO, a Congressional agency, replied, "A President may not through trade negotiations overturn or change a duly enacted law, absent other authority of law. However . . . the President feels—and we agree—that the enactment of section 103 will grant him sufficient authority to allow him to enter into agreements which could, in effect, change domestic law. . . . Congress may lawfully authorize the President to abrogate certain provisions of law. . . . Whether the exercise of such authority by the President would raise a constitutional question would depend on the statute involved. . . . Eliminating certain nontariff barriers on imports might result in discriminating against domestic competitors and thus raise a constitutional question."[82]

Congressman Vanik also wondered if the proliferation of environmental protection or food safety regulations would lead to more trade disputes with America's trading partners.[83] Only one witness echoed these concerns. Wayne Hawkins of the Florida Fruit and Vegetable Association noted, "The American consumer cannot determine different cultural practices distinguishing the types of fertilizer, spray materials, or packinghouse conditions." He stressed that U.S. customs inspections were inadequate to protect consumers from eating imported food sprayed with pesticides banned in the United States.[84]

Congressman Vanik was concerned about consumer safety (which is improved by regulation) as well as consumer welfare (which is often improved by trade liberalization). He called for an "escape clause . . . that would assure the rights of the consumer will not be transgressed upon through any operation of this act." But Agricultural Secretary Earl L. Butz refused to grant him that assurance, noting that "if the rights of the consumer become . . . unreasonable it may result in inadequate food supplies, higher prices." He cited consumer concerns about the use of pesticides and growth hormones (DES used to fatten beef) as examples of such unreasonable concerns.[85] In his view, these pesticides or additives simply made it cheaper to produce food. Congressman Bill Archer of Texas (seconded by Congressman Wagner) took the increasingly popular view that America's high regulations such as OSHA, EEOC, and EPA regulations make competition "unfair," because other nations don't have these many regulations and consequent high costs that American business must amortize.[86]

Most witnesses, however, were less concerned with the costs of complying with American regulatory standards than with minimizing the discriminatory impact of such regulations overseas. B. H. Jones, executive vice president of the National Livestock Feeders Association, stressed that NTBs were the principal restraint on agricultural trade. He noted that Germany required that its meat inspectors be located in the plants; thus, it was almost impossible to export to Germany. Jefferson Peyser of the Wine Institute noted that the European Community (EC) did not recognize many American grapes as wine grapes. As a result, U.S. wine producers could not sell California champagne or Bordeaux to Europeans as wine.[87]

The debate also revealed that Americans were increasingly divided as to how trade affects workers. Some members such as Congressman Duncan worried about "the exporting of low-wage rates to our country . . . through products manufactured in places like Taiwan and Korea and Japan by almost slave labor."[88] Union leaders were also divided about future trade policy. While the United Auto Workers (UAW) and the International Leather Goods, Plastics and Novelty Workers' Union called for international labor standards, Paul Jennings of the AFL-CIO opposed such labor standards because they were unenforceable without trade sanctions. The U.S. Catholic Conference called for such standards in concert with stronger unemployment assistance.[89] But Lazare Teper of the Garment Workers called this approach inadequate and too expensive.[90] I. W. Abel of the AFL-CIO called for a thorough revision to U.S. trade policy: "America needs an entire restructuring based on the recognition that the concept of free trade versus protectionism . . . is badly out of phase with the vastly changed world of the seventies."[91] In contrast, Leonard Woodcock, president of the UAW, noted, "the

UAW still supports liberal international trade policy," but he called for greater funding of "measures to protect workers and their families."[92]

Many of the witnesses and members suggested that trade policies would be improved if trade policy-making became more democratic, by involving a broader cross section of Americans. They were especially concerned about ensuring broader participation in NTB negotiations.[93] The Emergency Committee for Foreign Trade (a leading supporter of trade liberalization) suggested "the President consider the views of the public" on NTBs, since the president must gain public views before entering in tariff negotiations.[94] But these suggestions got nowhere in 1973. Despite days (and thousands of pages) of debate, the House never acted on the president's bill.

Congress Crafts a Compromise: The Trade Act of 1974 and the Birth of Fast-Track

On October 3, 1973, the House put forward its own bill, H.R. 10710. This bill permitted the president to enter into NTB agreements only after consulting with the Committee on Ways and Means and the Committee on Finance. The bill proposed greater public involvement (creating the first advisory committees) and congressional involvement and oversight. The House passed the revised bill on December 11, 1973.[95] In its report on the act, the House Ways and Means Committee concluded that "this major legislation would . . . provide the President adequate . . . authority to achieve reciprocal reductions of both tariff and nontariff barriers, within constitutional limits and subject to Congressional surveillance. At the same time, it provides adequate safeguards for the rights of United States workers, industries, farmers, and consumers."[96]

As the House found consensus, the Senate delayed its consideration of the bill. In closed deliberations, the Senate Finance Committee devoted some five months to dealing with NTBs. But political and economic conditions changed dramatically during this period. President Nixon resigned on August 9. After Gerald R. Ford took office, policymakers were more concerned about the success of OPEC in raising oil prices than about future trade policy.[97]

The Senate decided that it was appropriate for the United States to encourage NTB negotiations but said that a NTB trade agreement could not "enter into force" unless the president submits two bills: a bill authorizing negotiations and an "implementing bill." The implementing bill must contain the following provisions: approval of the trade agreement; changes or additions to domestic law necessary to implement the agreement; and, in recognition that NTB negotiations could forces changes to U.S. laws or regulations, a statement describing changes to administrative practice to implement the agreement. After these steps, Congress (by majority vote) must vote up or down on the bill within ninety days after the implementing bill (which could not be altered by Congress) was introduced. Finally, the special trade representative must continually consult with the Senate Finance Committee and House Ways and Means Committee on the negotiations. This approach became known as *fast-track*.[98] As part of this legislative package, the Finance Committee agreed "to refrain from the imposition of non-tariff barriers where such barriers are not currently imposed."[99] These changes would give Congress more control and information to make good decisions about the ever broader turf that trade negotiations would cover, but it came with a price: limited congressional action during the negotiating process. That price would make the fast-track process as well as the content of trade agreement legislation controversial in the future. In 1974, rather than focusing on these issues, the Senate Hearings focused on a provision of the bill linking trade concessions to human rights, the Jackson-Vanik amendment.

THE DEBATE ON THE 1974 TRADE ACT

Hearings on H.R. 6767: House Hearings
Focused on president's unprecedented request for NTB authority
Over 400 witnesses, not including letters
Government witnesses: 17

Hearings on H.R. 10710: Senate Hearings
Focused on emigration/trade link with the Soviet Union
Government witnesses: 6
Public witnesses: over 171

The Senate hearings were shorter, but often as vociferous as those in the House. Traditional protectionists such as the Glass Workers Protective League and the steel industry testified in force against the Senate bill.[100] Some witnesses and members of Congress questioned the economic and political ideas underpinning American support of the GATT system. For example, Senator Hartke called for an international standardized wage because in the United States "the minimum wage limits the exploitation of human labor."[101] But most senators recognized that the United States could not force its standards on the rest of the world; nor did the United States want to accept the standards of other countries.

I. W. Abel, president of the United Steelworkers of America, AFL-CIO, claimed that managed economies and monopolistic industries had relegated comparative advantage "to the scrap heap." Democratic Senator Ribicoff agreed that "the theory of comparative advantage certainly goes out the window."[102] Howard D. Samuel of the Amalgamated Union noted that federal funds designed to cushion unemployment from trade had enticed liberals into supporting "unrestricted free trade." But he urged liberals to find other solutions to reconcile trade and American social norms.[103]

The Senate debate did not spend much time developing such solutions, although some Americans had a lot to say about this problem. For example, the Florida Fruit and Vegetable Association wrote about the inconsistency between trade agreements and food safety standards. Mexico was the poster child nation for this debate. The association noted the ironies inherent in a study trip of some of its members to Mexico. The delegation members "were cautioned by the travel agency, the agricultural attache of the American embassy and others not to eat any fresh fruits or vegetables." The writer wondered why Americans visiting Mexico are instructed not to eat their produce, but the United States "opens its borders freely to the same commodities so American consumers can purchase them without warning." The writer reiterated concerns that Mexican vegetable imports had pesticides banned or untested in the United States. Ironically, however, the association noted that because "Mexico imposes very strict regulations on imports . . . it is impossible for Florida to ship fresh produce into Mexico."[104]

This was not the only writer to argue that environmental regulation in the United States came with costs to American exporters. Scott C. Whitney, a law professor at the College of William and Mary and a partner in the law firm of Bechloeffer, Snapp, wrote that these costs were impeding the competitiveness of U.S. firms. His views were seconded by Cyanamid, a producer of products "for human, animal and plant health on a global basis." In written testimony, Cyanamid called for harmonization of international standards. Until such harmonization, Cyanamid called for Congress to make allowances "to bring about comparative equity between the foreign and domestic producers. . . . This will also encourage other countries to upgrade their own pollution control standards."[105] Finally, Mr. Collins of the International Union of Electrical, Radio and Machine Workers complained about America's strong social contract: "Such things as the OSHA . . . that Congress has legislated for our benefit are not applicable" to Mexico. Thus, Mexico had become a magnet for U.S. jobs.[106]

The Senate debate focused on how trade sanctions and market access could be used to support American values overseas. President Nixon and his successor, President Gerald Ford, were committed to détente and consequently wanted a relatively clean trade bill without stringent standards linking U.S. market access to Soviet emigration policies. Their views were seconded by many liberals who were still in a cold war mind-set. These individuals saw trade as a tool to encourage a richer, more peaceful world and not a tool to make a better world. Finally, many big firms also wanted a clean bill because they hoped détente would yield millions of new consumers in these Communist countries.[107] However, many members of Congress in both houses wanted to link emigration rights to trade concessions. These strange bedfellows included Representatives Barry M. Goldwater Jr. (the noted conservative/libertarian) and Edward Koch (at the time known as a liberal), George Meany of the AFL-CIO, and Senator Henry (Scoop) Jackson. These members delayed consideration of the trade bill to ensure that they could achieve the linkages they wanted. But in this delay, some observers saw protectionist intent. They suspected that Jackson was doing Meany's dirty work, delaying the bill for protectionist reasons, rather than trying to forge an acceptable compromise on linking trade and emigration policies. Ultimately, the Ford administration found a compromise that did not force the Soviets to adhere to strict public emigration rules. This allowed the trade bill to go forward. The Jackson-Vanik amendment, which linked such trade concessions to human rights enhancement, has governed trade with nonmarket economies ever since.[108]

Some witnesses warned against using trade concessions to influence the internal policies of other nations toward their own citizens. They feared that by linking trade policy to social goals, they might open up a Pandora's box of requests. Trade policy could be hijacked by new special interest groups. During the Senate debate, other groups called for linking trade to other social policies. For example, the Society for Animal Protective Legislation wanted H.R. 10710 to be amended to require Soviet adherence to an additional moratorium of ten years on the commercial killing of whales to get normal trade privileges.[109]

Despite the many delays and complicated debate, both the House and Senate approved the Trade Act of 1974. The House voted 323–36 in favor; the Senate, 72–4 in favor. On January 3, 1975, President Ford signed PL 93–618.[110] This would allow the United States, the world's largest market, to participate in the seventh round of trade negotiations under the GATT, the Tokyo Round. During these negotiations, America and her trading partners would negotiate some codes governing the use of some NTBs, including standards, subsidies, and procurement regulations. For example, the standards code was designed to ensure that technical regulations and standards are not prepared, adopted, or applied in such a way as to obstruct international trade.[111] These codes went into effect in the 1980s, and soon thereafter, activists such as Ralph Nader began to pay greater attention to trade policies.

AFTER MONTHS OF DEBATE colored by a constitutional crisis, high inflation, and ad hoc economic policies, Congress finally passed a trade bill. This bill was historic for many reasons. It granted extraordinary power to the executive branch to negotiate NTBs to trade, such as standards. Moreover, it gave such authority to the executive branch after the nation saw President Nixon dismantle many government programs. Finally, it came at a time of dismay that the federal government could not solve many of America's economic problems, such as stagflation.

But this bill was not only about the traditional turf of trade policymakers, border measures such as tariffs or quotas. This bill had the potential to affect a wide range of domestic regulations and laws that shaped how goods and services were produced. If the president succeeded at negotiating global standards (e.g., product standards), U.S. laws or regulations might have to be changed. Ironically, although the legislation was designed to mitigate support for protection and protectionist use of NTBs, it would prove to be the impetus for a new generation of critics of trade agreements. These individuals, who included human rights advocates, environmentalists, and citizen and consumer rights advocates, would see deregulation of their national social compact in the GATT's attempt to address trade distortions of domestic regulations.

The bill was a first step in making trade policy more transparent, democratic, and more accountable. The circle of participants had grown larger to include, for example, human rights and religious leaders. The bill also broadened the involvement of Congress and business, agriculture, and labor advisers. However, the circle of participants was still relatively small, despite the growing importance of trade policy to the nation's economic and political health. Moreover, these changes could not guarantee that this expanded circle would develop more democratic or better trade policies.

Nevertheless, the bill made radical change to U.S. trade policy possible. By linking trade concessions to emigration (Jackson-Vanik), the Trade Act of 1974 explicitly made emigration/human rights achievement an acceptable goal for trade policy. Moreover, it also made the achievement of *results,* rather than solely the negotiation of *rules,* an acceptable strategy for trade policy. This would have important ramifications for trade policy in the 1980s.

CHAPTER 4

Back to "America First"

Deregulation, Economic Nationalism,
and New Rationales for Protection

FROM 1945 TO 1979, most Americans simply did not care about trade policy. It was not the stuff of headlines, front page news, or sixty-second sound bites. Trade policy was made in Washington and in Geneva by a relatively small circle of government officials, trade unionists, business leaders, and academics. Critics of trade policy were not visible to most Americans during these glory days of the U.S. economy. Although many Americans disagreed with certain aspects of U.S. trade policy, they expressed their disagreement in traditional venues—the halls of Congress or executive branch buildings. Critics of U.S. trade policy rarely took to the streets.

But by the 1980s, public frustration about trade "had become a familiar image to many TV viewers." Throughout the decade, in Flint and Detroit, Michigan, as well as in Washington, D.C., some Americans expressed their anger by demolishing Toyota and Datsun cars as well as Toshiba radios. These protesters were not just angry at Japanese companies and workers for their success in U.S. markets. They were angry at U.S. policymakers for not stopping the flood of imports. They blamed these imports for the economic devastation occurring in America's industrial cities.[1]

The streets were not the only venue where Americans vented their anger at U.S. trade policy. In churches, on Capitol Hill, and on talk radio, some blamed the government for letting foreigners "take over" America's market.[2] Meanwhile, other Americans demonized America's trading partners, particularly the Japanese.[3] A growing number of Americans concluded that the global trading system was unfair, that other nations were unfair traders, and that the U.S. government was not doing a good job in making the world a fairer place for U.S. producers.[4] They linked trade to the nation's economic and social problems, which included a soaring budget deficit, high interest rates that dampened investment, and high unemployment.[5]

Other Americans adopted a more radical view of the costs of trade. They saw foreign competition as a war that Americans were losing. They called on their fellow Americans to "fight against the disappearance of the independence of the United States through . . . economic integration."[6]

America's economic and political problems undermined national confidence. As the cold war rationale for freer trade dissipated, and as America continued to experience economic and social problems, it became increasingly acceptable to call for a nationalist trade policy that put Americans first. As imports became more visible, rising from 4.3 percent of GNP in 1953 to 10.6 percent in 1980, it also became acceptable to describe the policies and actions of other nations as unfair simply because they were different. At the same time, academics invented new justifications (such as strategic trade theory) to justify unilateral (as opposed to multilateral) or protectionist actions. Even strong advocates of laissez-faire in the business community and in the Reagan White House embraced new interventionist trade and economic policies in the name of restoring "competitiveness" to the American economy.

While producers had long been concerned about the effects of trade on jobs or specific sectors, new groups and individuals began to examine how trade policy affected the achievement of other policy goals such as protecting the global commons or ensuring consumer welfare. As noted in chapter 3, the Trade Act of 1974 authorized first President Gerald Ford and later President Jimmy Carter to negotiate rules, which were contained in codes, to govern NTBs. These barriers included product standards, procurement codes, and subsidies. As Congress considered the results of the Tokyo Round negotiations, some witnesses testified that these codes could be deregulatory.

THE TOKYO ROUND AND THE STANDARDS CODE

President Jimmy Carter, like presidents Nixon and Ford before him, was unable to revive the American economy to its postwar peak. America's economic stagnation seemed to mirror its declining global clout. In 1979, the Shah of Iran was overthrown and then admitted to the United States for medical treatment. Mobs stormed the U.S. Embassy in Iran, and for nearly two years some fifty Americans were held hostage. But the United

States was unable to rescue its hostages without a full-scale war that no one wanted. This situation left Americans feeling impotent as well as furious.[7]

This sense of political impotency was reflected in the economic policy-making sphere, too. Since the Great Depression, policymakers had learned how to use fiscal, budgetary, or monetary policy to encourage growth in recessionary times. But they did not know how to rescue the nation from stagflation, slow productivity growth, and a rising trade deficit.[8]

President Carter hoped that trade liberalization might spur U.S. economic recovery. He had chosen a shrewd political operator, lawyer Robert Strauss, to close the Tokyo Round. This round was much more complex than earlier rounds because so many nations participated and because negotiators focused on nontariff as well as tariff barriers to trade. Some ninety-nine nations participated in the negotiations. Although the United States was still the largest economy, it could not force its negotiating goals upon its trading partners. The European Community (EC) and Japan joined the United States in governing the direction and content of the negotiations.[9]

The ninety-nine nations found it difficult to reach common ground on harmonizing standards for two important reasons. Each participating nation had different regulations that it wanted to preserve and different approaches to developing and administering regulations. Some nations had centralized governments. These nations could easily adapt to global rules. But others such as the United States had a federal system, where regulations were made by federal, state, and local government authorities. Regulations at each level might distort trade and might have to be changed under global rules. Not surprisingly, policymakers at the local, state, and national levels protested that federalism could be undermined by economic internationalism.

To foster compromise among these different nations with diverse political systems, the GATT secretariat prepared a draft "Code for Preventing Technical Barriers to Trade." This draft code focused on product standards (the design and performance of a final product) and not on process standards (how goods are made). Moreover, this code was designed to fall outside the GATT. Nations did not have to adhere to it unless they agreed to. (It was one of several Tokyo Round Codes.) The director general of the GATT said that participants settled on this strategy for dealing with standards because GATT did not have the proper expertise to govern such standards. He noted technical regulations "were . . . not suitable for treatment and settlement under normal GATT rules."[10]

Thus, as early as the 1970s, the director general seemed to recognize that giving the GATT limited authority to regulate product standards could be controversial. However, in the United States, few citizens were aware of such negotiations, because, like all trade negotiations, the negotiations were conducted in secret, far away from the United States in Geneva, Switzerland (home of the GATT). Environmentalists, public health officials, and consumer advocates were not directly involved in the negotiations or the advisory process monitoring these negotiations.[11] Yet the Standards Code did discuss the nexus of trade and environment, stating that "no country should be prevented from taking measures necessary . . . for the protection . . . of the environment."[12] The negotiations were not often front page news (although they were covered on the business pages).

But trade negotiators kept members of Congress well informed on the negotiations related to NTBs. Staff at the Special Representative for Trade Negotiations prepared descriptions of the codes and lists of domestic statutes and regulations that might be affected. Congress sponsored hearings on the negotiations before the Tokyo Round was completed. The Finance Committee also made recommendations regarding changes to U.S. legislation so that the United States could adhere to these codes.[13]

Congress held hearings in 1979 on the completion of the Tokyo Round. In presenting the round to Congress, Special Trade Representative Strauss was modest in his assessment of how it might impact the U.S. economy: "Will it cure all our problems? Of course not. . . . It's the first chapter in a long, long book called trade."[14] The Office of the Special Trade Representative anticipated that the code on standards would be controversial, especially vis-à-vis federalism: the relationship between the federal government and the states.[15] But federalism was not the issue that bedeviled congressional review of the code. Witnesses focused on its inadequacy as well as whether it would lead to lower U.S. standards. Richard W. Roberts, the president of the National Foreign Trade Council (a business lobbying group supporting the GATT) worried about enforcing the codes at the local level because only central governments are bound by the code. He called for future negotiations, noting "the task of removing worldwide non-tariff barriers to trade begins rather than ends with the signing of the codes."[16] The Motor Vehicle Manufacturers Association agreed, calling for further harmonization of standards because they competed in a global marketplace for cars: "We hope that the Code will stimulate more active U.S. government participation (specifically by the National Highway Traffic Safety Administration and the Environmental

Protection Agency) in international harmonization. . . . The Code will provide a means by which manufacturers may seek the removal of standards that are unjustifiable trade barriers."[17]

One international union, the International Brotherhood of Electrical Workers (IBEW), saw the codes as the equivalent of international deregulation, believing other nations were not as vigilant about safety: "In the U.S., particularly with regard to electrification, the philosophy of the public has been one in which safety has always been paramount. In the European Community and in some other foreign countries, their philosophy . . . has not been one of the same penchant." The IBEW had strong reservations: "[If the bill becomes law] we will have subordinated the standards-making processes to the international arena. . . . We cannot avoid expressing serious concern about any process that holds a potential for subjecting U.S. standards to international review. . . . The product standards agreement states that developing countries may encounter special difficulty in the . . . application of technical regulations and standards . . . and then sets forth special and differential treatment for developing countries." The IBEW argued that such differential treatment would be an incentive to induce multinational corporations to establish more of their operations in developing countries, which could endanger U.S. workers and consumers. The IBEW concluded that if U.S. companies moved their manufacturing overseas and then exported to the United States, Congress should ensure that imported products conform to U.S. standards.[18]

Other witnesses complained that the Standards Code was confusing because its language was clear on product standards but unclear on process standards (how goods are made). The Office of the Special Trade Representative admitted "the code clearly covers such issues when product specifications are involved, but some countries, including the EC (European Community) believe the code does not apply to regulations on production processes." For example, the National Cattlemen's Association testified that the EC had unreasonable food safety requirements that impeded trade, such as annual physical examinations of all employees or separate facilities for meat cutting and packaging.[19] This issue of process standards would soon flare up regarding U.S. efforts to protect endangered species.

One witness linked labor standards (how workers are treated as they produce goods and services) to the standards code. David C. Williams, representing the Council on Hemispheric Affairs stated, "It is not fair international trade for our workers . . . when U.S. asbestos processors unwilling to meet the legal standards for occupational health and safety in the United States, transfer their 'dirty' operations across the border into Mexico. . . . And then they export their products back to the United States. . . . A study by the Congressional Office of Technology Assessment [warns that] U.S. pollution control laws and occupational health standards may soon lead to wholesale exodus in major industries as manufacturers move to avoid the large costs imposed here."[20] Williams did not see the contradiction inherent in his words. On the one hand, he argued it was unfair that U.S. workers might lose jobs because the United States gave their workers and the environment greater protections. On the other hand, he was unlikely to argue that such standards should be lowered in the United States to keep those jobs here. Yet Williams was also prescient; like the IBEW, he foresaw that companies would use trade as an excuse to press for deregulation.

Despite these concerns, the Trade Agreements Act of 1979 was approved overwhelmingly 395–7 in the House, 90–4 in the Senate. It became law on July 26, 1979.[21] The Standards Code, formally known as the Agreement on Technical Barriers to Trade (TBT) entered into force on January 1, 1980. According to the United States International Trade Commission (ITC), under the Code, "signatory governments are required to ensure that regulations and standards are not prepared, adopted, or applied in such a way as to obstruct international trade." The ITC acknowledged that the Code was a small step forward, but it did not foresee its implications for both democracy and global regulation. The ITC noted that the Code could further regulatory transparency. More important, the ITC noted that the standards code internationalized the regulatory process. To encourage further international agreement on standards, the TBT also "[sought] to further open national standards setting procedures to foreigners to comment on proposed standards."[22]

Some U.S. trade officials hoped that with the Code, the United States might encourage greater transparency of standards and increased acceptance of test data generated by other parties.[23] But the Standards Code did not achieve global acceptance. By 1987, it had only thirty-nine signatories (about 40 percent of GATT's membership at that time). According to the ITC, the United States was unable to find common ground internationally on how standards should be *used as the basis for government regulation.*[24] Increasingly, however, the United States and her trading partners would find the application of such standards "unfair." This notion of fairness would greatly color American trade policy during the presidency of Ronald Reagan.

UNDER THEIR THUMB?
HOW CHANGING WORLD CIRCUMSTANCES
INFLUENCED ATTITUDES TOWARD TRADE

Given America's diminished economic and political status, many voters in 1980 wanted a leader who could restore their confidence as well as America's economic and political vigor. They picked a former movie actor and governor of California, Ronald Reagan. Yet to many observers, Reagan was no better than Carter at fostering equitable economic growth. Reagan thought he had a three-pronged solution: get the government out of the economy as much as possible, cut taxes, and deregulate.

Reagan's chief advisers were influenced by "supply-side" economists. They believed that the most important precept of economic policy-making was to pay attention to how government policies affected individual decisions to work, save, and invest. They thought that sharp tax cuts would solve stagflation by stimulating both supply and demand.[25] However, according to economist David Calleo, "Reagan's massive rearmament made nonsense of his economic strategy." Soaring defense budgets, supply-side tax cuts, tight money, and a deep recession led to very large fiscal deficits. Heavy spending and tight money meant high interest rates and a strong appreciation of the dollar. This made it more difficult for firms to justify investment in people or new technologies because they had to ensure high returns. Higher capital costs also reduced U.S. firms' ability to invest in automation, research, innovation, and worker training.[26]

Americans were stuck in a vicious cycle. After almost two decades of rising inflation, Americans saved little. In the 1970s, they understood their money would be worth less tomorrow, so they spent it. They continued to spend, rather than save, even after inflation was defeated by the high interest rates of the early 1980s.[27] Some of that money went toward imports, thereby increasing the trade deficit and the need to borrow abroad to finance the standard of living Americans expected. At the same time, the overvalued dollar hurt American exports. Manufacturers and farmers cried out for protection.

President Reagan ignored these pleas for protection and continued to espouse market solutions to America's economic conundrum. The markets, however, were not yielding growth and prosperity for many voters in 1982. Unemployment hit some 10 percent, and more Americans were living in poverty (by 1982 some 34 million).[28] While many economists believed that tight money kept unemployment high, they argued about the role of other policies, such as high taxes, fiscal mismanagement, an overvalued dollar, extensive and excessive regulation, adversarial relations, or predatory trade practices. Although some 46 percent of Americans in 1985 thought our problems were of our own making, few corporate executives took responsibility and blamed themselves.[29] But others such as economist Pat Choate saw it differently, noting that "a kind of national sclerosis, a resistance to change" had set in, preventing Americans from adapting to these new challenges.[30]

In the late 1980s, the old world order abruptly ended. In 1989, East Germans repudiated their communist government. Soon young Germans scaled the Berlin Wall and dismantled the concrete block that had separated East and West Berlin since 1961. Communism collapsed throughout Eastern Europe, and the former Soviet Union was gradually dismantled.[31]

Some Americans openly wondered whether the American poor had paid an excessive price for America's cold war defense. They noted that money spent on defense could have been better invested in education, nutrition programs, public health programs, or infrastructure (such as roads and bridges). They worried about the costs of such excessive defense spending upon the competitiveness of American business. Moreover, they questioned the policies—especially trade and developing country debt policies furthered by the IMF, the World Bank, and the GATT—that helped encourage global economic growth and interdependence. After the Third World debt crisis broke in August 1982, debtor countries in Latin America and Asia were directed to "adjust" their economies, reduce their barriers to trade, and promote exports. These countries, which included Mexico, Brazil, Korea, Argentina, Thailand, and Indonesia, among others, increased their exports to the United States. The trade deficit reflected the success of these exporters as well as that of America's traditional trade partners in American markets. Although the United States remained a mighty exporter, the trade deficit in 1981 was $28 billion; by 1983, it was $67 billion, and by 1984, it was $112 billion.[32] However, to some observers, the trade deficit symbolized how American workers were paying a price for U.S. trade policies.

The greatest questioning about U.S. foreign economic policies seemed to come from individuals on the right. While many business leaders continued to support freer trade, some conservatives began to wonder whether freer trade had served American capitalism.[33] In the fall of 1990, the Heritage Foundation, America's leading conservative think tank, sponsored a discussion among conservatives who challenged freer trade and conservatives who touted it. The conference was funded by Grover Coors (an executive with Coors Beer and one of the founders and original funders of Heritage). Now that anticommunism had been toppled as the central rationale for American policy, the participants stumbled over finding common ground for the appropriate role of government in the economy.[34] Whereas many individuals of the left could justify an activist government in the domestic sphere (the social compact) and in the international sphere, those on the right have traditionally argued for limited government involvement in the economy. Conservatives concluded that the end of the cold war meant government should return to a limited role in both foreign policy and defense.

Meanwhile, some economic nationalists/conservatives developed a new overarching rationale for American policy. They noted that other nations (particularly Japan) were warlike in their quest for market share; they stressed that the United States often engaged in trade "wars" with such nations, and thus trade was equivalent to war. They saw Japan, France, and West Germany as interventionist, and they argued that the United States should also intervene to ensure that American markets favored American producers. In their view, true patriots support government intervention as a nationalist trade policy.[35] Alfred E. Eckes, historian and former Reagan administration international trade commissioner, was a leading theoretician of this view; he would educate politicians from Ronald Reagan to Pat Buchanan. He wrote, "The world is not peaceful. . . . Trade is not reciprocal. . . . Import dependence magnifies vulnerabilities and jeopardizes American independence in the same way that economic dependence did during the Napoleonic wars." Unless policymakers put America first, America would remain what Eckes called, "a third rate industrial power because of trade policy."[36] Other nationalists concurred with this view. To prove the point, they cited polls showing "Americans feel more menaced by Japan than the Soviet Union—72 to 20 percent."[37]

This perception of Japan as a threat seemed to grow throughout the 1980s, and among some Americans, it became an obsession. As example, the business best-seller lists were full of books showing what Americans could learn from Japan, as well as books bashing Japan for taking advantage of America and Americans.[38] In a very influential study, Clyde V. Prestowitz, former counselor to the secretary of commerce, described how Japan used intervention to gain domestic and foreign market share. Prestowitz established an influential think tank on trade (the Economic Strategy Institute) to put his ideas into action.[39] Author James Fallows also worried about Japan, but in contrast with Prestowitz he took a "glass is half full" approach. In a well-received book, he argued, "A society that is true to its own culture will usually have a healthy economy. It will have found the right way to elicit its people's best efforts." Fallows recommended that Americans tap "the resilience that has always distinguished this country. . . . Japan is strong because of its groups; America because of its individuals." Fallows concluded that we could recover our political and economic drive, not by becoming more like the Japanese, but by becoming "more like us."[40]

Others sought to explain America's decline by asking different questions. In a prize-winning book published in 1982, economist Mancur Olson found the answer in the power of vested special interest groups. He noted these groups (e.g., labor unions and steel industry executives) demanded and often received special benefits from government, despite the costs to society as a whole. Moreover, the general public rarely organized to challenge such special benefits. He concluded that the power of special interests made it difficult for American society to innovate and adapt.[41]

Economist Pat Choate also wrote about American political rigidity. Like Fallows, Choate was optimistic that the United States had the resilience to respond to the "powerful tide of creative destruction" engulfing America. But in his view, U.S. trade policy must also change to meet inevitable market change. Choate believed, "The starting point in devising such policies is to recognize the limits of both free trade and multinational negotiations. . . . The principal issue . . . is not free trade or protectionism but market access." He called for a more practical, more *results-oriented* trade policy because other nations, particularly Japan and Korea, "behaved" differently. The results should be assessed not by how well they seemed to adhere to GATT's rules but by how much market share American business captured overseas.[42]

Choate's results-oriented focus seemed to catch on as business leaders demanded that policymakers find new ways for Americans to win the market share they thought they deserved in countries such as Japan, Korea, Taiwan, and the European Community.[43] But many economists were uncomfortable with this approach. They believed that trade should be regulated by focusing on rules (such as those embodied in the GATT), rather than managed through agreements setting fixed quantitative trade outcomes (results). Moreover, these economists worried that such an approach would contradict America's commitment to free-market capitalism.[44]

While Choate focused on revamping trade policy, other analysts from America's left and right reexamined trade's effects on the American social compact. Alan Tonelson, a Princeton-educated writer and analyst (now at a nationalist think tank, the U.S. Business and Industrial Council) wrote frequently and eloquently about this issue. Early on Tonelson understood that trade transcended the traditional dividing lines between left and right, interventionists and isolationists, multilateralists and unilateralists. Others, such as political commentator Kevin Phillips and Harvard professor Robert Reich, saw global economic interdependence creating a new divide with business, professional and government elites on one side (the beneficiaries) and wage earners—especially unskilled workers—on the other (the losers).[45]

Although original in his assessment of the politics of trade, Tonelson did not posit an original solution. Protectionism such as tariffs and quotas were, in his view, a cheap way to maintain social stability. Citing figures from the Institute for International Economics (the most influential think tank on trade), he argued that protecting the national interest is relatively cheap "a mere $11 billion, a drop in the bucket in a $6 trillion economy." He argued that this frugal investment in protection could boost employment, preserve communities dependent on certain industries, and hold down welfare rolls.[46]

Tonelson's views were reminiscent of those expressed by skilled workers in the nineteenth century (see chapter 2). His solution, however, could keep the economy mired in the past. With protectionism, firms might get fat and lazy, stop innovating, or let quality and service decline. Moreover, consumers would likely pay the costs of such protection in the goods and services they buy. The only way to prevent the misuse of protectionism was for citizens to monitor it and for government officials to attach conditions and time frames when they grant such protection.

NEW AND OLD IDEAS ABOUT ECONOMICS

During the 1980s, computers, robots, fiber optics, and new plastics revolutionized not just the products Americans used but how they produced these products. These new technologies and production processes inspired some economists to rethink old ideas about economics. In the late 1970s, James Brander and Barbara Spencer at the University of British Columbia challenged the bedrock principle of free trade: the theory of comparative advantage. Comparative advantage purports that nations trade because of their differences, because each nation naturally produces some things more efficiently than others. Each nation will gain more if it specializes in those goods and services it can produce at the lowest relative cost and at greatest efficiency, rather than producing everything it needs. But comparative advantage changes over time, reflecting changes in markets. The two economists argued that government could play a role in making market conditions change so that their producers were favored.[47] In reading these conclusions, some analysts purported that this model seemed to fit Japan's and Korea's approach to technology trade.

Although these ideas were controversial, mainstream economists could not ignore their implications. A young scholar named Paul Krugman took these ideas further. In articles and a book, he fleshed out "strategic trade theory." He noted that governments could and did intervene successfully in high-tech markets to create early advantages for their companies. Such governments were often successful because many markets for high-tech goods (such as computers) were oligopolistic (a few main suppliers).[48] In fact, twentieth-century U.S. history illuminated the success of that strategy, in sectors as diverse as aerospace, pharmaceuticals, and computer software, among others.

Another young scholar, Laura Tyson, focused on the policy implications of this theory. In a widely read book written for the Institute for International Economics, Tyson argued, "New developments in trade theory have demonstrated that under conditions of increasing returns, technological externalities, and imperfect competition, free trade is not necessarily . . . the best policy. Promotional and protectionist policies by foreign governments can harm domestic economic welfare by shifting industries . . . away from domestic producers. Conversely, comparable policies at home can improve domestic economic welfare, sometimes at the expense of other nations." Tyson (who would later serve as chair of President Clinton's Council of Economic Advisors) described herself as a cautious activist who favored limited use of such policies. She was cautious because she recognized that "the theoretical assumptions behind these demonstrations are very restricted." Multilateral rules would be, in her view, a better solution.[49] Thus, Tyson was noting that governments *could* intervene, not that governments *should* intervene. As the president's chief economic adviser from 1992 to 1996, she consistently argued against such intervention.

Strategic trade theory stimulated a wide-ranging discussion in academic circles. One observer noted that strategic trade theory "shook the field of neoclassical trade theory, and it may one day win Krugman a Nobel Prize." But Krugman, however much he may have wanted this honor, virtually disowned his own theory, noting trade is about mutually beneficial exchange, not competition. In many publications he chastised strategic trade theorists. This argument spilled over to Capitol Hill. Krugman, who became one of America's leading economists and a great popularizer of economics, worried that his ideas were hijacked by people who did not understand economics, such as members of Congress.[50] However, Krugman should not have been surprised that members of Congress wanted results. They had to answer to constituents who were hurting and believed that trade was to blame for their problems. Moreover, as noted earlier, the U.S. government had long intervened to create comparative advantage.

TURNING IDEAS INTO ACTION ON CAPITOL HILL

Early in his administration President Reagan seemed relatively uninterested in trade policy. But on Capitol Hill, members of his own party demanded he pay attention. Senator John Heinz of Pennsylvania noted, "Our trade policy has turned the American dream into a nightmare of lost jobs, lost opportunities, and lost lives. . . . In 1973, it cost a worker 21 percent of his monthly pay for a mortgage on a new home, in 1984, . . . 44 percent."[51] Many of these workers Heinz was referring to had been Reagan Democrats, Democrats that had voted for Reagan. Heinz argued that America's steel and manufacturing towns were suffering and deserved protection.

In truth, the administration had provided some sector-specific protection. From 1981 to 1982, the United States induced a voluntary quota of 1.68 million Japanese cars (about 20 percent of the car market); increased protection on textiles; adopted quotas for sugar; and negotiated "voluntary" quotas with the European Community on steel products. These actions came on the heels of President Carter's use of orderly marketing agreements for shoes and televisions as well as steel protection.[52] But the administration constantly portrayed itself as devoted to laissez-faire, and administration officials actively discouraged congressional colleagues from seeking such protection.

As members of Congress debated whether it should provide such protection, new voices argued for more open markets. For example, service sector exporters (such as banks) and intellectual property rights holders (such as music, pharmaceutical, and software companies) wanted greater discipline in global trade rules. They argued that the administration should focus on new comprehensive trade talks that would include services and intellectual property protection. Moreover, by the 1980s, a wide range of manufacturers and farmers became aware of the costs of protection to their competitiveness. These farmers and manufacturers used imports of materials and machinery to produce commodities or goods. Moreover, these farmers and manufacturers worked hard to influence the policy-making process, hiring lawyers and lobbyists, joining associations and directing them to influence trade policy. At the same time, some emerging high-tech companies (such as Digital or Cray Computers) became more involved in the trade debate. Their Democratic representatives (often called "Atari Democrats") represented new growth regions of the United States such as Silicon Valley, Highway 128 in Massachusetts, and Austin, Texas. But many Democrats remained responsive to their traditional constituents, such as labor, who were calling for greater protection.[53]

However, by 1983, the Reagan administration became more responsive to protectionist entreaties. The world economy was experiencing slow or stagnant growth. At the same time, U.S. monetary policy facilitated imports. America's relatively high interest rates attracted foreign capital, which the nation needed to fund its high budget deficit. The dollar remained overvalued. From late 1978 to November 1982, the dollar rose by some 50 percent against the yen. This made Japanese imports relatively less expensive and made it harder for the United States to export. Throughout the 1980s, the U.S. trade balance was in deficit. As the United States imported more without increasing her exports, the trade deficit kept growing. The 1983 trade deficit of some $67 billion almost doubled in 1984 to $112 billion. By 1987, the trade deficit stood at $159 billion. As a share of gross domestic product (GDP), the trade deficit rose from .5 percent in 1980 to 2.5 percent in 1984; to a high of almost 3 percent in 1987, when it began to decline.[54]

The large trade deficit became a symbol of America's declining economic clout. Because many Americans thought that deficits per se were bad, they blamed trade for our economic problems.[55] Not surprisingly, protectionist ideas became more acceptable and visible.

Protectionism became more visible because of changes in procedure as a result of the 1974 Trade Act. Because the act authorized NTB negotiations, it could potentially affect a wide range of U.S. regulations, laws, and policies. As a result, a greater number of committees than those traditionally concerned with trade (e.g., finance, agriculture) held hearings on the impact of trade. Many members of these committees were devoted to economic internationalism and they spoke out. Trade scholar I. M. Destler surmised that between 1975 and 1980, congressional references to trade went up by 70 percent. Meanwhile, Congress made it easier to grant or receive protection. In 1974, Congress broadened the president's powers to take retaliatory actions and established a procedure by which individual citizens could complain to the U.S. government about trade and encourage the government to carry this complaint into international forums. In 1979, section 301 of U.S. trade law was strengthened to explicitly encourage the president to "enforce the rights of the United States under any trade agreement."[56] According to John H. Jackson, America's foremost legal scholar of the GATT, since the Trade Act of 1974 entered into force, "there have been approximately 31 formal complaints to the U.S. government under section 301." Thirty-one complaints may not sound like a lot but as Jackson noted, "U.S. law is possibly unique in that it provides a statutory right to citizens to petition their government, requires the government to respond within fixed time limits . . . and encourages the government to invoke the appropriate international procedure on its citizens' behalf."[57]

Protectionism was not only visible because it was easier to obtain as a result of changes in procedure. The new laws also required policymakers to respond forcefully to foreign barriers to trade. In 1984, Congress required the office of the USTR to issue reports documenting significant foreign barriers to U.S. exports. The report's main purpose was "to identify and analyze the most important barriers of major U.S. trading partners thus facilitating negotiations to reduce or eliminate such barriers." The report found some twelve different categories of trade barriers including standards, testing, labeling, and certification.[58]

These requirements in turn put greater pressure on the administration to act. In 1982, USTR William S. Brock warned that the forces supporting protection were stronger than at any other time in the postwar period. Some analysts stated that the USTR was increasingly receptive to limited protectionism in the hope that it would co-opt even greater protectionist rhetoric.[59] By granting some limited protection, the administration could say it was responding to the needs of specific sectors while maintaining the facade that it believed in open markets and laissez-faire. According to the Institute for International Economics, "the trend in the past five years has been . . . toward a net increase in protection—especially when defined broadly to include trade-distorting subsidies and government aids."[60]

Finally, protectionism became more visible because members of Congress were passing protectionist legislation. The 97th Congress (1981–82) had more than thirty bills calling for "reciprocity in foreign trade." These bills were written to ensure that U.S. producers found overseas access to foreign markets comparable to what foreign producers found in the United States. U.S. trade policy had long been based on reciprocity, but such reciprocity had traditionally been negotiated internationally. Yet these bills called for bilateral reciprocity. This meant that if Japanese steel producers had 12 percent of the U.S. market, U.S. producers should obtain approximately 12 percent of the Japanese market. Some of the bills demanded that if such access was not met, the United States could retaliate.[61] Economist William Cline feared that this strategy would totally negate previous trade commitments. He worried that if the United States acted unilaterally in this way, it could provoke foreign retaliation and force other countries to default on their existing trade commitments.[62] Moreover, it would undermine America's commitments under the GATT. Finally, this focus on market share results would imply major changes to U.S. economic policy. After all, the United States, as a supposedly capitalist nation, believed in the invisible hand of markets, rather than in the visible hand of policymakers.

Why were so many members of Congress willing to abandon multilateral and rules-based approaches to trade? Some members, such as John Danforth and John R. Heinz, seemed to believe that other nations had not really fully complied with their trade obligations. Moreover, they thought that the United States had led trade liberalization while other nations still had numerous restrictions. Senators John Danforth and John R. Heinz were key proponents of this approach. Their proposals also built on strategic trade theory, on the idea that some nations had created unfair advantages for their high-tech industries by intervention (such as subsidies).[63] So the only solution was to unilaterally use U.S. power to achieve market access.[64]

Other members of Congress were so focused on market share results that in 1984 Congress passed a general trade bill with a global import ceiling reflecting the "sense of Congress." Although this bill was not mandated, Congress had now signaled its growing receptivity to economic nationalism. Trade liberalization was no longer the best or most appropriate trade policy.[65] The public seemed to share these views. In a 1983 poll, Americans were asked which countries subsidized their trade industries; Japan was most frequently cited at 45 percent. In 1987, some 50 percent of those polled by Yankelovich thought the Japanese engaged in unfair trade practices.[66] Polling data revealed that Americans wondered if our nation's efforts on behalf of freer trade benefited American workers and communities as much as their counterparts in other nations such as Japan, West Germany, and Korea.[67] According to the Public Agenda Foundation, there was a widely held conviction that "something is wrong" with the U.S. economy, a "real fear that the country is skating on thin ice and that . . . we have lost something crucial to our success as a nation."[68]

Clearly the economic and political pressures stemming from America's economic problems would not "let Reagan be Reagan" and allow him to remain true to his self-described noninterventionist impulses. On September 23, 1985, the administration announced it would lower the dollar, combat unfair trade practices, and find ways to renew growth in developing countries. Talking the new language of trade, the president explicitly noted that "not just free trade, but free and fair trade is the major policy goal of the United States." This was a major policy change. The president made it clear that he would occasionally abandon laissez-faire in the interest of supporting American producers. Moreover, the president noted that his administration was investigating certain practices by Brazil, South Korea, and Japan. This was the first time that the administration initiated such complaints, rather than waiting for public complaints.[69] Finally, the president expressed his willingness to pass legislation promoting free and fair open markets. However, his notion of fairness had to do with promoting openness among our trading partners. It had nothing to do with promoting equity for workers.

The president's strategy of providing some limited protection and adopting protectionist rhetoric helped slow demands for protectionist trade legislation on Capitol Hill.[70] However, the president recognized that he needed a broader approach to co-opt protectionist and interventionist rhetoric in Congress and even in the business community. His advisers recommended that he examine the broad swath of policies from trade to fiscal policy to regulation that could affect American competitiveness.[71] With great reluctance, Reagan permitted his administration to study how the federal government could help American business regain its "competitiveness."

COMPETITIVENESS: A RUBRIC FOR PROTECTIONISM? OR A RATIONALE FOR DEREGULATION?

The Reagan administration was behind the curve in assessing the competitiveness of U.S. business. Academics and even members of Congress had worried about declining wages and productivity since the 1970s.[72] These men and women knew that ultimately a nation's competitiveness depends on how productively the private sector uses resources. But some representatives, such as Senator Lloyd Bentsen, also understood that government has an important role in encouraging

productivity. The right mix of public policies can encourage investment and growth and help ensure a rising standard of living for more
of its citizens.[73] These legislators made sure that the Trade Act of 1979
required a review of the U.S. competitiveness position, with particular
attention to how government policies might be improved.[74] As a result,
in 1980, Congress received a detailed interagency review of changes in
U.S. competitiveness. But "competitiveness" did not become a issue
until the early 1980s, when business, academic, and labor leaders began
to call for a coordinated program to examine whether U.S. government
policies could better facilitate American firms competing both domestically and abroad.[75] By the mid-1980s, it seemed that everyone in
Washington thought America was an economic dinosaur, and making
America competitive became a national obsession.[76]

On June 28, 1983, President Reagan issued Executive Order 12428
setting up the President's Commission on Industrial Competitiveness.
The commission was to be composed of members with "particular
knowledge and expertise concerning the technological factors affecting
the ability of the United States firms to meet international competition
at home and abroad." On August 4, he announced the commission's
leadership and members. He noted that by establishing this commission, chaired by John A. Young, the president of Hewlett-Packard Co.,
"we reaffirm this administration's commitment to making sure this government will be a help, not a stumbling block, as U.S. industries compete." He called on the commission to identify the problems and opportunities for the private sector to innovate and "to recommend policy
changes at all levels of government to improve the private sector's ability
to compete . . . and create opportunities for American workers."[77]

The thirty members of the commission included seventeen corporate CEOs or company presidents, three senior vice presidents; officials
from two unions—the AFL-CIO and the UAW; two partners of
law/consulting firms; four academics; and two government officials
(the New York state comptroller and the science adviser to the president). The members were divided into five groups to discuss five areas:
the strategic framework for dealing with international competition;
research, development, and manufacturing; capital resources; human
resources; and international trade and marketing. The strategy group's
first task was to develop a reasonable definition of national (as opposed
to corporate competitiveness). The members defined it as the degree to
which a nation can, under free and fair market conditions, produce
goods and services that meet the test of international markets while
expanding the real incomes of its citizens.[78]

Members of the commission agreed that competitiveness is the basis for a nation's standard of living, which in turn is fundamentally determined by the productivity of U.S. industry. From 1973 to 1983, America's average annual rate of productivity growth was roughly one-seventh of its major trading partners. Moreover, the commission members stressed that competitiveness is "fundamental to the expansion of employment opportunities and a nation's ability to meet its international obligations. . . . However, without free and fair market conditions, the fruits of productivity do not flow to the nations or sectors that achieve it."[79]

As the president's commission proceeded, other groups and individuals also began to discuss these issues. They included the Business Higher Education Forum (a study/lobbying group of big business and academic groups); the Business Roundtable (a study/lobbying group of Fortune 500 companies); think tanks such as the Brookings Institution; and prestigious academic institutions such as the Harvard Business School. Almost all the studies published by these groups noted that government regulations hindered U.S. competitiveness.[80] The president's commission encouraged these groups to focus on such policies.

The commission emphasized that the government's role in the economy is "to encourage private initiative by removing barriers and providing incentives."[81] Not surprisingly, the commission noted that regulations were a key barrier to competitiveness. It said that many regulations "emerged in an ad hoc way and have frequently sacrificed competitiveness in the pursuit of other goals."[82] The commission recommended that the United States should "modify or eliminate legislative or regulatory mechanisms that are not based on a global market definition or outlook." In short, the commission was arguing that deregulation could help achieve competitiveness.

The commission noted that under Executive Order 12291, "regulatory agencies are required to submit an impact analysis statement for proposed regulatory actions which explains how the benefits of the proposed action outweigh its costs . . . and the burden the proposed action will impose on the public."[83] However, "regulations raise costs and lengthen development times . . . and raise prices. . . . The issue is not whether regulations should exist. . . . The public supports the concept of regulation. . . . Existing regulations should be reexamined and the full consequences of potential new regulations should be reexamined . . . to balance the needs of science and technology with concerns about health, safety, and the environment."[84] To justify its recommendations, the commission noted that "in recent years a large number of well-documented economic and policy studies point to . . . the costs to the society of so much regulation . . . [that] could far exceed the apparent benefits. . . . A fundamental problem in our regulatory process is the failure to uniformly and properly balance safety concerns with the needs for innovation and industrial competitiveness."[85]

According to the commission, "A national consensus has emerged that inept federal regulation . . . has become more of a hindrance to progress than a solution. . . . In fact the last four Administrations have reviewed the problem. . . . Little has been achieved, however, in the review of existing health, safety and environmental regulations as they affect the innovation of new products."[86]

In making its case, the commission frequently cited the economic costs of such regulations. For example, the commission noted that the United States had taken the lead in developing genetically engineered products, such as disease resistant plants and microbes that clean up oil spills. Such genetically modified products could have great economic potential. However, the commission warned that the EPA could thwart that potential by its desire to regulate these organisms, thereby stifling innovation as well as exports.[87] The commission did not take the view that regulation might assuage a public that might be reluctant to accept such genetically modified innovation. The commission also focused on chemicals, which were "affected by an array of federal regulations." The commission noted that at least four studies have concluded these regulations hurt innovation, create business uncertainty, and delay production.[88] Finally, the commission spoke out on regulations of pesticides and pharmaceuticals: "Evidence clearly supports the proposition that health, safety, and environmental regulation . . . is a negative factor in . . . technological innovation. Chemicals, pesticides and pharmaceuticals are examples where the impact is particularly severe." The commission also noted that this was compelling chemical and pharmaceutical manufacturers to move their production overseas, unless regulations were eased.[89] Finally, the commission recommended: "Federal regulatory agencies must be required to assess the effects of their rules on a continuous basis. . . . A key goal for the new Administration should be to put review of health, safety, or environmental regulations . . . on the national agenda in 1985. . . . No health, safety or environmental regulation of new products should seek or purport to eliminate every possible risk."[90] To the commission, the United States was regulating in an impractical manner. The commission's solution was to place hurdles upon the regulatory process and encourage deregulation.

The president's report on competitiveness received widespread publicity when it was issued in 1985. The chairman of the commission, John Young, was determined that these ideas be debated and hopefully brought into action through a dialogue between representatives of business, labor, academia, and the American public and their elected representatives. As the work of the commission progressed, several groups were organized to lobby Congress on these issues. They included the Council on Competitiveness (in which John Young actively participated); Coretech (focused on tax credits for research and development); and the Congressional Leadership Institute (formed to assist the Congressional Competitiveness Caucus in reviewing policy recommendations). Existing groups such as the Business Roundtable, the National Association of Manufacturers (which had long called for less regulation), and the Competitiveness Enterprise Institute also tried to put the commission's recommendations into action.[91] Working together and separately, these groups made sure that the competitiveness agenda became public policy.[92]

The competitiveness groups differed in their priorities, strategies, and the importance in which they viewed deregulation and new approaches to trade policy. However, these groups were dominated by business executives who were often members of several of the groups. In general, environmental, religious, and community groups were not members of these organizations. Labor unions were, however, well-represented on the Council on Competitiveness, the most prominent of these groups.[93]

It was interesting that labor union leaders jumped on the competitiveness bandwagon. On the one hand, competitiveness could become a rubric for increased aid to business or increased protection, and workers could benefit from such taxpayer largesse. However, competitiveness also became a rubric for downsizing and for threatening workers in the United States (and other industrialized nations).[94]

Given the collective clout of these business and labor players, it's not surprising that Washington paid attention to competitiveness. The House Ways and Means Committee noted "national concern has focused on America's diminishing competitiveness." Speaker Jim Wright asserted early in this session of Congress that competitiveness "may be the dominant economic issue of the remaining years of the 20th century." President Reagan pledged in his 1985 State of the Union address that his administration would do "everything possible to promote America's ability to compete."[95] When Congress finally passed a trade bill authorizing U.S. participation in the next round of trade negotiations, the bill was called The Omnibus Trade and Competitiveness Act.[96]

Competitiveness and the new attitudes toward trade stimulated an environment supportive of putting America first—in trade policies as well as regulatory policies. But business leaders were not the only individuals turning to nationalistic solutions to global problems. In this period, support for economic nationalism grew among conservatives, libertarians (even those who advocated no government intervention in the economy), and especially America's more radical right (isolationist/militia movements). A newspaper called *The Spotlight* began to focus on the "new world order" of economic internationalist companies and institutions and called on its readers to resist it.[97]

At the same time, some groups on the left also began to focus on global governance. They noted that despite increased trade, the world still suffered from poverty, disease, illiteracy, inequality, and other ills. As they looked around the United States, they observed that many Americans were poor, sick, hungry, unemployed, or underemployed. Many individuals on the left concluded that trade agreements were not part of the solution to these important social problems.

The Left Turns Away
from Economic Internationalism

The 1980s were the worst of times (and to a lesser degree the best of times) for public interest groups on the left. Environmentalists and social activists saw deregulation in many Reagan era policies. They were especially concerned that the Reagan administration wanted to reverse many environmental, social, and consumer policies that had been put in place in the 1970s and early 1980s. During his first years in office, President Reagan used the budget deficit as a rationale to cut a wide range of social programs from school lunch programs to foreign aid, as well as regulatory staff and activities. He also used regulatory oversight to thwart new regulation and to slow down the pace of regulation. These groups found that they could use their opposition to the Reagan administration's actions to raise money to oppose his administration and set up Washington offices.[98]

Environmentalists and consumer activists were also concerned by the president's international activities. President Carter had made international environmental protection a priority. Just before he left office, President Carter issued Executive Order 12264, restricting the export of agricultural chemicals, pharmaceutical products, and assorted synthetic commodities too dangerous to be freely sold or distributed in the United States. Carter wanted to ensure that U.S. producers did not then dump these products on overseas markets. But the Reagan administration took the position that the United States should not extend its environmental policies and regulation to other nations through export controls. It rescinded and abandoned the Carter administration's focus on global environmental protection. The Reagan administration also financed exports of cigarettes and pesticides banned in the United States.[99] Moreover, when the issue of international trade in hazardous materials came before the General Assembly of the United Nations in January 1983, the United States cast the one dissenting vote; all the other nations in the General Assembly voted for the measure 146–1. The Reagan administration also obstructed Organization for Economic Cooperation (OECD) negotiations on regulation of toxic substances in international commerce.[100] To environmentalists, these international actions proved their worst fears: the Reagan administration was not only not interested in global public health, but it was no longer committed to improving the global commons.

Some environmentalists decided that they must build a stronger international environmental movement to ensure environmental protection. Others, however, decided they must focus their activities on defending America's social and environmental regulations on the home front. In an influential tract, economist Herman Daly and theologian John Cobb Jr. wrote, "There are . . . good reasons to favor a nationalist policy that reduces free trade . . . and interdependence. . . . Once community is devalued in the name of free trade, there will be a generalized competing away of community standards." The two men concluded that because Social Security, Medicare, and conservation standards raise costs like high wages, they will not survive the "standards-lowering competition" that is free trade.[101]

These ideas gradually spread among social activists in the United States and around the world, leading many activists to rethink their views about international organizations. Some environmentalists began to argue that the World Bank and the International Monetary Fund had encouraged environmental degradation in the interests of rapid development. They noted that these institutions had made only limited progress in alleviating poverty. In some nations, budgets were balanced and inflation was reined in at the expense of the poor and working class. Many on the left eventually concluded that the Bretton Woods Institutions had not fostered development or macroeconomic stability, but instead simply made these nations safe for big business.[102]

At the same time, other Americans argued that policymakers had spent too much money overseas while ignoring America's problems of growing crime, unemployment, and stagnant economic growth. Some communitarians, for example, called for a society based on values of social stability and justice rather than simply on market efficiency. They believed that economic internationalism (and in particular free trade) threatened the social contract between American workers and American business, where workers were rewarded with relatively high wages for sustaining labor peace and high productivity. Some analysts, such as Michael Lind, even saw trade and immigration as tools used by the overclass to keep the native-born working classes in its place. They noted trade's (and immigration's) impact on many minority communities, perpetuating crime, poverty, and drug abuse, as well as environmental degradation.[103] Beginning in the late 1980s and 1990s, these ideas influenced many internationalists who participated in and funded NGOs such as environmental, religious, and population groups in the United States and abroad.

Some Americans of the left adopted a simplistic negative view of trade policy—that it was by and for corporate interests. In 1990, Ralph Nader wrote, "[Although] there are many good liberalizations of trade in the GATT negotiations . . . there is a citizen vacuum that is being filled by corporate schemes. Take back this vacuum."[104] In 1990, the senior editor of the magazine *Greenpeace* warned that "free trade as defined by corporate interests" will take away America's authority to protect the environment, food, labor, and small business, and put it "in the hands of government-appointed trade ministers, multinational corporations and obscure international agencies."[105] The essayist Wendell Berry asserted, "Pressure for these revisions has come solely from . . . corporations. . . . There certainly has been no popular movement in favor of them—not in any country." These views were seconded by noted Canadian novelist Margaret Atwood and Mexican scholar Jorge G. Castañeda, among others.[106] In Canada, England, Germany, and France (and to a lesser degree in Australia), the critique of freer trade was part of a larger critique of capitalist democracy. In the United States, however, capitalism was a sacred tenet. It could only be attacked on the margins by attacking the philosophy of freer trade and the mechanism of trade agreements.[107]

Like their counterparts on the right, many Americans on the left feared that American sovereignty could be undermined by the Reagan administration's approach to economic internationalism. The same administration, under the rubric of competitiveness, had rolled back regulations that controlled capitalism and moved some of these regulations to international bureaucracies or business decision makers unaccountable to the people. They believed that only in a national democratic system could individuals ensure that government serves as a counterweight to business excess. On the right, however, many individuals seemed to believe that global governance by international organizations such as the GATT was unconstitutional. Beginning in the 1980s, these groups occasionally came together to oppose internationalist initiatives and institutions. Despite their different views about what government should do, members of these groups began to find common ground in the belief that American values could best be preserved by retreating from internationalism.

THE END OF THE COLD WAR and America's economic stagnation revealed a great schism as to what our economic policies should be and what our international role could be. But in problems came opportunity, and protectionists, economic nationalists, and others tried to forge new trade ideas. Many of these ideas had a significant impact on legislation and the thinking of a wide variety of Americans. These ideas also changed how protectionism was implemented.[108] Some individuals called for strategic or results-oriented trade policy. Others justified nationalistic trade policies as a means of preserving communities or opportunities for Americans.

America's economic problems also encouraged new rationales for deregulation. The Tokyo Round created codes to govern the use of regulatory standards. But this was not enough for some business leaders who wanted more efforts to reduce the costs of innovation. They used "competitiveness" as a rubric to rail against government regulations at the same time that individuals on the left and right alleged that trade with other nations would lower U.S. regulatory standards. Concerns about such standards were a key part of the debates over NAFTA and the Uruguay Round of the GATT. These debates are discussed in the chapters that follow.

CHAPTER 5

It Came from Canada

What Americans Learned About Trade and the
Social Compact During the FTA and NAFTA Debates

GEOGRAPHY, FOR MOST COUNTRIES and their citizens, is destiny. For Canadians, it is also a source of great ambivalence. On the one hand, they live next to the United States. The largest economy in the world is a great market for Canadian exports. On the other hand, Canadians live next to the United States. The largest economy in the world exports acid rain and occasionally erects barriers to Canadian products.

Canadian ambivalence about its southern neighbor and most important trading partner has a proud history. In the nineteenth century, when some Canadians proposed closer economic relations, they were challenged by fellow Canadians concerned about sovereignty. However, in September 1985, the Progressive Conservative government headed by Brian Mulroney formally invited the U.S. government to enter into negotiations on a free trade agreement.[1]

From 1985 to 1988, while most Americans greeted the prospect of a free trade agreement with a collective yawn, Canadians engaged in a wide-ranging debate. That debate over the free trade agreement (FTA) taught many Canadians that trade policies could affect a wide range of social and environmental policies. These policies (such as universal health care) made Canada's version of democratic capitalism distinct from its neighbor to the south. Many Canadians perceived that the Canadian social compact might be at risk from the FTA.

Although the two nations passed the FTA, Canadian social activists came to understand that they must educate their counterparts in other nations to the costs of trade agreements to policies and priorities they valued. When Mexico proposed a continent-wide free trade agreement among the three nations, Canadians such as environmentalist Steven Shrybman traveled to the United States to urge their sister environmental, consumer, and civic organizations to oppose such an agreement.

As policymakers from the three governments negotiated a North American Free Trade Agreement (NAFTA), Canadian and American social activists coordinated the first multinational nongovernmental organizational challenge to a trade agreement. Linked initially by phone and fax, this coalition brought public attention to the "terms" of trade agreements.

Lessons from Canada

When Prime Minister Mulroney proposed a free trade agreement with the United States, most Canadians were sympathetic. In 1984, some 78 percent of Canadians supported a process of encouraging free trade; only 17 percent were opposed. After all, the two nations were each other's most important trading partners. Canadian-U.S. tariffs were very low before the agreement. But as previous chapters have shown, in the 1980s the United States had become increasingly protectionist in some sectors such as forestry, steel, and agriculture. Nontariff barriers to trade had proliferated in both nations. Thus, many Canadians saw the FTA as a way to forestall U.S. protectionism, lessen regulatory impediments to trade, and cement closer economic relations.[2]

Canadians, however, were well aware that the FTA also came with costs. They worried about its potential impact on their jobs, on Canada's sovereignty, and on the environment. Not surprisingly, from the beginning, the FTA had some vociferous opponents, who had widely divergent views about its costs. These Canadians warned that the free trade agreement could allow U.S. multinationals to "rule" Canada and take over quintessential Canadian companies and institutions. They feared it would lead to too much foreign investment. Ironically, some labor unions feared that these same companies would leave Canada, leading to job loss due to disinvestment.[3] But whether the FTA would lead to increased investment or disinvestment, as the negotiations got under way and opponents got active, public support began to wither.

Canadian union leaders also worried about the FTA. These men and women had a lot of political clout. Canada had a relatively high union rate compared with the United States (35 percent vs. approximately 15 percent), a higher minimum wage, more comprehensive labor standards, and a stronger system of unemployment insurance.

They said that the FTA would encourage the movement of jobs to the lower-wage United States. Tax revenues would decline, and the government would not have the money to support public services. Canadian labor union leaders always noted they supported trade and did not argue that trade agreements were bad per se. However, they expressed concern about the FTA's potential impact on Canadian sovereignty and on how free trade could risk Canada's "more equal and decent society."[4]

Other groups and individuals also expressed concerns about the FTA's impact on Canadian sovereignty and values, but their concerns were new to the trade policy debate. For example, environmentalists, such as Steven Shrybman of the Canadian Environmental Law Association, thought of the FTA not solely as a trade agreement, but as more of "an environmental statute." He alleged that the Conservative government of Prime Minister Mulroney was trying to "conceal the deal's environmental significance." Shrybman's views were shared by other Canadian environmental groups that feared that the treaty could move Canada's energy and resource policy away from conservation toward greater extraction. Moreover, they thought that because of the importance of the U.S. market and the clout of the U.S. government, Canadian environmental policy would have to become more like American environmental policy, which they saw as less stringent. According to Shrybman, at the same time that Canadians were trying to move away from dependence on pesticides, the proposed Canada-U.S. trade agreement committed "Canada to a U.S. regulatory approach that . . . actually made it easier for certain pesticides to be licensed." This approach would weaken Canadian pesticide regulation and benefit the transnational chemical industry at the expense of the Canadian people.[5] Thus, Canadian environmental activists feared not only a loss of control over the environment, but also a harmonization that would yield an American rather than Canadian approach to environmentalism.

Canadian concerns about the environment were understandable. Throughout the 1970s and 1980s, the United States did little to resolve the long-standing problem of acid rain, pollution that flows across the permeable border between the two nations. Many Canadians resented not only the acid rain but also their dependence on the United States to address that problem.[6]

As these concerns seeped into public consciousness, Canadian support for the FTA declined significantly. By February 1986, only 46 percent favored the agreement. Some 38 percent of Canadians polled in 1986 believed that free trade would lead to an erosion of Canada's cultural identity, while some 40 percent worried that Canada's "political independence would be in jeopardy."[7]

In 1985, Maude Barlow, Bruce Campbell, and other Canadian social activists formed a coalition, the Council of Canadians, to focus on the FTA and the Canadian social compact. Its membership included a wide range of social, cultural, women's, environmental, labor, and church groups. The Council never saw its end goal as the defeat of a particular trade agreement, but rather to arouse public awareness of ways to preserve Canada's social compact.[8]

From the outset, the Council of Canadians understood the debate should not be limited to the halls of government. To take the debate to the people, they published a cartoon-style booklet highlighting the costs of trade to Canadian sovereignty and values. The booklet, "What's the Big Deal?" received a lot of attention and was widely distributed during the 1988 election. It played on Canadian fears that by joining the FTA, all that was uniquely Canadian could be lost, and Canada would simply become the fifty-first U.S. state.[9]

Opponents also alleged that Canadians would be forced to accede to American economic values. Maude Barlow wrote that "all Canadian institutions are now under intense pressure to operate as if they were businesses." Canada's social institutions, such as education, would be treated as commodities, although to Canadians they were essential services. She concluded that the FTA was "an attack on the history, culture, and values of the nation itself."[10] According to publisher Malcolm Lester, under the FTA, "The Americans will continue to claim our social policies, like medicare and unemployment insurance . . . are unfair subsidies; and they will continue to penalize us for such behavior." Lester warned that eventually Canada would be "a separate nation, in name only."[11]

The Canadian opponents of the FTA focused on how trade would hurt society's more vulnerable citizens. They argued that not only would the FTA ultimately end Canada's social welfare system, hurting the disabled and the elderly, but it would force reductions to social programs like Medicare or child care services. They alleged that disproportionate numbers of women might lose their jobs. According to Marjorie Cohen, an FTA opponent, "Women work in the very manufacturing and service industries that are most vulnerable in a free trade market," including textiles, clothing, small electrical products, sporting goods, toys and games, and leather products. These sectors accounted for some 42 percent of all women working in manufacturing.[12]

Although such concerns about the inequitable costs of the FTA were understandable, they were also exaggerated. Proponents responded to these arguments with fear tactics, too. They stressed that without the FTA, Canada's relatively small economy would stagnate and be isolated. Richard G. Lipsey, an economist at the centrist C. D. Howe Institute in Toronto, noted, "The U.S. offer of preferential access to their mass market has made Canada the envy of the trading world. Yet in a fit of national insecurity, Canadians may reject the offer."[13]

At that time, many of the Canadian FTA opponents were not opponents of trade or internationalism. They believed that Canada benefits from trade and the set of multilateral rules governing trade. Moreover, they saw internationalism as a counterweight to right-wing nationalism within Canada as well as a counterweight to U.S. power.[14] However, some Canadians saw the Uruguay Round of GATT and NAFTA as two of a kind—both using trade liberalization as a guise for deregulation. According to Tony Clarke, "Stateless corporations are effectively transforming nation-states to suit their interests. . . . Business coalitions mobilize facts, policy positions . . . opinion polls and organize citizen-front groups for their campaigns to change national governments and their policies. By campaigning for . . . privatization and deregulation, business coalitions have effectively dismantled many of the powers and tools of national governments." Clarke did not see trade agreements as tools to regulate business actions across national borders but as tools to unshackle business from national rules. Clarke and many other Canadian social activists believed the best way to counter such corporate domination was to build a social movement in which people reclaim their sovereign rights over big multinational corporations and banks.[15] But they did not think they could revamp trade agreements to help fulfill their goals.

Author Margaret Atwood had a different perspective on the FTA. She admitted, "I don't understand the full scope and implications of this agreement and I don't believe anyone else really does either." She warned that the only position the United States had "ever adopted toward us, country to country, has been the missionary position, and we were not on top." She urged Canadians to question the time frames for considering the agreement and ask whether Canada could get out of it. And she concluded, "Our national animal is the beaver, noted for its industry and its cooperative spirit. . . . It is also noted for its habit . . . of biting off its own testicles and offering them to its pursuer. I hope we are not succumbing to some form of that impulse."[16]

Ironically, in the hopes of motivating the Canadian public, Steve Shrybman invited American Ralph Nader to give a press conference on the implications of the FTA for citizens of both nations. On the eve of the vote, Nader warned Canadians that they were "underestimating the consequences of the free-trade agreement when multinational corporations start demanding cost reductions in the social service worker benefit and consumer protection areas as a price of staying in Canada."[17]

Although many Canadians had very real concerns about the agreement, they did not heed Nader's warning. The opposition Liberal Party forced an election over the free trade agreement, but the Conservative Party won a majority of seats. Although polling data revealed Canadian voters opposed the trade agreement, Parliament approved the treaty.[18]

Given public concerns about the free trade agreement, it seems surprising that it passed the Canadian parliament. Although many Canadians worried about the FTA's impact on the social compact, these concerns did not override the public's and policymakers' views about its benefits. Nor were critics of the FTA able to forge a broad-based left-right movement across Canada to oppose the FTA. Most of the FTA opponents tended to come from the Canadian left and traditional protectionist sectors. Individuals on the right, in contrast, saw the FTA and NAFTA as ways to rein in big government and make Canada more competitive. They supported the FTA in the hopes of becoming more like the United States.[19]

Meanwhile, the FTA sailed through the U.S. Congress. Although some farm groups and labor union representatives expressed concerns, the American social compact was not an issue in the FTA. In fact, Americans paid little attention to the agreement. The U.S. Congress overwhelmingly approved the FTA, in the House 366–49 and in the Senate 83–9. The FTA went into effect January 1, 1989.[20]

Many social activists in Canada hoped the aftermath of the FTA would actually build Canadian and U.S. support for their concerns. In 1987, Shrybman wrote to U.S. environmental groups warning them of the costs of the FTA to the achievement of environmental policy goals. He received one polite response. But in the spring of 1988, Mark Ritchie, the president of the Institute of Agriculture and Trade Policy (IATP), a Minneapolis think tank concerned with farm, trade, nutrition, and environmental issues, wrote to Shrybman, inviting him to give a talk about his views on trade and the environment to an audience of social activists in Washington, D.C. (Ritchie would be the first to sound the alarm among U.S. citizen activists about the GATT—see next chapter). The meeting was attended by representatives of various U.S. consumer, civic, and environmental groups.[21]

These groups were just waking up to the global nature of environmental and public health problems. In 1987, the World Commission on Environment and Development, chaired by Norwegian Prime Minister Gro Brundtland, issued a report that called for reconciling economic growth with policies sustaining the environment (sustainable development). Partly because of this report, some activists were motivated by Shrybman's speech to become more active. Consumer, civic, and environmental activists began to look more closely at trade agreements. These groups would come to understand that opposition to trade agreements could reenergize many of their supporters[22] (see next chapter). Environmental issues became a hot political issue as Americans and Canadians debated expanding the FTA to Mexico.

The Path to NAFTA

Geography was destiny as well as a source of ambivalence for Mexicans, too. Like Canada, Mexico had a complicated history of wanting both closer ties with and distance from the United States. However, the Canada-U.S. FTA put pressure on Mexico to develop a similar free trade arrangement with the United States.

Leaders of the three nations had different reasons to support a continent-wide free trade agreement. After the debt crisis of 1985–1986, Mexico had adopted new policies to spur foreign investment and trade. Mexican leaders hoped that such an agreement could spur foreign investment and economic diversification as well as enhance Mexico's international prestige. The Canadian government hoped that the agreement could encourage Mexican economic growth, while not undermining the economic benefits obtained under the FTA. The Bush administration saw it as a lever to encourage Mexico to continue to pursue market-oriented policies. Moreover, it might have positive spillovers. With greater economic growth, fewer Mexicans might migrate illegally to the United States. Thus, low-skilled workers might find greater numbers of opportunities and even higher wages. But that is not how Bush administration officials talked about the potential agreement to the American people.[23]

The Bush administration was not the first to call for closer economic ties among the three nations. Congress had called for such a free trade area between Canada, Mexico, and the United States in 1979.[24] This idea initially sounded good to Americans of many political stripes. During the 1980 presidential campaign, both Republican candidate

Ronald Reagan and Democrat Jerry Brown expressed support for a North American Common Market. (Brown, however, would become a vociferous opponent of NAFTA.)[25]

Trade and the Social Compact
Social Indicators for Canada, Mexico, and the United States in 1990

	Canada	Mexico	United States
Percentage of people under 15	21.1	37.8	21.6
Infant mortality	0.7	2.1	0.8
Life expectancy	77.7	69.4	75.8
Persons per physician	51.4	12.42	4.73
Adult illiteracy (%,1985)	*	10	*

Source: Data from the World Bank, World Development Report 1991.
*Less than 5%.

In February 1991, President George Bush announced the three countries would begin negotiations on NAFTA, and trilateral negotiations commenced in Toronto on June 12, 1991. President Bush then submitted an action plan for dealing with border problems.[26]

Any trade agreement would wake up protectionists, economic nationalists, and isolationists. NAFTA was no different in this regard. But NAFTA was a different type of trade agreement. This was the first time that two wealthy industrialized countries were negotiating a free trade agreement with a much poorer nation (see the accompanying chart).[27] Moreover, because NAFTA brought to the fore issues of the social compact, NAFTA woke up a broader swath of Americans, including social and community activists, environmentalists, development advocates, consumer advocates, and human rights advocates.[28] These groups were energized in all three countries to talk about what NAFTA could and should be. In October 1990, they began to work together to forge a common strategy. These NAFTA critics focused both on the proposed content of the NAFTA agreement and what they saw as the secretive nature of the negotiations.

FAST-TRACK: THE PLACE TO START

NAFTA was particularly controversial in the United States. This was not simply because of the potential content of the agreement, but because of the path to NAFTA acceptance. The president needed first to get congressional approval to negotiate (fast-track authority) the trilateral trade agreement. The president also needed fast-track to continue the eighth round of trade negotiations, the Uruguay Round (which had begun in 1986). This meant that the two negotiations would always be linked, even though the two trade agreements were very different. NAFTA was devised to link the North American continent; the Uruguay Round was devised to reduce trade barriers among some one hundred nations around the world.

The process of fast-track approval was complicated. The Democratic chairs of Senate Finance and House Ways and Means (Senator Lloyd Bentsen and Congressman Dan Rostenkowski) were strong backers of GATT and generally approved of NAFTA, but they had several important concerns about it. They asked President Bush to provide them with written assurances that NAFTA would not hurt the U.S. economy. They also asked him to detail its effects on the environment, jobs, and worker rights. In this way, these Democrats forced the Republican president to acknowledge that trade policy could affect other important policy goals. On May 1, 1991, the Bush administration promised that it would provide assistance through an adjustment assistance program to workers who might lose their jobs as a result of NAFTA. The statement also praised Mexican efforts to enforce labor standards and worker rights. Finally, the administration promised that it would negotiate side agreements to ensure that environmental and labor standards would be protected by NAFTA.[29]

This promise set an important precedent. The Bush administration had acknowledged that trade, worker rights, democracy, and the environment were linked. Moreover, it was the first time that a trade agreement included such safeguards within side agreements for such important supposedly "nontrade" policy goals. But as readers of this book know, these issues had long been trade issues.

Some Americans, however, did not like either the side agreements approach or the fast-track process that facilitated NAFTA negotiations. They feared that fast-track would allow the Bush administration to negotiate and sign trade deals that could override domestic laws, such as environmental regulations. Members of Public Citizen (the Nader-affiliated consumer and environmental NGO), the Sierra Club, and Friends of the Earth (environmental NGOs), and the Community Nutrition Institute (a food safety NGO), among others, attempted to convince Congress that both the negotiations and the fast-track process undermined democracy, given the breadth of issues under negotiation. They argued that Congress should hold separate hearings on NAFTA's potential impact on labor, food safety, and human rights, and not just its economic impact.[30] They gained the support of a key Democrat, David Bonior, the Democratic Whip. But on May 9, 1991, his boss, House Speaker Richard Gephardt, announced his support for the side agreements approach to NAFTA. Nonetheless, Gephardt warned, "If the administration sends to this Congress a trade treaty that trades away American jobs, or tolerates pollution of the environment or abuse of workers . . . we will amend it or reject it."[31] Congress soon agreed to extend fast-track, authorizing the president to begin NAFTA negotiations and to continue negotiations on Uruguay Round negotiations.[32]

Negotiations on NAFTA attracted press coverage and inspired a wide range of Americans to talk about trade. However, much of what the public heard about NAFTA was negative. Some individuals said NAFTA was a symbol of America's industrial decline. Others, including vegetable growers, textile producers, and labor union officials, saw it as a threat to their livelihood. For example, the AFL-CIO and the United Automobile Workers (UAW) saw NAFTA as "an economic and social disaster."[33] Human rights groups (such as Human Rights Watch, an international NGO) and development groups (such as the Development GAP) stated that NAFTA could not turn Mexico into a transparent, equitable, and fair democracy. Although President Salinas had taken steps to correct human rights abuses, Mexico still had disappearances, death threats, political prisoners, and a corrupt police force and judiciary. These groups argued the NAFTA could not help the Mexican people rid their nation of corruption, disappearances, or human rights abuses. Like union leaders, many human rights and development activists saw NAFTA as a tool enabling manufacturers to shift labor-intensive or environmentally destructive production to lower-wage Mexico. Some opponents alleged that NAFTA was less a trade agreement than a "vehicle for facilitating investment flows."[34] These groups and individuals condemned NAFTA as the final fruit of a government captured by big business.

These allegations were understandable, but they were not quite true. American business had very different views about the benefits and costs of the NAFTA. Executives of most multinationals understood that they could achieve significant benefits from the trade agreement, but they also understood that they could never achieve NAFTA if they did not reassure Americans that our system and approach to government would not be undermined or changed. In October 1991, the president's Advisory Committee on Trade Policy and Negotiations (ACTPN), the highest-level trade advisory group, made its recommendations for the

NAFTA. In their "Negotiating Objectives for a North American Free Trade Agreement," the ACTPN counseled USTR Carla Hills that "to ensure an agreement in the interest of the private sector . . . enhanced standards and enforcement of labor-related and environmental laws and regulations are also a priority and should be negotiated in parallel with the NAFTA. . . . To achieve an NAFTA in the U.S. interest, our government must negotiate a comprehensive agreement."[35]

The ACTPN was dominated by executives of multinational business, who made a commitment that the trade agreement should not lower health and safety standards. They called for "strenuous enforcement and raised standards, where appropriate, of health and sanitary regulations" and "technical standards that are developed and maintained through [a] fair and transparent process and that do not limit trade unless necessary for plant, animal, and human health and safety or to achieve security and consumer protection objectives. . . . The ACTPN opposes any weakening of U.S. labor-related and environmental laws and regulations in the NAFTA."[36] But the business members of the ACTPN did not insist that these concerns be carefully met by placing them in the body of the agreement being negotiated. Thus, it is hard to ascertain if this commitment was simply rhetorical. Jack Sheinkman and Rudy Oswald, labor representatives on the ACTPN, expressed their opposition to President Bush's side agreements approach. They believed labor and environmental issues must be in the body of the trade agreement and not on the side.[37] They decided to oppose the NAFTA. They were joined in opposition by consumer advocate Ralph Nader, head of Public Citizen, and his colleague Lori Wallach. Nader had great visibility and international influence because of his reputation as America's leading consumer and civic activist.[38] Wallach, a Harvard-trained lawyer, became a key strategist and commentator on trade agreements.

RALPH NADER:
FROM CONSUMER ACTIVIST TO CITIZEN ACTIVIST

During the 1940s through the 1950s and 1960s, consumer groups (as well as groups involved in civic, veteran, and poverty issues) were prominent supporters of trade liberalization under the GATT.[39] They understood that citizens, especially the poorest consumers, often benefit from trade and trade agreements. Trade encourages competition between foreign and domestic producers and keeps American producers on their toes. American consumers benefit from that competition because they can purchase high-quality goods and services at competitive prices. By reducing trade barriers and limiting the use of protectionist measures, trade agreements have the potential to help all consumers. Moreover, by regulating protection, trade agreements are often most helpful to the poorest consumers. Lower-income families spend a greater share of their income on necessities such as clothing, shelter, furniture, and food. Because tariffs and quotas increase the prices of necessities, protectionism works like a regressive tax, hurting families with lower incomes more than rich or middle-class families. Thus, by regulating protectionism, trade agreements help make more goods more affordable.

In the 1970s, when Ralph Nader became America's preeminent consumer activist, he said nothing about protectionism or trade agreements. He did, however, attack multinational corporations for moving their manufacturing operations overseas. Another consumer activist, Simon Lazarus, thought Nader's views were bizarre, "a betrayal of his own constituency, since corporate emigration tends to bring . . . lower prices for consumers."[40]

But Nader challenged the view that consumers always benefit from trade and agreements to govern such trade. He thought that as business got bigger and achieved economies of scale, executives would move their operations to developing nations with low wages and loose environmental and social protections. These firms would not pass on their cheaper costs to consumers, but transform them into profits for shareholders. In this view, trade agreements increased business power against workers and consumers. Nader and other consumer activists determined to use democratic process and institutions to counter that power.[41]

Nader came to these views because he saw consumers not solely as economic actors. He thought consumers should not only express their views with their purchases but also become active citizens to ensure that the state does not collude with big business. To achieve this goal, he spawned a series of organizations staffed by idealistic and energetic lawyers such as Lori Wallach. According to a global study of consumerism by Yiannis Gabriel and Tim Lang, "The common themes of these organizations were a distrust of corporations, a defense of the individual against the giants, a demand that the state protect its citizens, and above all an appeal for Americans to be citizens, not just consumers. . . . The nature of commerce is stacked against the customer, unless regulations or standards of conduct are fought for."[42]

In the early 1980s, consumer and environmental organizations did not actively organize against trade agreements. But environmentalists and consumer activists were increasingly aware that trade agreements were affecting the achievement of other important policy goals. After 1980, GATT's Standards Code went into effect. These individuals did not like what they saw of GATT in action. Their negative view of trade agreements got worse in 1991, at the very time NAFTA and the Uruguay Round were being negotiated. In their minds, big business, ineffective governance, environmental protection, GATT, and Mexico were forever associated in the trade dispute some called GATTzilla versus Flipper.[43]

As noted in chapter 1, this dispute focused on America's attempt to apply high standards for dolphin protection upon all tuna sold in the U.S. market. To environmentalists around the world, this dispute seemed to threaten environmental progress. But to Nader, Wallach, and many environmental activists, the dispute and the GATT ruling threatened American sovereign control over the standards for goods sold in the U.S. market. They wondered how an unaccountable international bureaucracy (the GATT) could instruct the U.S. Congress to kill a U.S. law, change it, or pay sanctions to maintain it.[44] (In fact, under GATT rules, the United States did not have to do anything. Any member of GATT could block the decision, and the GATT had no ability to enforce a panel decision.)

Public Citizen was especially concerned that other nations were challenging American norms and regulations at the GATT. According to Lori Wallach, "Since 1980, when the Tokyo Round of GATT first included limitations on a country's domestic non-trade laws . . . the United States has lost 80% of the cases raised by other nations against our laws." She noted that the American people and their Congress, not officials at the GATT, should decide how to reconcile trade and the environment.[45] Trade policymakers responded that these worries were unfounded. But Nader, Wallach, and other activists determined to bring these concerns to the fore in the debate about trade and trade agreements. Consumer and environmental activists began to study the GATT's potential impact on policies they valued. They noted that America's environmental regulations, for example its air quality and food safety standards, were seen by other nations as trade barriers, no different from tariffs, rather than carefully erected democratically determined regulations. Their work coincided with greater research by other consumer groups on the implications of trade agreements on national systems of regulation (see next chapter).[46]

In 1990, some activists formed a small study group to examine these issues. This group, which met at the National Wildlife Federation in Washington, included Chuck Fox from Friends of the Earth; Howard Lyman of the National Farmers' Union; Segundo Mercado Llorens of the United Food and Commercial Workers Union; Lori Wallach of Public Citizen; Edy Dubrow of the International Ladies Garment Workers Union; Barbara Warden of the United Auto Workers; Pharis Harvey of the International Labor Rights Federation; John Cavanagh of the think tank Institute for Policy Studies; and Karen Hansen Kuhn of the Development GAP, a think tank working on development issues. The study group was diverse, with some focused on improving NAFTA, others focused on developing alternatives to NAFTA, and still others focused on lobbying against it.[47] Not surprisingly, the members of the study group soon divided on strategy.

The Views of Social and Environmental Activists

Environmentalists were never of one mind about NAFTA. While some were adamantly opposed from the start, others saw opportunity in NAFTA to improve border environmental conditions. But the environmentalists shared some broad concerns. Echoing labor unions worried about disinvestment, some environmentalists maintained that firms were moving to Mexico to avoid complying with U.S. environmental standards. They cited a study by the United States General Accounting Office (GAO), a congressional agency, showing that some twenty-two firms said they had moved, at least in part, to avoid stringent local air pollution standards.[48]

For a time this negative perspective of NAFTA gained ascendancy among environmentalists. They did not believe that as Mexico grew more prosperous and stable from the NAFTA, it would adopt and enforce more stringent environmental standards. Nor did they foresee that NAFTA, by elevating environmental standards, might give new political clout to Mexican environmentalists and environmental concerns.[49] However, while Mexican environmentalists saw opportunity in NAFTA, many Canadian environmentalists and social activists were furious about the costs of the FTA. They determined to oppose the NAFTA.

In 1991, Action Canada Network leaders contacted their counterparts in Mexico and the United States and proposed working together on trade and social issues. They met with two broad groups of NGOs concerned about trade policy. The first group was centered on labor rights and development issues. Its members included representatives from the Development GAP, the United Electrical Workers, the Washington Office on Latin America, the United Methodists, and the Institute for Policy Studies. The other group focused on sustainable development issues. Its members included family farm, environmentalist, and consumer groups, such as the Institute for Agriculture and Trade Policy, National Farmers Union, the UAW, the Sierra Club, the National Wildlife Federation, National Family Farm Coalition, and Public Citizen.[50] On January 15, 1991, these groups cosponsored a forum on Capitol Hill to express concerns that "preparations for the U.S. Mexico Free Trade Agreement are proceeding with little or no public debate over the effects of such an agreement." The organizers hoped to "stimulate and broaden debate around some environmental and social impacts of a free trade agreement prior to Congressional approval." They succeeded: the forum was held in the early days of the Gulf War to defend Kuwait from an Iraqi invasion, yet it was standing room only.[51]

These individuals adopted a two-prong strategy. On the one hand, they organized opposition to President Bush's approach to NAFTA; on the other hand, they determined to develop an alternative agreement that would protect the environment, workers, and human rights and spur trade. Meeting in the United States and later in Mexico, the civil society groups found common ground on their idea of an appropriate agreement. They contrasted their efforts with the official NAFTA negotiations. "Our reflections . . . are part of a process that began over a year ago, precisely when the negative effects of the free trade agreement caused a crisis among the people of Canada. . . . We do not oppose trade as such . . . however we reject a free trade agreement that responds only to the needs of transnational capital. . . . The secret and exclusive manner in which the official negotiations are taking place is in stark contrast with the open and pluralistic forum in which we have developed our forum."[52]

This strategy of developing an alternative NAFTA had little impact on the negotiations, but it did attract the attention of the press. In a story about this two-pronged strategy, the *Wall Street Journal* described the involved individuals as a motley group of activists opposed to trade agreements. So the U.S. component of this effort called themselves MODTLE (the Mobilization on Development, Trade, Labor and the Environment, pronounced "motley"). Their two-pronged strategy was widely supported by farm, religious, civic, development, and consumer groups; several unions; and a growing number of policymakers.[53]

On January 29, 1992, Representatives Marcy Kaptor, Peter DeFazio, and Don Pease, among others, wrote to USTR Carla Hills, endorsing the MODTLE statement on NAFTA. Soon thereafter, Representatives Henry Waxman and Richard Gephardt sponsored House Congressional Resolution 246, stating that "Congress will not approve legislation to implement any trade agreement if such agreement jeopardizes United States health, safety, labor, or environmental laws." By July the Resolution had some 218 House Members as cosponsors.[54]

Although the motley critics of NAFTA began to get press attention and political support, they were unable to change the USTR's strategy for the negotiations or to place social and environmental concerns into the heart of the agreement. Some of the members of these groups felt that the USTR treated them as if they were not "players" in trade policy, and they complained that the USTR refused to address their concerns. They tried to get the USTR to admit that because Mexico frequently violated the basic human rights of its citizens, it did not merit a free trade agreement. They also argued that the USTR ignored the needs of small family farmers in all three nations.[55]

These activists were not only concerned about the scope of NAFTA, but also outraged by the way the negotiations were conducted. Their outrage became news. The *Financial Times,* the world's leading paper on international trade and finance, quoted Craig Merillees, a Fair Trade Campaign organizer, who worked to develop grassroots opposition to NAFTA. He argued that trade negotiations should be more accessible to the public. "They can run but they can't hide. . . . This is not the right way to make a major policy decision in this country." Mr. Merillees's anger was understandable, but he clearly misunderstood the process of trade negotiations, which are always secretive to facilitate tough economic concessions and to protect confidential business information provided to the negotiators.[56] But the NAFTA critics were not able to bring the negotiations into the sunshine. Some Canadian NGOs eventually obtained stolen copies of the draft agreements, but the official negotiations remained secret.[57] The NAFTA negotiators pressed on, with no changes to their NAFTA strategy.

Division among Trade Agreement Critics

The American public did not share this outrage about the negotiations. To motivate them, Lori Wallach of Public Citizen, in tandem with other groups such as Friends of the Earth, organized a grassroots organization, the Citizen's Trade Campaign (CTC). The CTC was built on an earlier grassroots group formed in 1990, the Fair Trade Campaign. It was incorporated in 1992, and former Congressman Jim Jontz became its coordinator in December 1992. The CTC worked with members of Congress, raised money, and hired organizers to motivate citizens around the country against the trade agreement. But it also worked closely with other NAFTA critics, including MODTLE. Its participants included a wide range of environmental, farm, religious, and consumer/citizen groups (see the following).[58] Although the CTC was able to build greater public and congressional opposition to NAFTA, it was not able to coordinate a united front of groups, such as environmental organizations, to oppose NAFTA.[59]

MOVERS AND SHAKERS IN MODTLE AND CTC, 1992

MODTLE (Mobilization on Development,
Trade, Labor, and the Environment)
(This study group was policy oriented and internationalist.)

> Institute for Policy Studies
> International Labor Rights Education and Research Fund
> Development GAP
> Community Nutrition Institute
> Center of Concern (affiliated with the Jesuits)
> National Consumers League
> Presbyterian Church USA
> Maryknoll Fathers
> Institute for Agriculture and Trade Policy
> American Agriculture Movement
> National Lawyers Guild

Members of Citizens Trade Campaign
(This coalition of environmental, labor, family farm, consumer, and religious organizations promoting environmental and social justice in trade policy was action oriented, focused on the undemocratic nature of trade agreements, and more nationalist.)

> Friends of the Earth
> Public Citizen
> Sierra Club
> Institute for Agriculture and Trade Policy
> National Farmers Union
> National Consumers League
> United Auto Workers
> Rainbow Coalition
> Americans for Democratic Action

However, the CTC earned the ire of both proponents and opponents of NAFTA because of its tactics. The CTC used tactics widely accepted among environmentalists and unions, such as grassroots organizing, picketing, petitions, demonstrations, and litigation. Although petitions had long been used to influence the course of trade policy, litigation, grassroots organizing, and demonstrations were more unusual. These tactics got public attention, but they could do little to improve NAFTA. Moreover, they frustrated Bush and Clinton administration officials who wanted to find ways to reconcile trade and environmental goals.

The CTC did not confine its efforts to the continental United States; it worked closely with Maude Barlow and Tony Clark of Canada. The CTC also worked with MODTLE to bring Canadian and Mexican allies on to speak around the country and on Capitol Hill.[60] Meanwhile, members of MODTLE continued to focus on changing the content of the final agreement. Their actions gained considerable support on Capitol Hill among progressives such as Representatives Don Pease of Ohio, George Brown of California, Henry Waxman of California, Richard Gephardt of Missouri, Marcy Kaptor of Ohio, Peter DeFazio of Oregon, and Senator Paul Wellstone of Minnesota. Their work also attracted the support of protectionist members such as Congressman James A. Trafficant and the pundit Patrick J. Buchanan.[61] America's left and right had begun to feel more comfortable working together to oppose NAFTA.

In contrast with the U.S. focus of the CTC, the bulk of MODTLE's work was with its Canadian and Mexican counterparts. Many of its members collaborated with Common Frontiers, a Canadian NGO "concerned with the social and economic effects of North American economic integration" that worked with Mexican groups to improve working conditions, living standards, and the environment. They also kept close ties with Mexican opponents of NAFTA, such as the Mexican Network Against Free Trade, an association of sixteen national unions, two large campesino (small farmers) leagues, and several Mexican NGOs.[62] This internationalism fueled their willingness to continue to try to improve NAFTA, rather than simply oppose it.

One political benefit stemming from the NAFTA negotiations was already clear. As NAFTA was being negotiated, Mexican officials began to pay more attention to the social and environmental costs of trade. This is turn empowered environmental and labor rights activists within Mexico. In his history of NAFTA, William Orme argued that the NAFTA debate forced the Mexican government to confront environmental problems in a new way. He noted that NAFTA could not gain approval in Canada or the United States without some promise of enforceable environmental provisions. Robert Paarlberg, a political scientist, testified on Capitol Hill, "I don't think you would be able to engage the Mexican government in tough dialogue on environmental protection if you didn't have the anticipated NAFTA. . . . I don't think there would be too many better ways to strengthen environmentalist groups within Mexico than to institutionalize this sort of dialogue. . . . It encourages Mexico to tighten existing standards, to control pesticide applications." Moreover, it gave new leverage to environmentalists such as Ambassador Homero Aridjis who noted, "The bottom line for Mexico was that, GATT or no GATT, it could not sell tuna in the United States unless Mexican tuna boats made a sustained, verifiable effort to spare dolphins."[63] In June 1992, Mexico signed an accord committing Mexico to steady declines in dolphin mortality during tuna fishing. As they became aware of their increased leverage, human rights groups and democratic reform groups in Mexico also became more visible. Such groups understood that by working with U.S., Canadian, or international human rights groups and labor unions, they could gain publicity that would force Mexican policymakers at minimum to enforce its labor laws.[64] This view that the trade agreement might help Mexico improve its social compact was not unique to some members of MOD-TLE. It also gained credibility on Capitol Hill and among a growing number of church and environmental activists.

Nonetheless, many environmentalists and consumer groups remained concerned that the side agreements to NAFTA would be inadequate. They included a wide range of environmental and food safety groups, such as the Community Nutrition Institution, Defenders of Wildlife, Environmental Action, National Consumers League, Friends of the Earth, Institute for Agriculture and Trade Policy, National Audubon Society, Public Citizen, and the Sierra Club. In June 1992, these groups made several recommendations to ensure that environmental standards would not be compromised by the trade agreement. They proposed that NAFTA commit the three countries to provide sufficient funding to fully implement environmental laws and fund a clean-up throughout the continent.[65] But these recommendations went nowhere. To many of these groups, the Bush administration's commitment to environmental protection was rhetorical.

On August 12, 1992, the three nations announced that the NAFTA negotiations were completed. Yet the full text of NAFTA remained a secret. It was not released until September, when congressional hearings began. On October 3, 1992, 105 members of the House wrote Governor William Jefferson Clinton, the Democratic candidate for president, asking him not to endorse the Bush administration's NAFTA. But Clinton adopted a different strategy. On October 4, he gave qualified support for NAFTA but insisted on stronger supplemental agreements to address social, environmental, and agricultural issues. In this way he distinguished his views from those of House Majority Leader Richard Gephardt, who now called for starting afresh and for putting labor and the environment in the body of the agreement.[66]

On October 7, some forty-nine groups in the United States (jointly with citizen groups in Canada and Mexico) held a press conference to announce their views on the final NAFTA. They expressed their conclusion that this NAFTA would be harmful to the vast majority of the people of the continent. First, they noted that NAFTA would yield common standards, rather than national standards, that would be lower for the United States and Canada: "Free trade fosters an equalization of labor, environmental, and other social standards among member nations." They also noted that NAFTA would weaken workers' ability to collectively bargain versus continent-wide businesses: "NAFTA also fails—by omitting any provisions to guarantee respect for internationally recognized labor rights—to give workers the tools they need to defend themselves against a tri-national collapse in their living and working standards." They also alleged that NAFTA did not address bilateral immigration issues or human rights violations. Finally, the trinational group criticized the lack of public participation and access in the development and negotiation of the NAFTA: "Many citizen groups offered suggestions to government negotiators over the past year; almost [none] ended up in the text. [NAFTA] threatens to undermine sovereignty in all three nations and replace it with the dominance of unelected, unaccountable corporate dominated tribunals." Yet the signatories noted they were not opposed to a trinational economic agreement: "We recognize the growing ties among our nations and are committed to democratic and inclusive forums to build a continental initiative for North American development."[67]

Canadian trade agreement critics were especially concerned that their views were ignored. They argued that the free trade agreement with the United States had damaged the Canadian economy and the Canadian social compact. Action Canada and the Council of Canadians argued that Canada had already suffered significant job loss (23.1 percent of the manufacturing workforce) since the FTA went into effect. The FTA had enabled companies to move to the United States for lower wages, nonunionized workers, and lower health and safety standards. Moreover, the FTA had done nothing to stop the production of acid rain and its export to Canada. Although leaders of these Canadian NGOs participated in the process of developing an alternative NAFTA, the FTA experience radicalized them. Their critique had become a critique of capitalism, although in the Canadian way, it was not a critique of internationalism. But that was not the American way. In the United States, capitalism was sacrosanct, but it was easy to criticize economic internationalism for being undemocratic and a threat to U.S. sovereignty.[68]

U.S. trade agreement critics attacked both the content of NAFTA and the legislative vehicle for approving it (fast-track). The fast-track process set limits on the time that Congress and the president's advisory committees could examine the agreement. Once the agreement was completed and signed, the president had to develop implementing legislation. The implementing legislation would include congressional approval of the agreement, plus information delineating any changes necessary to U.S. law to implement the trade agreement. Under fast-track, Congress must vote yes or no ninety days after the implementing legislation is submitted by the executive branch.[69] Although the Tokyo Round had been negotiated and approved under this process, trade agreement critics argued that this time period was too short, given the complexity of NAFTA and its effects on other important policy goals. Congress could not fully examine the changes to U.S. laws that NAFTA might require. Traditional protectionists, such as labor unions and Florida tomato growers, joined in this two-front attack on NAFTA.

However, in the early summer of 1992, Public Citizen (on behalf of itself, the Sierra Club, and the Friends of the Earth) took an extraordinary step and asked the judiciary branch to step into the fast-track process. They sued in D.C. District Court and asked that NAFTA not be voted on until it had a comprehensive "environmental impact statement." The litigants argued that a trade agreement constituted a formal act by the federal government. Under the National Environmental Policy Act, the federal government is required to submit an environmental impact statement prior to implementation of such an act. But this strategy did not succeed in derailing NAFTA. The case continued for three years, although the Supreme Court refused to hear it. This stalling technique was lost on appeal.[70]

The tactic, however, had both positive and negative impacts on the strategy of the NAFTA critics. On the one hand, it forced trade policymakers to reiterate that trade agreements affected the achievement of other important policy goals such as environmental protection. Ultimately the Clinton administration did review NAFTA's potential effect on the environment. On the other hand, it alienated important proponents of linking trade agreements and environmental policies, who thought it was wrong to bring the judicial branch into the trade policy-making process. Moreover, it may have divided the environmental community even further. These stalling and confrontational tactics did little to improve the environmentalists' public image or to gain support for their approach to reconciling trade and sustainable development. While Public Citizen, the Humane Society, and the Sierra Club focused on thwarting NAFTA, the World Wildlife Fund, National Wildlife Foundation, and National Resources Defense Council decided to put pressure on the Bush administration (and later Clinton administration) to modify the environmental provisions of NAFTA. The latter groups also worked with members of Congress such as Congressmen Bill Richardson and Robert Matsui who would lead the administration's NAFTA push.[71] These groups thought they could improve the process by participating in it.

In the next few months, while Bill Clinton and George Bush were busy campaigning for the presidency, Clinton did not describe what changes he might make to NAFTA. After Clinton won the election, he signaled that he would make economic policy a priority. However, he said very little about his views on trade. Moreover, Clinton did not pick an established trade negotiator to lead trade negotiations. He chose Michael (Mickey) Kantor, a high-powered lawyer and close political friend. At first glance, Kantor seemed a reassuring choice to the trade agreement critics. He had started his career as a legal aid lawyer working to improve the conditions of migrant farm workers. But Kantor was little concerned about these issues in 1992. His priority was to use his assigned turf—trade—to ensure President Clinton's political success. His strategy, however, would alienate many moderate trade agreement critics who wanted to support NAFTA.[72] Kantor decided to use political chits and budgetary pork to achieve his goals, thereby giving the impression that the administration was horse-trading unrelated policy issues to achieve support for a trade agreement.

The Clinton NAFTA

With Kantor at the helm, Clinton's NAFTA strategy would bring triangulation to new peaks. Kantor sought to find a middle ground between the left, to whom he was increasingly less credible, and the business community, which he felt he had to court. In August 1992, Kantor and his staff finished negotiating the labor and environmental side agreements. Clinton formally endorsed what was now his trade agreement. On September 14, 1993, six major environmental groups (World Wildlife Fund, Environmental Defense Fund, National Wildlife Federation, National Resources Defense Council, National Audubon Society, and Conservation International) formally endorsed NAFTA. But grassroots organizations like the Sierra Club, Friends of the Earth, Greenpeace, Clean Water Action, the Humane Society, and Public Citizen still denounced NAFTA as inadequate. The environmental NGOs were now publicly divided, and relations become them became increasingly bitter. They argued over who really spoke for the American public on the environment and how best to balance trade and the environment.[73]

The differences among the environmental NGOs was not just about NAFTA, but about democracy. A few of the NGOs seemed to decide that they could help protect the environment by becoming trade policy players. That meant they had to be practical about policy, which often moves incrementally. For example, during the Ways and Means hearings held in September, Steward J. Hudson of the National Wildlife Foundation testified, "[NAFTA] has caused a great deal of pain . . . to the four environment groups you see before you. I want you to remember two things about this testimony. . . . A fair and objective reading of the NAFTA leaves you with one uncompromising conclusion: the environment is far better off with this NAFTA than without. Two . . . Those who want to kill NAFTA are hiding behind the environment."[74] Hudson was saying point-blank, some NAFTA opponents were protectionists because they did not believe that trade and environmental protection could be balanced.

While American environmentalists were divided, Canadian NGOs were united. The Council of Canadians and the Canadian Labor Congress quickly decided that the side agreements were "cosmetic" and inadequate.[75] They organized an anti-NAFTA movement among farmers, labor, women's groups, environmentalists, artists, intellectuals, and church and social activists. These groups provided a wide range of evidence that the FTA was forcing Canada to become, like the United States, a democratic capitalist nation without a strong safety net. But the Conservatives won a majority of seats in Parliament. Soon the Canadian parliament passed the NAFTA.[76]

Meanwhile, NAFTA garnered greater support among elites in Mexico. Polling data revealed, however, that most Mexicans had little understanding of the trade agreement that their leaders valued so much. For example, some 49 percent of Mexicans polled thought that NAFTA would facilitate their ability to work in the United States. These same Mexicans must have been amazed to learn that many Americans thought that NAFTA would lead their employers to shift production and jobs to Mexico.[77] However, Mexico's leaders never wavered in their support for NAFTA. According to Jose Cordoba, chief of staff to Mexico's president, "Most Mexicans have favored the NAFTA ever since . . . it was announced: it was perceived as an integral part of a general reform process that has received broad public support . . . 75 percent of the Mexican people believe that Mexico will be able to increase the quality of its goods. . . . There is no worry about negative cultural influences from the United States."[78]

In the United States, however, NAFTA would be a much harder sell. While producers and retailers prepared to sell Christmas presents in 1993, the White House prepared to sell NAFTA to the Congress. Clinton set up a war room in the White House, headed by William Daley of Chicago and former Republican Representative (and Brookings Institution scholar) William Frenzel. The war room staff also included key environmentalists such as Michael Waldman (once of Public Citizen) and Chuck Fox (formerly of Friends of the Earth). Yet the focus of the war room was not to meet the concerns of social and environmental activists, but to organize congressional support for NAFTA.

The war room seemed to come out of the Clinton team's approach to "economics" as a political issue. Clinton administration officials seemed to see trade policy as a battle to be won by convincing members of Congress, rather than educating Americans to the rationale for trade agreements.

The war room often worked in tandem with the business groups, such as USA-NAFTA. The administration and its business allies made bold promises of widespread economic growth and many new jobs as a result of NAFTA.[79] But to opponents of NAFTA and to many journalists, the White House and USA-NAFTA did not seem to be focusing on the merits of NAFTA. Instead, it seemed they traded concessions on other policies and pork (federal funding) to achieve votes for NAFTA. To some observers, it looked like the Clinton administration had allied with the Fortune 500 to buy the vote.[80]

Ironically, a leader from the Fortune 500 came to symbolize opposition to NAFTA. His involvement changed the tenor of the debate and diminished the clout of many of America's trade agreement critics. The media focused on H. Ross Perot and his sound bites, rather than the substantive arguments of the diverse critics of NAFTA.

PEROT STEALS NAFTA AND STRIKES OUT

In 1992, H. Ross Perot decided to run for president and use NAFTA as a key issue in his campaign. Perot was a billionaire businessman with libertarian sympathies, a tradition of public service, a spectacular record in business, and an idiosyncratic style. Perot not only criticized NAFTA but built a grassroots political movement denouncing America's fiscal and budgetary policies. Americans did not know what to make of this self-made billionaire. Perot's views on social, environmental, and economic issues were all over the map. He sounded like a libertarian who wanted government out of our lives, yet he had built a multinational business processing government (and business) data, Electronic Data Systems (EDS). He believed government should stay out of the bedroom (he was pro-choice) but believed taxpayers should fund a wide range of government programs such as Head Start and poverty programs, as well as a national industrial partnership to create long-range "strategic plans, industry by industry."[81]

Using a state-by-state petition drive, an electronic town hall, and a toll-free number, Perot in 1992 appeared to be truly concerned about the people's views and prepared to engage in a dialogue with them.[82] Perot's followers built a grassroots movement called "United We Stand." It would forge bridges both to the libertarian left and right; to centrists concerned about the budget deficit, such as the Concord Coalition; and to radical nationalist and isolationist groups. For a brief moment in time, Perot seemed to tap the "can do" ethos that has marked America in time of war or crisis. He inspired some Americans to attempt to solve the gridlock surrounding the budget deficit. Moreover, Perot called on his fellow Americans to attempt to change policies where "the people feel . . . that they have no voice in their government," such as NAFTA or campaign finance.[83]

Although he won only 19 percent of the 1992 vote for president, he continued to speak about NAFTA and trade in general. Perot talked about trade in ways many Americans could understand. In 1993, Americans were especially uninformed about NAFTA.[84] While supporters argued that NAFTA would create a single market of some 370 million people, encouraging high-wage, high-technology jobs and a more prosperous Mexico, opponents alleged the trade agreement would lead to job flight and environmental degradation. They pointed to the loss of manufacturing jobs in the Midwest and the horrible environmental and public health conditions on the U.S./Mexican border. But Perot's allegation that NAFTA would lead to "a great sucking sound" of lost jobs and industries became the sound bite of trade, turning the debate into a food fight about numbers: Would NAFTA create or destroy American jobs?

Perot attracted a wide range of Americans who felt anxious about the future and worried that the "middle-class dream" was dying.[85] Some people somehow saw in Perot's grassroots movement the forerunner to a new populism, although it had little in common with the self-help focus of the original nineteenth-century populists.[86] With this base, Perot was able to build a broad anti-NAFTA coalition. While some of his supporters saw NAFTA as a plot for global deregulation, others saw in it an attempt to build an ever greater interventionist state. Despite their many different and often contradictory views about what government should do, they banded together to forge an ad hoc political coalition of left and right. This coalition was unusual, because as Alan Tonelson observed, it linked "blue collar union members; white collar middle managers and small businessmen; family and community oriented immigrants; and grass-roots environmental activists."[87]

Perot worked with economist Pat Choate on a book about NAFTA, called *Save Your Job, Save Our Country: Why NAFTA Must Be Stopped—Now.*[88] The USTR was so disturbed by this book that it prepared a response, "Correcting the Record."[89] According to analyst John Audley, "Perot became the de facto leader of the anti-NAFTA campaign although most interest groups opposed to the agreement had not selected him to act as their spokesperson. Association with Perot meant access to his vast financial resources, but it also imposed political costs."[90] However, his self-anointed leadership of the anti-NAFTA movement, his imperiousness, and his inattention to detail began to alienate other NAFTA opponents. Environmentalists and civic activists had never seen him as representing their views on NAFTA. They worried about linking to "protectionist" coalitions and to the focus on jobs. They identified with other prominent NAFTA opponents such as ex-California governor Jerry Brown and Ralph Nader.[91] But these NAFTA critics did not have Perot's weird charisma, folksy accessible style, instant access to the media, or billions of dollars.

Many anti-NAFTA advocates were alienated by Perot's presentation of his views in the NAFTA debate with Vice President Gore on the *Larry King Show.* On November 9, 1993, Gore not only calmly defended NAFTA and trade, but he linked Perot (the man who created a high-tech industry) with old ideas and traditional fears of economic change, while linking supporters of free trade to the future.[92] After 1994, although Perot remained an important public figure, he was less vocal on trade. Pat Buchanan soon took up the mantle of the leading nationalist politician in opposing trade agreements.

Perot's role in the NAFTA debate, however, left an enduring legacy. His grassroots group, United We Stand, had innovated in using technology from faxes to the Internet to mobilize and unite widely dispersed Americans. Other grassroots groups, such as Public Citzen's Global Trade Watch and the Institute for Agriculture and Trade Policy, would adopt these tools, especially E-mail, to link and organize trade agreement critics around the world. Trade agreement critics also had learned by 1993 that strange bedfellows from the left and right could find common ground in opposing the tools and beneficiaries of globalization.

Nader, Wallach, and other social activists were determined to protect America's system of regulatory protection. Many of their new allies—protectionists and economic nationalists—were not fans of the big government intervention they were defending. Nonetheless, protectionists were not inherently uncomfortable with government intervention—after all, they thought government should protect specific sectors or producers from foreign competition. Moreover, trade agreement critics of left and right agreed that the consumer, worker, and environmental regulations were issues that only Americans should decide. Thus, they shared a nationalist perspective. Finally, left and right alike objected to the newfangled concepts of the "new world order" and globalization. Both were increasingly skeptical about international big government. In the years that followed, trade agreement critics of the left and right found that by ignoring their differences and pooling their efforts, they could achieve greater influence.[93]

Congress Weighs NAFTA

Despite the efforts of the trade agreement critics of the left and right, issues of sovereignty, democracy, human rights, and the environment were not the central issues of the 1993 NAFTA debate. As the vote drew closer, it became a debate about numbers. Instead of focusing on the agreement's actual content, policymakers focused on how many people supported the NAFTA or opposed it; how many jobs would be created or destroyed; and how many economists or former presidents supported the NAFTA.[94]

Testimony and congressional speeches began to sound just like earlier trade debates. Many NAFTA opponents sought to explain that they were not protectionists, and the debate was not "about protectionism versus free trade."[95] For example, the president of the National Family Farm Coalition, representing thirty-nine family farm and rural organizations across thirty-two states, said "[The] opposition to NAFTA cannot and should not be called protectionist, but rather represents the need for expanded economic opportunity . . . for all North American people, not just the giant corporations."[96] However, members could only vote up or down on NAFTA and thus had to choose sides. If you were a freer trader, then you had to support NAFTA; if you were a protectionist, you had to oppose it. Yet NAFTA and its side agreements did not fit this simple paradigm. Some proponents of freer trade found themselves opposing NAFTA because of the side agreements and what they saw as the elevation of nontrade issues. Some trade agreement critics (especially environmentalists) were willing to support NAFTA because they saw it as an important step toward reconciling trade and environmental objectives.[97]

Labor unions were caught in a bind. On the one hand, labor union officials were united in opposing NAFTA and believing it would yield lower standards, lower wages, and fewer jobs. On the other hand, the side agreements could increase the power of Mexican labor and help U.S. workers find common ground with those in Canada and Mexico. However, most union leaders could not transcend the traditional paradigm. With the exception of the former head of the UAW, Douglas Fraser, union leaders concluded that the side agreements were a fig leaf. They uniformly took a negative position on NAFTA.[98] Some environmentalists and consumer advocates also alleged that NAFTA would lower U.S. standards. They saw the Clinton administration's changes to NAFTA as ineffective "Band-Aids" or as promises that were already broken.[99]

Some trade agreement critics on the left began to sound like economic nationalists as they made their case. For example, Marcy Kaptor, an articulate and forceful member of Congress from Ohio, argued that the side agreements were not only inadequate but also undemocratic. She found proof by reading the text, which was full of the words *investors* and *competition*, but did not include the words *people, workers,* and *farmers.* Then, illuminating the strange bedfellow coalitions that trade agreements were inspiring, she quoted Pat Buchanan to make her case, saying NAFTA could undermine states' rights.[100] Echoing that sentiment, the Sierra Club noted that the NAFTA "is also a major step toward ending democracy in this country." This led Congressman Bill Thomas to accuse the left of demagoguing on this issue.[101]

In truth, despite shared concerns about the poor, human rights, and the environment, social activists were increasingly divided. On the one hand, the Sierra Club, Public Citizen, and some AFL member unions of the AFL-CIO demanded that the NAFTA be renegotiated.[102] They seemed overly optimistic that the United States and Canada could actually force a better agreement out of Mexico. On the other hand, as already noted, several environmental NGOs viewed the side agreements as a tool to encourage Mexico to improve its regulations and enforcement of its social compact. To Fred Krupp of the Environmental Defense Fund, representing more than a quarter of a million Americans, "There are real trade-related environmental problems. . . . These problems have occurred without NAFTA, and without NAFTA, they will get even worse. . . . If the side accord is adopted, a person or NGO who believes that a country is not enforcing its environmental laws will be able to make those allegations to the new Commission for Environmental Cooperation." He noted that NAFTA will not solve all environmental problems but had moved the process forward, "including setting the stage for long overdue reform of the GATT."[103] To Steward J. Hudson of the National Wildlife Federation, "The benefits of the NAFTA package stand in stark contrast to the status quo, where environmental concerns are largely ignored in commerce between nations, where lax enforcement . . . is unchecked and citizen input into trade and environmental issues is shut out."[104]

Many social and environmental activists now understood that, like other regulatory policies, trade policy moves forward incrementally. But other trade agreement critics could not accept incrementalism. For example, Pharis Harvey of the International Labor Rights Education and Research Fund noted that "the collusive relationship between the employers, union officials and the state has made it possible for Mexico to maintain what are among the lowest wages in the world for many kinds of . . . work, and to advertise these conditions as an incentive for foreign investment under a free trade agreement." Mexico needed radical reform, which NAFTA could not inspire.[105] However, to many proponents of trade liberalization, NAFTA was an important, albeit small, step forward. As a result, by 1993, they began to see many trade agreement critics on the left as perfectionist—no trade agreement would be good enough for them. According to Congressman Bill Thomas, by negotiating and improving the side agreements, President Clinton made an honest effort to meet the criticism posed by these groups, and yet these groups were using the side agreements "to defeat the very agreement." He asserted, "That is the reason both Mr. Perot and you folks are demagogues on this issue." Congressman Robert Matsui added, although he supported the environmental position on protecting dolphins, "Weren't we attempting to impose our environmental laws on other countries by extraterritorial actions? . . . Aren't we talking about economic nationalism? . . . And Jerry Brown, Pat Buchanan, your biggest supporters are the most vocal on this issue." Lori Wallach of Public Citizen responded that environmentalists don't want to control other countries' environmental laws, "but . . . the U.S. must maintain control of entry into its market to effectively enforce its existing policy measures."[106] At its essence, Wallach's argument was a nationalist argument to preserve the social compact, one that presumed that U.S. standards could not be maintained if foreign producers could get access to the U.S. market without meeting U.S. standards.

GATT was never far from the congressional debate over NAFTA. Opponents of NAFTA were divided not only on their views, but also on how to use NAFTA to change or attack GATT. Some members wondered about the implications of a potential NAFTA defeat for the conclusion of the GATT Round. GATT, after all, was politically and commercially more important to America. Congressman Robert Matsui speculated that if Congress couldn't pass NAFTA, other nations such as France would not take the political risks they needed to pass a strong comprehensive GATT. Thomas Donahue of the AFL-CIO disagreed, noting that Congress would easily pass GATT. After all, "GATT is something nobody understands and NAFTA is something everybody understands."[107] But to Lori Wallach of Public Citizen, Carl Pope of the Sierra Club, and many other environmentalists, GATT and NAFTA were inseparable and equally horrible.[108] "The reason why so many environmental groups, consumer groups, and other citizens groups are concerned about NAFTA and the Uruguay Round of GATT is that the substantive rules of those agreements have expanded into subject matters where trade agreements did not used to tread. . . . These are not just tariffs but a variety of nontariff issues that set down the rules for natural resources, food safety, environmental standards." But Congressman Bill Thomas noted that these groups had acted inconsistently by pushing for rules to govern these standards and then rejecting them: "It clearly indicates that you are using these arguments for other reasons."[109] Moreover, these groups seemed to presume that U.S. standards are always the highest and the most effective. This is not always true.[110]

As the NAFTA vote drew closer, policymakers and the public seemed to focus less on the social and environmental issues that many trade agreement critics concentrated on. After September 1993, much of the public debate and newspaper headlines focused on whether it would yield job losses or gains. The administration made its case based on NAFTA's macroeconomic benefits to the U.S. economy. But that is not how they convinced many members, especially Democratic members, of the benefits of NAFTA. Behind the scenes, they traded promises of a yes vote on NAFTA for pork for their districts or other favors. NAFTA proponents continued to characterize all NAFTA opponents as individuals fearful of change and defeatist. In this view, the social critics of NAFTA had become protectionists. By working with economic nationalists, isolationists, and protectionists, the social critics of NAFTA were less able to argue otherwise. Meanwhile, the divisions among the environmental community made it difficult to make environmental arguments against NAFTA. In the end, vote-buying and macroeconomic arguments sold enough members of Congress on NAFTA. The House narrowly passed NAFTA, by 34 votes, whereas the Senate went 61 to 38. On December 8, 1993, the president signed NAFTA into law.[111]

THE FTA AND NAFTA taught first Canadians and later Americans about the impact of trade on the social compact. Nongovernmental organizations forged a trinational movement that weighed issues of concern to social groups in all nations. However, in the United States, the NAFTA debate exposed divisions among these civic groups regarding whether one could be pro-trade liberalization and pro-environment/democracy/human rights and whether incremental reform proposals, such as that of the side agreements, were useful. This division seemed to foster the belief among analysts and policymakers that one was either pro-trade or protectionist, although the debate had become so much more complex.

By forging an alliance with economic nationalists, isolationists, and protectionists, some of these trade agreement critics had formed a powerful lobby to block forward movement on trade. However, many of their allies who wanted to reconcile trade and the environment began to see them as obstructionist and often labeled them "protectionist." At the same time, the Clinton administration's strategy of horse-trading votes for NAFTA with votes for other unrelated policies convinced trade agreement critics that trade and other policy goals must be reconciled.

NAFTA was a learning experience for critics of trade agreements and for trade policymakers in the United States and Canada. Trade policies and the strategies to affect them had divided social activists. But they would soon have another opportunity to influence the trade debate. The Uruguay Round of the GATT remained to be completed and weighed by governments, including the United States. Trade agreement critics were determined to influence both its content and the legislative vehicle—fast-track—for approving it.

CHAPTER 6

Gleaning the GATT

As HE SLOGGED through the Reagan administration's GATT proposals in the summer of 1987, Mark Ritchie was worried.[1] Ritchie was an agricultural policy analyst for the state of Minnesota. His job was to examine how global and domestic public policies might affect Minnesota's farmers.[2]

The members of the GATT had begun the eighth round of multilateral trade negotiations (the Uruguay Round) in 1986. U.S. officials had five areas of negotiating priority: agriculture, services, intellectual property rights, investment measures, and GATT dispute settlement. They hoped to strengthen GATT's rules governing the use of NTBs such as food safety standards. In their opinion, this would ensure that such national regulations would not be covertly used as tools of protection. Finally, U.S. officials wanted to ensure that no nation could adhere to GATT selectively. This phenomenon, called GATT à la carte, meant that nations would adhere to some of the codes negotiated during the Tokyo Round, but not others.[3] These officials hoped that such a comprehensive approach to trade liberalization under the Uruguay Round would strengthen the GATT and expand trade. Moreover, they argued that a more global and comprehensive approach to trade liberalization would be in the interests of the small family farmers that Mark Ritchie wanted to support.

Ritchie was not opposed to bringing agricultural trade under international rules, but he did not want these rules to result in the demise of small farmers. Nor did he want these rules to limit the ability of national or state level policymakers to use health and safety standards to protect consumers and producers.[4] He understood that sometimes national or state level regulations distorted trade among foreign and domestic producers. In his view, trade liberalization should ensure each member nation's rights to achieve the level of food self-sufficiency and consumer safety the individual nation deemed appropriate. But he feared that should the Reagan administration trade policy plans become reality, the GATT could become a backdoor tool for deregulating consumer, health and safety, and environmental regulations.[5]

In 1987, Mark Ritchie virtually stood alone in his fear about the potential implications of these GATT proposals.[6] Few Americans had heard of the oddly named GATT. Even fewer Americans read the Reagan administration proposals for a new round of multilateral trade negotiations.[7] Thus, most people were not cognizant that globalization put their national governments in a dilemma. As the United States and other nations opened themselves to global markets, their citizens demanded new and broader forms of regulation and social insurance to cushion them from the vicissitudes of global markets. But the state (seconded by taxpayers and investors) is less able to play that role without making itself less competitive in global markets. This is the "Catch-22" of globalization.[8]

In 1987, Ritchie did not seem to have much ability to influence those negotiations. He was not a "player" in U.S. farm policy during the Reagan/Bush era (1981–1992), nor was he well connected to the movers and shakers who made trade policy in Congress or the Reagan administration.[9] But he had experience organizing an international movement. He also was an effective educator and fundraiser, willing to use his considerable energy and public-speaking skills to explain his concerns to other farm, civic, environmental, religious, community, consumer activists, and foundation officials.[10]

After reading the proposals, Mark Ritchie became a twentieth-century Paul Revere, warning citizens and civil society groups that the Reagan (and later Bush) administration's trade policy plans could jeopardize national approaches to sustainable development, food self-sufficiency, and national systems of social regulation. After 1988, Ritchie became more like Johnny Appleseed. He saw his mission as organizing a domestic and international movement critical of trade agreements. He built bridges among development, farm, environmental, human rights, and labor groups and planted the seeds of trade agreement criticism.[11] As a result of his efforts (and those of many others), a wide range of individuals in Canada, the United States, Europe, and Asia formed links to influence the Uruguay Round, and in particular the U.S. trade proposals. Some activists thought the Reagan and Bush administrations were using the GATT as a tool to lower national regulatory standards. They came to that perspective not only because of the content of the trade policy plans, but also because of the context in which the Reagan and Bush administrations made their proposals: a time of economic uncertainty, protectionist rhetoric, and deregulation. By 1991, many of the trade agreement critics concluded that they must oppose trade liberalization under the GATT to preserve their regulatory protections. In the United States, some of these critics forged a political alliance with protectionists and economic nationalists to object to the trade agreement's impact on sovereignty.

The Message and the Messenger: Linking Environmental, Farm, and Consumer Protection Policies

Ritchie's fears about the Uruguay Round's impact on the environment and farmers had merit. In the forty years of GATT negotiations, GATT's contracting parties had not developed clear rules for trade in agriculture. As farmers became more efficient, they produced surpluses and became dependent on foreign consumers to buy their surplus production. At the same time, industrialized nations continued to protect their domestic agricultural sectors through subsidies, credit programs, tax incentives, price supports, production controls, and health and safety standards. As the world's farmers contended with declining prices and relatively high costs of protection, they came under greater pressure to use pesticides and biotechnology to produce efficiently.[12]

The pressure to farm almost every inch of arable land and to use pesticides was not the only irony affecting the world's farmers. Farmers were producing more food than ever, yet many people in the poorest nations of the world went hungry. This gap between demand and supply stemmed from a noble goal. All nations were determined to ensure a reliable and safe food supply for their citizens. Thus they protected their farmers but did little to ensure that food was always affordable and available to their needy citizens. In many nations, consumers and taxpayers subsidized farmers, and the price of such support programs continued to rise. In 1982, U.S. farm programs costs some $26 billion, while European Union farm subsidies and support measures were approximately $23 billion. These high costs pressed policymakers around the world to search for a global solution to reduce both overproduction and farm supports. They hoped to find one under the aegis of the GATT. In discussing the problems of America's farmers, Daniel G. Amstudz, the undersecretary of agriculture for international affairs and commodity programs, argued in 1986, "We must reject the 'go it alone' approach. . . . The international bargaining approach is where the solution lies."[13]

The Reagan trade policy plans, however, coincided with horrible upheaval in America's farm sector. Since the 1970s federal farm policy had discouraged soil conservation and encouraged many farmers to become dependent on global markets. America became "the breadbasket of the world," but reliance on global markets did not help many small farmers. As land and commodity prices fell throughout the 1980s, many farmers were unable to cover their losses. High interest rates and enormous debt loads forced many farmers into bankruptcy, fueling bitterness at the banks and anger at the federal government. The costs of supporting such farmers grew so high that policymakers and taxpayers demanded changes to farm policy.[14] As farmers tried to squeeze every last bushel out of their land to survive, soil erosion and groundwater contamination accelerated. At the same time, many family farms were liquidated. Rural communities throughout the United States were devastated and depopulated.[15] Some farmers became radicalized, joining extremist antigovernment groups (such as militia groups in Idaho, Michigan, and Montana).[16] Others determined to develop new farm policies through political activism, somewhat like the populist alliance of the late nineteenth century. Mark Ritchie was one of these activists, but his activism would transcend U.S. borders.

Like many agricultural economists, Ritchie believed U.S. farm programs tended to subsidize agribusiness and large corporate farmers who were most likely to use pesticides.[17] He was not opposed to international trade rules that could force the reduction of such subsidies. He was also not opposed to finding international common ground on health and safety standards (called sanitary and phytosanitary [S&P] regulations). But Ritchie felt strongly that the United States must recognize that "import controls, including quality and safety regulations, are necessary to protect the integrity of domestic food and farm programs."[18] In short, Ritchie wanted to ensure that food safety standards could continue to be used as a tool of protection. Although the United States had consistently taken the position that nations should use overt tools of protection such as tariffs to protect, it also had long used food safety regulations to protect American farmers as well as its consumers, as its trading partners had.[19]

FOOD SAFETY

America's system of food safety regulation is incredibly complex. There are twelve agencies with food safety responsibilities, but none has primary responsibility. The most important agencies are the Food and Drug Administration (FDA), the Department of Agriculture, and the Environmental Protection Agency (EPA). Given this complexity, Americans have repeatedly tried to reorganize the U.S. government's approach to protecting consumers from unsafe food and separate it from other functions such as expanding exports.[20] For example, in 1972, Ralph Nader's Center for Study of Responsive Law published Sowing the Wind, *saying the goal of government regulation of food safety should be to protect public health and not to promote U.S. farm products.[21] In the following years, civic groups and coalitions such as the Safe Food Coalition criticized both the strategy for and organizational structure of food safety regulation, but this criticism had little impact. The public was increasingly vulnerable to tainted food.[22]*

The American public strongly supports government regulation of food safety and has been especially concerned about the rising percentage of imported food that is not subject to regulation during production. Food safety advocates believe the first step is to improve domestic regulation of food safety. Europeans also want to find a more effective approach to food safety.[23]

In 1987, Mark Ritchie hoped to help the Reagan administration find a better balance between consumer welfare and producer protection. He believed the GATT system could and should be improved, stating, "As flawed as they are, GATT rules . . . are increasingly more, not less necessary."[24] He stressed, "The GATT talks will set the international economic agenda . . . far into the next century. They can be used to vastly improve the situation, or they can be a disaster."[25] This ambivalence toward trade agreements would shape his actions; he would adopt both a reformist and a rejectionist strategy.

Ritchie thought that the Reagan administration had developed lousy plans because they had not invited broad participation in developing the plans. This insularity, Ritchie concluded, and not some grand conspiracy, was to blame for the administration's approach. In his view, it could only be overcome by getting more of the public informed and involved in the process. But Ritchie did not adopt the traditional Washington approach of lobbying inside the Beltway or using the media to convey his views.[26] Instead, he moved his family to Europe and worked to build an international constituency to oppose the Reagan administration's approach to the Uruguay Round.

Ritchie had both a wide range of international contacts and experience in achieving major international change.[27] He had been a leader in one of the first international consumer campaigns: the boycott of the Nestlé company. In some developing nations in the late 1970s, Nestlé advertised that infant formula was a good (not exact) substitute for breast milk and the "modern way" to feed infants. But there are a lot of "ifs" in substituting formula for breast milk in developing nations. To mimic breast milk, the formula must be combined with the right amount of sterilized water and fed to babies in sterilized bottles with sterilized nipples.[28] Health care workers and missionaries (later joined by consumer advocates) called on Nestlé and other producers of infant formulas to make sure that consumers understood that the formula should not be diluted or mixed with unsafe water. But Nestlé did not respond.

Ritchie and other activists set up the Infant Formula Action Coalition (INFACT) in Minneapolis, which led a global boycott of Nestlé products. The results were slow in coming, but dramatic. The World Health Organization passed a code of conduct for the marketing and sale of infant formula, and Nestlé changed its marketing practices for infant formula.[29]

Most important, the baby formula campaign was a transnational social movement, linking doctors, nutritionists, development experts, missionaries, and other individuals across borders. It inspired other individuals and groups to work internationally (such as the disinvestment campaign to end apartheid in South Africa). It also encouraged Mark Ritchie to find global common ground among citizens' groups on ways to protect small farmers, consumers, and the environment, while encouraging trade.[30] This goal, he believed, required working with citizens and public officials of many nations.

Ritchie already had close relations with Canadian environmentalists, social activists, and farm groups. In 1987 he focused his efforts on European activists. He gave a speech at a conference in England sponsored by the Catholic Institute for International Affairs. This speech inspired some of the attendees to think differently about trade policy. Among those inspired were Kevin Watkins of the Catholic Institute for International Affairs (a development activist now with Oxfam), Tim Lang (a food safety and consumer expert), and Colin Hines (an environmental activist and now Green Party strategist).[31] All these individuals remain involved in the globalization debate.

Ritchie also worked with farmers from Canada, Japan, Europe, and some Third World countries to forge a common strategy. These farmers seemed to have little in common. However, at a December 1987 summit meeting in Geneva, the home of the GATT, these farmers called for an end to export dumping and issued proposals for countries to strengthen—not eliminate—import barriers. In 1988, thousands of farmers gathered in Montreal at the GATT midterm review and issued a joint statement, the "Montreal Charter." The charter opened with a statement expressing concern about "the chaotic state of agricultural trade" and proposed solutions to better link farmers' needs and environmental protection.[32] Thus, as early as 1988, farmers and advocates of small farmers were cooperating internationally to protect their national systems of regulatory protection. How were these farmers able to find such common ground? They believed most government programs provided benefits to large corporate farmers, rather than small farmers. In Europe, farmers were protected by high prices, which consumers absorbed, while in the United States, taxpayers subsidized farmers. In nations such as Argentina and Canada, farmers benefited from export subsidies, while in Europe and the United States, many farmers benefited from domestic subsidies. These strategies, however, had different environmental impacts. To environmentalists and food safety advocates, the Europeans seemed to do a better job of reconciling trade, consumer welfare, and environmental policy goals.[33]

Ritchie and his allies decided that they could develop alliances with negotiators from other countries. He became close to prominent European trade officials, such as Tran Van Thinh, the European Community's GATT negotiator, and the Jamaican negotiator, Anthony Hill. Ritchie saw these alliances as a useful way to publicize the concerns of small farmers, environmentalists, and other concerned groups and to build a broad international coalition. He recognized that the Europeans (especially the French) were very concerned about reducing protection for their farmers, who comprised an important political bloc. The European trade officials saw their alliance with Ritchie as a means of tempering the U.S. proposals, especially in the area of agriculture. Sometimes European trade policymakers leaked the American proposals to U.S. NGOs to advance European positions or disadvantage U.S. negotiators. Thus, the Europeans used the NGOs to play off the Americans, and the NGO activists used the European governments to press their positions with their home country negotiators.[34]

Not surprisingly, this strategy alienated some U.S. trade negotiators. Because Ritchie was hampering the progress of trade negotiations, they came to see Ritchie as a protectionist and a thorn in their side, instead of someone to work with.[35] But other Americans began to concur that U.S.

interests could work internationally to influence U.S. and global trade policy.[36] For example, the American Agricultural Movement, the League of Rural Voters, the National Farmers Organization, the National Farmers Union, and the National Save the Family Farm Coalition, in a joint press conference with the Japanese Central Union of Farmer Cooperatives (Zenchu), called for a less confrontational approach to trade. U.S. and European farm groups issued statements calling on policymakers to protect family farms instead of concentrating on reducing subsidies. But the Reagan administration conveyed that it did not approve of such nongovernmental internationalism. In 1988, Agriculture Secretary Richard Lyng criticized this cross-border organizing and called the farm groups "un-American."[37]

Meanwhile, Ritchie returned to the United States and began to lobby other NGOs concerned about agricultural, consumer, and human rights issues. In 1986, Ritchie organized a Minnesota think tank, the Institute for Agriculture and Trade Policy (IATP) to "give voice to the interests of small- and medium-sized farmers, along with the citizens who consume their products, in the global decision-making arena." The IATP received funding from internationalist and mainstream national foundations such as Ford, Kellogg, MacArthur, and Rockefeller Brothers, as well as left-leaning foundations such as Veatch, Tides, Bauman, and the Ruth Mott Fund.[38] It used these funds to write and disseminate a wide range of reports on the potential impact of the GATT. Ritchie tailored these reports to different audiences to arouse their concern about the Uruguay Round.[39]

Ritchie believed that U.S. citizens and interest groups would be most disturbed by the potential of the Uruguay Round to lower national health and safety standards. In 1989, he began to work closely with a Washington-based think tank, the Community Nutrition Institute (CNI), headed by Rod Leonard, a former agricultural department official. In joint publications, they warned citizens that big food corporations and agribusiness saw GATT as an opportunity to deregulate global food trade and harmonize, and thus lower, food safety standards.[40] Ritchie wrote to development groups, noting that the GATT proposals "are designed to force poor countries to abandon efforts to achieve . . . food self-reliance."[41] Many of these reports were overly negative and glossed over any potential benefits of finding common ground internationally on health and safety regulation. But they achieved what Ritchie wanted, which was to inspire a wide range of religious, farm, and consumer groups to examine and disseminate information about the potential impact of the Uruguay Round around the world.[42] These nationalist/internationalist efforts stimulated greater public interest in the direction of trade policy. But in 1989, trade policy was about to change. The new president, George Bush, had a different vision of how the GATT system should be revised. The Bush administration said that it wanted to harmonize global regulation on the basis of sound science.

THE BUSH ADMINISTRATION PROPOSALS

From 1987 to 1989, the Uruguay Round negotiations proceeded slowly because participants could not find common ground on agriculture, services, and many other issues. In 1989, to encourage the process, the Bush administration submitted its final version of a comprehensive agricultural proposal. Like the earlier Reagan proposals, this proposal was aimed at reducing government intervention in the agricultural sector. The Bush administration hoped to "prevent the many problems . . . of current agricultural policies," including "costs . . . that exceed $275 billion annually, incentives for overproduction . . . and import barriers that misallocate resources, reduce the level of food purchases and limit consumer choice." However, while the Reagan administration had proposed *"uniform food and health regulations around the world to prevent non-tariff barriers to agricultural trade,"* the Bush administration claimed that its proposals were designed to *"ensure that measures taken to protect animal, plant and human health are based on sound scientific evidence and recognize the principle of equivalency."* This was a significant change. The Bush proposals did not call for *uniformity,* which could preempt U.S. standards at the federal and state levels, but rather a *harmonization* of food regulations based on standards set by the Codex Alimentarius Commission, a subsidiary of the United Nations.[43]

Codex is an intergovernmental organization that sets guidelines and standards relating to such areas as food safety, pesticide residues, sampling, and testing methodologies. Delegates to Codex rely on scientific experts to set international standards. Bush administration policymakers thought that Codex would be perceived as fair and unbiased, because it had expertise at building an international consensus, based on internationally determined "sound science."[44]

Bush administration policymakers believed that this approach would not result in a lowest common denominator of regulations. Nations could maintain higher standards if they could provide scientific justification for such standards. However, these officials presumed that "scientific consensus could provide guidance" in sorting out which regulations are truly based on health or safety grounds and which are motivated by protectionist intent. But this strategy of reliance on "science" presented other problems to trade policymakers. According to Carol Kramer, associate director of the Resources and Technology Division of the U.S. Department of Agriculture, "Science is not always the exclusive factor in decision-making." There are divergent safety standards, different risk assessment methods, different tax and subsidies that encourage or discourage the use and development of certain agricultural inputs, and different food production processes. Scientists may not be able to find consensus at the national or international level. What may be determined to be sound science at Codex may not be perceived as equally "sound" at the national level. Finally, sometimes policymakers weigh factors other than science. Kramer was not the only U.S. government official to express such important concerns.[45]

The "terms" of the Bush administration's agricultural proposals did not receive a rousing reception around the world. Although agricultural exporting nations such as Australia, Argentina, and New Zealand welcomed this attempt to move the process forward, the Europeans made it clear that they disagreed with much of the administration's objectives and strategies.[46] However, the Europeans and representatives of other nations also were very concerned about a U.S. proposal to convert all NTBs into tariffs. This proposal may have made trade sense, but it seemed to threaten national flexibility on how to protect citizens or producers.[47] Some foreign government officials began to see the Bush administration plans as an attempt to force U.S. standards on the rest of the world as well as a threat to their national sovereignty. Ironically, international government concern about the U.S. proposal was mild compared with the furor expressed by some environmentalists, consumer advocates, farm organizations, and other trade agreement critics. They saw the Bush administration's proposals as a plot by multilateral big business, especially agribusiness, to remake U.S. agricultural policy. They called it "decoupling" because these critics saw it as a covert attempt to decouple support for small farmers from trade policy. The IATP described the Bush proposals as a plan by "Cargill and their supporters . . . to go around Congress by moving the debate and ultimate decision-making to the international trade negotiations at GATT." To prove their point, they cited as evidence the fact that "this global strategy" was developed by former Cargill executive and current Undersecretary of Agriculture Daniel Amstutz.[48] Their fears that Bush administration trade policy ignored the needs of small farmers was understandable, although that allegation did not prove their point.

The IATP, the CNI, and the National Toxics Campaign Fund joined together to scrutinize and publicize what they saw as the broad negative impact of the proposals. They hoped to use this information to educate the public and convince them that U.S. trade policy had been designed by and for big business.

Staff at many of these NGOs were suspicious of the administration's strategy of harmonization and its reliance on Codex to determine national standards. They alleged that Codex was captured by big business and only business representatives attended its meetings.[49] They obtained leaked documents showing that other nations did not concur with the U.S. strategy.[50] Finally, they organized an international opposition to the Bush administration agricultural trade proposals. In June 1989, some seventy farm leaders from forty-eight countries met in St. Paul, Minnesota, to oppose the official U.S. proposals.[51]

Food safety advocates in the United States and Europe were especially concerned about the administration's strategy. They acknowledged that S&P standards could be used to distort trade. But who should decide what was legitimate consumer protection and what was not? The beef hormone case provides a good example of this phenomenon. The Europeans had a long record of protecting their beef *producers.* But in the early 1980s, the European Community (EC) banned beef with hormone implants (in both imported and domestic beef). This ban came about as a result of *consumer* pressure (through the Bureau Europeen des Unions de Consommateurs—the European office of Consumers Unions). Although these hormones are naturally occurring, EC policymakers feared the long-term implications of eating beef grown with these synthetic hormones.[52] Many U.S. producers used these hormones to fatten their calves. The hormones made U.S. calves mature earlier, which in turn allowed U.S. producers to bring their beef to market earlier. Thus, with such hormones, the U.S. could produce beef more cheaply.

Clayton Yeutter, secretary of agriculture and former USTR under President Reagan, thought reliance on science would allow policymakers to distinguish between legitimate and illegitimate (i.e., protectionist) standards such as in the beef hormone case. In an interview with *Farm Journal,* he said, "A new GATT agreement will standardize health and safety rules on a global basis." If the rest of the world can agree on what the standard ought to be on a given product, "maybe the U.S. or E.C. will have to admit they are wrong when their standards differ."[53] But the Europeans did not quite see it that way. They had a different notion of sound science and how best to protect consumer welfare.

In 1989, the United States threatened retaliation for their ban on beef hormones. The Europeans refused to lift the ban.[54] Yeutter may have been relieved when it was reported that the head of the European Alliance for Safe Meat and a member of the European Parliament frankly admitted "the decision to ban these substances was made for political and commercial reasons and not, as the public was led to believe, for consumer protection." The case continued to bring out the worst in policymakers. When Texas Agriculture Commissioner Jim Hightower made arrangements to ship hormone-free beef from Texas to Europe, Yeutter threatened to prosecute him under the Logan Act for committing a treasonable offense.[55]

Some environmentalists and consumer advocates who had long been internationalists worried that the Bush administration food safety strategy would actually thwart finding common ground internationally. According to Mark Ritchie, "Nation states must retain the right to set more strict standards if they so choose. . . . In the end, the real danger of 'harmonization' is that if it does win approval by GATT negotiators, it may create the kind of consumer backlash in Europe, the United States, Japan, and other countries that could set back many important, positive gains of post-war multilateralism."[56] But the Bush administration did not see it this way.

Moreover, some U.S. government officials were concerned about the administration's trade strategy. In 1990, an EPA official publicly acknowledged that Codex's pesticide standards were often weaker than those of the United States. In an 1990 internal memo, EPA staff worried about the implications of letting Congress abdicate its powers to determine the level of safety appropriate to American society. At the same time, Health and Human Services Secretary Louis Sullivan encouraged states to come out with their own laws in the area of food labeling, in direct contradiction to the views and efforts being made by the USTR and the Department of Agriculture.[57]

Meanwhile, members of Congress were waking up to concerns about imported food and U.S. food inspection. The Subcommittee on Oversight and Investigations of the House Committee on Energy and Commerce described the FDA import inspection program as "fatally flawed." Some 40 percent of tested samples were contaminated with salmonella, pesticides, insects, and filth or decomposition.[58] The United States did not have its own consumer safety house in order.

In 1990, a coalition of environmental, consumer, and farm groups organized the Ad Hoc Working Group on Trade and Environmentally Sustainable Development to lobby the Bush administration to change its proposals. Its leaders seemed to understand that in order to reconcile the goals of trade expansion and consumer/environmental protection, they must distinguish between true consumer protection and traditional trade protection. On June 11, 1990, Eric Christiansen of the Natural Resources Defense Council (NRDC), wrote USTR Carla Hills, noting, "[We agree that] nations should not be allowed to impose protectionist measures disguised as health and safety regulations. We also urge the administration to reexamine the proposal of sanitary and phytosanitary standards submitted by the United States to GATT in October, and to add language that clearly protects the power of the United States and individual states to enact legitimate health and safety regulations."[59]

Members of the Ad Hoc Working Group on Trade and Environmentally Sustainable Development

American Agriculture Movement	U.S. Public Interest Research Group
Community Nutrition Institute	Center for Rural Affairs
Development Group for Alternative Policies	Consumer Pesticide Project
Environmental Defense Fund*	National Wildlife Federation*
Fair Trade Campaign	National Council of Churches
Foundation on Economic Trends	National Family Farm Coalition
Friends of the Earth	National Toxics Campaign
Institute for Agriculture and Trade Policy	Sierra Club
	Greenpeace

*Supported Clinton approach to NAFTA

This group began to get support on Capitol Hill. On May 21, 1990, some members of the ad hoc coalition urged Congress to pass the Scheuer resolution, which proposed the Congress not approve legislation implementing the Uruguay Round until key environmental objectives were met. The Scheuer approach suggested that international environmental standards "become a floor, not a ceiling" for state and national standards.[60] The Scheuer approach was less adamant than a competing proposal, the Swift proposal, which would block imports not meeting minimal environmental, consumer, and worker safety standards. Representative Swift hoped to protect U.S. producers from ecological dumping, where goods produced under lower environmental standards are shipped into the United States. Such goods may have a price advantage because producers did not have to bear the higher costs of environmental protection. Although the Swift resolution was first announced at a press conference sponsored by the Working Group, most of its members concentrated their efforts on passing the Scheuer resolution.[61] In 1990, the Working Group seemed determined to find a middle ground between environmental protection and protectionism masquerading as environmentalism.

Throughout 1990, a wide range of individuals raised questions about the administration's agricultural trade proposals. They were concerned about a wide range of issues, from the impact on regulation to federalism to consumer safety. For example, several members of Congress asked the GAO to review the differences between the Codex and EPA standards for pesticides.[62] The director of the Idaho Rural Council asked the USTR if the GATT would force policymakers to phase out water irrigation projects. Vermont legislators wondered what this proposal would do to dairy price supports.[63]

These questions became news. The press, the translators of trade policy to the public, were increasingly aware that trade regulation and social regulation were related. At a May 1990 speech at the National Press Club in Washington, D.C., USTR Carla Hills was asked, "Why doesn't your GATT proposal do more to protect the environment?" Ambassador Hills gave an answer, but it was not to the question posed. She replied, "We want objections raised to food to be based upon real scientific fact."[64]

The Bush administration wanted to reassure American activists that it would not use trade regulation to undermine democratically developed regulations. However, according to former EPA official Dan Esty, Bush administration officials were torn between two impulses: their desire to reconcile trade, environmental, and consumer considerations globally (to rationalize such regulations) and their desire to be responsive to legitimate concerns of U.S. consumer, environmental, and sustainable development groups.[65] They knew these individuals could exert significant political pressure, especially on the Democrats. Thus, Bush administration officials tried to appease them by meeting with them to hear out some of their concerns.

On August 9, 1990, some of the American trade agreement critics again met with government officials from USDA, FDA, USTR, and EPA concerning the GATT. They stressed that the administration had not made a compelling case for a new agreement on S&P measures. They argued the proposals must permit public participation: "To deny public access to international decision-making bodies such as GATT . . . is fundamentally undemocratic." Despite their strong words, the Bush administration's GATT proposals did not seem to change.[66] In the months that followed, many trade agreement critics concluded that the Bush administration shared the Reagan administration deregulatory objectives but simply cloaked them in a kinder, gentler, more responsive strategy.

The kinder, gentler strategy, however, was not yielding international consensus. Trade negotiators were talking in Geneva, but not reaching agreement. To move the process forward, on June 27, 1990, Aart de Zeeuw, chairman of the GATT Agricultural Negotiating Committee, circulated his proposal for the final framework agreement.[67] But this proposal barely reflected the concerns of environmental and consumer groups in the United States and Europe. Meanwhile, British food safety advocates made a detailed study of the Codex; they alleged that it was dominated by business, that its participants had many potential conflicts of interest, and that the participating NGOs tended to be business groups.[68] This evidence further soured critics of the Bush administration's proposals.

Slowly, trade agreement critics began to forge a global movement to oppose the U.S. GATT proposals. The National Toxics Campaign Fund in the United States and the Third World Network in Malaysia issued reports on GATT issues and processes. *The Ecologist* in Great Britain published articles by Steven Shrybman of the Canadian Environmental Law Association and Martin Khor Kok Penn (director of the Consumers Association of Penang Malaysia), among others, on the relationship between food safety, national self-sufficiency, environmental protection, and democracy. While Shrybman argued that the GATT must be amended to make the connection between environmental protection and resource conservation explicit in the GATT, Khor argued the only way to make sure GATT elevates environmental values is for our government and legislators "to play a balancing role." These trade agreement critics were raising a wide range of questions about trade agreements. In 1990, however, they did not want to hamper trade liberalization per se or to gut the GATT system.[69]

As this debate unfolded, activists in the United States demanded more, not less, environmental or consumer regulation. California voters passed a strict pesticide ban (Big Green), while several dairy states passed bans on bovine growth hormone in milk (similar to the growth hormones used in cattle). While the United States pushed harmonization within the GATT, the EC attacked such state-level regulation as a trade barrier, arguing that such regulation "fragments" the American market, making it harder for European producers to serve. They insisted that the United States harmonize its approach to regulation before demanding international harmonization.[70] Some environmentalists and consumer activists were very worried by this European view that state-level regulations were protectionist. They feared that U.S. negotiators might concede state powers over health and safety measures to get concessions in the EC's agricultural policies. Thus, they saw this approach to trade liberalization as a threat to state and federal environmental regulation and federalism per se.[71]

In July 1990, echoing the EC's concerns about Big Green, the administration decided to challenge California's higher levels for pesticide protection. In July 1990, USTR Carla Hills asked the International Trade Commission (ITC) to determine whether California's Big Green proposition could hurt trade relations, noting that the EC had threatened to list it as a trade barrier. This action infuriated many environmentalists and consumer safety activists. Supporters of the initiative accused the Bush administration of orchestrating the ITC hearing to help chemical and agribusiness interests whose costs would rise to meet California's higher standards. In a press conference objecting to the hearing, Senator Dianne Feinstein argued, "We Californians have a right to safeguard our own health and the health of our children. Under Big Green, our farmers can make a gradual transition to safer alternatives from cancer-causing alternatives."[72]

By year-end 1990, almost all the environmental groups opposed the Bush administration GATT proposals. Moreover, only Resources for the Future (an environmental group that tries to reconcile environmental protection and economic growth) still supported trade liberalization in agriculture. The International Organization of Consumer Unions (IOCU) stated that it supported the objectives of the Uruguay Round but objected to the notion that sound science should be the only criteria for determining food standards.[73] Representatives of these groups seemed increasingly frustrated by what they saw as the undemocratic nature of the trade policy-making process and its capture by "big business."[74]

Meanwhile, Ritchie, was still trying to find a middle ground. In 1990, the Dutch Centre for Agriculture and the Environment organized a conference. Participants came from twenty-one countries and included policymakers, scientists, environmentalists, and representatives of farmers' and consumers' organizations. They agreed that "the GATT, if properly applied, and amended on some points, could play a positive role towards a newer world, where fair trade does not interfere with the responsibilities of democratically chosen bodies, where food security is guaranteed . . . and where a highly productive . . . agriculture is integrated into a well-protected environment."[75]

The Uruguay Round negotiations were due to end in December 1990. But the GATT signatories were unable to reach an agreement on all the issues they had agreed to negotiate.[76] To move the process forward, Arthur Dunkel, the new director general of the GATT, set a deadline and presented governments with a complete revision of the Uruguay Round Final Act. The 392-page draft (the Dunkel text) included proposed compromise texts drawn up by GATT staff covering areas in which negotiators had not yet reached agreement.[77] The draft was supposed to be for contracting parties only and thus was not declassified. However, some citizen activists obtained the text of the draft and found it deeply disappointing. Like the Bush administration's proposals, the Dunkel draft provided that signatories would endeavor to apply only health measures based on scientific evidence and recognized nations' rights to use stricter standards. It also recognized the benefit of agreement on the equivalency of standards and included a reference to consumer concerns, animal welfare, and environmental protection.

The Dunkel draft was not widely available in the United States, furthering an impression that the process was undemocratic and secretive. As with the NAFTA text, trade agreement critics seized on this secrecy as a way of underscoring that the trade policy-making process was unfair. They insisted that the GATT negotiations be done in an open manner. They asserted that if trade agreements were going to regulate national regulations, the process of developing these regulations must be transparent. However, that was not how trade negotiations were conducted in the past. The negotiators presumed that secrecy was essential because it facilitated the process of granting concessions that might not be politically palatable at the national level without a complete Uruguay Round agreement. In addition, policymakers argued that they needed secrecy to protect proprietary business information given to government negotiators to facilitate negotiations. These same policymakers, however, did not foresee that this secrecy could undermine public support for the agreements they were trying to achieve.

The development of the Dunkel text did not move the process forward. Despite discussion between leaders of the United States, France, and Germany, no further agreement on the Uruguay Round was reached by mid-1992.

On June 19, 1991, Rod Leonard of the Community Nutrition Institute decided that if the trade agreement critics wanted to change the

Bush administration's strategy for the negotiations, these critics should develop a model of a better agreement.[78] Leonard, working with Eric Christiansen of the NRDC (a market-oriented environmental group), proposed basic principles for reconciling trade and the environment, including sustainable development as the touchstone of trade policy; greater public participation; consideration of the environmental impact of trade agreements; policies to prevent environmental dumping (where firms move to countries with weaker standards); preservation of local and national control; and formal recognition of environmental protection within the GATT.[79] On May 16, 1991, some of these individuals met with James D. Grueff, a key negotiator for the U.S. Department of Agriculture. They argued that environmental, health, and consumer protections should not be "unduly constrained" by the "niggardly interpretation" of the GATT.[80] They noted that the role of science in the regulatory process is advisory. They warned, "The U.S. trade proposal would change all of that. A scientific court would be accountable only to those individuals or interests that appoint the members of the court. . . . Science would no longer be an advisor, but would determine what is best."[81] They urged the administration to alter its approach to regulating consumer welfare.

By 1991, however, other individuals came to the fore of the trade debate. Some of these individuals did not share a reformist perspective and were less trusting of government and business. These activists were certain that U.S. trade policy was captured by big business and was designed to covertly lower U.S. standards. Lori Wallach became a prominent leader of this perspective. An energetic, articulate, and forceful young lawyer, she joined Public Citizen as a food safety lobbyist. Wallach had been a television producer before she went to law school. She knew how to use the media to raise public concern about trade issues.[82] Because she was skilled both as a strategist and a spokesperson, she became a formidable opponent of the Bush and Clinton's administrations' approach to trade. Working closely with Brent Blackwelder of Friends of the Earth, as part of the Citizens Trade Campaign (see previous chapter), these groups adopted a more confrontational approach. They were not afraid to be tagged as protectionists or to work with economic nationalists. These activists were willing to use lawsuits, petitions, and protests to derail the Bush administration's Uruguay Round proposals. But they also worked closely with more internationalist activists such as Mark Ritchie and Rod Leonard.

For example, Wallach, Ritchie, and Leonard, among others, went to Geneva to try to influence the course of GATT negotiations. In a series of meetings held in Stuttgart, Geneva, and Amsterdam, representatives of consumer, environmental, religious, and farm groups from Japan, Europe, and the United States met with a wide range of national government and GATT officials to present their views and learn about the Uruguay Round's progress. But although the GATT staff were willing to meet with these critics, they could not change the course of negotiations or change national positions. These trade agreement critics began to see GATT staff in Geneva (as well as U.S. officials) as biased against their concerns. They cited a statement by Jean Marc Luc, director of the agricultural division of the GATT. Recognizing that the United States has the only food safety law—the Delaney clause—that sets a zero tolerance for cancer-causing food additives, Luc noted, "World trade cannot survive with a zero tolerance." These individuals, however, misinterpreted Luc's remarks as part of a deliberate strategy by the GATT to undermine the U.S. approach to food safety and ultimately all regulations that could distort trade. The GATT had no power to do this, unless all of its member nations agreed to do so as part of a trade negotiation.[83]

By 1991, leaders of many of these groups had gradually concluded that they could neither remake the GATT to meet their concerns nor get the United States, the most powerful GATT contracting party, to force such changes. On July 8, 1991, Ralph Nader went before the IOCU and urged IOCU members to oppose the GATT, noting that "nothing less than the chance for economic self-determination . . . is at stake." He called on IOCU to oppose GATT, spread the word against it, and ask governments "why they are trading away citizens rights."[84] Nader also endorsed a strategy of working internationally to thwart what he and others saw as covert deregulation.

Meanwhile, ironically, the GATT did make some progress regarding trade and the environment. In February 1992, the GATT Secretariat published the organization's first-ever report on trade and the environment, noting that "even if a trade measure is discriminatory, a signatory may be able to justify its necessity under [the GATT's] article XX."[85] Policy moves forward in baby steps, but this step was too small for consumer advocates and environmentalists. These activists wondered, "Why . . . dirty your backyard, only to trumpet the virtues of cleaning it up?" They saw the GATT as consciously protecting the corporate elite and not the public good. Their negative view of GATT was strengthened by their view of GATT's mediation of trade disputes such as the beef hormone case. The GATT, in their view, represented only market values and devalued other values such as protecting the environment or workers.[86]

While GATT was stalled politically in 1992, NAFTA was moving forward. Individuals concerned with social justice, the environment, and family farms, among others, turned their attention toward influencing that process. These groups divided on NAFTA, and that division was deeply disturbing to some leaders, especially within the environmental community. To some degree, the more reformist and more international groups—those who still thought that trade could be reconciled with environmental or social goals—focused on NAFTA and paid less attention to GATT. This would include the members of the Alliance for Responsible Trade, which replaced MODTLE in 1993, and environmental groups such as NRDC, World Wildlife Fund (WWF), and the Environmental Defense Fund. The more confrontational and oppositional groups such as the Council of Canadians, Public Citizen, and the Sierra Club continued to speak out against GATT as well as NAFTA, and their views seemed to have gained ascendancy among progressives.[87] Meanwhile, in Europe, social activists were equally unhappy with the progress of the Uruguay Round and determined to oppose it by 1992.[88]

While European, Canadian, and American activists found common ground in their opposition to the proposed Uruguay Round, their governments were increasingly disputing trade. For example, in November 1992, as Americans prepared to vote for a new president, the United States and Europe argued about the trade distortions caused by EC oilseed subsidies. The United States threatened to retaliate against a billion dollars of EC exports. On November 5, 1992, the United States announced it would impose a 200 percent tariff on over $300 million of EC exports, primarily white wine. This threat of retaliation got the Europeans to the table. Trade and agriculture ministers from the United States and the European Union met at Blair House (near the White House) to compromise on agricultural subsidies. They achieved a breakthrough in November 1992, but news of the breakthrough led to a massive farm protest on December 1, 1992, in Strasbourg, France. These farmers did not think trade policy should force changes to farm policy. However, even that breakthrough did not yield a complete agreement. The Uruguay Round was still not complete when Democrat William Jefferson Clinton took office in January 1993.[89]

In 1993, public interest in GATT swelled around the world. The tuna dolphin case alienated many environmentalists. Environmental groups, such as the Sierra Club and Public Citizen, used the case to portray GATT as "GATTzilla," an enemy of the environment. They plastered posters in many U.S. cities and paid for full-page ads in major newspapers. Gretchen Stanton of the GATT received a small flood of letters protesting GATT interference with animal welfare and food safety decisions. In the United Kingdom, a coalition of ten environment and development agencies wrote letters of protest to members of Parliament. The UK National Consumer Council publicized the negative effects of the negotiations on European consumers. European NGOs concerned with food safety and sustainable trade also called on their governments to find ways to make "global trade be sustainable."[90] Opposition to GATT was also growing in developing nations. In 1992, grassroots social movements held a meeting in India and organized to fight the GATT. The Third World Network, headquartered in Malaysia, argued that the GATT should not be empowered to deal with trade and the environment.[91]

Meanwhile, individuals concerned with labor rights also were frustrated by their inability to change the GATT system. Congress directed that labor standards were a negotiating priority in the 1974 and 1988 trade bills authorizing international negotiations.[92] The Bush administration tried to push for these standards. In 1986, Bill Brock, former U.S. secretary of labor and former USTR, claimed, "Those countries which are flooding world markets with goods made by children, or by workers who can't form free trade unions . . . or who are denied even the most minimum standards . . . are doing more harm to the principle of free and fair trade than any protectionist group I can think of." Although the Reagan administration had tried to include labor standards in the Uruguay Round, India, Brazil, and Mexico, as well as many industrialized nations, objected. Officials from these nations saw labor standards as another protectionist strategy. The Bush administration also tried to move these issues before the GATT Council in 1987 and 1990, but other nations remained opposed.[93] Officials from these nations feared that by including the enforcement of labor rights in the GATT's rules, they would lose a key source of their competitive advantage and trade would thus decline. Trade agreement critics, however, saw this lack of progress as evidence that the Bush administration was only committed to rhetoric.

By 1992, many individuals of the left in the United States and abroad had developed an overwhelmingly negative view of trade agreements. Although trade had done much to bring economic growth and improve living standards around the world, they could only see its costs. They had seen little progress on labor rights, and they perceived the GATT proposals as deregulatory. Moreover, they saw GATT as a secretive and undemocratic institution. In the United States, twenty-six environmental and consumer groups called on Congress to reject the 1991 final act text. The signatories included many environmental and consumer groups that had a long commitment to international-ism.[94] Approximately one hundred and sixty NGOs from sixty countries wrote to their heads of government to oppose the Uruguay Round. Vandana Shiva of India, a biologist and food safety activist, and Martin Khor Kok of Malaysia, an influential consumer activist, also urged their governments to reject the Uruguay Round. Concern about the Dunkel text did not only come the left. Sir James Goldsmith of Great Britain, a Conservative member of the European Parliament, also lobbied to oppose the round. In Europe, he was joined by nationalists such as Le Pen of France's National Front and the Movement for France.[95]

CLINTON ROPES A TRADE ACCORD

This negative view of the GATT was not shared by President-elect Bill Clinton. Early on, Clinton won legislation extending the deadline for concluding the Uruguay Round to December 1993 (fast-track). This put pressure on other nations to emphasize their negotiating priorities and seemed to give the United States increased leverage. Japan and the European nations feared that Clinton could be more protectionist than his predecessors, and that fueled their interest in compromising and completing the round.[96]

Clinton did not use that leverage in ways that pleased many trade agreement critics of the left and right. First, he agreed to transform the informal GATT into a permanent umbrella institution: the WTO. The WTO charter provided legal authority for a secretariat, a director general, and a staff and strengthened and unified the trade regime's system of dispute settlement. With agreement on this new structure, the Uruguay Round was finally completed in December 1993 and participants signed the final act in Marrakesh on April 5, 1994.[97] However, to trade agreement critics of right and left, this new structure threatened to thwart national sovereignty.

Second, the president achieved the establishment of a working party on workers' rights designed to "explore the linkage between international trade and internationally recognized worker rights." The working party was to take into account differences in the level of development among countries, examine the effects on international trade of the systemic denial of such rights, and consider ways to address them. But in the view of human rights and labor rights advocates, worker rights had been examined to death over the last forty years; it was time for action. They saw it as a lost opportunity to use U.S. leverage on behalf of workers around the world. They argued that the United States should have tried harder to convince other GATT contracting parties of the benefits of including such worker protections within the GATT system, especially since the new agreement included intellectual property protection (protection of the intellectual product of workers).[98]

Third, the Clinton administration was able to obtain some modifications to the original Dunkel draft regarding S&P. Instead of saying that S&P measures must "not be maintained against available scientific evidence," the language was changed to state that "standards cannot be justified without sufficient scientific evidence." Thus, science would not be the only criteria for S&P standards. USTR Kantor noted the Clinton administration also safeguarded U.S. rights to establish higher levels of regulatory protection. The USTR published reports describing how the environment and consumer regulation would not be affected by the new GATT rules or the new system of dispute settlement.[99] The new rules, however, made it harder to justify import restrictions based on consumer environmental rationales. According to Dan Esty, the Uruguay Round agreement narrowed the GATT Article XX general exceptions, saying that environmental regulations should not be "more trade restrictive than necessary." "Necessary" means least inconsistent with the GATT.[100]

Finally, the preamble of the new WTO enshrined sustainable development as an objective of trade. This recognition was extremely important, but at that time many environmental activists saw it as mere rhetoric. In the United States, almost every labor union, consumer group, human rights group, and environmental group came out in opposition to the Uruguay Round.[101] The only consumer group publicly supporting the Uruguay Round was the IOCU and its U.S. affiliate, Consumers Union.[102] Thus, almost unanimously, trade agreement critics condemned the Uruguay Round and the WTO for a narrow focus on the commercial benefits of trade to the detriment of other important policy goals. But these trade agreement critics misunderstood that the GATT was deliberately designed to be narrowly focused and insulated from political pressure. The structure helped it sustain its long-term perspective and trade liberalizing mission in the face of challenges from special interests. Moreover, as chapter 2 notes, the GATT was limited to meet the narrow grant of authority approved by the U.S. Congress.

Trade agreement critics weren't the only parties capable of misunderstanding. As former EPA official and Yale Law professor Dan Esty wrote, "The GATT way of thinking failed to recognize the public's growing appetite for environmental protection, and other forms of social regulation."[103] By ignoring and appearing to devalue other important public policy concerns such as human rights, environmental protection, and consumer welfare, trade agreement proponents helped foster an opposition to multilateral trade liberalization. Moreover, by not early on addressing critics' concerns, advocates of trade liberalization helped perpetuate a negative image of the WTO as a heartless tool of big business. It became harder for economic internationalists of the left to make a progressive case for trade liberalization and to convince their allies on the left that the objectives of the social compact and trade expansion could be reconciled.

In 1994, the president submitted the results of the Uruguay Round to the Congress. But neither the president nor Congress moved rapidly to gain approval of the round in 1994. The president's top priority was health care reform. Republicans and Democrats alike found many reasons to stall development of the implementing legislation.[104] During the delay, a wide range of groups and individuals came out against the Uruguay Round. Democratic social activists were particularly disappointed. They saw the Clinton administration, a Democratic administration with a strong base of labor and environmental support, as unresponsive to their concerns and captured by international business.[105] But the administration, however much it may have shared the objective of reconciling trade liberalization with social and environmental protections, was unable to convince most GATT contracting parties of the merits of such objectives in 1993.

The trade agreement critics on the left were not able to bring their concerns center stage. Like the NAFTA debate, policymakers did not focus on social issues. Instead the debate turned on how the new WTO might affect American sovereignty. In the United States, trade critics of left and right alleged that this new powerful WTO could force changes to U.S. law if the United States lost a trade dispute.[106] But this was and is not true. If a WTO panel found the United States in violation of the trade rules established under the WTO, the United States had several options: it could change its laws or regulations; it could offer compensation through lowered trade barriers in other areas (or cash payments); or the United States could accept equivalent foreign retaliation through increased barriers to U.S. exports. These same options existed under the GATT, but they were not well understood by members of the general public or WTO opponents.[107] This focus on sovereignty allowed nationalists and traditional protectionists to again dominate the trade debate. Nationalist Patrick J. Buchanan was among the most forceful opponents of the Uruguay Round.

FIRE ON THE RIGHT

In the early 1990s, Buchanan came to believe that globalization was dividing America into a two-class system. That recognition, he said, transformed him: "The more I read of local businesses and factories shutting down, workers being laid off, towns dying, the more I began to ask myself, the price of free trade is painful, real, lasting—where is the benefit other than the vast cornucopia of consumer goods?"[108] While campaigning in New Hampshire for the Republican presidential nomination in 1991, Buchanan recalls, "Word had gone out that there would be further layoffs at the James River paper mill. [One man said to me], 'Save our jobs!' It went right through me." He decided, "We can do better by the norms of social justice—for all our people." Buchanan says he was transformed into a "conservative of the heart," determined to help the "Americans who make things with their hands, tools and machines who are paying the price of free trade."[109]

Buchanan concluded that increased trade was uprooting American norms. He noted that many women now had to work to keep family incomes up. With so many women working, families and society paid a price "in falling birthrates and rising delinquency, in teenage drug abuse, alcohol abuse, promiscuity, illegitimacy and abortions and in the high divorce rate among working parents. The American family is paying a hellish price for the good things down at the mall."[110] There was no evidence, however, that the American family agreed. They certainly liked their imported computers, clothes, chocolates, and other such items.

Buchanan argued that economic policies must be designed to benefit Americans; their international ramifications were irrelevant.[111] Economic considerations, such as the law of comparative advantage, were also irrelevant. In his view, the only considerations policymakers should weigh in making U.S. trade policy are whether it expands the nation's manufacturing base and whether it maintains its social and political stability.[112]

Buchanan was not the only conservative or nationalist to worry about the implications of trade liberalization for the American economy and American sovereignty. As discussed in chapter 4, some Americans were becoming more militant in their nationalism, resenting what they saw as the growing power of international organizations. Among the most vocal opponents were Phyllis Schlafly, a longtime conservative and proponent of "family values"; Republican Congressman Duncan Hunter; Michael

Lind, former conservative writer and social analyst (who became a senior editor at *Harpers Magazine*); conservative radio host Oliver North; and writer and economic analyst Alan Tonelson.

Tonelson's employer, a nationalist think tank funded by business, the U.S. Business and Industrial Council (USBIC), took the lead in publicizing the dangers of the Uruguay Round to American sovereignty. Kevin Kearns, president of the USBIC organized a press conference that brought Ralph Nader and Pat Buchanan together in opposition to the Uruguay Round agreement. Kearns argued that small- and midsized businesses had long feared government intervention, and that the new WTO was international intervention at its extreme.[113]

That press conference was an exception. Trade agreement critics of the left and right did not frequently appear together to herald their coalition. But they did cooperate behind the scenes to publicize concerns about the round and to coordinate strategy. For example, they published expensive full-page ads in major American papers to rail against the round.[114]

The very visible opposition of Buchanan, Perot, Schlafly, and North produced some interesting results among the Republicans whom Clinton counted on to support trade. The president and many business leaders presumed that Republicans would see the benefits of the GATT to economic growth. But many Republicans were truly concerned about what they perceived as the WTO's potential threat to sovereignty. Others were opposed to the new GATT superstructure. On Capitol Hill, Democratic Representative Jill Long and Republican Senators Larry Pressler, Jesse Helms, and Larry Craig, among others, expressed concern that this new WTO would be undemocratic, make decisions in a closed manner, and be staffed by unresponsive faceless bureaucrats. Fifty-five members of the Congress (both Democrats and Republicans) urged President Clinton to delay the vote on the Uruguay Round until July 1995.[115] Clinton refused because delay could have jeopardized congressional passage of the Uruguay Round. As mentioned earlier, under fast-track, once the president formally submits implementing legislation to the Congress, both houses must vote up or down on the bill without changes within ninety days. The fast-track time clock would prove to be a major problem for the GATT/WTO; its requirements would further an impression that the GATT/WTO as well as U.S. trade policy were undemocratic.

Congress Debates the GATT/WTO

Because the Uruguay Round was so broad and so controversial, many hearings were held on various aspects of the round during the 103rd

Congress.[116] But the implications of changing the GATT to the WTO were never far from the debate. While proponents of the round tried to focus the debate on its benefits and costs to the economy as a whole, much of the public and congressional debate focused on the WTO's potential impact on American sovereignty. The Senate Commerce, Senate Foreign Relations, and House Ways and Means Committees held specific hearings on the WTO and how this new institution might affect U.S. law.[117] This focus was a small victory for these trade agreement critics; although they had not achieved their goals within the negotiations, they did set the terms of congressional debate.

That debate sounded familiar. Sovereignty has long been a "trade" issue. For example, John Quincy Adams said "protection is the price of allegiance. When a government ceases to protect, it must cease to claim obedience or submission."[118] Thus, there was historical continuity to fears that the WTO could alter the ability of the American people to determine their destiny. But few individuals concerned about finding a complementary approach to expanding trade and investment as well as protecting the environment and workers' rights argued that nations must cede some degree of sovereignty in the interest of developing international rules to govern globalization. These individuals kept relatively quiet during the Uruguay Round debate.[119]

The debate over GATT/WTO raised important questions about whether or not American law and institutions should adapt to the global economy. Even supporters of strengthening the GATT infrastructure questioned the WTO's effects on sovereignty. Clyde Prestowitz, former trade negotiator and president of the Economic Strategy Institute, noted that "the environmentalists . . . are correct when they express their concern for the potential reversal of U.S. regulations via findings of the WTO."[120] To some opponents, the WTO would not only affect the ability of individuals to influence government, it would upset federal-state relations (federalism). One of the most interesting arguments used by WTO opponents was that of states' rights—the rights of states to preserve their standards for health and safety. On June 27, 1994, twenty-two state attorneys general wrote President Clinton asking the administration to "explain how states will be able to defend their laws from foreign challenges before World Trade Organization panels." They also asked if implementing legislation can guarantee that the federal government will accept trade sanctions rather than pressure states to change state laws that are successfully challenged in the WTO.[121] Sierra Club attorney Patti Goldman noted, "The current structure gives the federal government the power through preemption, withholding federal funds, and litigation to compel changes in state laws that conflict [with trade agreements]." Although the administration consults with state governments on state standards, the federal government has the power to "trump" state law. In advertisements opposing the WTO, the Sierra Club argued that foreign nations will use the GATT/WTO to challenge these laws, noting "every state is affected."[122]

Senator Bob Dole, the Republican leader, heard the concerns about sovereignty. On August 28, Senator Dole wrote an editorial in the *Wichita Eagle* suggesting that members of Congress take their time in assessing the GATT/WTO. Although Dole stated he was "not trying to hustle opposition to the GATT," he argued that the administration was ignoring legitimate concerns about how the GATT/WTO would affect American laws and practice. The senator said he was receiving about two thousand phone calls a day on GATT. GATT/WTO proponents were alarmed by Dole's actions, for he had long been a supporter of both internationalism and freer trade.[123]

Ambivalence about the WTO, especially among Republicans, served to legitimize fears about its potential impact on U.S. sovereignty.[124] To counter that ambivalence, the Clinton administration named names. In testimony to the House Ways and Means Committee, USTR Michael Kantor, noted that "everyone from Consumers Union, from . . . Jack Kemp to Judge Bork . . . have said that U.S. sovereignty is not affected, in fact may even be enhanced."[125] The administration distributed a letter to every member of Congress discussing its dispute settlement mechanisms, how decisions would be made in the WTO, and how these decisions would affect U.S. law.[126]

Throughout 1994, members of Congress remained concerned that the WTO could undermine U.S. laws. They raised questions about how it would affect the American system of social and environmental regulations.[127] But to many Republicans and business leaders, such linkages were anathema. Congressman Newt Gingrich pressed USTR Kantor about whether he would use the WTO "to expand labor and environmental standards," thereby transforming the GATT into more than a trade agreement. The USTR responded by saying that "addressing the intersection of labor standards and . . . environment and trade will only help enhance a world trading system." Ironically, many of the same "purists" in business and in Congress would find themselves defending a GATT/WTO that included a Committee on Trade and the Environment and congressional implementing legislation that would direct the president to seek a working party on labor standards within the WTO.[128]

The debate was also surprisingly ironic. For example, to encourage *American* opposition toward the WTO, Lori Wallach of Public Citizen cited the 1992 letter of three hundred *international* groups; she called it an "international movement against this agreement." As further evidence of how international these issues had become, Sir James Goldsmith, a member of the European Parliament, traveled to Washington to testify against the Uruguay Round. He justified his appearance before Congress by stressing, "Whereas I would never even consider making a comment on matters which concern U.S. domestic political matters, this is an international cooperative effort which affects us identically."[129]

Given this domestic and international concern, the Senate Committee on Government Affairs reported the bill "without recommendation," noting that the authority of the WTO does not supersede the sovereign powers of state governments or the federal government. However, the committee issued a warning about the WTO's potential impact on U.S. sovereignty: "This committee takes very seriously the issue of federalism." They promised to hold executive branch officials accountable to ensure that U.S. sovereignty is protected and that the WTO becomes more democratic.[130]

On September 27, 1994, final drafts of the implementing legislation were introduced in both houses and referred to the relevant committees of jurisdiction. The ninety-day time clock had begun, and it included the midterm election in November. But a Democratic senator, Ernest Hollings, stopped the clock, holding the implementing legislation in his committee, the Senate Commerce Committee, for forty-five days. The vote was delayed until after the congressional election. The House was scheduled to return on November 29, 1994, for the sole purpose of considering the Uruguay Round agreement. The Senate was now scheduled to reconvene on November 30 and to vote on December 1 on the agreement. While lame duck members of Congress might feel free to vote their opinion, supporters of the Uruguay Round bill worried that a lame duck session might not have the political will to approve U.S. participation in this new international organization.

This concern helped invigorate the GATT/WTO's proponents. Business groups, as usual, took the lead. They tried to keep the GATT/WTO from becoming an election-year issue, and they stepped up their lobbying with a multimillion-dollar print and television media campaign. The Alliance for GATT Now sent out press releases noting that former trade officials, forty governors, former presidents, and four hundred and fifty leading economists endorsed the Uruguay Round. They issued fact sheets on related issues such as sovereignty.[131] However, while they made macroeconomic arguments in support of the Uruguay Round, they made little mention of its effects on the social compact or on citizens' daily lives.

Meanwhile, WTO opponents forged a broad coalition well versed in influencing Washington. WTO opponents included neopopulists, the NAACP, United We Stand, small farmers, the AFL-CIO, small businesses, isolationists, business leaders, human rights activists, libertarians, environmentalists, and community activists. But the more internationalist environmental groups such as the WWF, the Environmental Defense Fund, and the NRDC seemed relatively muted.[132] The opposition lobbied and made the rounds of talk shows and community centers. While Public Citizen condemned GATTzilla, United We Stand protested "the general agreement on tyranny and treason." Lori Wallach, and devoted economic nationalist Bruce Warnick of United We Stand, worked hard to ensure that concerns about sovereignty got a lot of attention on Capitol Hill.[133] The arguments these critics made, about the Uruguay Round's effect on equity, sovereignty, and democracy, were easier for citizens to relate to and comprehend.

By 1994, the torch of trade agreement criticism had been passed to Lori Wallach of Public Citizen. She and her allies skillfully used the media to argue that congressional approval of GATT was undemocratic. They noted that most members of Congress hadn't read the implementing legislation and had no idea about the powers of the WTO. To get public attention, Ralph Nader, the founder of Public Citizen, challenged every lawmaker to take a quiz on the GATT. Only one senator, Hank Brown of Colorado, took him up on the quiz. To derail the GATT/WTO, opponents next looked to the 1994 congressional election.[134]

When the Republicans won a majority in both houses, from the White House, the Uruguay Round's fate looked iffy. The media interpreted the Republican victory as a repudiation of President Clinton's leadership. Some Republicans threatened to deny Clinton a victory to show their power, despite the fifty-year record of trade bipartisanship. Moreover, the administration could not necessarily count on the Democrats to vote for the Uruguay Round bill. No one knew how Democrats would vote. On the one hand, retiring and defeated members could vote however they wanted, without voter punishment. On the other hand, their vote could be discredited as not legitimately reflecting their constituents. Yet the White House said little to make the WTO more palatable to traditional Democratic constituents concerned about trade and workers, human rights, and the environment.[135]

Despite a growing nationalist backlash among Republicans, spawned by the opposition of Buchanan and Ross Perot, the Republicans came through for the president. The Republican party leadership and campaign finance donations from business supporters of the Uruguay Round kept members in line. Campaign finance donations also seemed to persuade some key Democrats. However, many Democrats understood the need to govern the global economy and the potential benefits of the more comprehensive WTO. Although they were scared of alienating key constituents, these Democrats felt that the Uruguay Round was a small step forward.[136]

Almost one month after the election, Congress overwhelmingly voted in favor of the GATT/WTO. Seventy-six percent of both houses voted in favor of the Uruguay Round Implementing Act on December 1, 1994. However, because the GATT was approved in lame-duck session, Pat Buchanan, Lori Wallach, and other trade agreement critics argued that it was rammed through the Congress.[137]

The Uruguay Round was controversial in other nations as well, such as India, Brazil, Mexico, and the Philippines. In these nations, some environmentalists, consumer activists, and farm groups also urged its defeat. But their leaders saw the Uruguay Round differently: as a way to further regulate industrialized country protectionism.[138] Meanwhile, European nations and Canada also approved the round in the hopes of fostering economic internationalism and expanded trade. With more than one hundred and twenty members, the WTO officially superseded the GATT on January 1, 1995.

WARNED BY MARK RITCHIE, an unusual alliance of consumer, civic, religious, farm, and environmental groups around the world came together to influence the Uruguay Round of the GATT. These activists worked both nationally and internationally. They forged an alliance that not only transcended traditional concepts of left and right, nationalism and internationalism, and freer trade and protectionism, and it also changed how trade policy was made. The activists protested in the streets, played off governments, and challenged the trade negotiating process as undemocratic and secretive.

In the end, the WTO did not include labor standards and had done little to place environmental considerations on a par with trade. But trade agreement critics had in fact made considerable progress. They had greatly shaped both the elite and the public debates over trade agreements. No longer could people argue that food safety, labor standards, and other aspects of the social compact were not trade issues.

However, what many trade agreement critics gleaned from the GATT debate was that trade agreements were deregulatory.

In January 1994, some of these activists decided that they had tackled only part of the problem by criticizing trade agreements. Maude Barlow and Tony Clarke of Canada, Edward Goldsmith and Helena Norberg-Hodge of the United Kingdom; Vandana Shiva of India; Martin Khor of Malaysia; and Lori Wallach, Jerry Mander, John Cavanagh, and Mark Ritchie of the United States, and other activists met in San Francisco to convene a new international organization, the International Forum on Globalization. These individuals aimed to "expose the multiple effects of economic globalization in order to stimulate debate" and "to reverse the globalization process by encouraging ideas and activities which revitalize local economies." These trade agreement critics noted that the world needs new international agreements "that place the needs of people, local economies and the natural world ahead of the interest of corporations." With this organization, trade agreement critics could find common ground on how to speak out against the real problem: "economic globalization."[139] Moreover, they offered an alternative strategy, a sort of *ecological nationalism.*[140] This broader critique did not alter their strategy of thinking locally and acting globally. These trade agreement critics remained determined to protect their national systems of consumer environmental, and worker protections.

CHAPTER 7

Thinking Locally, Acting Globally

ON A SUNNY JUNE AFTERNOON in 1996, some seventy economists, political scientists, reporters, and business and government officials from around the world gathered in a fancy Washington, D.C., hotel. They met to celebrate the work of the new international organization that governs trade, the World Trade Organization (WTO), and to examine trade barriers that might be reduced in future international negotiations among WTO member nations.

One of America's most respected trade scholars, I. M. Destler, took the floor to discuss the politics of trade in the world's most powerful trading nation, the United States. He stated that protectionist sentiment was waning because the economy was experiencing high employment and low inflationary growth. But he said nothing about how environmental, human rights, or food safety advocates had affected the development of the Uruguay Round or NAFTA. Like other analysts at that time, he did not see such activists as important players in the trade debate. (He later changed his views.)[1]

As he spoke, the sky exploded with rain, wind, and thunder. The extreme weather distracted his listeners. To lighten the mood, Ellen Frost, former counselor to USTR Mickey Kantor, openly wondered if the weather was God's punishment for paying short shrift to "new protectionists" who are concerned about such social and environmental issues. For as she knew, consumer and environmental activists had greatly influenced both the GATT and NAFTA negotiations.

This book has illuminated how a broad group of individuals— including environmentalists, civic leaders, health and consumer advocates, human rights advocates, and others—joined traditional protectionists including economic nationalists, some producer interests, and some labor unions to hinder trade liberalization in the United States, in other nations, and at the WTO. These trade agreement critics have reminded citizens around the world that trade policy is not simply about economic policy but also about the achievement of other important policy goals. However, that debate has gotten more complex because trade agreements regulate trade among different nations with different approaches to economic and political governance. Moreover, trade agreements not only place limits on how nations can use traditional border measures, but they also increasingly affect domestic regulations that may, without intent, distort trade.[2]

What has been the impact of these trade agreement critics? First, they have changed the content and structure of trade agreements. As a result of their protests, NAFTA has side agreements relating to the environment and labor standards. The WTO, which replaced the GATT in 1995, is more explicit about the nexus of trade and environmental issues. Its preamble states that sustainable development policies, which reconcile economic growth and environmental protection, should be an objective of trade.[3] Some trade disputes have provided clarification as to how nations can protect the environment without distorting trade (e.g., shrimp turtle). But WTO members have not formalized new rules that explicitly delineate how preserving the global commons and trade can be made complementary.

Second, trade agreement critics also have influenced the structure of the WTO. For example, some developing country can't afford the costs of representation in Geneva at the WTO offices. As a result of pressure from development activists and developing countries officials, WTO staff work to help developing countries better utilize the WTO system. In addition, by 1998, the WTO had a staff devoted to working with NGOs as well as personnel working on outreach. This staff made sure that a wide variety of NGOs were invited to participate in the 1999 Seattle trade talks, but it was up to governments to decide whether representatives of civil society should be included in their official delegations.[4]

Third, these critics have gotten more people talking about trade policy. Through demonstrations, teach-ins, and forums in the United States and around the world, they have stimulated discussions about NAFTA, GATT, and global economic interdependence. They have also changed *how* people talk about trade. Although issues of sovereignty and equity are not new to the debate, these issues have taken on greater coherence when trade agreement critics argue that trade agreements are essentially deregulatory.

Fourth, trade agreement critics have raised important questions about the relationship between trade regulation and social/environmental regulation. However, many critics have not completely thought through their arguments about trade agreements. While they condemn such agreements as deregulatory, few trade agreement critics admit that trade agreements *reregulate* some national regulations at the international level. Such global regulation may be increasingly necessary in a world where business, technology, and capital are global. For example, many trade agreement critics argue that nations such as Mexico do not have strong environmental laws. Yet these same activists have done little to promote the diffusion of more effective environmental regulation in countries such as Mexico.

Trade agreement critics also criticize trade agreements for not respecting or elevating industrialized country norms for how people and the environment should be treated as goods and services are produced. However, uniform regulatory standards may not be appropriate, obtainable, or desirable. As David Vogel has noted, nations may adopt distinctive standards or norms for many reasons, "some of which, such as different income levels or distinctive tastes, preferences, or priorities, may be legitimate, while others, such as the capture of regulatory authorities by producer interests are not."[5] While trade agreement critics demand that trade agreements not force lower standards upon nations such as the United States or Canada, they have not fully assessed whether they really want a global institution to uphold domestic norms internationally and whether the WTO should really be that institution.

Fifth, they have forced trade policymakers at the national and international levels to make their decisions openly and to make such decisions widely available. For example, many industrialized nations have searchable Web sites, where they disseminate a wide range of documents on trade. The European Commission and the governments of Canada and Australia use the World Wide Web to ask for citizen input into trade policy-making. These governments see their Web sites as a key part of a functional public affairs program on trade. The Canadian Web site stresses, "we want to hear from you." It sends a message that the public's views on trade policy matter. The European Commissioner for trade holds regular on-line chats with citizens of the EC. The Commission will also E-mail interested parties information on trade developments. The USTR, in contrast, uses the Web site strictly as a dissemination device, not as part of a broad strategy to explain and discuss trade policy. While other nations have become more opaque, the United States sends a message that it does not yet value broad public input.[6] It does not, for example, link its Web site to those of its critics so that citizens can come to their own conclusions about trade.

GUILT BY ASSOCIATION

Proponents of trade agreements in the United States and around the world have frequently described trade agreement critics as protectionists. Protectionists want government to shelter domestic producers from foreign competition. However, this is not the principal goal of many of the individuals who have been described in these pages. It does appear to be the goal of others described herein, from Sir James Goldsmith to Pat Buchanan. Individuals such as Mark Ritchie of the IATP or Rod Leonard of the CNI do not seem to have a direct economic interest at stake that could be undermined by trade liberalization. Their goals are political. They want to preserve national regulations that protect consumers, workers, and the environment, but they also want to protect their political influence over such regulations. Nonetheless, increasingly, these individuals and groups have an indirect economic interest; they raise money for their organizations by opposing trade agreements.

However, like traditional protectionists, many environmentalists, consumer, and other citizen activists are nationalists. While traditional protectionists want trade policy to benefit domestic producers, many of these trade agreement critics want regulatory policies that are affected by trade to remain national decisions, even if such an approach distorts trade, appears unilateral, or undermines the norms of other countries.

Many trade agreement critics on the left have said they don't oppose trade per se. For example, Herman Daly and Robert Goodland, early critics of trade agreements, argued that "protectionism is . . . viewed as the only alternative to 'free trade.' . . . Protecting . . . hard-won social gains from blind standards-lowering competition in the global market is what we are interested in—not the protection of some inefficient entrepreneur who wants to grow mangoes in Sweden."[7] Although they have different views about trade, many trade agreement critics have fostered alliances with protectionists and economic nationalists around the world and within nations as diverse as the United States, India, and France. But while these left-right coalitions seek to hamper trade and trade agreements (a protectionist strategy), they don't seek to protect the same interests.

For example, labor leaders, human rights activists, and development advocates all have called for including international labor standards in trade agreements. Labor union leaders have called for labor standards for economic reasons as well as humanitarian reasons: they want to protect the workers they represent from low-wage foreign competition. Human rights activists, in contrast, have called for labor standards in the belief that decent working conditions are a basic human right. They may have no direct economic interests motivating their demands for labor standards, although they may receive economic support or enhanced political clout by allying with labor unions on this issue. Finally, many development advocates have called for a middle ground, recognizing that citizens in developing countries must trade and that their low-cost labor is a source of comparative advantage. If developed countries demand that developing countries adopt higher labor standards, developing countries' labor costs may rise, and such countries may lose foreign investment and trade. However, development advocates also acknowledge that nations may need the outside incentive of trade agreements to get such worker protections on the books or to enforce existing labor standards.[8] Thus, while trade agreement critics may share a desire to include labor standards within the WTO system, they are motivated by different concerns and have different timetables and strategies for incorporating such standards. Given these diverse intentions, it seems illogical to lump all these interests into one category: protectionist. Nor can we describe all such trade agreement critics as nationalists.

ONE WORLD, MANY VISIONS

Trade agreement critics disagree on how to reconcile global capitalism with democratically determined rules. Most such critics are internationalists and share a belief that the world needs organizations to monitor and enforce environmental standards or worker health and safety. But they can't find common ground on whether all such regulations should be contained within the GATT/WTO system.

Building on long-standing global networks, environmental, consumer, and human rights NGOs have successfully played off governments and interest groups to advance their positions internationally. Yet that same internationalism sometimes has tempered their positions. NAFTA provides a good example. Leaders of NGOs from Mexico, Canada, and the United States found that the negotiation of NAFTA empowered environmentalists and labor activists within Mexico. From their international activities and attempts to find common ground, Canadian and U.S. NGO leaders learned how important trade was to their Mexican counterparts. Mexican government officials recognized they had to promise and deliver on improved environmental and labor rights standards. But this recognition of mutual international interests and their combined political clout did not inspire many trade agreement critics to support NAFTA and its side agreements. While some environmentalists saw the NAFTA side agreements as significant, others—especially in the consumer and development communities—condemned them as inadequate. In their opinion, even with its side agreements, NAFTA was no better than the GATT. They agreed with Ralph Nader: "NAFTA . . . subordinates important values—health, environmental protection, democracy and the like—to . . . the imperatives of international commerce." [9] But NAFTA at its core is a trade and investment agreement. That is how such agreements work.

While NGOs in the United States divided on NAFTA, many of these NGOs united in their concerns about the Uruguay Round of the GATT. Again, their international alliances tempered their positions. By working internationally, these trade agreement critics were able to coordinate a broader opposition to the Uruguay Round. However, this internationalization did not temper their negative view of the Uruguay Round. In the United States, only Consumers Union came out and explicitly supported the implementing legislation.

As mentioned in the previous chapter, the final text of the Uruguay Round agreements did not include labor standards and did little to place environmental considerations on a par with trade. Environmentalists and consumer advocates were especially disturbed that the Uruguay Round elevated the notion that environmental and food safety regulations should be based on the least-trade-restrictive principle. This convinced them that proponents of trade agreements thought trade should trump other policy goals.[10] Although this perspective is understandable, it ignores the history of and rationale for trade agreements. Such agreements were designed to encourage trade by reducing impediments to trade, including regulatory impediments. In their arguments, however, trade agreement critics diminish the importance of trade to economic growth and the need for policies and institutions dedicated to helping policymakers reduce barriers to trade.

THE POLITICS OF TRADE IN THE UNITED STATES

Trade policy has long attracted unusual political alliances; yet many Americans found it surprising that Ralph Nader, Pat Buchanan, Ross Perot, and Jerry Brown could find common ground on any issue. This alliance of strange bedfellows became a fluid and formidable political block, wedding citizens calling for limited government to citizens demanding interventionist government. This book first found a left-right alliance on the nexus of trade and human rights during the debate on the Jackson-Vanik amendment to the Trade Act of 1974. Libertarian Barry Goldwater found himself allied with Congressman Edward Koch and AFL President George Meany, supporting an amendment linking trade concessions to emigration from nonmarket economies. More recently, the joint opposition of Ralph Nader and Pat Buchanan has symbolized this alliance. Both men make a seductive and simplistic argument: Americans should only accept trade with countries with similar political institutions and legal protections. However, nations trade because of their differences. Moreover, many of the two critics' concerns about trade agreements are really concerns about trade policy. In 1789 as well as in 1998, citizens asked how to reconcile trade policy with goals such as promoting equity, facilitating democratic decision making, maintaining high-wage jobs, and preserving sovereignty. At their core, both men are nationalists.

Trade Agreements as Global Regulation

Trade is different from other market activities because it involves different languages, customs requirements, and currencies. But trade is a subset of capitalism. Global markets, like domestic markets, may fail. Trade agreements regulate such market failures by ensuring that importing nations can protect their producers from unfairly dumped steel or unsafe food. And they protect exporters by ensuring that importing nations do not apply protectionist regulations unduly or unfairly. To put it simply, they regulate how firms may trade and how nations may protect.

In truth, many trade agreement critics are really arguing that trade agreements do not regulate effectively or enough. For example, some environmentalists argue that companies may move to and export from nations because they have low environmental standards. High levels of disease and water pollution on America's border with Mexico illuminate the potential costs of inadequate regulation of trade and its effects on the environment of both nations.[11] Labor and human rights advocates have long argued that it is inequitable to treat workers unfairly as they make traded goods and services. One can also make a case for global labor or environmental standards on the basis of global efficiency. Human rights exploitation is inefficient, because it prevents individuals from reaching their economic and intellectual potential, and that in turn thwarts economic growth.[12]

In short, critics and proponents of trade agreements are talking about issues of efficiency or equity—issues endemic to regulation. Nations continually enact new regulations or alter existing ones. Some of these regulations may affect the competitive position, costs, or market share of foreign producers. Policymakers have attempted to coordinate regulations within regional and multilateral trade agreements in the hopes of making regulation more effective and to reduce the potential trade distortions of regulations. Where trade agreements once only included rules governing border measures, today they include rules governing trade related to investment, procurement, research subsidies, and food safety regulations, among others. When producers meet national standards to facilitate trade or negotiate international standards, they are helping national regulatory systems to converge. Trade agreement critics allege this will lead to a race to the bottom. They may be right. They may also be wrong. As political scientist David Vogel has noted, when rich nations such as the United States and Germany enact stricter product standards, their trading partners must meet these standards to serve these markets. This process often encourages consumer or environmental organizations in the exporting country to demand similar standards at home. Thus, national standards can be driven upward as integration increases.[13]

A similar phenomenon occurs when nations dispute trade. The beef hormones or tuna dolphin cases illuminated the search for common ground on trade. Ultimately, these disputes also grew the GATT/WTO regulatory system. At the GATT/WTO, policymakers struggled to define how and when nations might be justified in protecting their citizens or consumers in the interest of protecting the global commons or public health. At the national level, policymakers had to attempt to ensure that such regulations achieved their public policy goals, did not distort trade, and were uniformly applied to exporting nations.[14]

TRADE AGREEMENTS AS DEREGULATION

Many critics of trade agreements believe that including regulations within trade agreements has led to a lower common denominator of regulation. They argue that trade agreements have been used by business to achieve deregulation that would be politically unattainable at the national level. Such deregulation, they say, not only has been achieved in an undemocratic manner (by the covert mechanism of trade agreements), it also offers citizens no mechanisms for accountability.[15] Is this true? As chapter 3 showed, the Committee for Economic Development in 1969 suggested that "governments should investigate . . . existing foreign regulations before initiating new laws in the field of public health and safety."[16] The CED was suggesting that too much regulation would impede trade. But the CED's views that trade should trump other regulations were not shared by other business leaders. For example, both Cyanamid and the Motor Vehicle Manufacturers Association wanted to harmonize product safety regulations internationally. They were not calling for lower standards, but they recognized that it would be cheaper to amortize the costs of such regulations if all nations had the same regulations, whether higher or lower. Moreover, it might give them a source of competitive advantage against smaller competitors.[17]

In the 1980s and 1990s many trade agreement critics became convinced that trade agreements were one of many tools to lower national standards. As chapter 4 delineated, clearly many business leaders wanted to lower U.S. environmental, worker, and health regulations. But the primary source information currently available reveals no evidence that U.S. business leaders, in concert with government officials, sought to deliberately lower such standards through trade agreements.[18]

In fact, some evidence indicates that business groups were beginning to recognize the importance of upholding such regulations. For example, in 1991, the International Chamber of Commerce endorsed the principle of sustainable development as a global priority.[19] The president's principal advisory group on trade policy, the ACTPN, consistently stated that international harmonization should not lead to downward harmonization. Business leaders dominated the ACTPN, although it also had civil society, farm, and labor leaders. ACTPN members took a strong position on preserving U.S. regulation and expressed the view that trade agreements should not weaken U.S. health, safety, or environmental law.[20] Executives on the ACTPN said that they did not want trade regulation to mean domestic deregulation, but they did not oppose global reregulation. At the same time, however, these executives may have preferred global regulation that set a ceiling, rather than a floor for national regulations.

THE INTERSECTION:
TRADE REGULATION AND SOCIAL REGULATION

To understand why so many trade agreement critics see trade agreements as deregulatory, we must understand the evolution of trade agreements. In the first years of this century, some visionary leaders understood that growing economic interdependence made it difficult for nations to effectively regulate alone. Thus, the United States, Britain, Australia, and Canada banned traded goods made by convict labor; signatories to the Berne Convention of 1905 banned trade in phosphorus matches; and the United States, Russia, Japan, and Great Britain signed the Fur Seal Treaty of 1911 to regulate the hunting and importation of seals. U.S. officials also tried to apply U.S. law to foreign nations (extraterritoriality). For example, in 1932, some Americans hoped to use the Smoot-Hawley tariff as a stick to change the treatment of workers in the Soviet Union. But, in general, Congress did not want to regulate international markets or cede its control of trade policy or the social compact. Congress found, however, that trade policy influenced social policies made by Congress. In the late nineteenth century, when some European nations banned U.S. pork, Congress developed new regulations to reassure foreign (and domestic producers) about the safety of such pork. In this case, regulation was inspired by the need to trade, but the need to trade did not inspire lower tariffs.

It was not until 1934 that policymakers explicitly began to link social and trade policies within trade legislation. The Reciprocal Trade Agreements Act (RTAA) called for bilateral negotiations to reduce trade barriers and thus expand global markets for U.S. goods. The preamble linked trade to job creation. But the act could do little to reduce protectionist use of NTBs, such as food safety or procurement regulations. These were considered domestic policies in the United States (as well as in many other nations). Congress soon made it very clear that it objected to subjecting such policies to international negotiations.

World War II limited the potential of this act, but the war years did allow policymakers to experiment. They used the lend-lease agreements to induce America's allies to liberalize barriers to trade. They developed an agreement to govern commercial policy (the GATT) and a broader international institution, the ITO, to link social and foreign economic policies. The ITO charter allowed nations to restrict trade to protect the safety of citizens, workers, and consumers. It also allowed nations to restrict trade to conserve the environment. But the business community was divided on the ITO, and to get congressional approval, President Truman would need business support. He had other important legislative priorities, like NATO, and so he decided to focus on the more limited GATT agreement. Congress did not disagree and never voted on the ITO.

The GATT was designed to regulate only commercial policy. It was tailored to fit the grant of authority under the 1945 extension of the RTAA. Under this law, U.S. policymakers could negotiate trade agreements governing tariffs and quotas, but it could do nothing about other policies that could distort trade. In the years that followed, a growing number of nations joined the GATT and participated in trade agreements. But the GATT did not govern NTBs such as procurement rules or health and safety standards. More and more nations seemed to be using these NTBs to protect their producers and consumers.

During the 1960s to 1970s, citizens in the United States and many other industrialized nations demanded a broad system of regulations to govern the workplace, the marketplace, discrimination, and the environment. Congress also gave consumers, citizens, and workers new legal rights to challenge business. A wide range of citizens groups such as Public Citizen and the Sierra Club became expert in such regulations. They also had a direct economic and political stake in maintaining such regulations.

Many environmental and social regulations were popular with the public. But many business leaders worried about the costs of such regulations to economic efficiency. Moreover, some business leaders, economists, and trade policymakers worried about the trade distortions stemming from the growing use of such regulations. They called on Congress to allow policymakers to negotiate rules to govern the trade distortions of such national regulations. In 1974, Congress passed the Trade Act of 1974, a major change to U.S. trade policy.

The Impact of the Trade Act of 1974

The floodlights of history reveal many ironies in this bill. It was debated as Congress deliberated the fate of President Richard Nixon, yet it gave his successor broad new powers to negotiate the reduction of some NTBs. This was the first time Congress gave the executive branch power to negotiate trade agreements that could affect a broad swath of U.S. laws and regulations. It was designed to mitigate support for protection, but by granting the executive branch powers to negotiate NTBs, it helped inspire new trade agreement critics. It was a first step in making trade policy more transparent and democratic by providing new ways for Congress and interest groups to advise on the process. But the law set strict time frames and requirements, such as no amendments when Congress considered trade agreements (fast-track). These adjustments to the legislative process furthered the view among trade agreement critics that the process was also undemocratic and problematic.

Yet this same bill explicitly linked trade and human rights (Jackson-Vanik). By so doing, it gave trade agreement critics hope as well as precedent. Moreover, by demanding emigration results, this portion of the legislation may have influenced results-oriented trade legislation.

Large numbers of citizens did not wake up to the intersection of trade and the social compact until the 1980s. This decade was a time when many Americans tried to find a rationale for the nation's declining competitiveness. Some scapegoated Japan, and others became more receptive to protectionist sentiment. In the late 1980s, they were educated by their friends to the north. Canadians taught Americans how trade could affect the social compact. Canadian, Mexican, and U.S. consumer and environmental, development, labor rights, and civic groups joined with religious groups to criticize the NAFTA. During the debate on the Uruguay Round, these groups became more convinced that trade liberalization was deregulation.

CONCLUSION: A DIFFERENT FOCUS

This book has argued that we need to start talking about trade agreements as tools to regulate the global economy. This approach, I believe, will produce greater understanding about what we do when we negotiate trade agreements and why such agreements are necessary. Moreover, thinking about trade agreements in this way may help us find new approaches to trade policy that maintain national standards while minimizing costs to economic efficiency.

For example, understanding the broad impact of trade agreements may inspire policymakers and citizens to rethink how the executive branch and the Congress share responsibility for trade policy-making. Under the fast-track process, the Congress delegates authority to the executive branch to negotiate trade agreements, including agreements that can affect America's system of regulation. According to law professor David Wirth, some individuals have argued, "[Fast track has led to an] unprincipled sort of horse-trading among issues such as the safety of imported food and intellectual property that would rarely be so linked in a typical legislative session. . . . These amendments to the patent and food inspection laws . . . represented major public policy initiatives that ought to have received a full domestic airing." However, they were bundled in a trade agreement negotiation.[21] Thus, it is not surprising that trade agreement critics saw such agreements as deregulation. Moreover, the timetable associated with fast-track made some individuals see the process, as well as trade agreements, as essentially undemocratic. As Wirth noted, there is a "cognitive dissonance between, on the one hand, our domestic legal traditions of openness and accountability and, on the other, the very closed policies pertaining to negotiation and implementation adopted under these agreements."[22]

U.S. proponents of trade agreements might find common ground with trade agreement critics on a different approach to granting such authority. For example, Congress could authorize fast-track for a limited time, but condition its renewal on progress on the environment or labor standards. Moreover, Congress could create a new executive-congressional body to review such progress, composed of a broad range of citizens.

Thinking about trade agreements as regulations may inspire trade agreement critics to make some important decisions about what they really want. Trade agreement critics of left and right allege that trade agreements such as the WTO have transferred power from the people to global corporations. Yet many trade agreement critics (with the prominent exception of labor rights groups such as the National Consumers League or Global Exchange) have devoted relatively little energy to developing incentives and disincentives to reward and punish global corporations for their behavior across borders. This is especially ironic. Ralph Nader made his reputation criticizing the auto industry's disregard for customer safety. The Paul Revere of this movement, Mark Ritchie, cut his teeth helping to organize the boycott of baby formula makers such as Nestlé. More recently, a growing number of NGOs such as Amnesty International, ANPED of the Netherlands, Oxfam, and Friends of the Earth have begun to focus more of their efforts on developing an international code of business practices, such as the nonbinding social compact (the Global Compact) sponsored by the United Nations or the more comprehensive (and potentially more effective) OECD Guidelines for Multinational Enterprises.[23] The OECD Guidelines are the only multilaterally endorsed and comprehensive code of business practices that governments have committed to promote. They were also the only voluntary global code agreed to by some 33 governments—the world's leading investor nations. These governments agree to promote the Guidelines among all their firms: large and small, domestic and multinationals; and to use their good offices to investigate alleged violations of the Guidelines. But such codes will only have an impact if they are implemented and monitored by business, labor, government, and civil society. Some corporate executives in the United States and abroad are receptive to this approach. They don't want a patchwork of regulation at the national level. Moreover, they understand that by adhering to these Guidelines, their consumers can be reassured that such firms care about the conditions in which workers produce goods and services. To that extent, the Guidelines are an incentive-based approach, which might prove a more effective alternative to humanizing globalization than demagoguing trade agreements.

Thinking about trade agreements as regulations may help many trade agreement critics find other strategies to ensure that their concerns are being taken seriously. Environmentalists have long argued that to foster the environment, one must think globally, but act locally. But recently, trade agreement critics have been thinking locally and acting globally. If many of society's problems are global in reach, society must find global solutions. This requires that those concerned about trade work first nationally and then internationally—a difficult, time-consuming, and frustrating process. Trade agreement critics must participate by being involved in the trade policy-making process, by taking a place at the table. After all, they are the ones who made it possible for environmentalists and consumer advocates to sit at the table.[24] Sitting at the table enhances their power to affect regulation at both the national and international levels.

Yet many trade agreement critics do not seem truly committed to improving the regulatory process to fit global markets. Although some trade agreement critics have worked hard to distinguish their views from those of economic nationalists and isolationists, many (including the AFL, the Sierra Club, and Public Citizen) continue to cooperate politically with these groups. This is understandable, as this strategy has helped these groups gain funds, public attention, and greater political clout. However, it is also dangerous. It seems strange that some individuals argue that they want to reconcile trade agreements and national systems of social regulation, yet they work closely with individuals clearly opposed to extending and improving such systems of social regulations.

Some trade agreement critics proudly claim the protectionist mantle (e.g., Ross Perot, Alan Tonelson, Pat Buchanan, and Sir James Goldsmith). But it makes many on the left uncomfortable. A few, such as Britain's Colin Hines and Tim Lang, say their protectionism differs from the old protectionism because they seek to protect the world's majority against the free-trading elite. Using this language, however, perpetuates the dialectic that there is no middle ground between free trade and protectionism. It has never been that simple, as individuals from Congressman William M. Springer in 1882 to Minority Leader Richard Gephardt in 1997 have argued.[25] Using these terms prevents the public from understanding that we are really talking about global governance, not just trade.

Trade agreement critics may find that using this divisive language also may thwart their objectives of making the world and the United

States a better place. Equity provides a good example. By definition, protectionism is inherently inequitable, favoring the interest of some communities and producers over the general populace. Protectionists "export" the issue of equity, arguing that foreigners are treating Americans unfairly, and thus, the federal government should intervene to protect U.S. producers from unemployment or lost opportunities. But trade agreement critics concerned about the social compact should examine equity arguments carefully. Is it equitable to favor special interests at a cost to most taxpayers and consumers? Moreover, does governmental responsibility for equity end at the U.S. border? Is it equitable for U.S. policymakers to deny imports, jobs, and a potentially rising standard of living to citizens of other nations?

Moreover, trade agreement critics have not assessed whether protectionist solutions can achieve their goals. The preservation of small family farms provides a good example. Mark Ritchie and advocates from other farm groups have questioned much of U.S. and global trade policies and argued that they have led to overproduction and the demise of small family farms. They need to ask if protectionism is a better alternative. How would protectionism truly improve the situation of family farmers? History may provide a useful example. For much of U.S. history, farmers supported low tariffs. However, in the nineteenth century, as farming in the United States and abroad grew increasingly efficient, crop yields increased and prices declined for many agricultural products. After World War I, agricultural prices fell dramatically and exports slumped. Many farmers called on Congress for protection. In 1921, President Harding urged "instant tariff enactment" and imposed high duties on forty agricultural products, including wheat and apples. In 1922, however, the Tariff Commission found the tariff did not raise farm prices. According to economist William Kelly, higher tariffs had instead curtailed farmers' foreign markets and raised prices for imported and domestic products. When farmers went into bankruptcy, many left their farms for the city.[26] One might argue that higher tariffs actually hurt labor as well as farmers, as these former farmers sought industry jobs, flooding the labor pool. Ritchie and other small family farm advocates might call for more tailored solutions to assist small farmers. However, they recognize that such solutions may not be attainable, due to congressional spending limits. Protectionism is generally off-budget, and thus in their view, protectionism may be the most politically viable solution.

Some individuals are rethinking their ideas about trade policy. Many Americans think of Minority Leader Richard Gephardt as the consummate protectionist. Yet in a 1997 letter to his democratic colleagues, Gephardt urged his colleagues to rethink their ideas about trade policy: "Labels denigrate the debate. . . . What is needed is an honest debate about the real issue . . . how to continue the process of economic integration in a way that is truly a force for progress for all involved." To paraphrase Gephardt, global society must find ways to reconcile trade rules with social and environmental regulations, domestically and internationally.[27]

GLOBAL ECONOMIC INTERDEPENDENCE is here to stay. Those who want to make the world a better place have a choice. They can condemn globalization or develop strategies to hold global business accountable, while fostering the much needed investment, technology, competition, employment, and products that global business brings. They can throw bricks at the WTO, NAFTA, and other trade agreements, or they can use these bricks to remodel and rebuild trade agreements.

Notes

Chapter 1

1. N.a., "The New Trade War," *Economist,* 4 December 1999, 25–26; www.ictsd.org/wto_daily/index.htm, David E. Sanger and Joseph Kahn, "A Chaotic Intersection of Tear Gas and Trade Talks," *New York Times,* 1 December 1999, A14; and Mercury News Wire Services, "Notebook," *San Jose Mercury News,* 30 November 1999.

2. N.a., "The Battle in Seattle," *Economist,* 26 November 1999; and Bruce Ramsey, "Morality vs. Right to Choose in Trade Debate," *Seattle Post Intelligencer,* 24 November 1999.

3. Susan Ariel Aaronson, "The Word on the Street," www.intellectualcapital.com/issues/issue316/item7094.asp.

4. Excerpts from press conference by President William Jefferson Clinton, 8 December 1999; and excerpts from press briefing by Joe Lockhart, 6 December 1999, both on WTO Third Ministerial Conference Web site, www.wto.org.

5. Statement by Michael Moore at www.wto.org/wto/new/press160.htm.

6. Editorial, "WTO: Disaster in Seattle," and Guy de Jonquieres and Frances Williams, "Seattle: A Goal Beyond Reach," both in *Financial Times,* 6 December 1999.

7. A. V. Ganesa, former commerce secretary of India, "WTO Protesters Didn't Speak for Me," *Washington Post,* 5 December 1999; Anne Swardson, "A Rorschach Test on Trade," *Washington Post,* 3 December 1999, A32; John Burgess and Rene Sanchez, "Clinton's Remarks on Sanctions Open Rift," *Washington Post,* 3 December 1999; and Helene Cooper, "Poor Countries Are Demonstrators' Strongest Critics," *Wall Street Journal,* 2 December 1999.

In the United States, many business leaders and some Republican members of Congress do not think trade policies should address social issues such as food safety or labor standards. I. M. Destler, *American Trade Politics: System Under Stress* (Washington: Institute for International Economics, 1995), 285–86; and Geza Feketekeuty with Bruce Stokes, *Trade Strategies for a New Era: Ensuring U.S. Leadership in a Global Economy* (New York: Council on Foreign Relations, 1998), 259–98.

8. On the Boston Tea Party, see Terrence H Witkowski, "Colonial Consumers in Revolt: Buyer Values and Behavior During the Nonimportation Movement, 1764–1776," *Journal of Consumer Research* 16 (September 1989): 219–20; on the slave trade protests, see Margaret E. Keck and Kathryn Sikkink, *Activists Beyond Borders: Advocacy Networks in International Politics* (Ithaca: Cornell University Press, 1998), 41, esp. n. 3.

9. "Time for Another Round," *Economist*, 3 October 1998; "China: WTO Gathering Marred by Globalization Protests," *China Daily*, 8 July 1998; "Supplement: What Limits to Free Trade?" *Le Monde*, 25 May 1998; and "WTO Prepares Key Events Amid Street Protests, Asian Troubles," *Agence France Presse International*, 15 May 1998.

10. Guy de Jonquieres, "Rules for the Regulators," *Financial Times*, 2 March 1998, 19.

11. Keck and Sikkink, *Activists Beyond Borders*, 41–47; and Percy W Bidwell, *The Invisible Tariff: A Study of the Control of Imports into the United States* (New York: Council on Foreign Relations, 1939), 106–7, 109–11.

12. President's Council of Economic Advisors, *Economic Report of the President 1993* (Washington: GPO, 1993), on reducing services, 109–12; on deregulation, 24, 170–73; on trade, 311, 315, 318.

13. Steve Charnovitz, "Environmental and Labour Standards in Trade," *World Economy* (May 1992): 335–55; John Judis, "Campaign Issues: Trade," *Columbia Journalism Review* (November/December 1992): 38–39: and David Vogel, *Trading Up: Consumer and Environmental Regulation in a Global Economy* (Cambridge, MA: Harvard University Press, 1997), 20.

14. David W Pearce, ed., *The MIT Dictionary of Modern Economics*, 4th ed. (Cambridge, MA: MIT Press, 1992), 425.

15. Patrick J Buchanan, *The Great Betrayal: How American Sovereignty and Social Justice Are Being Sacrificed to the Gods of the Global Economy* (Boston: Little, Brown, 1998), 107, 264–69, 313; and Ralph Nader, "Introduction," in Ralph Nader et al., *The Case Against Free Trade* (San Francisco: Earth Island, 1993), 1–12.

16. Save Our Sovereignty, "Opposition to World Trade Organization Grows Across Political Spectrum," press release, 13 June 1994. Save Our Sovereignty was a coalition of economic nationalists and conservative activists run out of the U.S. Business and Industrial Council, 122 C St. NW, #815, Washington, DC 20001.

17. On GATT, see Susan Ariel Aaronson, *Trade and the American Dream* (Lexington: University of Kentucky Press, 1996), 147–66. On NAFTA, see John J. Audley, *Green Politics and Global Trade* (Washington: Georgetown University Press, 1997), 155–63. On Schlafly, see www.eagleforum.org/column, for 29 February 1996 and 31 October 1996.

18. On Jerry Brown and concerns of the left, see Edmund G. Brown Jr., "Free Trade is not Free," in *The Case Against Free Trade*, 65–69. Edmund G. Brown is Jerry Brown.

19. On these strange bedfellows, see editorial, *Wall Street Journal*, 9 September 1993, A20. On Milliken, see Buchanan, *The Great Betrayal*, 94–97.

20. An early influential example is E. E. Schattschneider, *Politics, Pressure and the Tariff: A Study of Free Private Enterprise in Pressure Politics as Shown in the 1929–1930 Revision of the Tariff* (New York: Prentice Hall, 1935). A more recent example is Daniel Verdier, *Democracy and International Trade: Britain, France, and the United States, 1860–1990* (Princeton: Princeton University Press, 1994).

21. Interview with Colin Hines, Green Party, 23 September 1998; and Sir James Goldsmith, "Global Free Trade and GATT," excerpt from *Le Piege*, 1994.

22. Nancy Dunne, "Consumer Protest at World Trade Plan," *Financial Times*, 11 December 1992, 5; Tim Lang and Colin Hines, *The New Protectionism: Protecting the Future Against Free Trade* (New York: New Press, 1993), 49; and Dani Rodrik, *Has Globalization Gone Too Far?* (Washington: Institute for International Economics, 1997), 1–7.

23. "India Rejects EU. Plan for Fresh WTO Talks on Trade," *Agence France Presse*, 11 September 1998; "Indian Farmers Attack WTO Import Rules," Reuters, 15 August 1998; and "A Time for Another Round," *Economist*, 3 October 1998, 3.

24. Bruce Campbell, Canadian Centre for Policy Alternatives, interview, 16 September 1998 and Steven Shrybman, Canadian Environmental Law Institute, interview, 22 August 1998.

25. On Australia, Kate Gilmore, Amnesty International; Judy Henderson, Oxfam International; Phyllis Campbell, Greenpeace; and Liam Phelen, Aidwatch, all interviews, 16 June 1997 in Sydney, Australia.

26. Lang and Hines, *The New Protectionism;* and Colin Hines, interview, 23 September 1998.

27. One of the first cross-border organizing efforts against the GATT was at the GATT ministerial session in Brussels, Belgium, in December 1988; see Mark Ritchie, "Cross-Border Organizing," in *The Case Against the Global Economy and for a Turn Toward the Local,* ed. Jerry Mander and Edward Goldsmith (San Francisco: Sierra Club, 1996), 494–500; notes from Lori Wallach, Global Trade Watch to Susan Aaronson on draft book, March 1999; and R.C. Longworth, "Activists on Internet Reshaping Rules for Global Economy," *Chicago Tribune,* 5 July 1999.

28. Lori Wallach, director of Public Citizen's Global Trade Watch, first used this term to describe her work on trade in the United States and overseas (Lori Wallach, interview, 2 July 1998). Wallach believes the term was created by Wallach's Indian colleague, Vandana Shiva, who is director of the Research Foundation for Science, Technology and Natural Resource Policy in Dehradun, India.

29. Vogel, *Trading Up,* 3.

30. Ibid., 5, 8.

31. Douglas A Irwin, *Against the Tide: An Intellectual History of Free Trade* (Princeton: Princeton University Press, 1996), 6.

32. Ibid., 4–5; and Mario Broussard and Steven Pearlstein, "Reality Check: Great Divide, Economists Vs. the Public," *Washington Post,* 13–15 October 1996, A1, A6.

33. Broussard and Pearlstein, "Reality Check," A6. Also see Paul Krugman, *Pop Internationalism* (Cambridge, MA: MIT Press, 1997).

34. United States Trade Representative, *A Preface to Trade* (Washington: GPO, 1982), 149.

35. Jagdish Bhagwati, *Free Trade, "Fairness" and the New Protectionism: Reflections on an Agenda for the World Trade Organisation* (London: Institute of Economic Affairs, 1995) and Edward John Ray, *U.S. Protectionism and World Debt Crisis* (New York: Quorum, 1989), 13–27; and Nancy Dunne, "Alarm Over Protection with a New Bite in '97," *Financial Times,* 23 February 1997.

36. For historical evidence that the public sees trade as a dialectic, see polls from 1930–95, Aaronson, *Trade and the American Dream,* 249–50, and analysis, 169–71, 175–76. For more recent polls, see Jackie Calmes, "Despite Buoyant Economic Times, American Don't Buy Free Trade," *Wall Street Journal,* 10 December 1998 and EPIC/MRA poll for Women in International Trade, May 1999, at www.embassy.org/wiit/survey.htm.

37. Zedillo is quoted in Mortimer B. Zuckerman, "Editorial: A Bit of Straight Talk," *U.S. News & World Report,* 3 July 2000, 60. Mexicans may have gained a more transparent political system with the 2000 election of Vincente Fox. Views of many of the protesters, in William Greider, "The Battle Beyond Seattle," *The Nation,* 27 December 1999. According to the noted trade economist Jagdish Bhagwati, "fairness" in the American sense relates to the process by which "competition for economic success takes place." Americans are focused on procedure; Europeans on results. See Jagdish Bhagwati, "The Demands to Reduce Domestic Diversity Among Trading Nations," in *Fair Trade and*

Harmonization: Prerequisites for Free Trade? ed. Jagdish Bhagwati and Robert E. Hudec (Cambridge: MIT Press, 1995), 18, 32.

38. Judith Goldstein, *Ideas, Interests, and American Foreign Policy* (Ithaca: Cornell University Press, 1993), 1–22.

39. The United States also uses retaliatory protection to induce trade liberalization See Press releases on USTR Web site, www.wto.gov. Press Releases 35, 58, 60, and 41, USTR Announces Results of Special 301 Annual Review.

40. Deirdre McGrath, "Writing Different Lyrics to the Same Old Tune: The New (and Improved) 1997 Amendments to the Marine Mammal Protection Act," *Minnesota Journal of Global Trade 7:* (Spring 1999) 431, 437, 452.

41. The definition of mercantilism is from Ruppert Pennant-Rea and Bill Emmott, *Pocket Economist* (Oxford: Basil Blackwell, 1983), 146

42. Alfred E. Eckes, *Opening America's Market: U.S. Foreign Trade Policy Since 1776* (Chapel Hill: University of North Carolina Press, 1995), 29; and Alan Tonelson, "US Nationalists versus Free-Trade Theorists," *Singapore Business Times,* 5 March 1996.

43. Three good overviews of the history of protection are Eckes, *Opening America's Markets;* Tom E. Terrill, *The Tariff, Politics, and American Foreign Policy* (Westport, CT: Greenwood, 1973); and John M. Dobson, *Two Centuries of Tariffs* (Washington: GPO, 1976).

44. Goldstein, *Ideas, Interests,* 163–77; and Aaronson, *Trade and the American Dream,* 169–71, 175–76.

45. Council of Economic Advisors, *Economic Report of the President 1998* (Washington: GPO, 1998), 216–17. Trade is a much smaller component of the U.S. economy than in most countries.

46. John Immerwahr, Jean Johnson, and Adam Kernan Schloss, *Cross-Talk: The Public, the Experts and Competitiveness: A Research Report from the Business Higher Education Forum and the Public Agenda Foundation* (Washington: Public Agenda, 1991)

47. C. Michael Aho and Jonathan David Aronson, *Trade Talks: America Better Listen* (New York: Council on Foreign Relations, 1985), 27.

48. Aaronson, *Trade and the American Dream,* 57–60, 134–36, 169–71.

49. Immerwahr et al., *Cross-Talk.*

50. Council of Economic Advisors, *Economic Report of the President, 1993,* 27–30.

51. Murray Weidenbaum, *Business, Government and the Public* (Englewood Cliffs, NJ: Prentice Hall, 1990), 23; and Mark Green and Norman Waitzman, *Business War on the Law: An Analysis of the Benefits of Federal Health/Safety Enforcement* (Washington: Corporate Accountability Research Group, 1979), 1–2.

52. David Vogel, "The 'New' Social Regulation," in *Regulation in Perspective: Historical Essays,* ed. Thomas K. McCraw (Cambridge, MA: Harvard, 1981), 180–85.

53. Weidenbaum, *Business, Government,* 39–41.

54. Vogel, "The 'New' Social Regulation," 180–85.

55. "Politics Brief, Ex Uno plures," *Economist,* 21 August 1999, 44–45.

56. Martha Derthick and Paul J Quirk, *The Politics of Deregulation* (Washington: Brookings Institution, 1985), 1.

57. Mansel G. Blackford and K. Austin Kerr, *Business Enterprise in American History* (Boston: Houghton Mifflin, 1994), 330–31, 374–83.

58. Weidenbaum, *Business, Government,* 19–31.

59. Derthick and Quirk, *The Politics of Deregulation,* 58; and Blackford and Kerr, *Business Enterprise,* 330–31, 374–83.

60. Norman J. Vig and Michael E. Kraft, *Environmental Policy in the 1980s: Reagan's New Agenda* (Washington: Congressional Quarterly, 1984), 21 and Na, *The American Economy: Government's Role, Citizen's Choice* (Alexandria, VA: Close Up, 1991), 18.

61. Vig and Kraft, *Environmental Policy*, 3–26; Samuel P Hays, *Beauty, Health and Permanence: Environmental Politics in the United States, 1955–1985* (New York: Cambridge University Press, 1987), 491–526.

62. Rodrik, *Has Globalization Gone Too Far?* 7.

63. Derthick and Quirk, *The Politics of Deregulation,* 9–10; and Michael Pertschuk, *Revolt Against Regulation: The Rise and Pause of the Consumer Movement* (Berkeley: University of California Press, 1982), 5–45.

64. Pertschuk, *The Revolt,* 5–6.

65. Pietro S. Nivola, "American Social Regulation Meets the Global Economy," in *Comparative Disadvantages: Social Regulations and the Global Economy,* ed. Pietro S. Nivola (Washington: Brookings Institution, 1997), 16–97; Green and Waitzman, *Business War,* see ads in appendix A; and David Vogel, "The 'New' Social Regulation," 178.

66. Nivola, "American Social Regulation," 16–97.

67. Karl Polanyi, *The Great Transformation: The Political and Economic Origins of Our Time* (Boston: Beacon, 1944).

68. William B. Kelly, Jr., ed., *Studies in United States Commercial Policy* (Chapel Hill: University of North Carolina Press, 1963), 54–68.

69. World Trade Organization, "10 Benefits of the WTO Trading System" (Geneva: WTO, 1999), 1, 5, 8–12, 15; and Patrick Lane, "Time for Another Round," *Economist,* 3, 4.

70. For current information on the WTO and its members, see www.wto.org.

71. Francis Masson and H. Edward English, *Invisible Trade Barriers Between Canada and the United States* (Washington: National Planning Association and Private Planning Association of Canada, 1963), 2, 3.

72. Bidwell, *Invisible Tariff* 3–4; and Hoekman, "Trade Laws," 34.

73. John H. Jackson, *World Trading System: Law and Policy of International Economic Relations,* (Cambridge, MA: MIT Press, 1997), 75, 153–55.

74. Edward John Ray, *U.S. Protectionism and the World Debt Crisis* (New York: Quorum, 1989), 23.

75. Bidwell, *Invisible Tariff,* 111–15.

76. Aaronson, *Trade and the American Dream,* 3–6.

77. Robert E. Hudec, *Enforcing International Trade Law: The Evolution of the Modern GATT Legal System* (Salem, NH: Butterworth Legal, 1993), 45–46, 203; and Robert E. Hudec, *The GATT Legal System and World Trade Diplomacy* (New York: Praeger, 1975), 63, 355, 356, n. 17.

78. U.S. Tariff Commission, *Operation of the Trade Agreements Program,* 2nd report, April 1948–March 1949, 19–21, 20, n. 4.

79. S. Concurrent Resolution 100, 89th Cong., 2d sess. (1966) in Michael J. Glennon et al., *United States Foreign Relations Law: Documents and Sources International Economic Regulation,* Vol. 4 (London: Oceana, 1984), 4–10.

80. According to USTR, a "codes of conduct" approach was adopted because it allowed negotiators to deal with the various impediments to trade without dealing with the rationale for such impediments; USTR, *A Preface,* 6.

81. William R. Cline, ed., *Trade Policy in the 1980s* (Washington: Institute for International Economics, 1983), 69–71, 723, 735, 752, 771; Aho and Aronson, *Trade Talks,*

28–29; and Twentieth Century Fund Task Force on the Future of American Trade Policy, *The Free Trade Debate* (New York: Priority Press, 1989), 82.

82. USTR, *1987 National Trade Estimate Report on Foreign Trade Barriers* (Washington: GPO, 1987), 4; Council of Economic Advisors, *Economic Report of the President 1993* (Washington: GPO, 1993), 323.

83. GATT Secretariat, "Final Act Embodying the Results of the Uruguay Round of Multilateral Trade Negotiations," 15 December 1993, Annex IV, 91.

84. Lori Wallach, Director, Public Citizen's Global Trade Watch, interview, 14 March 1995; and Mark Ritchie, President, Institute for Agriculture and Trade Policy, interview, 17 April 1996.

85. Henry J. Tasca, *The Reciprocal Trade Policy of the United States: A Study in Trade Philosophy* (Philadelphia: University of Pennsylvania Press, 1938), 17–25.

86. Hudec, *Enforcing International Trade Law,* 45–46; and Robert M. Hudec, *The GATT Legal System* 356, n. 3 and n. 17; and Aaronson, *Trade and the American Dream,* 134.

87. Glennon et al., *United States Foreign Relations Law,* 45–49.

88. Lori Wallach and Tom Hilliard, "The Consumer and Environmental Case Against Fast-Track," *Public Citizen's Congress Watch* (May 1991): 7.

89. Patrick Lane, "Time for Another Round," 8–9, 22–28; GATT, *Analytical Index of the GATT* (Geneva: WTO, 1995), 771–87; and Hudec, *Enforcing International Trade Law,* 273–586.

90. Robert Collier and Glen Martin, "US. Laws Diluted by Trade Pacts Rulings Stir Criticism Across Political Spectrum," *San Francisco Chronicle,* 24 July 1999.

91. Deirdre McGrath, "Writing Different Lyrics," 433–36.

92. Ibid., 434–37, n. 35, 439.

93. Ibid., 439, 440, n. 55.

94. Interview with Lori Wallach, Public Citizen, 2 July 1998.

95. McGrath, "Writing Different Lyrics," 451, n. 133, n. 134, 452, n. 141.

96. McGrath, 456, n. 163–68.

97. James Harvey Young, *Pure Food: Securing the Federal Food and Drugs Act of 1906* (Princeton: Princeton University Press, 1989), 33–65.

98. Daniel C. Esty, *Greening the GATT: Trade, Environment and the Future* (Washington: Institute for International Economics, 1994), 1–27.

99. Ibid., 46–53.

100. Interview with Lori Wallach, Global Trade Watch, 2 July 1998.

101. Nader, "Introduction," 1–12.

102. Buchanan, *The Great Betrayal,* 284–85, 313.

103. Audley, *Green Politics,* 27–40.

104. Aaronson, *Trade and the American Dream,* 143–44; William Branigin, "Wal-Mart Assailed on Foreign-Made Clothes," *Washington Post,* 30 July 1998; and Madelaine Drohan, "How the Net Killed the MAI: Grassroots Groups Used Their Own Globalization to Derail Deal," *Toronto Globe and Mail,* 29 April 1998.

105. As an example, Public Citizen's Global Trade Watch tends to lead the opposition to trade agreements from the left, according to Linda Gordon Kuzmack, foundation officer, Public Citizen Foundation; letter to author, 9 January 1997, Public Citizen's Global Trade Watch 1996–1997 received funds from the Ford Foundation; Foundation for Ecology and Development; Patagonia Foundation; the C.S. Fund; the National Association of Public Interest Lawyers; Institute for Agriculture and Trade Policy; and the Preamble Collaborative (the Bauman Family Foundation). The Community Nutrition

Institute, which is a leading food safety group, received funds from the Bauman Family Foundation; C. S. Fund; Pew; Ruth Mott; Jessie Smith Noyes; and the German Marshall Fund. Jake Caldwell, letter to author, 17 February 1998. Earth Justice Legal Defense Fund (formally Sierra Club Legal Defense Fund), which wrote many of the briefs and helped direct the legal strategy affecting trade and environmental issues, received funds from over forty foundations, including the Altman; C. S. Fund; George Gund Foundation; John D. and Catherine T. MacArthur Foundation; Charles Stewart Mott Foundation: John Merck Fund; Surdna Foundation; and the Turner Foundation. However, like Public Citizen, most of its funds came from individual contributions. Ford, MacArthur, the Rockefeller Brothers Foundation and the Mott Foundation (internationalist foundations) tend to be among the most common sources for these groups. This book was also funded by the Ford and German Marshall Funds.

The leading economic nationalist think tank is the United States Business and Industrial Council. Alan Tonelson, a nationally recognized trade scholar, was kind enough to send me the 1997 annual report, which noted the financial support of the following major corporations and foundations: Anschutz Foundation; Alfred DuPont Foundation; St. Joe Foundation; True Foundation; Armstrong Foundation; and Stranahan Foundation. Corporate funders included Broyhill Investments; Cincinnati Companies; Chrysler Corporation; and Milliken and Company. Some reporters (including John Judis of *The New Republic*) argued that Milliken also funds much of the intellectual arguments for economic nationalism and even funds Public Citizen; John Judis, interview 21 May 1998. The lobbyist for that company, John (Jock) Nash, refused to tell me what groups they fund. As the company is privately held, he is not legally required to make this information public; Jock Nash, Milliken and Company, interview, 22 May 1998. However, Lori Wallach argues that Public Citizen takes no corporate or government funds. Its lobbying work is supported by membership fees from its 150,000 members; Lori Wallach, comments on Aaronson book draft, March 1999. For an interesting, albeit incorrect assessment of the funders of the trade agreement critics, see www.truthabouttrade.org.

106. Aaronson, *Trade and the American Dream*, 134–44; Audley, *Green Politics*, 135–63; and Vogel, *Trading Up*, 196–217.

107. Congressman Richard A. Gephardt, "Linking Trade with Worker Rights and the Environment," Economic Perspectives, March 1998 at www.asia.gov/journals/ites/0398/ij33/ejgep.htm.

108. Destler, *American Trade Politics*, 5.

109. "United States Challenges WTO to Build on Foundations to Meet 21st Century Needs," press release at www.ustr.gov; and "Barshefsky, Ruggiero Seek Boost in Transparency of WTO Process," *Inside U.S. Trade*, 17 April 1998, 8; and E. J. Dionne Jr., "Globalism With a Human Face," *Washington Post*, 29 May 1998, A27.

110. Drohan, "How the Net Killed the MAI," *Toronto Globe and Mail*, 29 April 1998.

111. To see USTR's Web site, go to www.ustr.gov. The site was recently revamped, but it is not as user-friendly as other government sites on trade. The EU, as example, has a list server on trade—it comes to its visitors, rather than insisting that they come to it.

Chapter 2

1. Franklin's letter to M. Leroy in 1789 is available at Bartlett's on the Web: www.columbia.edu/acis/bartleby/bartlett/245.html.

2. Thomas K. McCraw, "Mercantilism and the Market," in *The Politics of Industrial Policy*, ed. Claude E. Barfield and William A. Schambra (Washington: American En-

terprise Institute, 1986), 34–35. Today, policymakers have a panoply of tools from tax incentives to subsidies that they can tailor to encourage the growth of a particular sector.

3. In the nineteenth century, government's role in stimulating economic growth was minimal. See Robert M. Lively, "The American System: A Review Article," *Business History Review* 19 (March 1995): 81–96.

4. Eckes, *Opening America's Market*, 72–73, quotation; also see 75–77.

5. Eckes, *Opening America's Market*, xi–xxi, 278–89; Alan Tonelson, "Globalization: The Great American Non-Debate," *Current History* 96, no. 613 (November 1996): 353–59; and Aaronson, *Trade and the American Dream*, 169.

6. Bidwell, *Invisible Tariff*, 2.

7. Aaronson, *Trade and the American Dream*, 98–113, esp. fnn. 1, 6, on 216–17. Also see Raymond A. Bauer, Ithiel de Sola Pool, and Lewis A. Dexter, *American Business and Public Policy: The Politics of Foreign Trade* (New York: Atherton, 1963), 86–91; and Susan Aaronson, "The Truth About Trade: A Historical Rebuttal of Protectionism," *New Democrat* (September/October 1997): 12–14.

8. Terrence H. Witkowski, "Colonial Consumers in Revolt: Buyer Values and Behavior During the Nonimportation Movement, 1764–1776," *Journal of Consumer Research* 16 (September 1989): 219.

9. These acts included the Sugar and Currency Acts of 1764, the Stamp Act (repealed in 1766), the Declaratory Act, and the Coercive or Intolerable Acts of 1775. These acts greatly helped the colonists understand that their economic interests were different from their counterparts in Great Britain.

10. Interestingly, the nonimportation movement lasted until 1776. The movement attempted to use patriotism to get buyers to avoid buying British-made goods and tried to link patriotism and trade policies. Witkowski, "Colonial Consumers in Revolt," 220; and Dana Frank, *Buy American: The Untold Story of Economic Nationalism* (New York: Beacon, 1999).

11. W. E. B Du Bois, *The Suppression of the African Slave-Trade to the United States of America, 1638–1870* (New York: Dover, 1979), 2–3, fn. 2.

12. Ibid., 53–62.

13. Ibid.; 63–65 discusses the response in the pamphlets of the day, 65–69 delineates the response of state conventions.

14. Douglass C. North, *The Economic Growth of the United States, 1790–1860* (New York: Norton, 1966), 22–23; and John M. Dobson, *Two Centuries of Tariffs: The Background and Emergence of the United States International Trade Commission* (Washington: GPO, 1976), 8–9.

15. Dobson, *Two Centuries*, 71; and James A. Field Jr., "All Economists, All Diplomats," in *Economics and World Power: An Assessment of American Diplomacy Since 1789*, ed. William H. Becker and Samuel F. Wells Jr. (New York: Columbia University Press, 1984), 31.

16. Dobson, *Two Centuries*, 31.

17. Field, "All Economists, All Diplomats," 7.

18. Dobson, *Two Centuries*, 71; and Field, "All Economists, All Diplomats," 31.

19. Young governments often rely on indirect taxation because they lack the administrative resources and/or legitimacy to extract taxes directly from the citizenry. Cynthia A. Hody, *The Politics of Trade: American Political Development and Foreign Economic Policy* (Hanover: University Press of New England, 1996), 40–41; Dobson, *Two Centuries*, 8; and Field, "All Economists, All Diplomats," 12–13.

20. Hamilton is quoted in Eckes, *Opening America's Market*, 16.

21. Irwin, *Against the Tide*, 122.

22. Kelly, *United States. Commercial Policy,* 25.

23. Robert A. Pastor, *Congress and the Politics of U.S. Foreign Economic Policy, 1929–1976* (Berkeley: University of California Press, 1980), 73–74; and Dobson, *Two Centuries,* 8. The classic study on tariffs is by the first chairman of the Tariff Commission, Frank M. Taussig, *The Tariff History of the United States* (New York: Putnam, 1931).

24. Clay quoted in Eckes, *Opening America's Market,* 25.

25. Eric Foner, *Free Soil, Free Labor, Free Men: The Ideology of the Republican Party Before the Civil War* (New York: Oxford University Press, 1970), 18–19.

26. Foner, *Free Soil,* 20.

27. The U.S. government occasionally acted to open foreign markets in support of special trade interests, but such actions were "exceptional and cautious." Kinley J. Brauer, "The Diplomacy of American Expansionism," in *Economics and World Power,* ed. Becker and Wells, 113–14.

28. Kelly, *United States. Commercial Policy,* 3. The "American government apparatus was not developed in ways that allowed policy makers to pursue state interests." John G. Ikenberry, "Conclusion: An Institutional Approach to American Foreign Economic Policy," in *The State and American Foreign Economic Policy,* ed. John G. Ikenberry, David A. Lake, and Michael Mastanduno (Ithaca, NY: Cornell University Press, 1988), 232.

29. North, *Economic Growth,* 67–71.

30. Eckes, *Opening America's Market,* 66.

31. The abolitionist movement began in Great Britain. In 1787, British abolitionists launched a public campaign against the slave trade. Keck and Sikkink, *Activists Beyond Borders,* 41, esp. fn 3. The debate in the United States is well described in Du Bois, 94–130.

32. Brauer, "The Diplomacy of American Expansion," 71; and Keck and Sikkink, *Activists Beyond Borders,* 42, fnn. 6–9.

33. Du Bois, *Suppression of the African Slave-Trade,* 2–3, fn. 2.

34. Ibid., 152–55, 174.

35. Keck and Sikkink, *Activists Beyond Borders,* 42.

36. Charles Chatfield, "Intergovernmental and Nongovernmental Associations to 1945," in *Transnational Social Movements and Global Politics: Solidarity Beyond the State,* ed. Jackie Smith, Charles Chatfield, and Ron Pagnucco (Syracuse: Syracuse University Press, 1997), 21.

37. Keck and Sikkink, *Activists Beyond Borders,* 44–47, fnn. 21, 22, 30.

38. Dobson, *Two Centuries,* 13.

39. Charles P. Kindleberger, "The Rise of Free Trade in Western Europe," in *International Political Economy: Perspectives on Global Power and Wealth,* ed. Jeffrey A. Frieden and David A. Lake (New York: St. Martins, 1991), 86–88.

40. Polanyi, *Great Transformation,* 3–19, 178–81, 191–202; and Martin J. Sklar, *The Corporate Reconstruction of American Capitalism, 1890–1916: The Market, the Law and Politics* (Cambridge: Cambridge University Press, 1988), 13–20.

41. Foner, *Free Soil,* 43–35.

42. Foner, *Free Soil,* 21–33, quotation, 21.

43. On views of some workers, see Keck and Sikkink, *Activists Beyond Borders,* 180; and Susan Previant Lee and Peter Passell, *A New Economic View of American History* (New York: Norton, 1979), 103–4, 214, 220–33, 321.

44. Mill workers in Great Britain also did not see a link between their work conditions and those of the slaves that picked the cotton. Keck and Sikkink, *Activists Beyond Borders,* 41, 77, fn. 171.

45. Du Bois, *Suppression of the African Slave-Trade,* 192–93, 288.

46. Paul Wolman, *Most Favored Nation: The Republican Revisionists and U.S. Tariff Policy, 1897–1912* (Chapel Hill: University of North Carolina Press, 1992), 1; quotation, 3; and Hody, *Politics of Trade,* 41.

47. Congressman Springer was quoted in Tom E. Terrill, *The Tariff, Politics, and American Foreign Policy* (Westport, CT: Greenwood Press, 1973), 66–67.

48. Lawrence Goodwyn, *The Democratic Promise: The Populist Moment in America* (New York: Oxford University Press, 1976), 180.

49. David M. Pletcher, "Growth and Diplomatic Adjustment," in *Economics and World Power,* ed. Becker and Wells, 123; and Hody, *Politics of Trade,* 41, 61.

50. Terrill, *Tariff, Politics,* 70–71; Robert H. Wiebe, *The Search for Order* (New York: Hill & Wang, 1967), 111–32, 232–39; and Alan Trachtenberg, *The Incorporation of America: Culture and Society in the Gilded Age* (New York: Hill & Wang, 1982), 161–81.

51. Organized labor was divided and remained divided on trade. Leaders and members alike recognized that many workers produced goods and services that were exported. However, they called for domestic policies to assist workers hurt by trade. Charles William Vear, "Organized Labor and the Tariff" (Ph.D. diss., Fletcher School of Law and Diplomacy, October 1955).

52. Dobson, *Two Centuries,* 69.

53. Wolman, *Most Favored Nation,* xix–xxi; quotation on xix. On the populists, see Goodwyn, *Democratic Promise.*

54. Terrill, *Tariff, Politics,* 41, 48, 52–53. Interestingly, Terrill shows that there were plenty of Southern protectionists in the 1880s and 1890s (122–23).

55. Eckes, *Opening America's Market,* 42.

56. Robert H. Wiebe, *Businessmen and Reform: A Study of the Progressive Movement* (Cambridge: Harvard University Press, 1962), 20.

57. Eckes, *Opening America's Market,* 56.

58. Ibid., 33.

59. Terrill, *Tariff, Politics,* 56–60, 99.

60. Pletcher, "Growth and Diplomatic Adjustment," 133–34.

61. Rodrik, *Has Globalization Gone Too Far?,* 7–8; Jeffrey G. Williamson, "Globalization and Inequality Then and Now: The Late 19th and Late 20th Centuries Compared," NBER Working Paper 5491 (March 1996): 8–9, 14–15, 19; and Emma Rothschild, "Globalization and the Return of History," *Foreign Policy* 115 (summer 1999): 106–16.

62. Hody, *Politics of Trade,* 54–55.

63. Paul Bairoch and Richard Kozul-Wright, "Globalization Myths: Some Historical Reflections on Integration, Industrialization and Growth in the World Economy," UNCTAD, no. 113 (March 1996): 7–9. According to economic historians Paul Bairoch and Richard Kozul-Wright, rising protection was the common trend in the developed world (including nations as diverse as Japan and Sweden).

64. Terrill, *Tariff, Politics,* 203–4; and John L. Gignilliat, "Pigs, Politics and Protection: The European Boycott of American Pork, 1879–1891," *Agricultural History* 35, no. 1. (January 1961): 3.

65. Peter Alexis Gourevitch, "International Trade, Domestic Coalitions and Liberty," in *International Political Economy,* ed. Frieden and Lake, 97–100. According to Peter Gourevitch, "international political rivalries imposed concern for a domestic food supply."

66. Gourevitch, "International Trade," 100–101.

67. Bairoch and Kozul-Wright, "Globalization Myths," 7–9; and Peter H. Lindert, "The Rise of Social Spending, 1880–1930," *Explorations in Economic History* 31, no. 1 (January 1994): 1–37.

68. Bidwell, *Invisible Tariff*, 105–7.

69. Bidwell, *Invisible Tariff*, 111–15.

70. Bidwell, *Invisible Tariff*, 111–15.

71. Steve Charnovitz, "Environmental and Labour Standards in Trade," *World Economy* 15, no. 3 (May 1992): 337–39.

72. Keck and Sikkink, eds., *Activists Beyond Borders*, 39–66, 122.

73. Louis L. Snyder, "The American-German Pork Dispute, 1879–1891," *Journal of Modern History* 17, no. 1 (March 1945): 18–19, 25; and Gignilliat, "Pigs, Politics," 3.

74. The law was extremely weak; microscopic exams were on already boxed pork products, and such exams were not compulsory. Snyder, "The American-German Pork Dispute," 24–28; and Vogel, *Trading Up*, 20.

75. Gignilliat, "Pigs, Politics," 7.

76. Terrill, *Tariff, Politics*, 178–79; Snyder, "The German-American Pork Dispute," 26–28; and Gignilliat, "Pigs, Politics," 5, 8.

77. Snyder, "The German-American Pork Dispute," 26–27.

78. Terrill, *Tariff, Politics*, 81.

79. Eckes, *Opening America's Market*, 70–74, 75–85 on 1890–1914.

80. Terrill, *Tariff, Politics*, 89.

81. Eckes, *Opening America's Market*, 74–84, quotation on 84.

82. Dobson, *Two Centuries*, 83–89; and Wolman, *Most Favored Nation*, xi.

83. To both the United States and Britain, "questions of tariff rates were purely domestic issues." Kelly, *United States Commercial Policy* 24, 27, 29, 69; and Hody, *Politics of Trade*, 40.

84. Wiebe, *Businessmen and Reform*, 114.

85. Michael A. Bernstein, *The Great Depression: Delayed Recovery and Economic Change in America, 1929–1939* (New York: Cambridge University Press, 1987), 218.

86. Bernstein, *Great Depression*, 10; and Charles P. Kindleberger, *The World in Depression, 1929–1939* (Berkeley: University of California Press, 1973), 292–93.

87. Melvyn P. Leffler, "Expansionist Impulses and Domestic Constraints," in *Economics and World Power*, ed. Becker and Wells, 227–28, 231.

88. Bidwell, *Invisible Tariff*, 208–15, quotation on 215.

89. Bidwell, *Invisible Tariff*, 106–7, 109–11. Bidwell quotes the *New York Times*, February 17, 1939, on the view that because they were dictatorships, Germany and the Soviet Union used forced labor. Interestingly, the United States had abrogated the Russo-American Treaty of 1832 because of the pogroms and czarist prison camps. See Naomi W. Cohen, "The Abrogation of the Russo-American Treaty of 1832," *Jewish Social Studies* 25, no. 1 (January 1963): 3–41.

90. Bidwell, *Invisible Tariff*, 208–15, quotation on 215.

91. See E. E. Schattschneider, *Politics, Pressures and the Tariff: A Study of Free Private Enterprise in Pressure Politics, as Shown in the 1929–1930 Revision of the Tariff* (New York: Prentice Hall, 1935), 141–43.

92. Harry C. Hawkins and Janet L. Norwood, "The Legislative Basis of U.S. Commercial Policy," in *United States Commercial Policy*, ed. Kelly, 85.

93. Aaronson, *Trade and the American Dream*, 21, 31.

94. Dr. Strong's testimony on amending the Plant Quarantine Act was on March 17, 1936, quoted in Bidwell, *Invisible Tariff*, 251–52.

95. Stephen Haggard, "Institutional Foundations of Hegemony," in *State and American Foreign Economic Policy*, ed. Ikenberry et al., 93–94; Kelly, "Antecedents," in *United States Commercial Policy*, ed. Kelly, 73–75; and Aaronson, *Trade and the American Dream*, 21.

96. Aaronson, *Trade and the American Dream*, 21–22, 186.

97. Kelly, "Antecedents," 24–25.

98. Kelly, "Antecedents," 80–83; and Aaronson, *Trade and the American Dream*, 145–67.

99. Robert M. Hathaway, "Economic Diplomacy in Time of Crisis," in *Economics and World Power*, ed. Becker and Wells, 296–99.

100. Ibid., 326–29.

101. Aaronson, *Trade and the American Dream*, 30–33.

102. Aaronson, *Trade and the American Dream*, 25–35.

103. Tariff Commission for Committee on Ways and Means, *Report on the Havana Charter for an International Trade Organization* (Washington: Tariff Commission, 1949), 4; on employment and economic activity, 14; on labor standards, 60–61.

104. Aaronson, *Trade and the American Dream*, 68.

105. Aaronson, *Trade and the American Dream*, 87–89, fnn. 23–36; and Steve Charnovitz and John Wickham, "Non-Governmental Organizations and the Original International Trade Regime," *Journal of World Trade* 29, no.5 (October 1995): 113–22.

106. Esty, *Greening the GATT*, 47; and Steve Charnovitz, "The Moral Exception in Trade Policy," *Virginia Journal of International Law* 38, no. 4 (summer 1998): 689–94.

107. I take this language from Charnovitz, "Environmental and Labour Standards in Trade," 341, 348.

108. Ibid., 338–39.

109. Charnovitz and Wickham, "NGOs and the Original International Trade Regime," 121–22.

110. Article 7 of the ITO Charter stated, "Members recognize that measures relating to employment must take fully into account the rights of workers. . . . The Members recognize that unfair labour conditions, particularly in production for export, create difficulties in international trade." The ITO was supposed to cooperate with the ILO. Office of the Special Trade Representatives for Trade Negotiations (after 1980, the U.S. Trade Representative), "Labor Standards and International Trade," TSC D-122/64, Rev.1, 12, 9 August 1964, attachment C, in box 4, RG 364.1. I am grateful to Tab Lewis, archivist at the National Archives for his help with these records.

111. Office of the Special Trade Representative, "Labor Standards and International Trade," TSC D-122/64, box 4, RG-364.1.

112. Trade Executive Committee (TEC), "International Fair Labor Standards," 15 April 1968, Box 4TEC D-4/68, appendix I, box 4, RG 364.1.

113. "Labor Standards and International Trade"; "International Fair Labor Standards"; "Minutes: Trade Executive Committee Meeting," 1 April 1968, box 4, RG 364.1. In 1968, the United States decided not to push closer cooperation between the GATT and the ILO on labor standards. George L. P. Weaver, assistant secretary for international affairs, Labor Department, to William H. Roth, 23 April 1993, in box 4, RG 364.1.

114. Aaronson, *Trade and the American Dream*, 82, 134; and Michael J. Glennon, Thomas M. Franck, and Robert C. Cassidy Jr., *U.S. Foreign Relations Law: International Economic*

Regulation, vol. 4 (London: Oceana, 1984), 3. On GATT disclaimer, see Robert E. Hudec, *The GATT Legal System and World Trade Diplomacy* (New York: Praeger, 1975), 356, n. 3. The disclaimer was included in the 1953, 1954, 1955, 1958, and 1974 extensions of the RTAA.

115. B. A. Jones of the *New York Times* was quoted in Robert E. Baldwin, *Nontariff Distortions of International Trade* (Washington: Brookings Institution, 1970), 2, fn. 3.

116. Kelly, "Antecedents," 58–59. Tariffs were reduced from about 59 percent on average in 1932 to 7 percent in the early 1970s. Edward John Ray, "Changing Patterns of Protectionism: The Fall in Tariffs and the Rise in Non-Tariff Barriers," in *International Political Economy,* ed. Frieden and Lake, 342, quotation on 350.

117. Aaronson, *Trade and the American Dream,* 169–71, 176.

118. William L. Batt (industrialist and head of the Committee for the ITO), in Rubber Manufacturers Association, *Pros and Cons of the ITO,* 10 January 1950, 89–90.

119. Robert A. Pollard and Samuel F. Wells Jr., "Era of American Economic Hegemony," in *Economics and World Power,* ed. Becker and Wells, 385–387; quotation on 387.

120. John Gerard Ruggie, "Trade, Protectionism and the Future of Welfare Capitalism," *Journal of International Affairs* 48, no. 1 (summer 1994): 4–5.

121. In 1948, Congress also required that the Tariff Commission report the peril points, the lowest rate of duties that could be fixed without threatening serious injury to American producers. Aaronson, *Trade and the American Dream,* 70, 111–12.

122. House Committee on Ways and Means, *Extension of the Reciprocal Trade Agreements Act, Hearings on HR. 1211: A Bill to Extend the Authority of the President Under Section 350 of the Tariff Act of 1939, as Amended and for Other Purposes,* 81st Cong., 1st sess., 24 January–1 February 1949, 282, 305–6, 315–16, 344–45, 411–12; and Senate Committee on Finance, *Hearings on H.R. 1211, An Act to Extend the Authority of the President under Section 350 of the Tariff Act of 1930, as Amended and for Other Purposes,* 81st Cong., 1st sess., 17 February–8 March 1949, 8, 11, 217, 436, 645.

123. Senate Committee on Finance, *Hearings on H.R. 1211,* 180–81; 869–75; House Committee on Ways and Means, *Hearings on H.R., 1211,* 369, 375.

124. Eckes, *Opening America's Market,* 148. For a recent example, see remarks of Mr. Underwood and Mr. Engel, *Congressional Record,* 29 December 1994, H11495.

125. Eckes, *Opening America's Market,* 170–77, quotations on 176–77.

126. Aaronson, *Trade and the American Dream,* 121–22.

127. Jacob Viner, "Conflicts of Principle in Drafting a Trade Charter," *Foreign Affairs* 25, no. 2 (January 1947): 613.

Chapter 3

1. Ralph Nader, *Unsafe at Any Speed* (New York: Grossman, 1965).

2. Rogene A. Buchholz, William D. Evans, and Robert A. Wagley, *Management Response to Public Issues: Concepts and Cases in Strategy Formulation* (Englewood Cliffs, NJ: Prentice Hall, 1989), 10–11; Murray L. Weidenbaum, *Business, Government, and the Public* (Englewood Cliffs, NJ: Prentice Hall, 1990), 402–403. Also see Nader's affiliated Web sites: www.ref.usc.edu/~tbelt/web/nader/nader.html, www.autosafety.org, and www.mojones.com/election_96/nade.html.

3. Michael Pertschuk, *Revolt Against Regulation: The Rise and Pause of the Consumer Movement* (Berkeley: University of California Press, 1982); and Samuel P. Hays, *Beauty, Health and Permanence: Environmental Politics in the United States, 1955–1985* (Cambridge: Cambridge University Press, 1987).

4. Rodrik, *Has Globalization Gone Too Far?* 7. In some cases, the United States was in the forefront of such regulations. In other areas, other nations such as Sweden or Germany were ahead.

5. Evans, *The Kennedy Round,* 299–300; and comments of American Importers Association, Inc., in Subcommittee on Foreign Economic Policy of the Joint Economic Committee, *The Future of U.S. Foreign Trade Policy,* 90th Cong., 1st sess. (Washington: GPO, 1967), 423.

6. Bidwell, *Invisible Tariff,* 2–3, 7–8, 15; and Evans, *The Kennedy Round,* 87–112. Robert E. Baldwin, former chief economist at the Office of the Special Trade Representative, defined NTBs as "any measure (public or private) that causes internationally traded goods and services, or resources devoted to the production of these goods and services, to be allocated in such a way as to reduce potential real world income." Robert E. Baldwin, *Nontariff Distortions of International Trade* (Washington: Brookings Institution, 1970).

7. On U.S. receptivity to new ideas in culture see Ian Whitcomb, "Confessions of a British Invader," *American Heritage* 48, no. 2 (December 1997): 68–86; and Allen J. Matusow, "Rise and Fall of a Counterculture," in *A History of Our Time: Readings on Postwar America,* ed. William H. Chafe and Harvard Sitkoff (New York: Oxford, 1991), 378–99. Statistics on gross domestic product and real wages come from the President's Commission on Industrial Competitiveness, *Global Competition: The New Reality,* vol. 2 (Washington: GPO, 1985), 8–11, see charts 1–3 and table 1. A good example of these attitudes is in David Halberstam, *The Reckoning* (New York: Morrow, 1986), 726–28; and Jean Jacques Servan-Schreiber, *The American Challenge* (New York: 1968), 3, 10, 11.

8. Council of Economic Advisors, *Economic Report of the President, 1997* (Washington: GPO, 1997), table B-101, "U.S. International Transactions, 1946–1996," 414; and President's Commission, *Global Competition,* 14–15, 17.

9. These activists built on the ideas and work of individuals in the 1930s–1960s such as Louis Mumford, Dorothy Day, and Rachel Carson. Chafe and Sitkoff, eds., *A History of Our Time,* 341–43; and Joseph Youngerman, "The Passing of Passions," both in *Yale Alumni Magazine* 61, no. 8 (summer 1998), 21.

10. Spiro Agnew's speech, "Impudence in the Streets," address at Pennsylvania Republican Dinner, 30 October 1969, in Chafe and Sitkoff, eds., *A History of Our Time,* 397.

11. Nader on the Diane Rehm show on WAMU/National Public Radio. The transcript was on ic.net/~harvey/greens/rn-npr.txt. For a good understanding of the debate over consumer safety, see John Schwartz, "Debate From the '60s Echoes Today: Some See Courage, Others Luck in the FDA's Original Actions on Thalidomide," *Washington Post,* 17 July 1998, A15.

12. See Mansel G. Blackford and K. Austin Kerr, *Business Enterprise in American History,* 3d ed. (Boston: Houghton Mifflin, 1994), 325–32; and Weidenbaum, *Business, Government,* 39–42. On Nader's influence in the environmental and public health organization, see Samuel P. Hays, *Beauty, Health and Permanence: Environmental Politics in the United States, 1955–1985* (Cambridge: Cambridge University Press, 1987), 460–61, 577, fn. 27.

13. Hays, *Beauty, Health,* 32–35.

14. Hays details these changes in *Beauty, Health,* 33–35, 512. Also see Paul Wapner, *Environmental Activism and World Civic Politics* (Albany: State University of New York Press, 1996).

15. Subcommittee on Foreign Economic Policy, *The Future,* 220–21.

16. Figures from Council of Economic Advisors, *Economic Report of the President 1999* (Washington: GPO, 1999), Table B-103, 444. For a good overview of America's economic problems in this period, see Commission on International Trade and Investment Policy (hereafter Williams Commission), *United States International Economic Policy in an Interdependent World* (Washington: GPO, 1971), 4–6 and David P. Calleo, "Since 1961: American Power in a New World Economy," in Becker and Wells, *Economics and World Power*, 390–434, esp. 402.

17. For views of trade from the left, see Karin Ashley, "You Don't Need a Weatherman to Know Which Way the Wind Blows," reprinted statement of the Weatherman Manifesto, in Chafe and Sitkoff, eds., *A History of Our Times,* 352. For the views of Congress, see Evans, *The Kennedy Round in American Trade Policy,* 1, 303–7.

18. Ray, "Changing Patterns," 349.

19. Francis Masson and H. Edward English, *Invisible Trade Barriers Between Canada and the United States* (Washington: National Planning Association and Private Planning Association of Canada, 1963), 2, 3.

20. Bidwell, *Invisible Tariff,* 2, 15–17.

21. Masson and English, *Invisible Trade Barriers,* 4.

22. See "U.S. Proposals for Consideration by the GATT Subcommittee on NTBs and Other Special Problems." This is the title of memos dated 5 October 1963, TEC D-19/63, and 23 October 1963, both in box 2, RG 364. Also see Memo to William T. Gossett, Deputy Special Representative for Trade Negotiations, 1 March 1963, in box 2, RG 364.

23. This system, called the American Selling Price, was a tariff, but because it was based on domestic prices and not on the price of the exporting producer, foreign producers saw it as a NTB. Eckes, *Opening America's Market,* 198–99.

24. S. Concurrent Resolution 100, 89th Cong., 2d sess. (1966), listed in Michael J. Glennon et al., *United States Foreign Relations Law: Documents and Sources International Economic Regulation,* vol. 4 (London: Oceana, 1984), 4–10. The official document is Committee on Finance, U.S. Senate, *Antidumping Act of 1921 and the International Antidumping Code: Consistent or Not? A Critique by the Staff,* 90th Cong., 2d sess. (Washington: GPO, 1968).

25. Kent Higgon Hughes, *Trade, Taxes and Transnationals: International Economic Decision Making in Congress* (New York: Praeger, 1979), 1–2.

26. Subcommittee on Foreign Economic Policy, *The Future,* 302.

27. Subcommittee on Foreign Economic Policy, *The Future,* 1.

28. Ibid., quantitative restrictions, 303–45; Mr. Hemmendinger's report, 345–57.

29. Ibid., 99. Joseph A. Greenwald was a deputy assistant secretary of state in 1967. Also see views of William Diebold, Council on Foreign Relations, 220; Richard N. Cooper, professor of economics, Yale University, 225; and David Rockefeller, President, Chase Manhattan Bank, 291. Diebold saw the solution to the proliferation of NTBs in dispute settlement rather than negotiations. Lawrence C. McQuade, acting assistant secretary of commerce for domestic and International Business on how the United States handled its NTBs, 67, 98.

30. Ibid., 220–21.

31. Ibid., 136.

32. Ibid., 99.

33. Ibid., 224–25. Baldwin was professor of economics at the University of Wisconsin.

34. Committee for Economic Development, *Non Tariff Distortions of Trade* (Washington: CED, 1969), 28–29. This study was prepared in association with the European committee for Economic and Social Progress, the Political and Economic Planning (Britain); Japan Committee for Economic Development; the Committee for Economic Development of Australia; and the Industrial Council for Social and Economic Studies (Sweden).

35. This history of the surveys of NTBs is from the Williams Commission, *United States International,* 683, 718. Draft Memo W. B. Kelly Jr., 9 May 1969, p. 3, D-4/69 in box 5, RG 364.

36. Eckes, *Opening America's Market,* 201–2.

37. Allen J. Matusow, *Nixon's Economy: Booms, Busts, Dollars and Votes* (Lawrence: University of Kansas Press, 1998), 4, 7.

38. For a good history of how labor rights evolved as human rights, see International Labor Rights Education and Research Fund, *Trade's Hidden Costs: Worker Rights in a Changing World Economy* (Washington: Institute for Policy Studies, 1988), 41–48.

39. In 1961, the Joint Economic Committee studied the question of using trade to help encourage political liberalization in the Soviet Union and Eastern Europe. In February 1965, the Committee on Foreign Relations sponsored hearings on East-West trade. Some unions, civic groups, and farm groups seemed supportive. Committee on Foreign Relations, United States Senate, *Hearings on East West Trade,* 89th Cong., 2d sess., 24–26 February 1965; on history, 2–3; on trade as a political vehicle, 8; on views of labor, 9, 214–15, 248–51; on civic groups, 253; on farms, 253.

40. Paula Stern, *Water's Edge: Domestic Politics and the Making of American Foreign Policy* (Westport, CT: Greenwood, 1979), xviii–xix, 4–11.

41. Stern, *Water's Edge,* xviii–xix, 4–11, 39, 62, 69, 191. On the first successful linkage of Jewish pressure to abrogate a commercial treaty, see Naomi W. Cohen, "The Abrogation of the Russo-American Treaty of 1832," *Jewish Social Studies* 25, no. 1 (January 1963): 3–41.

42. Council of Economic Advisors, *Economic Report of the President, 1999* (Washington: GPO, 1999), table B-103, "U.S. International Transactions, 1946–1998," 444. Imports began to increase significantly in 1965; and Council of Economic Advisors, *Economic Report of the President, 1998* (Washington: GPO, 1999), 216.

43. Thomas J. Zeiler, *American Trade and Power in the 1960s* (New York: Columbia University Press, 1992), 54–55, 64–65; Eckes, *Opening America's Market,* 199–201; and Steve Dryden, *Trade Warriors* (New York: Oxford University Press, 1995), 45.

44. Anne Krueger, *American Trade Policy: A Tragedy in the Making* (Washington: American Enterprise Institute Press, 1995), 2.

45. See comments of Senator Barry Goldwater in 1964, in Dryden, *Trade Warriors,* 83.

46. Dryden, *Trade Warriors,* 81.

47. Eckes, *Opening America's Market,* 192.

48. Robert E. Baldwin, "Nontariff Distortions of International Trade," in Williams Commission, *United States International,* Compendium of Papers: Vol. I, 641.

49. Dryden, *Trade Warriors,* 84.

50. Calleo, "American Power in a New World Economy," 402.

51. Williams Commission, *U.S. International,* Compendium, 620–21, 681, list on 683–700. History of review of NTBs, 683, 718. Nixon understood that because of the constitutional separation of powers between the federal government and the lack of an adequate role for the federal government in product standardization, he could not act.

52. *The Trade Act of 1969*, H.R. 14870, 91st Cong., 1st sess., 1969 and *The Trade Act of 1970*, H.R. 18970, 91st Cong., 2d sess., 1970.

53. Williams Commission, *United States International*, Compendium, iii, list of members on v–vi. There were no members from civic, human rights, or environmental groups. The commission heard from Congress, foreign governments, trade associations and business, and academics, and foreign officials, ix–x.

54. Williams Commission, *United States International*," 2–3.

55. Williams Commission, *United States International*, 720–21.

56. Williams Commission, *United States International*, 682–83, 717.

57. Ibid., 682–99; 716–19.

58. Williams Commission, *United States International* 12–15, 138–139.

59. I take this clever term from Pietro S. Nivola, ed., *Comparative Disadvantages? Social Regulations and the Global Economy* (Washington: Brookings Institution, 1997).

60. Williams Commission, *United States International*, Compendium, 65. Commission members did not include minimum wages as a core labor standard because they believed such wages should be determined by local economic conditions, not international rules.

61. Matusow, *Nixon's Economy*, 117, 306–8; Council of Economic Advisors, *Economic Report 1997*, table B-101, on 414; and Calleo, "American Power," 419–21.

62. Hughes, *Trade, Taxes*, 2–3.

63. Hughes, *Trade, Taxes*, 30–31. Interview with Kent Hughes, February 13, 1998. Hughes left Congress to head the Council on Competitiveness.

64. Vear, "Organized Labor and the Tariff," 3–5.

65. Hughes, *Trade, Taxes*, 21–23.

66. Some Americans have long labeled our trading partners as unfair, but this seemed to become more common after the 1970s. Hughes, *Trade, Taxes*, 32–33.

67. Hughes, *Trade, Taxes*, 161.

68. Matusow, *Nixon's Economy*, 219, 221; and Calleo, "American Power in a New World Economy," 425–28.

69. Matusow, *Nixon's Economy*, 217–18.

70. For a good overview of food policy as foreign economic policy (and on this issue), see I. M. Destler, *Making Foreign Economic Policy* (Washington: Brookings Institution, 1980), 19–35.

71. Committee on Ways and Means, *Hearings on H.R. 6767, The Trade Reform Act of 1973*, 93rd Cong., 1st sess., part 1, 9 May 15–June 1973, 5. United States Trade Representative Bill Eberle in Congressional testimony on this authority, 346, 351; Statement of Frederick W. Hickman, assistant secretary for Tax Policy, Treasury Department, 498–99.

72. Jonathan Schell, "Watergate," in Chafe and Sitkoff, eds., *A History of Our Time*, 419–38.

73. Hughes, *Trade, Taxes*, 12–13, fn. 12.

74. Destler, *Making Foreign*, 165.

75. Ways and Means, *Hearings on H.R. 6767*, Congressman Collier, 392–93.

76. Ways and Means, *Hearings on H.R. 6767*, 352–53. Ambassador Pearce's comments on 395. Also see summary of government officials comments on the basic authority, 5175–76. Administration officials were well aware of the congressional implications of negotiating NTBs. See W. B. Kelly Jr., 9 May 1969, 3–10, in D-4/69, Box 5 in RG 364.

77. Ways and Means, *Hearings on H.R. 6767*, 327–31, 5176–77.

78. Ways and Means, *Hearings on H.R. 6767*, 713; summary of Congressional views on granting such authority, 5176–77; remarks of Congressman Frelinghuysen, 5054–55;

discussion with Congressman Burke, 5058–5061. Also see statement of Congressman Thomas M. Rees, 5109.

79. Groups expressing concern included the American Importers Association, the United Auto Workers, and the Committee for National Trade Policy (a coalition of business supporters of trade). Ways and Means, *Hearings on H.R. 6767*, 765 (testimony of American Importers Association); UAW concern, 851, 875; and Committee for a National Trade Policy, 792.

80. Ways and Means, *Hearings on H.R. 6767*, remarks of Chairman Ullman, 446–48.

81. Ways and Means, *Hearings on H.R. 6767*, Congressman Corman to Secretary Dent, 588, 326–31.

82. Ways and Means, *Hearings on H.R. 6767*, 756–59.

83. Ways and Means, *Hearings on H.R. 6767*, 763.

84. Ibid., 4281.

85. Ways and Means, *Hearing on H.R. 6767*, 557–58.

86. Ibid., 1181; Congressman Wagner, 655.

87. Mr. Jones, however, dismissed U.S. health and safety standards as protectionist. Ibid., 2813–15; and on wine grapes, 3046.

88. Ways and Means, *Hearings on H.R. 6767*, Congressman Duncan, 641–42; UAW testimony, 873–74; International Leather Goods . . . , 4779, 5301; Union of Dolls, Toys . . . , 4789–01; also see remarks of Lazare Teper, research director, International Ladies' Garment Workers' Union, and Congressman Claude Pepper, 4955.

89. Ibid., 1416; Catholic Conference, 1531. Interestingly the UAW only wanted temporary quotas for cars. This union was an internationalist union with many Canadian members as well as members from the export-oriented aircraft industry. Thus, it stayed supportive of trade longer than, for example, the AFL-CIO.

90. Ibid., 3879–81.

91. Ibid., 1210, 1215.

92. Ways and Means, *Hearings on H.R. 6767*, 849.

93. The League of Women Voters urged that the interests of consumers be given serious consideration when national trade policy is discussed. Ways and Means, *Hearings on H.R. 6767*, 370, 461, 2997 and 5305; comments of Robert B. Schwenger (a former trade negotiator) 4468–89; V. J. Adduci, president, Electronic Industries Association, 3268; Mr. Graubard, 1092; National Council of Jewish Women, Inc., 2954. For a good summary of opinion of witnesses see on the authority, 5177–93. On attitudes toward NTB negotiations, see 5193–5204.

94. Ways and Means, *Hearings on H.R. 6767*, view of Emergency Committee for Foreign Trade, 660, 668.

95. Glennon et al., *United States Foreign Relations Law*, 40–45.

96. Ways and Means, *Brief Summary of H.R. 10710: The "Trade Reform Act of 1973," A Report to the House on October 10, 1973* (Washington: GPO, 1973), 55.

97. Hughes, *Trade, Taxes*, 164–65.

98. Glennon et al., *United State Foreign Relations Law*, 45–49; and Memorandum to the Honorable Herman E. Talmadge from Finance Committee Staff, June 5, 1974, 64–65.

99. Press release, "Finance Committee Continues Action on Trade Reform Bill," Section 102, 1.c in Glennon et al., *United States Foreign Relations Law*, 91.

100. Committee on Finance, U.S. Senate, *Hearings on H.R. 10710: An Act to Promote the Development of an Open Nondiscriminatory and Fair World Economic System to Stim-*

ulate the Economic Growth of the United States and for Other Purposes (Washington: GPO, 1974); on Glass Workers, 2349; on steel, 1093.

101. Ibid., Senator Hartke, 1099–1101.

102. Committee on Finance, *Hearings on H.R. 10710,* 1330–31; can't move to new high-tech jobs, 1899; can't all be astronauts, 1923.

103. Ibid., 2878.

104. Ibid., 2356–57.

105. Ibid., Whitney, 2013–14; Cyanamid, 2348–49.

106. Ibid., Mr. Collins, 1692–93.

107. Ways and Means, *Hearings on H.R. 6767,* Donald M. Kendall, chair of Pepsico, 690.

108. Stern, *Water's Edge,* 32, 133, 177–79; and Destler, *Making Foreign* 189–90, fn. 63. Other vociferous supporters on the House side included the National Interreligious Task Force on Soviet Jewry, National Conference on Soviet Jewry, B'nai Brith, and the Union of Councils for Soviet Jews; see Ways and Means, *Hearings on H.R. 6767,* 5304–7; for Congressional support, see 4955–5013, 5145.

The Jackson-Vanik Amendment, Section 401 of Title IV of the Trade Act of 1974, as amended (PL 93–618), governs trade with nonmarket economies. It was designed to assure the continued dedication of the United States to fundamental human rights.

109. Committee on Finance, *Hearings on H.R. 10710,* Stanley Lubman, 2585; link most favored nation (MFN) privileges to environment 2649–59. "Most favored nation" privileges are normal trade privileges. They apply to all of America's trading partners, except terrorist/communist nations.

110. See Senate Finance Committee, "Congressional Votes on International Trade Bills," provided by Debbie Lamb, Chief Minority Trade Counsel; in possession of author, 1998. The House voted 319–80 to include the entire Jackson-Vanik amendment in the trade bill, which then passed the House by 272–140.

111. ITC, *Operation of the Trade Agreements Program, 37th Report,* 76.

Chapter 4

1. Bob Secter and James Risen, "Postwar Admiration of U.S. Fading in Japan, Jobless Americans Slow to Blame Tokyo," *Los Angeles Times,* 26 April 1987, 1; Editorial, "Japan-Bashers, On the March," *New York Times* 4 April 1984, 30. McNeil-Lehrer News Hour transcript of 7 April 1992.

2. John M. Culbertson, "Free Trade Harms the U.S.," in *Trade: Opposing Viewpoints,* ed. William Dudley (San Diego: Greenhaven, 1991), 60–61. Culbertson was a professor at the University of Wisconsin, Madison. This wonderful book is a compilation of the debates in the 1980s and early 1990s. Summary of views, 13–14, Representatives James H. Quillen, and nationalist William H. Gill, 69. For more moderate or left views about trade, see former Representative Don Bonker, "The U.S. Is the Victim of Unfair Trade Practices," and Senator Daniel Patrick Moynihan, "The U.S. Should Retaliate Against Unfair Trade Partners," in ibid., 71–77, 102–5. Also see Gerald W. Sazama, "Free Trade vs. Protectionism" *Christianity and Crisis,* 4 April 1988.

3. According to the national director of the Japanese-American Citizens League, Dennis Hayashi, "Products associated with Japan, and by association, Japanese people . . . are becoming the enemy." McNeil Lehrer transcript of 7 April 1992. In 1989, a joint CBS News/CNN report found some 46 percent of 1,601 voters polled by telephone thought Japan posed a serious threat to the United States position in international trade.

Taiwan and West Germany were next at 12 percent. Accession 0016511, 8 April 1989, Public Opinion Online.

4. Joan E. Twiggs, *The Tokyo Round of Multilateral Trade Negotiations: A Case Study in Building Domestic Support for Diplomacy* (Lanham, MD: University Press, 1987), 3.

5. AFL-CIO, "The Trade Deficit Creates Massive Unemployment," in *Trade: Opposing Viewpoints,* ed. Dudley, 188–195. During this period, unemployment ranged from 6.3 percent in 1980 to a high of 10.4 percent in 1982 to less than 5 percent in 1988, rising again in 1992 to 7.3 percent. Council of Economic Advisors, *Economic Report of the President 1993* (Washington: GPO, 1993), 43; and Bennet Harrison and Barry Bluestone, *The Great U-Turn: Corporate Restructuring and the Polarizing of America* (New York: Basic Books, 1988), 21–52.

6. See fn.2, Culbertson, "Free Trade," 60–61 for quotation.

7. Mary Beth Norton et al., *A People and a Nation* (Boston: Houghton Mifflin, 1994), 978–79.

8. Polling data throughout the 1970s and 1980s revealed that Americans were increasingly pessimistic about their economic future. See George H. Gallup, *The Gallup Poll: Public Opinion 1972–1977* (Wilmington: Scholarly Resources, 1978), 81, 621. On the 1980s, see John Immerwahr et al., *Cross-Talk.*

9. Director General of GATT, *The Tokyo Round of Multilateral Trade Negotiations* (Geneva: GATT, 1979), 1.

10. Director General of the GATT, *The Tokyo Round,* 29, 64–68. In Europe, regulatory bodies are not as powerful or as respected. Michael Spector, "Europe, Bucking Trend in U.S. Blocks Genetically Altered Food," *New York Times,* 20 July 1998, A1.

11. Glennon et al., *U.S. Foreign Relations Law,* 160–61, n. 2. According to a study of the procedures and legal documentation by Glennon et al., the only information made available to the public during the negotiations was contained in Ways and Means Committee prints that did not get widely circulated. Members of Congress did occasionally speak with the advisory committees, but there was no direct public debate during the negotiations about these codes.

12. The records of the Tokyo Round Negotiations have not yet been fully declassified and made available to researchers. On lack of environmental interest and quote from Standards Code, see Vogel, *Trading Up,* 99.

13. Committee on Finance, "Press Release," 2 May 1979 in Glennon et al., *U.S. Foreign Relations Law,* 160–61, fn.2; and Committee on Finance, U.S. Senate, 8 May 1979, "Finance Committee Recommendations for Legislation," in Glennon et al., *U.S. Foreign Relations Law,* 478–79. The trade scholar I. M. Destler concluded that the NTB negotiations "proved remarkably smooth, a tribute to the innovative procedures provided for in section 151 of the Trade Act of 1974." See Destler, *Making Foreign Economic Policy,* 203.

14. Steve Dryden, *Trade Warriors* (New York: Oxford University Press, 1995), 246–47.

15. Memorandum to Senator Russell B. Long, Chair, Senate Committee on Finance from Trade Staff, 11 April 1978; and Charles A. Vanik, Chair, Subcommittee on Trade to Members of the Committee on Ways and Means, 10 May 1978, in Glennon et al., *U.S. Foreign Relations Law,* 166–67, 170–72, 182; Tom Graham to Richard Rivers of the Office of the Special Representative for Trade Negotiations, 26 June 1978, 180–83.

16. Subcommittee on International Trade, Senate Committee on Finance, *Hearings on S. 1376: A Bill to Improve and Implement the Trade Agreements Negotiated under the Trade Act of 1974, and for Other Purposes* (Washington: GPO, 1979), 10–11 July 1979, 579, 583 (Roberts). Also see 541–44.

17. Ibid., 604–5.

18. Ibid., 588–89.

19. Ibid., 186–90; 619–20.

20. *Hearings on S. 1376,* 633–35.

21. Destler, *Making Foreign Economic Policy,* 203.

22. United States International Trade Commission, *Operation of the Trade Agreements Program,* 37th report (Washington: GPO, 1986), 76.

23. Ibid., 77.

24. United States Trade Representative, *1987 National Trade Estimate Report on Foreign Trade Barriers* (Washington: GPO, 1987), 343–44 and 4. Also see GAO, "Current Issues in U.S. Participation in the Multilateral Trading System," GAO/NSIAD-85-118, 4, 29.

25. Lawrence Lindsey, *The Growth Experiment: How the New Tax Policy Is Transforming the U.S. Economy* (New York: Basic Books, 1990), 6–7.

26. David P. Calleo, "American Power in a New World Economy," in *Economics and World Power,* ed. Becker and Wells, 440–43.

27. However, some argue, I think persuasively, that Americans saved by investing in their homes.

28. Norton et al., *A People and a Nation,* 1035–36.

29. In 1995, when asked what caused the trade deficit, 46 percent blamed problems of our own making (high wages, restrictive U.S. government policies, inefficient management and labor practices), and 36 percent attributed the deficit to actions of other countries (lower wages, artificial barriers that kept our exports out, other unfair trading practices) making it difficult for the United States to compete internationally. Gallup Organization poll of 1,350 adults for Potomac Associates, funding provided by the Henry Luce Foundation, Accession Number 0148343 on Public Opinion Online.

30. Pat Choate and J. K. Linger, *The High Flex Society* (New York: Knopf, 1988), 4–5; quotation, 6.

31. Norton et al, *A People and a Nation,* 909–13.

32. John Williamson, "Introduction," in *Latin American Adjustment: How Much Has Happened?* ed. John Williamson (Washington: Institute for International Economics, 1990), 1–3, 14–15; and John Williamson, ed. *The Political Economy of Policy Reform* (Washington: Institute for International Economics, 1994), 3–7, 527–95. On the increase in imports after the Tokyo Round, see statistics on the trade deficit in table 103, U.S. international transactions, 1946–1998, Council of Economic Advisors, *Economic Report of the President, 1999* (Washington: GPO, 1999), 444.

33. Patrick J. Buchanan, foreword to John P. Cregan, *America Asleep: The Free Trade Syndrome and the Global Economic Challenge* (Washington: United States Industrial Council Education Foundation, 1991), xi.

34. John P. Cregan, "The Free Trade Syndrome and America's Economic Disarmament," in Cregan, *America Asleep,* 28–31.

35. Cregan, "Free Trade Syndrome," 31. To Cregan, "a government role does not mean or imply a major new federal intervention in the domestic economy." However, Pat Buchanan thought because the government imposes wage and hour laws and tough environmental standards, the government should also provide protection. See Pat Buchanan, foreword to Cregan, *America Asleep,* xi. Also see William Gill, *Trade Wars Against America* (New York: Praeger, 1990), 281.

36. Alfred E. Eckes, "A Republican Trade Policy: Reviving the Grand Old Paradigm," in Cregan, *America Asleep,* 86–87.

37. Anthony Harrigan, "U.S. Trade Policy: A Tragedy of Errors," in Cregan, *America Asleep,* 169, 179.

38. These books included Chalmers Johnson, *MITI and the Japanese Miracle: The Growth of Industrial Policy, 1925–1975* (Stanford: Stanford University Press, 1982); and Karel Von Wolferen, *The Enigma of Japanese Power: People and Politics in a Stateless Nation* (London: Macmillan, 1989). For an insightful, albeit smug, critique of these books, see Brink Lindsey and Aaron Lukas, "Revisiting the 'Revisionists': The Rise and Fall of the Japanese Economic Model," *CATO Trade Policy Analysis*, 3 July 1998, no. 3.

39. Clyde V. Prestowitz Jr., *Trading Places: How We Allowed Japan to Take the Lead* (New York: Basic Books, 1988). Also see, Ronald Dore, *Taking Japan Seriously: A Confucian Perspective on Leading Economic Issues* (Stanford: Stanford University Press, 1987); Thomas K. McCraw, ed., *America vs. Japan* (Boston: Harvard Business School Press, 1986); James C. Abegglen and George Stalk Jr., *Kaisha: The Japanese Corporation* (New York: Basic Books, 1985).

40. James Fallows, *More Like Us: Making America Great Again* (New York: Houghton Mifflin, 1988), 5, 11, 208–10.

41. Mancur Olson, *The Rise and Decline of Nations: Economic Growth, Stagflation and Social Rigidities* (New Haven: Yale University Press, 1982).

42. Choate and Linger, *The High-Flex Society,* 63–64.

43. Council on Competitiveness, *Roadmap for Results: Trade Policy, Technology, and American Competitiveness* (Washington: Council on Competitiveness, 1993), 1.

44. Jadish Bhagwati, *The World Trading System at Risk* (Princeton: Princeton University Press, 1991), 46.

45. Kevin Phillips, *Arrogant Capital: Washington, Wall Street and the Frustration of American Politics* (Boston: Little, Brown, 1994); Robert B. Reich, *The Work of Nations: Preparing Ourselves for 21st Century Capitalism* (New York: Vintage, 1992); and Alan Tonelson, "Beyond Left and Right," *National Interest* 10, no. 34 (winter 1993/1994).

46. Alan Tonelson, "Beating Back Predatory Trade," *Foreign Affairs* (July/August 1994): 60–61; and Alan Tonelson, interview, 6 August 1998.

47. James Brander and Barbara Spencer, "Export Subsidies and International Market Share Rivalry," *Journal of International Economics* 18, no. 1–2 (February 1985): 85–100.

48. Paul R. Krugman, ed., *Strategic Trade Policy and the New International Economics* (Cambridge: MIT Press, 1986).

49. Laura D'Andrea Tyson, *Who's Bashing Whom: Trade Conflict in High Technology Industries* (Washington: Institute for International Economics, 1992), 3–4, 116.

50. On the uproar over strategic trade, see Eyal Press, "The Free Trade Faith: Can We Trust the Economists?" *Lingua Franca* (January. 1998): 34–35. For a good sense of Krugman's repudiation of his earlier views, see Paul Krugman, *Pop Internationalism* (Cambridge: MIT Press, 1996) and *Peddling Prosperity: Economic Sense and Nonsense in the Age of Diminished Expectations* (New York: Norton, 1994).

51. Committee on Finance, United States Senate, *Report: Omnibus Trade Act of 1987,* 100th Cong., 1st sess., 12 June 1987, 268–69.

52. William R. Cline, ed., *Trade Policy in the 1980s* (Washington: Institute for International Economics, 1983), 7–8. Carter had provided reference pricing for steel to determine if the Japanese were dumping steel.

53. Susan Schwab, *Trade-Offs: Negotiating the Omnibus Trade and Competitiveness Act of 1988* (Boston: Harvard Business School Press, 1994), 54–56; and I. M. Destler, John S. Odell, and Kimberly Ann Elliot, *Anti-Protection: Changing Forces in United States Trade Politics* (Washington: Institute for International Economics, 1987), 28–31, 35–59.

54. Council of Economic Advisors, *Economic Report of the President, 1999*, 444. For trade deficit as a percentage of GDP, see Council of Economic Advisors, *Economic Report of the President, 1996* (Washington: GPO, 1996), chart 8–3, 252.

55. Ibid., 84–87.

56. Destler, *American Trade Politics*, 76, 80–83, nn. 23, 24.

57. John H. Jackson, "GATT and the Tokyo Round Agreements," in *Trade Policy in the 1980s*, 184–85.

58. Office of the United States Trade Representative, *1987 National Trade Estimate Report on Foreign Trade Barriers* (Washington: U.S. GPO, 1987), 1–2, 344. The report summarized Reagan administration concerns about the Standards Code. "Several Standards Code provisions could be improved to enhance its functioning and make it more advantageous to U.S. exporters. In particular, code coverage of approval procedures, 'processes and production methods' test data and dispute settlement could be strengthened. The code does not simplify the procedures used to approve products. Nor does it set rules for accepting test data generated in one signatory nation by regulatory authorities in another."

59. Destler, *Making Foreign Economic Policy*, 203.

60. Brock was quoted in the *Wall Street Journal* on 5 January 1982, cited in Bergsten and Cline, "Overview," 60; and Cline, "Introduction and Summary," both in Cline, ed., *Trade Policy in the 1980s*, 8–9.

61. Bergsten and Cline, "Overview," 87; C. Fred Bergsten and John Williamson, "Exchange Rates and Trade Policy," 113–15; and William R. Cline, "Reciprocity: A New Approach to World Trade Policy?" all in William R. Cline, *Trade Policy in the 1980s*, 121. Also Ray Ahearn, Congressional Research Service, interview, 29 July 1998.

62. According to Cline, critics of the new reciprocity saw it as thinly disguised protectionism, but sponsors saw it as an alternative to protection because it was designed to address exports rather than increase barriers to imports. Cline, "Reciprocity," 121–22.

63. Cline, "Reciprocity," 153–56.

64. John H. Jackson, "GATT and the Tokyo Round Agreements," in *Trade Policy*, ed. Cline, 162.

65. Destler, *American Trade Politics*, 88.

66. Roper poll in August 1983, Accession no. 0123277 from Public Opinion Online. In a similar poll in August 1981, Japan again was number one at 42 percent. See Accession no. 0120879 by Roper of some two thousand adults in August 1981. Also see Yankelovich, Clancy, Shulman Poll, 6 April 1987, in author's files.

67. Daniel Yankelovich, "Foreign Policy After the Election," *Foreign Affairs* (fall 1992): 2–12.

68. Public Agenda Foundation, "Cross-Talk," 18–19; and Rosita Thomas, "Public Opinion on Trade," *CRS Review* (February/ March 1992): 17. Thomas cites a *New York Times* /CBS News poll of June 1991 and a CBS News/Tokyo Broadcasting News poll of May 1988. Also see Michele Galen and Mark N. Vamous, "Portrait of an Anxious Public," *Business Week*, 13 March 1995, 80.

69. United States International Trade Commission, *Operation of the Trade Agreements Program*, 37th report (Washington: GPO, 1986), 9–15, esp. 11.

70. On public opinion on trade, see *L.A. Times* telephone poll 2 February 1984 of 1,021 registered voters, by Yankelovich, Skelly, and White, Accession no. 0080028, Public Opinion Online. In 1984, voters were asked how important trade was to their decision to support a particular candidate; 53 percent ranked trade as a lot of influence. In

1983, 42 percent ranked trade as very influential. Accession no. 0136335; 1,000 registered voters polled in December 1983 by Time Yankelovich.

71. According to Kent Hughes, who went on to lead the Council on Competitiveness, Reagan was no great supporter of competitiveness. He did not want the government intervention he thought it implied. Kent Hughes, interview, 3 August 1998.

72. For example, President Nixon asked the International Trade Commission to examine the impact of imports on the competitiveness of various U.S. sectors. Draft letter, R. M. Nixon to Glenn W. Sutton, 30 June 1970, box 4/ M/6/70; RG 364.1

73. Ways and Means, *Hearings on H.R. 6767,* Congressman Casey, "[For] competitiveness in steel, textile, manufacture . . . [w]e will have to look more to high technology," 536. Also interview, Hughes.

74. Subcommittee on International Trade, Senate Committee on Finance *Hearings on S. 1356, The Trade Agreements Act of 1979,* 10–11 July 1979, 155.

75. In this period, some scholars of business brought competitiveness to the fore. Among the most influential was Michael Porter of the Harvard Business School. See President's Commission on Industrial Competitiveness, *Global Competition: The New Reality,* vol. II (Washington: GPO, 1985), 6, 8, 9.

76. This is my observation. Economist Paul Krugman thought this focus was misguided. Paul Krugman, "Competitiveness: A Dangerous Obsession," *Foreign Affairs* 73 (March/April 1994): 28–30.

77. Executive Order 12428, 28 June 1983, in President's Commission, *Global Competition,* vol II, 245 and Statement by the President, 4 August 1983, 248.

78. President's Commission, *Global Competition,* 6, 8, 9.

79. President's Commission, *Global Competition,* 6–8.

80. Think tanks' or study groups' studies on these issues include: The Business Higher Education Forum, *America's Competitive Challenge: The Need for a National Response* (1983) and The Heritage Foundation, *A Blueprint for Jobs and Industrial Growth* (1983). Academic studies include Robert Z. Lawrence, *Can America Compete?* (Washington: Brookings Institution, 1984) and Bruce R. Scott and George C. Lodge, eds., *U.S. Competitiveness in the World Economy* (Cambridge: Harvard Business School Press, 1985). Business group studies include: The Business Roundtable, "Strategy for a Vital U.S. Economy" (1984); Labor-Industry Coalition for International Trade, "International Trade, Industrial Policies, an Future of American Industry" (1983); National Association of Manufacturers, "Agenda for Regaining America's Initiative" (1983). Congressional studies include: Congressional Budget Office, "The Productivity Problem: Alternatives for Action" (1981) and House Republican Research Committee, "An Agenda for Regaining America's Initiative" (1983). Labor studies include: AFL-CIO, Industrial Union Department, "Deindustrialization and a Two-Tier Society" (1984). See President's Commission, *Global Competition,* 52–53. Sixty percent of these reports noted that government regulations hinder competitiveness.

81. President's Commission, *Global Competition,* list of commission members, vii–viii; tasks, x–xii.

82. Ibid., 27.

83. Ibid., 182.

84. Ibid., 259–60.

85. President's Commission, *Global Competition,* 279. It quoted studies by the Advisory Committee on Industrial Innovation, U.S. Department of Commerce *Final Report* (1979) and H. G. Grabowski and J. M. Vernon, *The Impact of Regulation on Industrial In-*

novation, (Washington: National Academy of Sciences, 1979). Also see Business-Higher Education Forum, *A Statement on Federal Regulatory Reform*, February 1981, 14.

86. President's Commission, *Global Competition*, 280, n. 6, 294. The commission cited one source for this consensus: American Council on Education, Business-Higher Education Forum, *A Statement on Federal Regulatory Reform*, February 1981.

87. President's Commission, *Global Competition*, 281–83.

88. Ibid., 285–86. The commission cited studies by the consulting groups Arthur D. Little (1978) and ICF (1980), the Chemical Manufacturers Association and the Chemical Specialties Manufacturing Association, 294–95. It noted that R&D budgets are directed at environmental and health activity instead of actual innovation, 285.

89. Ibid., 286–87, 289.

90. Ibid., 291–93.

91. See Council on Competitiveness, Policy Statement, "Restoring America's Trade Position," April 1987, 12. It listed guiding principles including principle 9: "Regulatory policies should be changed to reflect the new global markets within which U.S. firms operate." Also see the Business Roundtable, "American Excellence in a World Economy: Summary of the Report," *The Business Roundtable*, 15 June 1987, 8–10. "Public Laws and policies should . . . reflecting the realities of global competition, and avoid mandating benefits and actions that increase business costs. . . . Foreign competitors often do not face the same obstacles. A major objective in the Uruguay Round should be the elimination of non-tariff barrier agreements made outside the GATT framework. . . . [The United States should have as a negotiating goals] improved standards."

92. Susan Ariel Aaronson, "Competitiveness Study for LTV Corporation," 20 May 1987, 18–19. I did this study as a consultant to LTV.

93. Ibid., 26.

94. Aaronson, *Are There Trade-offs?* 48; and Maude Barlow and Bruce Campbell, *Take Back the Nation 2* (Toronto: Key Porter, 1991), 9.

95. House of Representatives, *Report: Trade and International Economic Policy Reform Act of 1987* Report 100–40, part 5, 100 Cong., 2d sess., 6 April 1987, 70.

96. For a short time in the 1980s, competitiveness seemed also to become a rubric for totally revamping governance. Some Americans joked that competitiveness became an excuse for changing a wide range of policies that were totally unrelated to trade such as entitlement reform (entitlements include government programs such as social security or welfare). Interview with Nancy Dunne, correspondent, *Financial Times*, 3 August 1998.

97. *The Spotlight* is on the Web at www.spotlight.org/html/order.

98. Norman J. Vig, "The President and the Environment," in *Environmental Policy in the 1980s*, ed. Vig and Kraft, 88–89. This process was designed to slow agency rule making. On the explosion of public interest and consumer lobbyists in opposition to Reagan administration policies, see Destler et al., *Antiprotection*, 28–29, fnn. 8–9.

99. Lynton K. Caldwell, "The World Environment," in *Environmental Policy in the 1980s*, ed. Vig and Kraft, 319–21, 323–24. Reagan rescinded Carter's Exec. Order 12264 on 17 February 1981, shortly after taking office.

100. Maurice Strong of the United Nations remarked that in a reverse of history, the nation that had led global environment cooperation now "suspected that global environmental proposals were surreptitious attempts to thwart the growth of the American economy." See Caldwell, "The World Environment," 332, 335, fn. 32.

101. Herman Daly and John Cobb Jr., "International Free Trade Exploits Poor Nations," in *Trade: Opposing Viewpoints*, ed. Dudley, 42. Cobb is professor emeritus at

Claremont School of Theology; Daly is an economist formally with the World Bank, now at the University of Maryland.

102. These groups helped force the multilateral development banks to weigh environmental issues in their debt plans. They began to get clout on Capitol Hill in the 1990s. See letter, Senator Robert W. Kasten to Carla A. Hills, 31 July 1990, in author's possession. On views of the left toward the Bretton Woods Institutions, see Herman E. Daly, "From Adjustment to Sustainable Development: The Obstacle of Free Trade," in Nader et al., *The Case Against Free Trade* 121–32. Also see Walden Bello, "Structural Adjustment Programs: 'Success' for Whom?" 285–96; and Carlos Heredia and Mary Purcell, 'Structural Adjustment and the Polarization of Mexican Society," 273–84, both in Mander and Goldsmith, eds., *The Case Against the Global Economy.*

103. Michael Lind, *The Next American Nation: The New Nationalism and the Fourth American Revolution* (New York: Free Press, 1995); Christopher Lasch, *The Revolt of the Elites and the Betrayal of Democracy* (New York: Norton, 1994); Michael Lind, "Spheres of Affluence," *American Prospect* (winter 1994): 91–99; and Joel Kotkin, "Nativists on the Left," *Wall Street Journal,* 25 July 1995, A12.

104. Ralph Nader, "GATT Could Get Us," *The National Forum,* 16–22 July 1990.

105. Robert Schaeffer, "Environmental Concerns Should Restrict Trade," in *Trade: Opposing Viewpoints,* ed. Dudley, 155–61.

106. Wendell Berry, "A Bad Big Idea," 229–30; Margaret Atwood, 92–97; and Jorge Castañeda, 78–91; in *The Case Against Free Trade*; Walter Russell Mead, "Bushism Found," *Harpers* 285 (September 1992): 37–45; Aaronson, *Trade and the American Dream,* 136–40, 227.

107. See interview with Kate Gilmore, Amnesty International Australia, 16 June 1997; interview with Mark Ritchie, President, Institute for Agriculture and Trade Policy (IATP), 17 April 1996; interview with James Cameron, FIELD(England), 24 September 1998; and interview with Kevin Watkins, Oxfam, England, 24 September 1998.

108. Patrick D. Chisholm, "Chalk Up One for Protectionists," *Wall Street Journal,* 22 November 1995, A10.

Chapter 5

1. According to Marc Gold and David Leyton Brown of Canada's York University, "The history of Canada-U.S. relations has been a succession of cautious moves toward free trade followed by the retreat from the brink." Marc Gold and David Leyton-Brown, eds., *Trade-Offs on Free Trade: The Canada-U.S. Free Trade Agreement* (Toronto: Carswell, 1988), ix; and Dobson, *Two Centuries,* 71–72.

2. Judith H. Bello and Gilbert R. Winham, "The Canada-USA Free Trade Agreement," in *Negotiating and Implementing a North American Free Trade Agreement,* ed. Leonard Waverman (Toronto: Fraser Institute, 1992), 55–57; and Steven Shrybman, Canadian Environmental Law Association (CELA), interview, 21 August 1998. On fears of U.S. protectionism, see Andrew Jackson and Bob Baldwin, "Lessons of Free Trade: A View from Canadian Labour," n.d., 13.

3. The Job Loss Register compiled by the Canadian Labour Congress in 1989 and 1990 documented "literally hundreds of examples of U.S. and Canadian companies shifting all or part of their manufacturing operations to the U.S." They also documented greater Canadian investment in the United States than U.S. investment in Canada. "Fast Facts, Let's Make Canada Work for People, Trade Ties with the United States," Canadian Centre for Policy Alternatives, 3, 5, 7. Also see submission by the Canadian Labour Congress on the North American Free Trade Agreement to the Sub-Committee on In-

ternational Trade of the Standing Committee on External Affairs and International Trade, Canadian Parliament, 26 January 1993, 3. Copy in possession of the author.

4. According to Andrew Jackson and Bob Baldwin, Canadian Labor Federation economists, "Most Canadians have taken pride in the fact that we have had a more generous welfare state and better developed set of public services than in the U.S. and thus a more equal and decent society." Jackson and Baldwin, "Lessons of Free Trade," 3, 7.

5. Steven Shrybman, "Selling Canada's Environment Short: The Environmental Case Against the Trade Deal," 1988, 16; and Vogel, *Trading Up*, 219.

6. Canada has a more decentralized approach to environmental regulation than the U.S. federalized approach, while its provinces have greater discretion than the U.S. states. See Marc Landy and Loren Cass, "U.S. Environmental Regulation in a Competitive World," in *Comparative Disadvantages? Social Regulations and the Global Economy*, ed. Pietro S. Nivola (Washington: Brookings Institution, 1997), 237.

7. Bello and Winham, "The Canada-USA Free Trade Agreement," 1, 53–59; and Donna Dasko, "Canadian Public Opinion: Sources of Support and Dissent," in *The Free Trade Papers*, ed. Duncan Cameron (Toronto: Lorimer, 1986), 27–28.

8. See www.canadians.org for a description of the Council of Canadians. The council remains influential some ten years later because it also works to safeguard Canada's social programs and advance "alternatives to corporate-style free trade." It works closely with Public Citizen in the United States.

9. According to a very thorough study of Canadian views of trade, this comic book became the movement's most successful educative piece. The booklet was designed as a counterweight to the government's $30 million campaign to promote the trade agreement. It educated the public and was accessible to people below university reading levels. Some 2.2 million copies were distributed. Jeffrey M. Ayres, *Defying Conventional Wisdom: Political Movements and Popular Contention against North American Free Trade* (Toronto: University of Toronto Press, 1998), 94–95. Also see Murray G. Smith, "Dealing with Nontariff Barriers," in *Negotiating and Implementing a North American Free Trade Agreement*, ed. Leonard Waverman, 138–39.

10. Maude Barlow and Heather Jane Robertson, "Homogenization of Education," in *The Case Against the Global Economy*, ed. Mander and Goldsmith, 60–70.

11. See, for example, George Hoberg, "Sleeping with an Elephant,: The American Influence on Canadian Environmental Regulation," *Journal of Public Policy* 1, no. 2 (January/March 1991): 107–32, esp. 108; Peter A. Cumming, "Impact of the FTA in Public Policy," 426, 433; and Donald Smiley, "A Note on Canadian-American Free Trade and Canadian Policy Autonomy," 442–45; both in *Trade-Offs*, ed. Gold et al. On how the FTA will lead to challenging the Canadian social compact, see Malcolm Lester, "Free Trade and Canadian Book Publishing," in *Trade-Offs*, 368.

12. Marjorie Cohen, "Women and Free Trade," in *The Free Trade Papers*, ed. Cameron, 144–45.

13. Alan M. Rugman, "Multinationals and the Free Trade Agreement," 4–12, and Richard G. Lipsey, "The Free Trade Agreement in Context," in *Trade-Offs*, 67, 74.

14. Jackson and Baldwin, "Lessons of Free Trade," 13.

15. Tony Clarke, "Mechanisms of Corporate Rule," in *The Case Against the Global Economy*, ed. Mander and Goldsmith, 298–300, 307–8. On seeing GATT and NAFTA as two of a kind, see Steven Shrybman, CELA, interview, 22 August 1998; Daniel Schwanen, Senior Policy Analyst, C. D. Howe Institute, interview, 9 June 1997; Bruce Campbell, Canadian Centre for Policy Alternatives, interview, 16 September 1998; and Steven Shrybman, "International Trade and the Environment," October 1989.

16. Margaret Atwood, "Blind Faith and Free Trade," in *The Case Against Free Trade,* ed. Ralph Nader et al., 92–96, originally published in *The Ottawa Citizen.*

17. Craig Macinnes, "Trade Deal Will Render Canada a Colony of U.S., Nader Warns," *Toronto Globe and Mail,* 15 November 1988.

18. The Progressive Conservatives won 43 percent of the vote while the Liberals won 32 percent of the vote and the NDP got 20 percent. Although the opposition Liberals and NDP won a total 52 percent of the vote, this did not translate into a majority antitrade agreement vote. Ayres, *Defying Conventional Wisdom,* 114–15.

19. Bruce Campbell, Canadian Centre for Policy Alternatives, interview, 16 September 1998; and U.S. House Committee on Ways and Means and Subcommittee on Trade, *North American Free-Trade Agreement (NAFTA) and Supplemental Agreements to the NAFTA,* 103rd Cong., 1st sess., 14–23 September 1993, 256.

20. The FTA became U.S. law as PL 100–449, on 28 September 1988. Vote count from Debbie Lamb, Senate Finance Committee. Also see Vogel, *Trading Up,* 219–21.

21. Steven Shrybman, counsel to CELA, interview, 22 August, 1998, and Mark Ritchie, IATP, interview, 23 March 1998.

22. Esty, *Greening the GATT,* 10, 183–84: and Mark Ritchie, IATP, interview 23 March 1998.

23. Bruce Michael Bagley, "U.S. Policy Toward Mexico," in *Mexico and the United States: Managing the Relationship,* ed. Riordan Roett (Boulder: Westview, 1988), 224.

24. Committee on Finance, "Press Release," 2 May 1979 in Glennon et al., *Making Foreign Policies,* 478–79.

25. Bagley, "U.S. Policy," 224.

26. Jeffrey J. Schott and Gary Clyde Hufbauer, "NAFTA: Questions of Form and Substance," in *Negotiating and Implementing,* ed. Leonard Waverman, 61–63, 65.

27. The European Union had grown to include Portugal and Spain, but their living standards were much higher than Mexico's. However, their entry in the European Union was also controversial.

28. Robert A. Pastor, "NAFTA as the Center of an Integration Process: The Non-trade Issues," in *Assessing the Impact: North American Free Trade,* ed. Nora Lustig, Barry P. Bosworth, and Robert Z. Lawrence (Washington: Brookings Institution, 1992), 177. On the first trinational coalitions, see Ayres, *Defying Conventional Wisdom,* 124.

29. President George Bush, *Report to the Congress on the Extension of Fast Track Procedures, Pursuant to Section 1103 (b) of the Omnibus Trade and Competitiveness Act of 1988,* 1 March 1991, 16–24; and President George Bush, *Response of the Administration to Issues Raised in Connection with the Negotiation of a North American Free Trade Agreement,* 1 May 1991. Also see Destler, *American Trade Politics,* 99–103.

30. Lori Wallach and Tom Hilliard, "The Consumer and Environmental Case Against Fast Track," Public Citizen's Congress Watch, May 1991, 1.

31. William A. Orme Jr., *Briefing Book: Continental Shift: Free Trade and the New North America* (Washington: Washington Post, 1993), 55–63; and Destler, *American Trade Politics,* 99–103.

32. Orme, *Continental Shift,* 70–71.

33. Development Group for Alternative Policies (GAP), *Look Before You Leap: What You Should Know About a North American Free Trade Agreement* (Washington: Development GAP, 1991), 1. This group is an international not-for-profit development policy and resource organization.

34. Ibid., 1.

35. James D. Robinson II and Kay R. Whitmore, letter to Ambassador Carla Hills, 8 October 1991. Robinson, CEO of American Express, was the chair of the ACTPN; and Whitmore, CEO of Eastman Kodak, was the chair of the NAFTA Task Force.

36. President's Advisory Committee for Trade Policy and Negotiations (ACTPN), "Negotiating Objectives for a North American Free Trade Agreement," October 1991, 1–3, 5, 10–11, 15, 17.

37. Jack Sheinkman and Rudy Oswald, "Dissent from the ACTPN Report on Negotiating Objectives for a North American Free Trade Agreement," 2 October 1991.

38. The International Forum on Globalization Web page notes that Nader has repeatedly been rated in national polls as "the most respected person in America." www.peacenet.org/Teach-in/naderbio.

39. Lazarus, *Genteel Populists,* 151–52, and Aaronson, *Trade and the American Dream,* 77, 111, 174.

40. Lazarus, *Genteel Populists,* 151–52.

41. To understand changes in the consumer movement over time, see Yiannis Gabriel and Tim Lang, *The Unmanageable Consumer: Contemporary Consumption and Its Fragmentations* (London: Sage, 1995), 159–65.

42. Ibid., 159–62.

43. Lori Wallach, Public Citizen's Global Trade Watch, "Trade Implications of Congressional Action on U.S. Dolphin Protection Laws," testimony before the Senate Committee on Commerce, Science and Transportation, Subcommittee on Oceans and Fisheries, 30 April 1996, 2, in possession of the author.

44. Lori Wallach's notes accompanying Aaronson book draft, March 1999; interview with Lori Wallach, 2 July 1998; interview with Segundo Mercado Llorens, the United Food and Commercial Workers, 8 November 1997.

45. Wallach, "Trade Implications," 7.

46. Interviews with Lori Wallach, 2 July 1998 and 17 March 1995.

47. Lori Wallach's notes accompanying Aaronson book draft, March 1999; and interview with Lori Wallach 2 July 1998 .

48. Orme, *Continental Shift,* 113–14. However, twenty-three of the twenty-eight companies told GAO that direct payroll costs had led them to move south.

49. Ibid., 118–24.

50. Mark Ritchie, IATP, interview, 17 April 1996; and John Cavanagh, Sarah Anderson, and Karen Hansen Kuhn, "Tri-national Organizing for Just and Sustainable Trade and Development, Some Lessons and Insights," unpublished paper in possession of author, 2. Cavanagh and Anderson are affiliated with the Institute for Policy Studies, Hansen Kuhn is with the Development Gap.

51. "U.S.-Mexico Free Trade: Opening Up the Debate," A Public Forum on Agricultural, Environmental, and Labor Issues, 15 January 1991. The groups initiating the forum included the AFL-CIO, Child Labor Coalition, the Development GAP, Fair Trade Campaign, Institute for Policy Studies, National Consumers League, National Family Farm Coalition, and the United Methodist Board of Church and Society. Also Karen Hansen Kuhn, the Development GAP, interview, 3 August 1998.

52. International Forum, "Public Opinion and the Free Trade Negotiations—Citizen's Alternatives," Zacatecas, Mexico, 25–27 October 1991. The signatories were the Action Canada Network; the Mobilization for Development Trade, Labor and the Environment (USA); and the Mexican Action Network on Free Trade.

53. Mobilization on Development, Trade, Labor and the Environment (MODTLE), "Development and Trade Strategies for North America," October 1991; and Hansen Kuhn, interview.

54. *NAFTATHOUGHTS* 2, no.1 (Feb. 1992): 3 and *NAFTATHOUGHTS* 3, no.3 (July 1993): 2.

55. Brent Blackwelder, president, Friends of the Earth, interview, 3 September 1998; and Lori Wallach, interview, 2 July 1998. Also see Lori Wallach notes on Aaronson draft, March 1999; and *NAFTATHOUGHTS* 2, no. 1 (February 1992): 3.

56. *NAFTATHOUGHTS* 2, no. 1 (February 1992) and Nancy Dunne, "Pact Opponents Claim 'Secret' Negotiations," *Financial Times,* 5 February 1992. Lori Wallach, interview, 2 July 1998.

57. Interview with Brent Blackwelder, 3 September 1998.

58. Lori Wallach notes on Aaronson draft text, March 1999.

59. Lori Wallach's notes accompanying Aaronson book draft, March 1999; interview with Lori Wallach 2 July 1998; and interview with Karen Hansen Kuhn, Development Gap, 31 August 1998.

60. Lori Wallach notes on Aaronson draft text, March 1999.

61. Lynden Peter, "Congressman Chides NAFTA with New Trade Proposal," *NAFTATHOUGHTS* 2, no. 3 (July 1992): 7; Nancy Dunne, *Financial Times* interview, 30 September 1998; Ray Ahearn, Congressional Research Service, interview, 31 July 1998; and Bill Cooper, Congressional Research Service, interview, 31 July 1998.

62. Ken Traynor, "Common Frontiers," *Briarpatch* (September 1991): 45–46.

63. Orme, *Continental Shift,* 105–11; and Pastor, "NAFTA as the Center of an Integration Process," 180.

64. Keith Bradsher, "President and Congress Square Off on North American Trade Accord," *New York Times,* 9 August 1992; *NAFTATHOUGHTS* 2, no. 4 (October 1992): 1–2.

65. Thirteen environmental organizations published a report in June 1992 with recommendations on NAFTA. *NAFTATHOUGHTS* 2, no. 3 (July 1992): 6.

66. Keith Bradsher, "President and Congress Square Off on North American Trade Accord," *New York Times,* 9 August 1992; and *NAFTATHOUGHTS* 2, no. 4 (October 1992): 1–2.

67. "U.S. Citizen Groups Call for Recasting of North American Agreement in Broader, More Democratic Talks," in *NAFTATHOUGHTS* 2, no. 4 (October 1992): 3–5. The signatories included development, religious and farm groups, union groups, papers, policy organizations, unions, and an occupational safety and health center.

68. Steven Shrybman, Canadian Environmental Law Association, interview, 22 August 1998; and Mark Ritchie, interview, 23 March 1998. On Campbell's view, see *NAFTATHOUGHTS* 2, no. 1 (February 1992): 5.

69. Destler, *Renewing Fast-Track,* 7–8; and Destler, *American Trade Politics,* 224.

70. Audley, *Green Politics and Global Trade,* 76.

71. Audley, *Green Politics,* 70–71.

72. Destler, *American Trade Politics,* 220–21. Recent presidents had also not chosen experienced trade negotiators. Mr. Kantor refused to be interviewed for this book in 1997. Ellen Frost, interview, 30 September 1998. Dr. Frost served as Counselor to Ambassador Kantor during the first Clinton administration; she was responsible for policy development.

73. House Ways and Means, Subcommittee on Trade, *North American Free Trade Agreements: NAFTA and Supplemental Agreements to the NAFTA,* 103rd Cong., 1st sess., 14–23 August 1993, 348–68; and Audley, *Green Politics,* 89–91.

74. Ways and Means, *North American Free Trade,* 368.

75. They concluded that the side agreements did not specify a common set of minimum worker standards, establish an independent investigation or adjudication procedure, or establish true sanctions for firms that mistreated their workers. Bob White, Canadian Labor Congress, "NAFTA Side-Deal Changes Nothing for Workers," 25 August 1993, and Bruce Campbell, Canadian Center for Policy Alternatives, interview, 11 September 1998.

76. Bruce Campbell, Canadian Center for Policy Alternatives, interview, 11 September 1998.

77. Centro Interamericano de Investigaciones, A.C. and Mexican Institute of Social Studies, "Public Opinion in Mexico City," October 1992; and Robert Pastor, "NAFTA as the Center of an Integration Process," 190–99.

78. Jose Cordoba, "Mexico," in *The Political Economy of Policy Reform,* ed. John Williamson (Washington: Institute for International Economics, 1994), 264; polling data on 265.

79. Destler, *American Trade Politics,* 224–28; Audley, *Green Politics,* 72–74; Aaronson, *Trade and the American Dream,* 140–41; and Lori Wallach comments on Aaronson draft, March 1999.

80. Interview with Lori Wallach, 2 July 1998; and Cavanagh, Anderson, and Hansen Kuhn, "Tri-national Organizing," 21.

81. Richard Morin, "What Americans Think: Americans Speak Their Minds About Ross Perot," *Washington Post National Edition,* 8–14 June 1992, 37; Gallup Poll News Service, "Week in Review: Perot Ties Bush in Gallup Poll," 24 May 1992; Times Mirror Center for the People and the Press, "Campaign '92: Bush/Clinton/Perot: An Analysis of the Standings," 8 May 1992; Walter Shapiro, "President Perot?," *Time,* 25 May 1992, 27–43; and Tom Shales, "Perot's Paradox: He's Slippery, but Not Slick," *Washington Post,* 9 June 1992, E1, E9; and "Issues: Filling in the Blanks," *Newsweek,* 15 June 1992. An example of Perot's contradiction: on the economy Perot complained that "television wants everything complicated short. . . . [but] all of these things are so simple." He criticized the notion that money is the answer to education, but "if you have to spend more, spend more."

82. Tom Mathews, "President Perot?," *Newsweek,* 15 June 1992, 18.

83. Henry Muller and Richard Woodbury, "Working Folks Say. . ." *Time,* 25 May 1992, 36–43; and Thomas B. Edsall, "Disaffected White Male Viewed as Most Likely Backer of Perot," *Washington Post,* 3 June 1992, A15.

84. Keith Bradsher, "Free Trade Pact Is Still a Mystery to Many in the United States," *New York Times,* 12 July 1993, A1.

85. "Anxious Swing Voters," *U.S. News & World Report,* 8 June 1992, 22–26; Shales, "Perot's Paradox," and Mark Clements, "What Worries Voters Most," *Parade,* 3 May 1992, 4–6. *Parade* found that some 88 percent of voters surveyed said they were worried about maintaining their income or having enough cash.

86. Lee Walczak, "The New Populism," *Business Week,* 13 March 1995, 73–80.

87. Tonelson, "Beyond Left and Right," 17.

88. Ross Perot (with Pat Choate), *Save Your Job, Save Our Country: Why NAFTA Must Be Stopped—Now!* (New York: Hyperion for United We Stand America, 1993).

89. USTR, "Correcting the Record," 2 September 1993.

90. Audley, *Green Politics and Global Trade,* 101.

91. As an example of environmentalist discomfort with Perot, see remarks of Carl Pope, president, Sierra Club, in Ways and Means, "NAFTA and Supplemental Agree-

ments," 376. Mr. Pope said, "I do not agree with Mr. Perot on everything. I stand by our statements, not Mr. Perot's statements." Also see Audley, *Green Politics,* 101, 109, 111, fnn. 14, 15. Public Citizen wanted to brief Perot, but he did not accept their offer. According to Audley, Friends of the Earth issued a press release saying that Perot did not act as their spokesperson. Also see Aaronson, *Trade and the American Dream,* 141–42; and Destler, *American Trade,* 98–101, 222–28.

92. Aaronson, *Trade and the American Dream,* 141–42; and Walczak, "New Populism," 73.

93. See, for example, on the right, *The American Protectionist, A Monthly Newsletter Magazine about the Authentic American Economic System,* January 1996, 3–7; on the left, see Mander and Goldsmith, *The Case Against the Global Economy.*

94. Senate Committee on Finance, *NAFTA and Related Side Agreements,* 103rd Cong., 1st sess., 15–28 September 1998. On numbers (create or destroy jobs) 4, 5, 18, 25, 31, 54, 56, 70–71, 149, 164–165 223, 334. On the numbers of supporters vs. opponents, Ambassador Mickey Kantor noted every living ex-president, 41 of 50 governors, 284 economists, and six environmental groups representing 7.5 million Americans or 80% of the membership of U.S. environmental organizations, support NAFTA. Compare to remarks of Lori Wallach, Public Citizen, who noted that some 300 state and local groups oppose NAFTA, comprising some 8 million citizens, 137.

95. Thomas R. Donahaue, secretary/treasurer, AFL, statement before Ways and Means, *NAFTA and Related Side Agreements,* 511.

96. Curt Rohland, president, National Family Farm Coalition, Senate Finance, *NAFTA and Related Side Agreements,* 137; also see 138–44.

97. Senate Finance, *NAFTA and Related Side Agreements,* 138–44.

98. Senate Finance, *NAFTA and Related Side Agreements,* on support of former UAW President Douglas Fraser, 105; on labor standards declining and job anxiety, see 59, 76, 131; on wages declining, 100–101; and testimony of Thomas R. Donahue, Secretary-Treasurer, AFL-CIO, 83–101.

99. House Committee on Agriculture, *Review of Issues Related to the North American Free-Trade Agreement—NAFTA,* 8 April–30 September 1992, quote of EPA Administrator William Reilly, quoted in Linda J. Fisher, assistant administrator, EPA, 495. Reilly described NAFTA as the "greenest trade agreement ever negotiated." Were they broken promises? In the Senate Finance Committee Hearing, Senator Donald Riegle asked Labor Secretary Reich what the difference was between the Bush administration's Memorandum of Understanding on Labor versus the Labor Side Agreement noted by the Clinton administration. The Bush Memorandum, signed on 3 May 1991, set out a list of cooperative activities between the United States and Mexico. The Clinton side agreement made all activities trilateral, created an institutional structure to ensure that the three nations cooperate, communicate, and "scrutinize the enforcement of each other's labor laws." The agreement also established a process to discuss and dispute labor law and "for the first time opens Mexican labor law procedures and enforcement up to public scrutiny." Senate Finance, *NAFTA and Related Side Agreements,* 249–50.

100. Ways and Means, *North American Free Trade,* 253–56.

101. Congressman Bill Thomas in a discussion with Carl Pope of Sierra Club, Andrea Durbin of Friends of the Earth, and Lori Wallach of Public Citizen in Ways and Means, *NAFTA and Supplemental Agreements,* 376–77.

102. Ways and Means, *North American Free-Trade,* 320, 346, 357, 534.

103. Senate Finance, *NAFTA and Related Side Agreements,* 115–16.

104. House Ways and Means, *NAFTA and Supplemental Agreements,* 369.

105. Pharis J. Harvey, "Labour Has Few Rights in Mexico," *Briarpatch* (September 1991): 25; and Pharis J. Harvey, Prepared Statement, Ways and Means Committee, 20 February 1991.

106. Ways and Means, *NAFTA and Supplemental Agreements,* 376–79.

107. Ways and Means, *NAFTA and Supplemental Agreements,* 527–37; Donahue quote, 536.

108. Ibid., Pope, 376, Wallach, 377; Congressman Bill Thomas interpretation of their views, 381–82.

109. Ibid., 377–78, 381–82.

110. According to congressional testimony of Mr. Peter F. Guerrero, associate director, environmental protection issues, General Accounting Office, "In some cases U.S. standards were higher, in other cases Codex standards were higher. We don't always have the most stringent standards." House Agriculture Committee, *Review of Issues Related to the North American Free-Trade Agreement—NAFTA,* 174.

111. In a study of NAFTA, John Audley found that 308 of 434 members who voted on the NAFTA implementing legislation issued comments on their votes. He found that not one of the opponents of NAFTA mentioned the environment as part of their justification for opposing NAFTA, but supporters cited NAFTA's environmental provisions as a reason for supporting it. Audley, *Green Politics,* 96, 110, fnn. 1–5.

Chapter 6

1. Ritchie had received a leaked copy of the proposals. Executive Office of the President, "United States Proposals for Multilateral Trade Negotiations on Agriculture," 6 July 1987. He believed they were leaked by Senator Jesse Helms. Interview with Mark Ritchie, 18 October 1998.

2. Several individuals in the United States and from overseas identified Mark Ritchie as the individual who first sounded the alarm about the potential impact of the GATT on national systems of regulation. Lori Wallach, Public Citizen, interview, 17 March and 21 March 1995; Steve Charnovitz, now of the law firm Wilmer Cutler, then research director, Competitiveness Policy Council, interview, 2 August 1994; Steven Shrybman, Canadian Environmental Law Association, interview, 22 August 1998; Kevin Watkins, Oxfam (England), interview, 24 September 1998.

3. International Trade Commission (ITC), *Operation of the Trade Agreements Program, 38th Report* (Washington: GPO, 1987), 1-2–1-7; ITC, *Operation of the Trade Agreements Program, 39th Report* (Washington: U.S. GPO, 1988), 2-4–2-5; and Jeffrey J. Scott, *The Uruguay Round: An Assessment* (Washington: Institute for International Economics, 1995), 4–5.

4. Mark Ritchie, "Trading Away Our Environment," May 1990, 2.

5. E-mail from Mark Ritchie to Susan Aaronson, 24 August 1998.

6. Another individual who early on became concerned about the relationship of trade and the environment was Konrad von Moltke, a professor at Dartmouth College. Interview with David Schorr, World Wildlife Fund, 1 December 1998.

7. Aaronson, *Trade and the American Dream,* chapters 9–10.

8. Rodrik, *Has Globalization Gone Too Far?* 5, 53, 65.

9. Ritchie became a member of President Clinton's Trade and Environment Policy Advisory Committee. Thus, one could say he became a "mover and shaker."

10. Also see Mark Ritchie, "Canada-U.S. Free Trade Agreement: The U.S. Perspective," *Review of European Community and International Environmental Law* 1, no. 1 (1992): 48. Writing about Ritchie, one observer noted, "Trade, per se, was simply not

on the activist non-profit or progressive philanthropic screen." In documents prepared nominating Ritchie for a MacArthur Genius award, the anonymous nominator wrote, he "brought the trade issue to a boil." "Anonymous Nominator's Excerpt: Mark Ritchie," in possession of the author.

11. "IATP contributes research and analysis on the economic, environmental, and cultural impacts of contemporary trade policy and practices. . . . IATP has made it a priority to effectively use fax, telephone, and computer technologies to gather information, inform, coordinate, and mobilize." Institute for Agriculture and Trade Policy (IATP), *Annual Report: 1996–1997,* 3–4.

12. Interview with Mark Ritchie, 17 April 1996; Mark Ritchie, "Globalizing the Farm Crisis: A Dangerous World Food Situation Demands Education/Action," *Christian Social Action* 3 (1998): 22–26; and Mark Ritchie, "Democratizing the Trade-Policy Making Process: The Lessons of NAFTA and Their Implications for the GATT," *Cornell International Law Journal* 27, no. 3 (1994): 749–53.

13. ITC, *Operation of the Trade Agreements Program 38th Report,* 1–5, 2–19–2-20; and Paarlberg, *Leadership Abroad,* 67–69, quotation on 69.

14. Interview with Kevin Brosch, Office of the General Counsel, Department of Agriculture, 2 September 1998. Brosch was a lead negotiator on agriculture during the Uruguay Round.

15. Ritchie, "New Perspectives on Ecologically Compatible Agriculture"; and Brosch, interview, 2 September 1998.

16. Devin Burghalter of Prairie Fire, interview, 13 July 1998. Prairie Fire was a religious and political support groups for small farmers in the Midwest.

17. Paarlberg, *Leadership Abroad,* 67.

18. Interview with Mark Ritchie, 17 April 1996; Mark Ritchie, "Trading Away Our Environment," IATP, May 1990, 2.

19. For example, in 1972, an assistant secretary of agriculture once justified a decision to restrict the flow of imported tomatoes into the United States not to ensure the tomatoes were safe to eat, but rather "the primary purpose of the act . . . is to protect the purchasing power of U.S. farmers." Lazarus, *Genteel Populists,* 101, 130–31; Ritchie, interview, 17 April 1996; and Donna U. Vogt, "Food Safety: Recommendations for Changes in the Organization of Federal Food Safety Responsibilities, 1949–1997," Congressional Research Service (CRS) 98-400, 21 April 1998, 7, 36, 44.

20. Vogt, "Food Safety," 7, 36, 44; and Community Nutrition Institute (CNI), "GATT Proposal May Weaken U.S. Right to Set Standards," 30 August 1990, 4.

21. Harrison Wellford, *Sowing the Wind: A Report from Ralph Nader's Center for Study of Responsive Law on Food Safety and the Chemical Harvest* (New York: Grossman, 1972).

22. The Safe Food Coalition was composed of members from the American Public Health Association, Center for Science in the Public Interest, Consumer Federation of America, Consumers Union, AFL-CIO, National Consumers League, Public Citizen, and the United Food and Commercial Workers International Union. Vogt, "Food Safety," 36, 44.

23. A series of polls throughout the 1980s noted that some 89.8 percent of those surveyed agreed (or strongly agreed) that keeping food safe should be a high government priority. Carol S. Kramer, "Food Safety: Consumer Preferences, Policy Options, Research Needs," in *Consumer Demands in the Marketplace: Public Policies Related to Food Safety Quality and Human Health,* ed. Katherine L. Clancy (Washington: Resources for the Future, 1988), 148 (poll cited, also see 150–61 for additional polls). The European nations had different food safety priorities and concerns. For example, compared with

U.S. consumers, Europeans were more concerned about hormones than pesticides; but food safety was also an important priority to Europeans in the 1980s. See David O'Beirne, "Issues in the European Community," also in *Consumer Demands,* 171–85.

24. Henk Lof, "GATT, Agriculture and Environment: Towards a Positive Approach," Centre for Agriculture and Environment, Utrecht, November 1990, Comments of Mark Ritchie, 9. Copy in possession of the author.

25. Mark Ritchie, "The Environmental Implications of the GATT Negotiations," RONGEAD Infos (autumn 1989): 12.

26. Interview with Mark Ritchie, 13 October 1998, and comments to author, 30 December 1998.

27. Ritchie was named one of the *Utne Reader*'s 100 visionaries in 1995. "Ritchie is GATT and NAFTA's worst nightmare. . . . He has spent the past 20 years working on the economic, social, and environmental issues facing family farms and small towns worldwide." John Spade and the editors of *Utne Reader,* "100 Visionaries Who Could Change Your Life," *Utne Reader* (January/February 1995): 73.

28. In many of these nations, sterilized water was not available. Fuel or electricity to sterilize the water was also expensive or unavailable. The formula (coupled with the bottles) was very expensive to citizens in developing nations. Thus, parents might be tempted to dilute the formula, which would lower its nutritional value.

29. George A. Lopez, Jackie G. Smith, and Ron Pagnucco, "The Global Tide," *Bulletin of Atomic Scientists* (July/August 1995): 33–35. The Nestlé case became a case study in corporate social responsibility. Rogene A. Buchholz, William D. Evans, and Robert A. Wagley, *Management Response to Public Issues: Concepts and Cases in Strategy Formulation* (Englewood Cliffs: Prentice Hall, 1989), 149–62; and Rafael D. Pagan Jr., "Corporate Strategies for Effective Crisis Management: Corporate Decision Making and Corporate Public Policy Development," in *Business and Society: Dimensions of Conflict and Cooperation,* ed. S. Prakash Sethi and Cecilia M. Falbe (Lexington, MA: Lexington Books, 1987), 432–49.

30. Mark Ritchie, "Introduction," in *1991 IATP Annual Report,* 3.

31. Tim Lang, professor, Centre for Food Policy, Thames Valley University, interview, 25 September 1998; Colin Hines, independent author and Green Party strategist, interview, 23 September 1998; and Kevin Watkins, Oxfam, interview, 24 September 1998. On organizing by farmers, see IATP, "The De-coupled Approach to Agriculture," September 1998, 28.

32. International Summit of Agricultural Producers Concerned with GATT, "Strengthening the Agricultural Trade Disciplines of the General Agreement on Tariffs and Trade," 2 December 1987.

33. Paarlberg, *Leadership Abroad,* 67; Mark Ritchie, IATP, interview, 13 October 1998; David Schorr, World Wildlife Fund, interview, 1 December 1998; and Nancy Dunne, *Financial Times,* interview, 18 November 1996.

34. Interviews with Lori Wallach, Public Citizen, 2 July 1998; Ambassador Tran Van Thinh, 16 October 1998; interview with Myrian Van Stichele, Stichting Onderzoek Multinationale Ondernemingen (SOMO; Centre for Research on Multinational Corporations), 29 May 1999; and Ricardo Melendez, Director, International Center for Trade and Sustainable Development, 27 May 1999.

35. Interviews with Amy Porges, Office of the General Counsel, USTR, series of interviews, May–December 1997; Laura Kneale Anderson, USTR, 4 August 1998; and Nancy Dunne, 18 November 1996.

36. Mychal Wilmes, "Europeans Need to Win Battle Over the Elimination of Farm Subsidies," *Agri-News,* 17 March 1998; and interview with Lori Wallach, Public Citizen, 2 July 1998.

37. Lane Palmer, "U.S. Farm Groups Heat Up the Trade War," *Farm Journal,* mid-March 1988, 32; Dan Miller, "Viewpoints: When Talking Works," *Iowa Farmer Today,* 5 March 1988.

38. The institute became a hub for a "network of farm, consumer, environmental, citizen, church, labor, and development organizations in the United States and abroad." In publicizing and fund-raising for the institute, Ritchie made contact with a wide range of foundations, churches, and media groups. By 1991, the institute had a budget of almost half a million dollars and a full-time staff of nine analysts. IATP, *1991 Annual Report,* 3, 6.

39. IATP, "Consumer Dangers in GATT," and "GATT Mid-Term Agreement," 14 April 1989; IATP, "The De-Coupled Approach to Agriculture," September 1988; IATP, "The Environmental Implications of the GATT Negotiations," 1989(?); Mark Ritchie, "Global Agricultural Trade Negotiations and Their Potential Impact on Minnesota," *Journal of the Minnesota Academy of Science* 54 (November 1989): 4–8. On views of farmers, see Mark A. Edelman, "Extension News: Iowa State," 23 December 1987, which reported that some 66 percent of 1,920 Iowa farmers polled supported developing domestic markets for farm products and de-emphasizing trade as a solution to low prices.

40. Rodney E. Leonard founded the Community Nutrition Institute in 1969. CNI focus on providing policy analysis, information, and education to consumers and government officials on a sustainable food supply, consumer protection, and sound federal diet and health policies.

41. IATP, "Consumer Dangers in GATT," n.d., 1.

42. Marta Cleaveland, "Ag Organizations to Form Coalition," *Times News* (Idaho), 19 April 1989; and "1988 Resolution Opposing GATT Agricultural Agreement," both in files of Mark Ritchie. The resolution was signed by farm groups from the states of North Dakota, Minnesota, and Montana. Also Devin Burghalter, interview, 13 July 1998; Lori Wallach, interview, 2 July 1998.

43. USTR, "Submission of the United States on Comprehensive Long-Term Agricultural Reform, Final U.S. Proposal, October 1989," 1, 3–6.

44. On Codex, see CRS, Donna U. Vogt, "Sanitary and Phytosanitary Measures Pertaining to Food in International Trade Negotiations," CRS-6, 11 September 1992.

45. Carol S. Kramer, "Implications of the Hormone Controversy for International Food Safety Standards," *Resources* (fall 1991): 12–14; and Vogt, "Sanitary and Phytosanitary Measures," CRS-6, 11 September 1992.

46. The United States and the Cairns Group (major agricultural exporters such as Argentina, Australia, Brazil, Canada, Chile, Hungary, Indonesia, Malaysia, New Zealand, Philippines, Thailand, and Uruguay) sought specific reduction of domestic support and export subsidies. The European Community, Japan, and other countries sought to focus reduction commitments on domestic support programs, but they would not specific policy specific commitments. ITC, *Operation of the Trade Agreements Program: 42nd Report 1990,* 13. Also see Ray MacSharry, European Community to Vermont House Representative Andrew Christiansen, 22 December 1989; and Acting USTR Jules Katz to Honorable Andrew Christiansen, 19 November 1989, from files of Mark Ritchie.

47. On the U.S. proposal to convert all NTBs into tariffs, see Farmers Union, "U.S. Seeking 'Tariffication' at GATT Talks," *Milk Matters,* 31 July 1989; National Farmers Union, "World Farm Leaders Oppose Decoupling, Want Supply-Management," 13 June

1989, and GATT, "Discussion Paper on Tariffication Submitted by the United States," MTN.GNG/NG5/W/97, 10 July 1989.

48. "Unofficial Report of Remarks by Daniel Amstuz, Undersecretary of Agriculture," 13 October 1988; and "A Framework for Agricultural Reform Submitted by the United States," 7 November 1988, in files of Mark Ritchie, IATP. Also see IATP, "The De-coupled Approach to Agriculture," September 1988, 21–22. The undersecretary of agriculture is also the chief agricultural trade negotiator.

49. See, for example, Natural Resources Defense Council (NRDC), "Bush Trade Proposal Threatens U.S. Pesticide Regulation," 24 Mary 1990; Greenpeace Action, "Harmonization of Global Pesticide Standards Proposed Under GATT: Threat to Safety of US Food Supply"; IATP, "GATT SCAN: Special Edition on Harmonization," 6 May 1990; and Ritchie, "Trading Away Rights." Dona Vogt of CRS refuted these allegations by noting that the U.S. government representatives were charged with representing the United States and not interest groups. She also found that some consumer groups, including CNI, Public Voice, and Consumers Union, had opportunities to attend Codex meetings. Vogt, "Sanitary and Phytosanitary Measures," CRS-7.

50. GATT Secretariat, "Common Language Developed from Country Proposals on Sanitary and Phytosanitary Regulations and Barriers," Revision 1, 29 May 1990; and "Submission of the European Communities on Sanitary and Phytosanitary Regulations and Measures," December 1989. The European Community fully supported the objective of harmonization but had a different strategy to achieve it.

51. Jonathan Harsch, "Washington Farm Scene," 13 May 1988, 6; and Pam Baldwin "Idaho Farm Future at Stake in Geneva," *Idaho Statesman,* 9 June 1989.

52. In 1981, some infant foods based on Italian veal containing synthetic hormones caused abnormal swelling of the mammary glands of young boys. David O'Beirne, "Issues in the European Community," in *Consumer Demands in the Marketplace,* ed. Clancy, 183.

53. Marcia Zarley Taylor, *Farm Journal,* May 1989, 10; and Leo Van Beek, "Yeutter Asks for International BGH Policy," *Agri-View,* 30 September 1989.

54. According to a U.S. government press release, "While the E.C. has joined other countries in calling for greater uniformity . . . of national health regulations, it appears less willing than other GATT members to agree that an effective dispute settlement process is needed for when a country fails to comply with this harmonization." U.S. Mission Daily Bulletin, "Governments Use Health Regulations to Limit Imports," 17 January 1989, given to me by Gretchen Stanton of the WTO staff. Also Gretchen H. Stanton, WTO, interview, 7 October 1998. She was the lead GATT staffer on S&P standards negotiations.

55. Ironically, the European Alliance for Safe Meat found that some 64 percent of Europeans polled have no problem with growth promotants as long as the resulting meat is certified safe for human consumption. See "Pro Farmer," 21 May 1990; and "Global Harmonization," 1; both in the files of Mark Ritchie, IATP. This example supports the official view that the Europeans were using health and safety standards strictly for trade protection, as in the 1870s (chapter 2). On Yeutter and Hightower, see James Ridgeway, "Who Was That Masked Man Anyway?" *Voice* 29 February 1989, 18; Texas Department of Agriculture, "Press Release: Texas Ships First Load of Hormone Free Beef to Europe," 31 July 1989; and Jess Blair, "Hightower Put in Hot Seat Over Beef Hormone Issue," *Feedstuffs,* 24 April 1989.

56. "Global Harmonization," in files of Mark Ritchie; and Gretchen Stanton, WTO, fax to Susan Aaronson, 13 October 1998, on S&P standards protests.

57. CNI, "GATT Proposal," *Nutrition Week*, 30 August 1990, 5. In May 1990, some EPA staff wrote an internal memo arguing that some standards are not based on sound science but on policy judgments, and thus, sound science should not be the only criteria for assessing legitimacy of domestic regulation. In a press briefing on May 4, 1990, Anne Lindsay, an EPA official, said that some 16 percent of the pesticide tolerance standards set by Codex are weaker than current U.S. tolerances. See "U.S. Agricultural Practices Change Predicted If CODEX MRLs Adopted," *Pesticide and Toxic Chemical News*, 9 May 1990, 1. On Louis Sullivan's view, see *Food Chemical News*, 16 April 1990, 45–46.

58. Subcommittee on Oversight and Investigations, House Committee on Energy and Commerce, "Hard To Swallow: FDA Enforcement Program for Imported Food" (Washington: GPO, 1989), 1. In 1989, GAO also did a study. It noted that the United States imported about 9 percent of its food supply in 1987 and inspected some 9 percent of those imports. GAO, "Imported Foods: Opportunities to Improve FDA's Inspection Program," GAO/HRD 89–88, April 1989, 2.

59. Eric Christiansen, NRDC, on behalf of Stewart Hudson, National Wildlife Federation; Alex Hittle, Friends of the Earth; Mark Ritchie, Fair Trade Campaign; Mark Floegel, Greenpeace; Craig Merrilees, National Toxics Campaign Fund; and Rod Leonard, Community Nutrition Institute, letter to USTR Carla Hills, 11 June 1990.

60. The Scheuer resolution was H.R. 336, 101st Cong., 2d sess., 1990. The resolution also urged Congress to find ways to better integrate environmental and economic decision-making. Hobart Rowan, "Are Food Imports Safe?" *Washington Post*, 31 May 1990, A23; and Ritchie, "Trading Away," 11.

61. Rowan, "Are Food Imports Safe?" A23; Bob Lewis, "Bob Lewis's Farmletter," 31 May 1990; and Ritchie, "Trading Away," 16. The Swift resolution was H.R. 371, 29 March 1990. The Swift resolution was announced at a press conference sponsored by the Ad Hoc Working Group on Trade and Environmentally Sustainable Development.

62. Greenpeace Action, "Harmonization of Global Pesticide Standards Proposed Under GATT: Threat to Safety of U.S. Food Supply" and NRDC, "Bush Trade Proposal Threatens U.S. Pesticide Regulation," 24 May 1990; GAO, "International Food Safety: Comparison of U.S. and Codex Pesticide Standards," GAO/PEMD-91-22, August 1991; and Ad Hoc Working Group on Trade and Environmentally Sustainable Development, letter to Members of Congress, 21 May 1990.

63. Phil Lansing, director, Idaho Rural Council, letter to Keith Higgenson, director, Water Resources, State of Idaho, 15 June 1990; and Leonard W. Condon, deputy assistant, U.S. Trade Representative for Agricultural Affairs, letter to Phil Lansing, director, Idaho Rural Council, 9 July 1990; both from files of Mark Ritchie. Also see Farmers Union Milk Marketing Cooperative, "FUMMC Urges Congress to Insist on Adequate Food Safety Standards Under GATT," 15 May 1990.

64. Carla Hills, USTR, transcript, National Press Club ballroom speech, 24 May 1990.

65. Dan Esty, Yale Law School, interview, 18 November 1998. Mr. Esty was a special assistant to EPA administrator William Reilly during the Bush administration and later served in senior positions.

66. Eric Christiansen, NRDC, on behalf of the Community Nutrition Institute and National Wildlife Federation, letter to Sharon Bylenga, Department of Agriculture, 23 August 1990, from files of Jake Caldwell and Ron Leonard, CNI.

67. GATT Negotiating Group on Agriculture: Working Group on Sanitary and Phytosanitary Regulations and Barriers, *Draft Text on Sanitary and Phytosanitary Measures*. MTN.GNG/NG5/WGSP/7; Geneva, Switzerland, 20 November 1990. The areas of dis-

agreement were marked by brackets. Also see Fair Trade Campaign, "GATT Focus," 10 July 1990.

68. Natalie Avery, "Fears Over Food Quality Standards," *Pesticide News* 20 (June 1993): 3; Rod Leonard, CNI, interview, 9 December 1997; Professor Tim Lang, interview, 24 September 1998; and Natalie Avery, Martine Drake, and Tim Lang, *Cracking the Codex: An Analysis of Who Sets World Food Standards* (London: National Food Alliance, 1993).

69. N.a., "GATT Could Jeopardise Food Self-Reliance," *Crosscurrents* 8, 28 August 1991, 7; and Dutch Alliance for Sustainable Development, "Towards Sustainability, a Dutch NGO Perspective," Utrecht, July 1991. Draft in possession of author. Jane Ayers, "Martin Khor: Fighting to Save Rain Forests and the World Environment," *ISEE Newsletter,* May 1991, 8.

70. Commission of the European Communities, "Report on United States Trade Barriers and Unfair Practices 1991: Problems of Doing Business in the U.S.," 15 March 1991, 7.

71. N.a., "Memorandum: Restriction of State Powers in International Trade Agreements," 24 June 1991, 1–6; and N.a., "Global Harmonization of Food Safety Standards: A Threat to Consumers, Farmers and the Environment," 1991, both in files of Mark Ritchie, IATP.

72. N.a., "Environmental Proposition Opposed," *Merced Sun Star* (California), 24 August 1990; Senator Dianne Feinstein, statement, 16 July 1990.

73. The position of the IOCU was reported in *Codex Coordinating Committee Report,* obtained by Rod Leonard of CNI, dated December 1991; copy in file of author, from files of Mark Ritchie of the IATP.

74. N.a., "Bush Administration Opens Backdoor to Gut Health, Safety Standards Via Trade Pacts," *Public Citizen,* October 1992, 14–16.

75. Centre for Agriculture and Environment, "GATT, Agriculture, and Environment," 1; and Henk Lof, "GATT, Agriculture and Environment: Towards a Positive Approach, Report on a Conference on September 14–15, 1990, Utrecht, Netherlands, November 1990.

76. Some progress had been made regarding nontariff barriers, but the EC and the United States could not find a common framework to reduce subsidies as well as trade barriers. They did achieve some movement on S&P, but they had not agreed whether nations had a right to their own regulatory approval procedures. ITC, *Trade Agreements Program 42nd Report, 1990,* 1–5, 14–15.

77. The draft final act was GATT Secretariat, MTN.TNC/W/35/Rev.1. In its request for fast-track authority, the administration noted that the draft final act was not attached to the president's report on its request for fast-track due to its considerable length. Thus, few people, even members of Congress, saw it until it was leaked. A limited number of copies were available at the Office of Public Affairs, USTR. President George Bush, "Report to the Congress," Attachment D.

78. Interview with Rod Leonard, 9 December 1997.

79. Rod Leonard and Eric Christiansen, "Basic Environmental Principles for Trade Agreements," proposal to NRDC, NWF, FOE, Audubon, EDF, Sierra Club, and Greenpeace, 19 June 1991.

80. Eric Christiansen, CNI, letter to James D. Grueff, group leader, U.S. Department of Agriculture, on behalf of Rodney E. Leonard, CNI and Alex Hittle, Friends of the Earth, 23 May 1991. The letter was copied to Senators Bentsen, Wirth, Gore, Leahy, and Lautenberg.

81. CNI, "New Trade Rules to Replace Health, Safety Standards in Federal Law," *Nutrition Week*, 3 May 1990, 4.

82. Interview with Lori Wallach, Public Citizen, 9 April 1999.

83. Wallach said she became an opponent of GATT when she found the doors closed to her—although I found evidence that GATT staff did meet with her. Lori Wallach, interview, 2 July 1998; Gretchen Stanton, interview, 7 October, 1998 and Gretchen Stanton, WTO letter to Susan Aaronson, 13 October 1998. Also see Postman and Mapes, "WTO in Seattle: Why WTO United So Many Foes," *Seattle Times,* 6 December 1999.

84. Ralph Nader, 13th World Congress of the International Organization of Consumers Unions, remarks, 8 July 1991.

85. The report was called "GATT, Trade and the Environment," GATT/1529, derestricted 2/2/1992." See IT, *The Year in Trade,* 21, 27.

86. Lang and Hines, *New Protectionism,* 11, 53.

87. Interviews with Mark Ritchie, IATP, 13 October 1998; Justin Ward, NRDC, 18 November 1998; Karen Hansen Kuhn, the Development GAP, interview, 2 August 1998; Steven Shrybman, Canadian Environmental Law Institute, 22 August 1998; and Stewart Hudson, formerly World Wildlife Fund, 22 October 1998.

88. Interview with Colin Hines, 23 September 1998; interview with Kevin Watkins, Oxfam, 24 September 1998; and interview with Myriam Vander Stichele, SOMO, 29 May 1999.

89. Destler, *American Trade Politics,* 218–11; and Council of Economic Advisors, *Economic Report of the President 1993* (Washington: GPO, 1993), 317; on oilseeds, 318–19. Mark Ritchie, IATP, interview, 13 October 1998. On protests, see Justin R. Ward, "Environmental Strategies for Agricultural Trade," in *Trade and the Environment: Law, Economics, and Policy,* ed. Durwood Zaelke, Robert Housman, and Paul Orbach (Washington: Earth Island Law, 1993), 247.

90. "Towards Sustainability: A Dutch NGO Perspective," Position paper on behalf of NAPED, first draft, Utrecht, July 1991, 34.

91. Gretchen Stanton, letter to Susan Aaronson, 13 October 1998; Gretchen Stanton, WTO, interview, 7 October 1998; Lori Wallach, letter to Gretchen Stanton, 16 November 1992; and Lori Wallach, Public Citizen, interview, 2 July 1998. The tuna dolphin report came out on 3 September 1991. On India meeting see, Terry Allen, "In GATT They Trust," *Covert Action* 40 (spring 1992): 60–65.

92. Section 1101 of the Omnibus Trade and Competitiveness Act of 1988, (14) Worker Rights states: the principal negotiating objectives of the United States regarding worker rights are to promote response for worker rights; to secure a review of the relationship of worker rights to GATT articles, objectives, and related instruments; and "to adopt, as a principle of the GATT, that the denial of worker rights should not be a means for a country or its industries to gain competitive advantage in international trade." Committee on Ways and Means, U.S. House, *Overview and Compilation of U.S. Trade Statutes 1997 edition,* 853, 855.

93. Charnovitz, "Environmental and Labour Standards," 335–56; Congressman Donald Pease, "A View from a Former Congressman," 53, quoting USTR Bill Brock; and Mickey Kantor, "The Perspective of the U.S. Trade Representative," 16; both in U.S. Department of Labor, *International Labor Standards and Global Economic Integration: Proceedings of a Symposium* (Washington: GPO, 1994).

94. The letter urging representatives to reject the Dunkel draft included seventeen environmental groups; five consumer groups; nine labor groups; five citizens groups;

six farm groups; and three religious groups. Many of these same groups had expressed concerns about NAFTA. See Citizen Trade Watch Campaign, "Consumer and Environmental Briefing Packet on the December 20, 1991 Uruguay Round GATT 'Final Act Text,'" spring 1992.

95. Lang and Hines, *New Protectionism*, 48–49; Nancy Dunne, "Consumer Protest at World Trade Plan," *Financial Times* 11 December 1992, 5; Colin Hines, interview, 23 September 1998; N.a., "Citizens' Groups Raise Concerns About GATT," *NAFTATHOUGHTS* 4, no. 1 (April 1994): 9; Kevin Watkins, Oxfam, interview, 24 September 1998; "France's Right: An Utter Mess," *Economist*, 19 August 1998; and James Goldsmith, "Global Free Trade and GATT," 1994.

96. Destler, *American Trade Politics*, 219–21; Schott, *The Uruguay Round*, 6–7; and Hines and Lang, *New Protectionism*, 47.

97. GATT Secretariat, "Final Act Embodying the Results of the Uruguay Round of Multilateral Trade Negotiations," 15 December 1993. The information on the WTO is in Annex IV, 91.

98. Committee on Ways and Means, *Overview and Compilation of U.S. Trade Statutes*, 855, Sections 131, 132, 135, and 315 of the Uruguay Round Agreements Act, as amended; Kantor, "The Perspective," 16; and interviews with Trim Bisell, National Coordinator, Campaign for Labor Rights, 2 December 1997; and Pharis Harvey, Executive Director, International Labor Rights Fund, 6 May 1997.

99. Interview with Jennifer Haverkamp, assistant USTR for Trade and the Environment, 31 July 1998; Laura Kneale Anderson, director for trade and the environment, USTR, 4 August 1998; and Bobbi Dresser, associate director for international standards, FDA, 16 September 1998. Also see USTR, "The Uruguay Round and U.S. Food Safety," June 1994.

100. Vogel, *Trading Up*, 191; and Esty, *Greening the GATT*, 49–52.

101. Esty, *Greening the GATT*, 53–54. Also interviews with David Schorr, WWF, 1 December 1998; Jennifer Haverkamp, Assistant USTR for Trade and the Environment, 31 July 1998; and Nancy Dunne, *Financial Times*, 7 July 1998.

102. Senate Committee on Commerce, Science, and Transportation, *Hearings on S. 2467: GATT Implementing Legislation*, 103rd Cong., 2d sess., 4 October–15 November 1994, 198–205. The Consumers Union noted it had certain problems with the Uruguay Round Agreements but hoped they would be addressed in the future work program of the WTO.

103. Esty, *Greening the GATT*, 53–54.

104. Aaronson, *Trade and the American Dream*, 145–46; and President of the United States, *Message Transmitting the Uruguay Round Trade Agreements, Texts of Agreements Implementing Bill Statement of Administrative Action and Required Supporting Statements*, 27 August 1994.

105. Interviews with Lori Wallach, Public Citizen, 2 July 1998; and Brent Blackwelder, Friends of the Earth, 3 August 1998.

106. Catherine Fields, Office of the General Counsel, USTR, telephone interview, 1 May 1994; and Omnibus Trade and Competitiveness Act of 1988, PL 100–418. The first trade negotiating objective for the United States in the act was "to provide for more effective and expeditious dispute settlement mechanisms and procedures." Also see President Bill Clinton, *Memorandum for the United States Trade Representative, Subject: Trade Agreements Resulting from the Uruguay Round of Multilateral Trade Negotiations*, 15 December 1994, 26.

107. Aaronson, *Trade and the American Dream*, 147; and Council of Economic Advisors, *Economic Report of the President, February 1995* (Washington: U.S. GPO, 1995), 205–14.

108. Patrick J. Buchanan, *The Great Betrayal* , 17–19.

109. Ibid., 19, 43, 62.

110. Ibid., 8–9, 113.

111. Susan Ariel Aaronson, "Circle the Wagons: Pat Buchanan's Illogical Campaign to Protect America from the Foreign Hordes," *New Democrat* (July/August 1998): 21–23.

112. Susan Dentzer,"The Buchanan Trade Winds," *U.S. News & World Report,* 26 February 1996, 31.

113. Save Our Sovereignty, "Opposition to World Trade Organization Grows Across Political Spectrum," press release, 13 June 1994. See Senate Committee on Commerce, *Hearings on S2467,* 93–95, testimony of Michael Lind; and 121–27, testimony of Kevin Kearns.

114. Reporters wondered how these groups could afford these ads and if the funding came from wealthy nationalists or corporate sources. I had heard that Milliken and Company paid for these ads, but I was not able to corroborate this. Milliken is privately held and does not legally have to reveal this information. Jock Nash, Milliken and Company, interview, May 20 1998; and Nancy Dunne, *Financial Times,* interview, 18 November 1996.

115. Congressman Lane Evans and fifty-four other members to President William Jefferson Clinton, request to delay vote, 28 April 1994; Kevin L. Kearns, president, United States Business and Industrial Council, statement, 13 June 1994; all in *Inside U.S. Trade,"* 12, no. 18, 6 May 1994, 12–13. Also see Senator Larry Pressler, *Congressional Record,* statement, 6 April 1994, S5344–S5346.

116. The 1994 hearings on the round included hearings held in January, February, and June by the House Ways and Means; March and April hearings by the House Agriculture Committee; and February, March, and June hearings by the House Foreign Affairs Committee. On the Senate side, the Finance Committee held hearings in February and March; the Commerce Committee held hearings in October and November; and the Foreign Relations Committee held hearings in June.

117. The Senate Foreign Relations Committee held hearings under the request of Senators Helms and Pressler. Senators Jesse Helms and Larry Pressler, letter to Senator Claiborne Pell, chair, Senate Foreign Relations Committee, 4 May 1994. Some of the Senate Commerce Committee hearings were held after the election, when Congress was in recess.

118. Adams is quoted in Thomas K. McCraw, "Mercantilism and the Market," 37.

119. Thus it was interesting that labor rights activists such as Pharis Harvey did not testify on the Uruguay Round. The Alliance for Responsible Trade was not as vocal on the Uruguay Round as it was on NAFTA.

120. Collins and Bosworth, *The New GATT,* 78–79.

121. Bureau of National Affairs, "State Officials to Ask Clinton for Trade Consultation Summit," *Daily Report for Executives,* 24 June 1994, A121; and *Inside U.S. Trade,* 1 July 1994, 11.

122. Patti Goldman, "Resolving the Trade and Environment Debate: In Search of a Neutral Forum and Neutral Principles," *Washington and Lee Law Review* 49, no. 4 (fall 1992): 1279; and Patti Goldman, telephone interview, 29 June 1994.

123. Thomas L. Friedman, "Dole Explains Trade Treaty Stand," *New York Times,* 13 August 1994, D2; "Administration Weighing Dole Proposal for Review of WTO Deci-

sions," *Inside U.S. Trade,* 18 November 1994, 1, 22, 23; and U.S. Senate, *Report 103–412:* Title I, Subtitle C, Sections 123–30, 20–27. To meet Dole's concerns, the Clinton administration agreed to establish a panel of judges to review WTO panel decisions.

124. Gingrich was quoted on the NBC program "Meet the Press." John Maggs, "Sovereignty Issue Threatens Trade Pact, As Fears of 'World Government' Voiced," *Journal of Commerce,* 26 April 1994; and Senate Commerce Committee, *Hearings on S.2467,* 4–32.

125. Committee on Ways and Means, *Hearings on the World Trade Organization,* 103 Cong., 2d sess., 10 June 1994; testimony of USTR Kantor, 9, 38, 44.

126. The letter also included an analysis by conservative law professor Robert Bork and Heritage Foundation economist Joe Cobb.

127. Committee on Ways and Means, *The World Trade Organization,* 38–43. Lori Wallach, telephone discussion, 17 March 1995. On better coordination of domestic and foreign economic policies see Clyde Prestowitz in *The New GATT,* eds. Collins and Bosworth, 78–80, 82; and Council on Competitiveness, *Roadmap for Results,* 5–20, 73–90.

128. Committee on Ways and Means, *Hearings on the World Trade Organization,* 28–32; "U.S. Drops Plan to Monitor Compliance With China Business Principles," *Inside U.S. Trade,* 11 November 1994; Michael Bergsman, "ACTPN to Call for Short-Term Focus in APEC," and "House Letter on Indonesia Worker Rights," both in *Inside U.S. Trade,* 28 October 1994, 23–24; Council of Economic Advisors, *Economic Report of the President, 1995,* 249–50; and David E. Sanger, "Trade Agreement Ends Long Debate But Not Conflicts," *New York Times,* 4 December 1994, A1. Environmentalists were also divided; some wanted an international organization to cover the environment, others wanted to include trade and environmental considerations in the GATT.

129. Committee on Commerce, *Hearings on S. 2467,* 77, Wallach quotes; 78, 83, Sir James Goldsmith.

130. U.S. Senate, Committee on Governmental Affairs, *Report 103–412 on S. 2467,* 221–23.

131. Alliance for GATT Now, "Statement of Purpose"; "Pro-GATT Editorials"; "America's Leading Economists Endorse Uruguay Round"; "Governors Voice Support to GATT Trade Pact"; "Alliance for GATT Now Membership," and "Voices in Support of the Uruguay Round"; and Michael E. Carpenter, attorney general of Maine, letter to Honorable Michael Kantor, 27 July 1994. Also see "Fact Sheets on the Senate Budget Waiver," "The Costs of Delay," and "Why Pass the Uruguay Round Implementing Bill This Year." All these documents were provided to me by Paula Collins of the Alliance for GATT Now. I am grateful for her assistance.

132. "Green Group Calls on Administration to Back Reform of GATT Rules," and Defenders of Wildlife, letter, *Inside U.S. Trade,* 28 October 1994, 15–17. Interview with John Audley of NWF, 22 October 1998; David Schorr, World Wildlife Federation, 1 and 2 December 1998; and Justin Ward, NRDC, interview, 18 November 1998. David Schorr of the WWF did issue mild support of the agreement, but he also criticized its content. Shorr's boss, Kathryn Fuller, served on the ACTPN.

133. Lori Wallach, interview, 21 March 1995.

134. *Public Citizen,* January/February 1995.

135. "Senate Letter on GATT Delay," *Inside U.S. Trade,* 18 November 1994, 20. "Clinton Urges Bipartisan Support for GATT Amid Conflicting GOP Signals," *Inside U.S. Trade,* 11 November 1994, 1, 16.

136. See, for example, remarks of Senator Barbara Mikulski, *Congressional Record,* 30 November 1994, S15102.

137. In the Uruguay Round vote, 167 Democrats and 121 Republicans voted for (288) the agreement and 89 Democrats and 56 Republicans voted against (and one independent) (146) the agreement in the House. In the Senate, 41 Democrats and 35 Republicans voted for, 14 Democrats and 10 Republicans voted against. Debbie Lamb, "Congressional Votes on International Trade Bills." Also see David E. Sanger, "Trade Agreement Ends Long Debate But Not Conflicts," *New York Times,* 4 December 1994, A1; and Patrick Buchanan, "An American Economy for Americans," *Wall Street Journal,* 11 September 1995.

138. William Drozdiak, "Poor Nations Resist Tougher Trade Rules," *Washington Post,* 14 April 1994; N. Vasuki Rao, "Developing States to Map Opposition to Trade Curbs," *Journal of Commerce,* 31 March 1994; John Zarocostas, "Environmental Proposal for WTO Met Coolly," *Journal of Commerce,* 19 September 1994.

139. On the International Forum on Globalization, see "History of the IFG," and IFG Associates at www.ifg.org/about.html; and www.ifg.org/assoc.html.

140. Interviews with Victor Mennoti, International Forum on Globalization, 25 August 1998; with Lori Wallach, 9 April 1999; and Colin Hines, 23 September 1998.

Chapter 7

1. Aaronson observation of Institute for International Economics Conference, June 1996. On I. M. Destler's views, see I. M. Destler, *American Trade Politics,* 3d ed. (Washington: Institute for International Economics, 1995), 7, 177, 316; I. M. Destler, John S. Odell, and Kimberly Ann Elliot, *Anti-Protection: Changing Forces in United States Trade Politics* (Washington: Institute for International Economics, 1987), 1–7; and I. M. Destler and Peter J. Balint, *The New Politics of American Trade: Trade, Labor, and The Environment* (Washington: Institute for International Economics, 1999), 1–13. Many analysts shared Destler's views. See Julie Kosterlitz, "Betting on Good Times," *National Journal,* 21 June 1997, 1266–69.

2. Polanyi, *The Great Transformation,* 204, 206.

3. WTO, "WTO Focus: WTO Holds High Level Trade Symposia on Environment and Development," March 1999, 5.

4. "WTO Environmental Panel Likely to Allow Public Access to Some Papers," *Inside U.S. Trade,* 2 December 1994, 13; "U.S. Calls on WTO Members to Open Dispute Mechanism to Public," *Inside U.S. Trade,* 6 November 1998, 8.

5. David Vogel, *Barriers or Benefits? Regulation in Transatlantic Trade* (Washington: Brookings Institution, 1997), 6, 62–66.

6. The USTR Web site is www.ustr.gov; Canada's Web site is www.dfait-maeci.gc.ca/tna-nac/why-e.asp; Austalia's Web site is www.dfat.gov.au; and Europe's Web site is www.europa.eu/int/comm/trade/misc/.

7. Daly and Goodland were quoted in Lang and Hines, *New Protectionism,* 115.

8. Human rights groups, however, may receive funding from labor unions and their affiliates.

9. Ralph Nader, "The Corrosive Effects of NAFTA," *Washington Post,* 15 November 1993.

10. David K. Schorr, World Wildlife Fund, testimony before the Subcommittee on Foreign Commerce and Tourism, Commerce Committee, U.S. Senate, 3 February 1994, 3–4 (in possession of the author).

11. On the other hand, developing nations may view developed country environmental standards as unfair because they force foreign producers to comply with overly stringent rules. Industrialized country standards may not only be expensive; they may

be difficult for foreign producers to understand and meet. From a developing country perspective, such standards may be inequitable.

12. Robert V. Reich, secretary, Department of Labor, in *International Labor Standards and Global Economic Integration: Proceedings of Symposium*, 1–5.

13. Suzanne Berger, "Introduction," in *National Diversity and Global Capitalism*, ed. Suzanne Berger and Ronald Dore (Ithaca: Cornell University Press, 1996); Vogel, *Trading Up*, 3–22; and Vogel, *Barriers and Benefits*, 3–7.

14. Aaronson, "What About Trade?" 44–48.

15. Wallach, interview, 9 April 1999; and Hines and Lang, *New Protectionism*, 25–26.

16. Committee for Economic Development, *Nontariff Distortions*, 28–29.

17. See chapter 3 and Hines and Lang, *The New Protectionists*, 104–5. They noted that large corporations "may . . . argue for higher standards to cut out medium and small firms."

18. The evidence thus far is incomplete, since the preliminary work of the Uruguay Round and the actual negotiations will not be declassified and available to researchers at the National Archives until the year 2011 at the earliest.

19. International Chamber of Commerce, *Business Charter for Sustainable Development*, 1991.

20. On NAFTA, the ACTPN recommended that "liberalized trade and environmental health cannot be separated." ACTPN, *ACTPN NAFTA Report*, September 1992, 81–83; ACTPN, *ACTPN Uruguay Round Report*, January 1994, 108, 115.

21. David A. Wirth, "International Trade Agreements: Vehicles for Regulatory Reform?" *Chicago Legal Forum* (1997): 354–55.

22. Ibid., 365–66.

23. Edward Alden, "Global Labor Standards Pledge," *Financial Times*, 30 July 2000; and OECD, "New OECD Guidelines for Multinational Enterprises Reinforce Framework for the Global Economy," www.oecd.org/media/release/nw))-68a.htm. These Guidelines are recommendations on responsible business conduct addressed by governments to multinational enterprises operating in or from the thirty-three countries that have agreed to adopt them. They were first published in 1976, but they have been revised several times since to meet changes in the global economy. At the United Nations, a wide range of companies agreed to nonbinding standards for human rights and environmental practices under the global impact. See Susan Ariel Aaronson, "Compassionate Globalization," *American Prospect Online*, www.prospect.org/webarchives/00-08/aaronson-00821.html.

24. The ACTPN included Rhoda Karpatkin of Consumers Union and Kathryn Fuller of the World Wildlife Fund in the NAFTA/Uruguay Round years, 1993–1995.

25. For example, see chapter 2 on the comments of Congressman William M. Springer and Jacob Viner. Also see Congressman Richard A. Gephardt to Democratic colleagues, 27 February 1997, 2. This letter was widely publicized, copy in author's possession.

26. Kelly, "Antecedents," 1–10.

27. Congressman Richard A. Gephardt to Democratic colleagues, 27 February 1997, 2.

Bibliography

Primary Sources

Archival Documents

Records of the Office of the United States Trade Representative, Record Group 364.1
Records of the Committee for Reciprocity Information, 364.2
Records of the Office of the Special Representative for Trade Negotiations, Record Group 364.3

Government Publications

Congressional Hearings on the Development of the GATT

House Committee on Ways and Means. *Extension of the Reciprocal Trade Agreements Act, Hearings in HR. 1211: A Bill to Extend the Authority of the President Under Section 350 of the Tariff Act of 1939, As Amended and for Other Purposes.* 81st Cong., 1st sess. 1/24–2/1, 1949.

Senate Committee on Finance. *Hearings on H.R. 1211: A Bill to Extend the Authority of the President Under Section 350 of the Tariff Act of 1930, As Amended and for Other Purposes.* 81st Cong., 2d sess., 2/17–3/8, 1949.

Congressional Hearings Related to the Kennedy Round

Committee on Foreign Relations, U.S. Senate. "East West Trade." 89th Congress, Part 1, 3/13–4/9, 1964.

Committee on Foreign Relations, U.S. Senate. "East West Trade." 89th Congress, Part 2, 2/24–26, 1965.

Subcommittee on Foreign Economic Policy of the Joint Economic Committee, Joint Economic Committee. "The Future of U.S. Foreign Trade Policy." Vol I, 90th Cong., 1st sess., 7/11–20, 1967.

Congressional Hearings Related to the 1974 Trade Act

Committee on Finance, U.S. Senate. *Hearings on H.R. 10710.* Part 1–15, 93rd Cong., 2d sess., 3/4–4/10, 1974.

Committee on Ways and Means. *Hearings on H.R. 6767, The Trade Reform Act of 1973,* Parts 1–15, 5/9–6/15, 1973.

Committee on Ways and Means. *Brief Summary of H.R. 10710: The "Trade Reform Act of 1973," As Report to the House on October 10, 1973.* Washington: GPO, 1973.

Congressional Hearings Approving the Tokyo Round

Subcommittee on International Trade, Committee on Finance, U.S. Senate. "Trade Agreements Act of 1979," 7/10–11, 1979.

Subcommittee on Trade, Committee on Ways and Means. "U.S. Trade Policy," 6/26–7/21, 1980.

Congressional Hearings Related to the Uruguay Round (GATT/WTO)

House Committee on Energy and Commerce, Subcommittee on Oversight and Investigations. "Hard to Swallow: FDA Enforcement Program for Imported Food." Washington: GPO, 1989.

House Committee on Ways and Means. *Trade Agreements Resulting From the Uruguay Round of Multilateral Trade Negotiations, Hearings.* 103rd Cong., 2d sess., 1/26–2/22, 1994.

———. *The World Trade Organization, Hearing.* 103rd Cong., 2d sess., 6/10/1994. Senate Committee on Commerce, Science, and Transportation. *S.2467, GATT Implementing Legislation, Hearings.* 103rd Cong., 2d sess., 10/4–11/15/1994.

Senate Committee on Finance. *Uruguay Round of Multilateral Trade Negotiations, Hearing.* 103rd Cong., 1st sess., 11/10/1993.

———. *Results of the Uruguay Round Trade Negotiations, Hearings.* 103rd Cong., 2d sess., 2/8–3/23, 1994.

———. "Chairman's Proposal: Legislation Implementing the Uruguay Round of Multilateral Trade Negotiations," 7/19/1994.

———. "Committee on Finance Action on the Uruguay Round Implementing Legislation," 8/5/1994.

———. *Uruguay Round Agreements Act: Joint Report of the Committee on Finance, Committee on Agriculture, Nutrition, and Forestry, and Committee on Governmental Affairs, to Accompany S. 2467.* 103rd Cong., 2d Sess., Report 103–412, 11/22/1994.

Senate Committee on Foreign Relations. *Transcript, Hearings on the World Trade Organization and U.S. Sovereignty,* 6/14/1994.

Additional Congressional Hearings

Committee on Ways and Means, Subcommittee on Trade, U.S. House of Representatives. "The Proposals to Terminate Trade Adjustment Assistance Programs for Workers and Firms." 104th Cong., 2d sess., 3/15/1996.

NAFTA Hearings

Committee on Agriculture, U.S. House. "Review of Issues Related to the North American Free Trade Agreement—NAFTA." 102nd Cong., 2d sess., 4/8–9/30/1992.

Committee on Ways and Means and Subcommittee on Trade, U.S. House. "North American Free-Trade Agreement (NAFTA) and Supplemental Agreements to the NAFTA." 103rd Cong., 1st sess., 9/14–9/23, 1993.

Committee on Finance, U.S. Senate. "NAFTA and Related Side Agreements," 103rd Cong., 1st sess., 9/15–9/28, 1993.

Congressional Hearings Related to Human Rights and Trade Linkage

Committee on Foreign Relations, U.S. Senate. "East-West Trade." 88 Cong., 2d sess., Part 1, 3/12–4/9, 1964 and 88th Congress, Part 2, 2/24–2/26, 1965.

Hearings on Competitiveness

Committee on Finance, U.S. Senate. *Report on the Omnibus Trade Act of 1987,* 100th Cong., 1st sess., Report 100–71, 6/12/1987.

Committee on Ways and Means, U.S. House. *Trade and International Economic Policy Reform Act of 1987,* 100th Cong., 2d sess.

House of Representatives. *Report: Trade and International Economic Policy Reform Act of 1987* Report 100-40, Part 5, 100th Cong., 2d sess., 4/6/1987.

U.S. Government Documents

Commission on International Trade and Investment Policy. "United States International Economic Policy in An Interdependent World." Washington: GPO, 1971.

Committee on Finance, U.S. Senate. *Antidumping Act of 1921 and the International Antidumping Code: Consistent or Not? A Critique by the Staff.* 90th Cong., 2d sess. Washington: GPO, 1968.

Committee on Ways and Means and the Tariff Commission, U.S. Congress. *Report in the Havana Charter for an International Trade Organization.* Washington: GPO, 1949.

Congressional Research Service, Donna U. Vogt. "Sanitary and Phytosanitary Safety Standards for Foods in the GATT Uruguay Round Accords." 6/21/1994.

———. "Sanitary and Phytosanitary Measures Pertaining to Food in International Trade Negotiations." 9/11/1992.

Council of Economic Advisors. *Economic Report of the President 1993.* Washington: GPO, 1993.

———. *Economic Report of the President, 1997.* Washington: GPO, 1997.

General Accounting Office. "Current Issues in U.S. Participation in the Multilateral Trading Sysem." GAO/NSIAD 885–118.

———. "Imported Foods: Opportunities to Improve FDA's Inspection Program." GAO/HRD 89–88, 4/1989.

———. "International Food Safety: Comparison of U.S. and Codex Pesticide Standards." GAO/PEMD 91–22, 8/1991.

Office of the United States Trade Representative. *1987 National Trade Estimate Report on Foreign Trade Barriers.* Washington: GPO, 1987.

———. "Submission of the United States on Comprehensive Long-Term Agricultural Reform, 10/1989,-Rinal U.S. Proposal." 10/1989.

———. "The Uruguay Round and U.S. Food Safety." 6/1994.

Peter G. Peterson. *The United States in the Changing World Economy, Vol. II. Background Material.* Washington: GPO, 1971, Chart 26.

President George Bush. "Report to the Congress on the Extension of Fast Track Procedures, Pursuant to Section 1103 (b) of the Omnibus Trade and Competitiveness Act of 1988." 3/1/1991.

President George Bush. "Response of the Administration to Issues Raised in Connection with the Negotiation of a North American Free Trade Agreement." 5/1/1991.

President of the United States (William Jefferson Clinton). "Message Transmitting the Uruguay Round Trade Agreements, Texts of Agreements Implementing Bill Statement of Administrative Action and Required Supporting Statements." 8/27/1994.

President Bill Clinton. "Memorandum for the United States Trade Representative, Subject: Trade Agreements Resulting from the Uruguay Round of Multilateral Trade Negotiations." 12/15/1994, 26.

President's Advisory Committee for Trade Policy and Negotiations. "Negotiating Objectives for a North American Free Trade Agreement." 10/1991.

President's Commission on Industrial Competitiveness. *Global Competition: The New Reality,* vol. II. Washington: GPO, 1985.

U.S. Congress, Congressional Budget Office. *The GATT Negotiations and U.S. Trade Policy.* Washington: GPO, 1987.

U.S. Congress, Office of Technology Assessment. *U.S. Mexico Trade: Pulling Together or Pulling Apart.* Washington: GPO, 1992.

———. *Technological Innovation, and Health, Safety, and Environmental Regulation.* Washington: GPO, 1981.

U.S. Department of Labor. *International Labor Standards and Global Economic Integration: Proceedings of a Symposium.* Washington: GPO, 1994.

———. *Worker Rights in U.S. Policy,* May 1991.

———. *Worker Rights and U.S. Trade Policy: An Evaluation of Worker Rights Conditionality Under the General System of Preferences.* September 1989.

———. *Institutionalizing Constructive Competition: International Labor Standards and Trade, Economic.* Discussion Paper 32, September 1988.

———. *Reconciling Labor Standards and Economic Goals: An Historical Perspective.* September 1989.

U.S. Department of State, Bureau of Intelligence and Research. "The Developing Institutional Character of the GATT." Report No. 562, 8/16/1962.

U.S. International Trade Commission. *Operation of the Trade Agreements Program.* Washington: GPO.

———. "Review of Trade and Investment Liberalization Measures by Mexico and Prospects for Future United States-Mexican Relations," Investigation No. 332–282, Phase I, USITC Publication 2275. Washington: GPO, 1990.

Canadian Government Documents

Canadian Labour Congress. *Submission on the North American Free Trade Agreement to the Sub-Committee on International Trade.* 1/26/1993.

European Government Document

Commission of the European Communities. "Report on Unites States Trade Barriers and Unfair Practices 1991: Problems of Doing Business in the U.S." 3/15/1991.

International Government Publications

GATT. "Discussion Paper on Tariffication Submitted by the United States," MTN.GNG/NG5/W/97 7/10/1989.

———. *The Tokyo Round of Multilateral Trade Negotiations.* Geneva: GATT, 1979.

———. *Trade Policy Review: The United States of America, 1989.* Geneva: GATT, 1990.

GATT Secretariat. "Final Act Embodying the Results of the Uruguay Round of Multilateral Trade Negotiations." 12/15/1993.

International Labour Office. *Defending Values, Promoting Change: Social Justice in a Global Economy.* Geneva: International Labor Organization, 1994.

SECONDARY SOURCES

Books

Aaronson, Susan Ariel. *Trade and the American Dream.* Lexington: University of Kentucky Press, 1996.

———. *Are There Trade-Offs When Americans Trade?* Alexandria, VA: Close Up, 1996.

Aho, C. Michael, and Jonathan David Aronson. *Trade Talks: America Better Listen!* New York: Council on Foreign Relations, 1985.

Bairoch, Paul. *Economics and World History: Myths and Paradoxes.* Chicago: University of Chicago Press, 1993.

Baldwin, Robert E. *Non-tariff Distortions of International Trade.* Washington: Brookings Institution, 1970.

Baldwin, Robert E., and J. David Richardson, eds. *NBER Conference Report: Issues in the Uruguay Round.* Cambridge: NBER, 1988.

Barlow, Maude. *Parcel of Rogues: How Free Trade Is Failing Canada.* Toronto: Key Porter, 1991.

——— and Bruce Campbell. *Take Back the Nation 2: Meeting the Threat of NAFTA.* Toronto: Key Porter, 1991.

Barnet, Richard J., and John Cavanagh. *Global Dreams: Imperial Corporations and the New World Order.* New York: Simon & Schuster, 1994.

Bartlett, Donald L., and James B. Steele. *America: Who Stole the Dream?* Kansas City: Andrews and McMeel, 1996.

Batra, Ravi. *The Myth of Free Trade: A Plan for America's Economic Revival.* New York: Scribner's, 1993.

Bauer, Raymond A., Ithiel de Sola Pool, and Lewis Anthony Dexter. *American Business and Public Policy.* New York: Atherton Press, 1963.

Berger, Suzanne, and Ronald Dore. *National Diversity and Global Capitalism.* Ithaca: Cornell University Press, 1996.

Bhagwati, Jagdish. *Free Trade, "Fairness" and the New Protectionism: Reflections on an Agenda for the World Trade Organisation.* London: Institute of Economic Affairs, 1995.

Bidwell, Percy. *The Invisible Tariff: A Study of the Control of Imports Into the United States.* New York: Council on Foreign Relations, 1939.

Blackford, Mansel G., and K. Austin Kerr. *Business Enterprise in American History,* 3d ed. New York: Houghton Mifflin, 1994.

Brecher, Jeremy, and Tim Costello. *Global Village or Global Pillage: Economic Reconstruction from the Bottom Up.* Boston: South End, 1994.

Bucholz, Rogene A., William D. Evans, and Robert A. Wagley. *Management Response to Public Issues: Concepts and Cases in Strategy Formulation.* Englewood Cliffs, NJ: Prentice Hall, 1989.

Business-Higher Education Forum. *America's Competitive Challenge: The Need for a National Response.* Washington: Business-Higher Education Forum, 1983.

Cameron, Duncan, ed. *The Free Trade Papers.* Toronto: Lorimer, 1986.

Celsi, Teresa. *Ralph Nader: The Consumer Revolution.* Millbrook: New Directions, 1991.

Chafe, William H., and Harvard Sitkoff, eds. *A History of Our Times: Readings on Post-war America.* New York: Oxford, 1991.

Choate, Pat, and J. K. Linder. *The High Flex Society.* New York: Basic Books, 1988.

Clancy, Katherine L., ed. *Consumer Demands in the Marketplace: Public Policies Related to Food Safety, Quality and Human Health.* Washington: Resources for the Future, 1986.

Cline, William R., ed. *Trade Policy in the 1980s.* Washington: Institute for International Economics, 1983.

Committee for Economic Development. *American Workers and Economic Change: A Statement by the Research and Policy Committee of the Committee for Economic Development.* New York: CED, 1996.

———. *Non-Tariff Distortions of Trade.* Washington: CED, 1969.

Compa, Lance A., and Stephen F. Diamond. *Human Rights, Labor Rights, and International Trade* (Philadelphia: University of Pennsylvania Press, 1996).

Cregan, John P., ed. *America Asleep: The Free Trade Syndrome and The Global Economic Challenge.* Washington: United States Industrial Council Educational Foundation, 1991.

Croomme, John. *Reshaping the World Trading System: A History of the Uruguay Round.* Geneva: WTO, 1995.

Crowther, Samuel. *America Self-Contained.* New York: Doubleday, 1934.

Daly, Herman E., and John B. Cobb Jr. *For the Common Good: Redirecting the Economy Toward Community, the Environment, and a Sustainable Future.* Boston: Beacon Press, 1989.

Dawley, Alan. *Class and Community: The Industrial Revolution in Lynn.* Cambridge: Harvard University Press, 1976.

Denver Research Institute. *The Impact of EPA Administrative Practice on the Innovation Process in U.S. Companies: A Case Study of Regulatory Barriers to Innovations.* Denver: Denver Research Institute, 1976.

Derthick, Martha, and Paul J. Quirk. *The Politics of Deregulation.* Washington: Brookings Institution, 1985.

Destler, I. M. *Making Foreign Economic Policy.* Washington: Brookings Institution, 1980.

———. *American Trade Politics,* 3d ed. Washington: Institute for International Economics, 1995.

Destler, I. M., and Peter J. Balint. *The New Politics of American Trade: Trade, Labor, and the Environment.* Washington: Institute for International Economics, 1999.

Dobson, John M. *Two Centuries of Tariffs: The Background and Emergence of the U.S. International Trade Commission.* Washington: GPO, 1976.

Douglass, Frederick. *Life and Times of Frederick Douglass.* New York: Collier, 1962.

DuBois, W .E. B. *The Suppression of the African Slave-Trade to the United States of America, 1638–1870.* New York: Dover, 1970.

Dudley, William. *Trade: Opposing Viewpoints.* San Diego: Greenhaven, 1991.

Dugger, William M. *Corporate Hegemony.* New York: Greenwood Press, 1989.

Ebeling, Richard M., and Jacob G. Hornberger. *The Case for Free Trade and Open Immigration.* Fairfax: Future of Freedom Foundation, 1995.

Eckes, Alfred E. *Opening America's Market: U.S. Foreign Trade Policy Since 1776.* Chapel Hill: University of North Carolina Press, 1995.

Evans, John W. *The Kennedy Round in American Trade Policy: The Twilight of the GATT?* Cambridge: Harvard University Press, 1971.

Fallows, James. *More Like Us: Making America Great Again.* New York: Houghton Mifflin, 1989.

Frank, Dana. *Buy American: The Untold Story of Economic Nationalism.* Boston: Beacon, 1999.

Frieden, Jeffry A., and David A. Lake, eds. *International Political Economy: Perspective on Global Power and Wealth.* New York: St. Martin's, 1991.

Foner, Eric. *Free Soil, Free Labor, Free Men: The Ideology of the Republican Party Before the Civil War.* New York: Oxford University Press, 1970.

Gill, William J. *Trade Wars Against America: A History of United States Trade and Monetary Policy.* New York: Praeger, 1990.

Glennon, Michael J., Thomas M. Franck, and Robert C. Cassidy Jr. *United States Foreign Relations Law: Documents and Sources International Economic Regulation,* vol. 4. London: Oceana, 1984.

Gold, Marc, and David Leyton Brown, eds. *Trade-Offs on Free Trade: The Canada-U.S. Free Trade Agreement.* Toronto: Carswell, 1988.

Goodwyn, Lawrence. *The Democratic Promise: The Populist Movement in America.* New York: Oxford University Press, 1976.

Grabowski, H.G., and J. M. Vernon. *The Impact of Regulation on Industrial Innovation.* Washington: NAS, 1979.

Graham, Otis L. *Toward a Planned Society.* New York: Oxford University Press, 1976.
———. *One World, Ready or Not.* New York: Simon & Schuster, 1996.

Green, Mark, and Norman Waitzman. *Business War on the Law: An Anlaysis of the Benefits of Federal Health/Safety Enforcement.* Washington: Corporate Accountability Research Group, 1979.

Greider, William. *Who Will Tell the People? The Betrayal of American Democracy.* New York: Simon & Schuster, 1992.

Halberstam, David. *The Reckoning.* New York: Morrow, 1986.

Hathaway, Dale E. *Agriculture and the GATT: Rewriting the Rules.* Washington: Institute for International Economics, 1987.

Hays, Samuel P. *Beauty, Health and Permanence: Environmental Politics in the United States, 1955–1985.* Cambridge: Cambridge University Press, 1987.

Hodgson, James G. *The Reference Shelf: Economic Nationalism.* New York: H.W. Wilson, 1933.

Hudec, Robert E. *Enforcing International Trade Law: The Evolution of the Modern GATT Legal System.* Salem, NH: Butterworth, 1993.

Hughes, Kent Higgon. *Trade, Taxes, and Transnationals: International Economic Decision Making in Congress.* New York: Praeger, 1979.

Ikenberry, G. John, David A. Lake, and Michael Mastanduno. *The State and American Foreign Economic Policy.* Ithaca: Cornell University Press, 1988.

Irwin, Douglas. *Against the Tide: An Intellectual History of Free Trade.* Princeton: Princeton University Press, 1996.

Johnson, Chalmers. *MITI and the Japanese Miracle: The Growth of Industrial Policy, 1925–1975.* Stanford: Stanford University Press, 1982.

Kaplan, Edward S. *American Trade Policy, 1923–1995.* Westport: Greenwood, 1996.

Keck, Margaret E., and Kathryn Sikkink. *Activists Beyond Borders: Advocacy Networks in International Politics.* Ithaca: Cornell University Press, 1998.

Krueger, Anne O. *The WTO as an International Organization.* Chicago: University of Chicago Press, 1998.

Krugman, Paul. *Peddling Prosperity: Economic Sense and Nonsense in the Age of Diminished Expectations.* New York: Norton, 1994.

———. *Pop Internationalism.* Cambridge, MA: MIT Press, 1997.

———, ed. *Strategic Trade Policy and the New International Economics* Cambridge: MIT Press, 1986.

LaFeber, Walter. *The American Age: United States Foreign Policy at Home and Abroad Since 1750.* New York: Norton, 1989.

Lang, Tim, and Colin Hines. *The New Protectionism: Protecting the Future Against Free Trade.* New York: New Press, 1993.

Lasch, Christopher. *The Revolt of the Elites and the Betrayal of Democracy.* New York: Norton, 1994.

Lawrence, Robert Z. *Can America Compete?* Washington: Brookings Institution, 1984.

Lazarus, Simon. *The Genteel Populists.* New York: Holt, 1974.

Lee, Susan Previant, and Peter Passell. *A New Economic View of American History.* New York: Norton, 1979.

Lemco, Jonathan, and William B. P. Robson, eds. *Ties Beyond Trade: Labor and Environmental Issues Under the NAFTA.* Washington: Canadian American Committee of NPA, 1993.

Lind, Michael. *The Next American Nation: The New Nationalism and the Fourth American Revolution.* New York: Free Press, 1995.

Lindsey, Lawrence. *The Growth Experiment: How the New Tax Policy Is Transforming the U.S. Economy.* New York: Basic Books, 1990.

Lodge, George C., and Ezra F. Vogel. *Ideology and National Competitiveness: An Analysis of Nine Countries.* Boston: Harvard Business School Press, 1987.

Lovett, William A., Alfred E. Eckes Jr., and Richard L. Brinkman. *U.S. Trade Policy: History, Theory and the WTO.* Armonk, NY: M.E. Sharpe, 1999.

Low, Patrick. *Trading Free.* New York: 20th Century Fund Press, 1993.

Lustig, Nora, Barry P. Bosworth, and Robert Z. Lawrence, eds. *Assessing the Impact: North American Free Trade.* Washington: Brookings Institution, 1992.

Lusztig, Michael. *Risking Free Trade: The Politics of Trade in Britain, Canada, Mexico, and the United States.* Pittsburgh: University of Pittsburgh Press, 1996.

Masson, Francis, and H. Edward English. *Invisible Trade Barriers Between Canada and the United States.* Washington: National Planning Association and Private Planning Association of Canada, 1963.

Matusow, Allen J. *Nixon's Economy: Booms, Busts, Dollars and Votes.* Lawrence: University of Kansas Press, 1998.

McConnel, Grant. *Private Power and American Democracy.* New York: Knopf, 1967.

McCraw, Thomas K. *Prophets of Regulation: Charles Francis Adams: Louis D. Brandeis, James M. Landis, Alfred D. Kahn.* Cambridge: Belknap, 1984.

———. *Regulation in Perspective: Historical Essays.* Cambridge: Harvard University Press, 1991.

Metzger, Stanley D. *Trade Agreements and the Kennedy Round.* Fairfax: Coiner, 1964.

Nader, Ralph. *Unsafe at Any Speed.* New York: Grossman, 1965.

Nader, Ralph, Mark Green, and Joel Seligman. *Taming the Giant Corporation.* New York: Norton, 1976.

Nivola, Pietro, ed. *Comparative Disadvantages: Social Regulations and the Global Economy* (Washington: Brookings Institution, 1997).

North, Douglass C. *The Economic Growth of the United States, 1790–1860.* New York: Norton, 1966.

Norton, Mary Beth, David M. Katzman, Paul D. Escott, Howard P. Chudacoff, Thomas O. Paterson, and William M. Tuttle Jr. *A People and a Nation.* Boston: Houghton Mifflin, 1994.

Olson, Mancur. *The Rise and Decline of Nations: Economic Growth, Stagnation and Social Rigidities.* New Haven: Yale University Press, 1982.

Orme, William A. Jr. *Briefing Book: Continental Shift: Free Trade and the New North America* (Washington: Washington Post, 1993).

Paarlberg, Robert L. *Leadership Abroad Begins at Home: U.S. Foreign Economic Policy After the Cold War.* Washington: Brookings Institution, 1995.

Pastor, Robert A. *Congress and the Politics of U.S. Foreign Economic Policy.* Berkeley: University of California Press, 1980.

Perot, Ross (with Pat Choate). *Save Your Job, Save Our Country: Why NAFTA Must Be Stopped—Now!* New York: Hyperion for United We Stand America, 1993.

Pertschuk, Michael. *Revolt Against Regulation: The Rise and Pause of the Consumer Movement.* Berkeley: University of California Press, 1982.

Phillips, Kevin. *Arrogant Capital: Washington, Wall Street and the Frustration of American Politics.* Boston: Little, Brown, 1994.

Preeg, Ernest H. *Traders in a Brave New World.* Chicago: University of Chicago Press, 1995.

Prestowitz, Clyde V. Jr. *Trading Places: How We Allowed Japan to Take the Lead.* New York: Basic Books, 1988.

Raner, Sidney. *The Tariff in American History.* New York: Van Nostrand, 1972.

Reich, Robert B. *The Work of Nations: Preparing Ourselves for 21st Century Capitalism.* New York: Vintage Press, 1992.

Roett, Rhiordan, ed. *Mexico and the United States: Managing the Relationship.* Boulder: Westview, 1988.

Ross, Robert J. S., and Kent C. Trachte. *Global Capitalism: The New Leviathan.* Albany: State University of New York Press, 1990.

Sanderson, Fred, ed. *Agricultural Protectionism in the Industrialized World.* Washington: Resources for the Future, 1990.

Schattsschneider, E. E. *Politics, Pressures and the Tariff: A Study of Free Private Enterprise in Pressure Politics, as Shown in the 1929–1930 Revision of the Tariff.* New York: Prentice Hall, 1935.

Schott, Jeffrey J. *The World Trading System: Challenges Ahead.* Washington: Institute for International Economics, 1996.

Schwab, Susan C. *Trade-Offs: Negotiating the Omnibus Trade and Competitiveness Act.* Cambridge: Harvard Business School Press, 1986.

Scott, Bruce R., and George C. Lodge. *U.S. Competitiveness in the World Economy.* Cambridge: Harvard Business School Press, 1985.

Servan-Schreiber, Jean Jacques. *The American Challenge.* New York: Atheneum, 1968.

Sheehan, James M. *Global Greens: Inside the International Environmental Establishment.* Washington: Capital Research, 1998.

Silk, Leonard, and Mark Silk, eds. *Making Capitalism Work.* New York: New York University Press, 1997.

Sklar, Martin J. *The Corporate Reconstruction of American Capitalism, 1890–1916, the Market, the Law, and Politics.* New York: Cambridge University Press, 1988.

Skocpol, Theda. *Protecting Soldiers and Mothers: The Political Origins of Social Policy in the United States.* Cambridge: Belknap, 1992.

Smith, Jackie, Charles Chatfield, and Ron Pagnucco. *Transnational Social Movements and Global Politics: Solidarity Beyond the State.* Syracuse: Syracuse University Press, 1997.

Stanwood, Edward. *American Tariff Controversies.* New York: Houghton Mifflin, 1903.

Stein, Herbert. *The Fiscal Revolution in America.* Washington: AEI, 1996.

Stern, Paula. *Water's Edge: Domestic Politics and the Making of American Foreign Policy.* Westport, CT: Greenwood Press, 1979.

Strasser, Susan. *Satisfaction Guaranteed.* New York: Pantheon, 1989.

Taussig, Frank W. *Tariff History of the United States.* New York: Putnam, 1913.

Terrill, Tom E. *The Tariff, Politics and American Foreign Policy, 1874–1901.* Westport: Greenwood Press, 1973.

Trachtenberg, Alan. *The Incorporation of America: Culture and Society in the Gilded Age.* New York: Hill & Wang, 1982.

Twiggs, Joan E. *The Tokyo Round of Multilateral Trade Negotiations: A Case Study in Building Domestic Support for Diplomacy.* Lanham, MD: University Press, 1987.

Vig, Norman J., and Michael E. Kraft. *Environmental Policy in the 1980s: Reagan's New Agenda.* Washington: Congressional Quarterly, 1984.

Vogel, David. *Lobbying the Corporation: Citizen Challenges to Business Authority.* New York: Basic Books, 1978.

———. *Trading Up: Consumer and Environmental Regulation in a Global Economy.* Cambridge, MA: Harvard University Press, 1997.

Von Wolferen, Karel. *The Enigma of Japanese Powers: People and Politics in a Stateless Nation.* London: Macmillan, 1989.

Wapner, Paul. *Environmental Activism and World Civic Politics.* Albany: State University of New York, 1996.

Waverman, Leonard, ed. *Negotiating and Implementing a North American Free Trade Agreement.* Toronto: Fraser Institute, 1992.

Weidenbaum, Murry L. *Business, Government, and the Public.* Englewood Cliffs: Prentice Hall, 1990.

Wellford, Harrison. *Sowing the Wind: A Report from Ralph Nader's Center for Study of Responsive Law on Food Safety and the Chemical Harvest.* New York: Grossman, 1972.

Wiebe, Robert H. *Businessmen and Reform: A Study of the Progressive Movement.* Cambridge: Harvard University Press, 1962.

Wiltse, Charles M. *The New Nation: 1800–1845.* New York: Hill & Wang, 1961.

Yergin, Daniel, and Joseph Stanislaw. *The Commanding Heights: The Battle Between Government and the Marketplace That Is Remaking the Modern World.* New York: Simon & Schuster, 1998.

Young, James Harvey. *Pure Food: Securing the Federal Food and Drugs Act of 1906.* Princeton: Princeton University Press, 1989.

Zaelke, Durwood, Robert F. Housman, and Paul Orbach. *Trade and the Environment: Law, Economics and Policy.* San Francisco: Island Press, 1993.

Zeiler, Thomas W. *American Trade & Power in the 1960s.* New York: Columbia University Press, 1992.

Journals/Articles

Aaronson, Susan Ariel. "Circle the Wagons: Pat Buchanan's Illogical Campaign to Protect America from the Foreign Hordes." *New Democrat* (July/August 1998): 21–23.

Allen, Terry. "In GATT They Trust." *Covert Action* 40 (spring 1992): 60–65.

Bluestone, Barry, and Rose Stephen. "Unraveling an Economic Enigma: Overworked and Underemployed." *The American Prospect* 31 (March/April, 1997): 58–69.

Brander, James, and Barbara Spencer. "Export Subsidies and International Market Share Rivalry." *Journal of International Economics* 18, no. 1–2 (February): 85–100.

Charnovitz, Steve. "Strengthening the International Employment Regime." *Intereconomics* 30 (September/October 1995): 221–23.

Charnovitz, Steve. "Environmental and Labour Standards in Trade." *World Economy,* 15 no. 3 (May 1992): 335–56.

———. "Promoting Labor Standards." *Washington Quarterly* (summer 1995): 167–90.

———. "The Moral Exception in Trade Policy." *Virginia Journal of International Law* 38, no. 4 (summer 1998): 689–745.

Cohen, Naomi W. "The Abrogation of the Russo-American Treaty of 1832." *Jewish Social Studies* 25, no. 1 (January 1963): 3–41.

Faux, Jeff, and Thea Lee. "The Effect of George Bush's NAFTA on American Workers: Ladder Up or Ladder Down?" Economic Policy Institute, 1992.

Gignilliat, John L. "Pigs, Politics and Protection: The European Boycott if American Pork, 1879–1891." *Agricultural History* 35, no. 1 (January 1961): 3.

Goldsmith, Sir James. "Global Free Trade and GATT." Excerpt from *Le Piege,* 1994.

Hoberg, George. "Sleeping with an Elephant: The American Influence on Canadian Environmental Regulation." *Journal of Public Policy* 1, no. 2 (January/March 1991): 107–32.

Kramer, Carol S. "Implications of the Hormone Controversy for International Food Safety Standards." *Resources* (fall 1991): 12–14.

Krugman, Paul. "The Accidental Theorist," on the Internet, *Slate* week of 2/24/1997.

Lind, Michael. "Spheres of Affluence," *American Prospect* (winter 1994): 91–99.

Lively, Robert M. "The American System: A Review Article." *Business History Review* 19 (March 1955): 81–96.

Masahiro, Sakamoto et al. "The Policy Recommendations on the WTO System and Japan." Tokyo: Japan Forum on International Relations, 1996.

McGrath, Deidre. "Writing Differ Lyrics to the Same Old Tune: The New and Improved 1997 Amendments to the Marine Mammal Protection Act," *Minnesota Journal of Global Trade* 7 (Spring 1999): 404–60

Ritchie, Mark. "The Loss of Our Family Farms: Inevitable Results or Conscious Policies?" Minneapolis: League of Rural Voters, 1979.

———. "Global Agricultural Trade Negotiations and Their Potential Impact on Minnesota." *Journal of the Minnesota Academy of Science* 54 (November 1989): 4–8.

Ruggie, Gerard. "Trade, Protectionism and the Future of Welfare Capitalism." *Journal of International Affairs* 1 (summer 1994): 1–11.

Snyder, Louis L. "The American-German Port Dispute, 1879–1891." *Journal of Modern History* 17, no. 1 (March 1945): 16–28.

Spar, Deborah. "Trade, Investment and Labor: The Case of Indonesia." *Columbia Journal of World Business* 31, no. 4 (winter 1996): 31–39.

Swinnerton, Kenneth A. "An Essay on Economic Efficiency and Core Labor Standards." Draft, September 1996.

Tonelson, Alan. "What Is the National Interest?" *The Atlantic* 268, no. 1 (July 1991): 39.

———. "Beating Back Predatory Trade." *Foreign Affairs* (July/August 1994): 60–61.

———. "Beyond Left and Right." *National Interest,* no. 1 (winter 1993/1994): 39.

———. "The Perils of Techno-Globalism." *Issues in Science and Technology* (summer 1995): 1–8.

Viner, Jacob. "Conflicts of Principle in Drafting a Trade Charter." *Foreign Affairs* 25, no. 2 (January 1947).

Whitcomb, Ian. "Confessions of a British Invader." *American Heritage* 48, no. 8 (December 1997): 68–86.

Wirth, David A. "International Trade Agreements: Vehicles for Regulatory Reform?" *Chicago Legal Forum* (1997): 331–73.

Witkowski, Terrence H. "Colonial Consumers in Revolt: Buyer Values and Behavior During the Nonimportation Movement, 1764–1776." *Journal of Consumer Research* 16 (September 1989): 216–26.

Yankelovich, Daniel. "Foreign Policy After the Election." *Foreign Affairs* (fall 1992): 2–12.

Working Papers, Monographs, and Pamphlets

Avery, Natalie, Martine Drake, and Tim Lang. *Cracking the Codex: An Analysis of Who Sets World Food Standards.* London: National Food Alliance, 1993.

Bairock, Paul, and Richard Kozul-Wright. "Globalization Myths: Some Historical Reflections On Integration, Industrialization and Growth in the World Economy." No. 113, UNCTAD, March 1996.

Baldwin, Robert. "The New Protectionism: A Response to Shifts in National Economic Power." NBER Working Paper No. 1823.

Bergsten, C. Fred. "Competitive Liberalization and Global Free Trade: A Vision for the Early 21st Century." Institute for International Economics, #96–15.

Business-Higher Education Forum. "Statement on Federal Regulatory Reform." February 1981.

Canadian Labour Congress. "Manufacturing Jobs Vulnerable to Relocation Under NAFTA." June 1993.

Citizens Trade Campaign. "GATT Media Packet—The World Trade Organization's National Policy Prerogatives." June 1994.

Council on U.S. International Trade Policy. "Agriculture and International Trade." The Council on U.S. International Trade Policy, February 1988.

Development GAP (Group for Alternative Policies). "Look Before You Leap: What You Should Know About a North American Free Trade Agreement." Washington: Development GAP, 1991.

Green Party. "Act Local, Act Global: Greening the European Union—A Challenge to Globalization," by Colin Hines.

International Summit of Agricultural Producers Concerned with GATT. "Strengthening the Agricultural Trade Disciplines of the General Agreement on Tariffs and Trade." 12/2/1987.

Lindsey, Brink, and Aaron Lukas. "Revisiting the 'Revisionists': The Rise and Fall of the Japanese Economic Model: CATO Trade Policy Analysis." 7/3/1998, no. 3.

Remarks of Ralph Nader, International Organization of Consumers Union., 7/8/1991.

Ritchie, Mark. "Trading Away Our Environment." 5/1990.

Rodrik, Dani. "Why Do More Open Economies Have Bigger Governments?" NBER Working Paper No. 5537.

Shrybman, Steven. "Selling Canada's Environment Short: The Environmental Case Against the Trade Deal."

Tanzi, Vito, and Ludger Schuknecht. "The Growth of Government and the Reform of the State in Industrial Countries." *IMF Working Papers,* December 1995, WP/95/130.

Wallach, Lori, and Tom Hilliard. "The Consumer and Environmental Case Against Fast-Track." Public Citizen's Congress Watch, 5/1991.

White, Bob. Canadian Labor Congress, "NAFTA Side-Deal Changes Nothing for Workers," 8/25/1993.

Williamson, Jeffrey G. "Globalization and Inequality Then and Now: The Late 19th and Late 20th Centuries Compared." NBER Working Paper No. 5491.

Conference Proceedings

Allen, Kristen, and Katie Macmillan, eds. *U.S. Canadian Agricultural Trade Challenges: Developing Common Approaches.* Washington: Resources for the Future, 1998.

Council on Competitiveness. "Restoring America's Trade Position." Policy statement, April 1987, 12.

Rubber Manufacturers Association. "Pros and Cons of the ITO." 1/10/1950.

Unpublished Papers and Dissertations

Aaronson, Susan Ariel. "Competitiveness Study for LTV Corporation." 5/20/1987.

Cavanagh, John, Sarah Anderson, and Karen Hansen Kuhn. "Tri-national Organizing for Just and Sustainable Trade and Development: Some Lessons and Insights." 9/27/1998.

Harvey, Pharis. "Overview: U.S. Laws Linking Labor Rights and Trade." LASA Conference, 3/11/1994.

Jackson, Andrew, and Bob Baldwin. "Lessons of Free Trade: A View from Canadian Labour." n.d.

Vear, Charles William. "Organized Labor and the Tariff." Ph.D. diss., Fletcher School of Law and Diplomacy, 10/1955.

Web Sites

Government Web Sites

www.ustr.gov
www.itc.gov
www.wto.org

Trade Critics Web Sites

www.citizen.org/gtw: Global Trade Watch/Public Citizen
www.tradewatch.org
www.nlcnet.org
www.oneworld.org/ni: The New Internationalist Magazine
www. compugraph.com/clr
www.ref.usc.edu/~tbelt/web/nader/nader.html
www.autosafety.org
www.mojones.com/election_96/nade.html
ic.net/~harvey/greens/rn-epr.txt
www.theamericancause.org (Pat Buchanan web site)
www.basenet/~eagle
www.canadians.org/
www.summersault.com/ (Campaign for Labor Rights)
www.iatp.org (food safety and environment)

Polls

Clements, Mark. "What Worries Voters Most." *Parade,* 3 May 1992, 4–6.

Gallup, Dr. George H. *The Gallup Poll: Public Opinion 1972–1977.* Wilmington: Scholarly Resources, 1978.

Gallup Poll News Service. "Week in Review: Perot Ties Bush in Gallup Poll." 5/24/1992.

Immerwahr, John, Jean Johnson, and Adam Kernan-Schloss. "Cross-Talk: The Public, the Experts, and Competitiveness: A Research Report from the Business-Higher Education Forum and the Public Agenda Foundation." Washington, D.C., 1991.

Roper Center. University of Connecticut Public Opinion Online. Reviewed 1960–1998.

Teixeira, Ruy. "Living Standards as a Values Issue." 2/12/1997 draft lent to author.

Times Mirror Center for the People and the Press. "The Vocal Minority in American Politics." 7/13/1993. (This is especially good on talk radio.)

Newsletters

Campaign for Labor Rights
Inside U.S. Trade
WTO/OMC Focus
IATP/BRIDGES
NAFTATHOUGHTS

Interviews

On Food Safety or Agricultural Negotiations

Kevin J. Brosch, Attorney, U.S. Department of Agriculture, Office of the General Counsel, 9/2/1998.

Jake Caldwell and Rod Leonard, Community Nutrition Institute, 11/26/1997 and 12/9/1997.

Gary Blumenthal and Carol Brookins, World Perspectives, Inc., 1/9/1998.

Bobbi Dresser, Assistant Director, International Affairs, FDA, 9/16/1998.

Suzanne Early, Assistant USTR for Agriculture, 9/6/1998.

Dan McGraw, director of International Affairs, EPA, 8/25/1998.

Donna Vogt, Congressional Research Service, 7/31/1998.

Jennifer Haverkamp, Assistant USTR for Trade and the Environment, 7/31/1998.

Laura Kneale Anderson, Director for Trade and the Environment, USTR, 8/4/1998.

On Labor Standards

Tim Bissell, National Coordinator, Campaign for Labor Rights, 12/2/1997.

Brad Feigel, NIKE, Director of Government Affairs and International Trade Counsel, 12/15/1997. (Also formerly Chief Counsel, International Trade, Senate Finance under Senator Robert Packwood)

Pharis Harvey, Executive Director International Labor Rights Fund, 5/6/1997.

Jon Rosenbaum, USTR, 9/18/1998.

Ellen Frost, Former Counselor to the USTR under Mickey Kantor, 9/30/1998.

On Protectionist Impact on Capitol Hill

Steve Charnovitz, now of Wilmer, Cutler, then Research Director, Competitiveness Policy Council, 8/2/1994.

Kent Higgons Hughes, Associate Deputy Secretary, Department of Commerce, on Burke Hartke, 2/13/1998.

Debbie Lamb, Chief Counsel, Senate Finance Committee, series of interviews, 1996–1998.
Mary Jane Wignot, Trade Negotiator 1964–1974; Deomcrats on House Ways and Means, 1/6/1998.
Amelia Porges, USTR, series of interviews, May–December 1997.
Ray Ahearn, Congressional Research Service (a congressional agency, 7/29/1998).
Bill Cooper, Congressional Research Service, 7/31/1998.

On the Evolution of Trade Agreement Critics and Protectionism in the United States

Sara Anderson, Institute for Policy Studies, 9/17/1998.
Dr. Brent Balckwelder, President, Friends of the Earth, 9/3/1998.
Devin Burgharter, on the militia movement, Pat Buchanan, and trade critics, 7/13/1998.
John Cavanagh, Institute for Policy Studies, series of interviews in 1995, 1996.
Steven Charnovitz, former Research Director, Competitiveness Policy Council, 8/2/1994.
Nancy Dunne, trade correspondent, *The London Financial Times,* series of interviews 1997–1998.
Dan Esty, Yale Law School, 11/18/1998.
John Judis, *The New Republic,* 5/19/1998.
Bill Goold, Chief of Staff, Congressman Bernie Sanders, 9/19/1997.
William Greider, National Correspondent, *Rolling Stone,* 6/20/1997.
Karen Hansen Kuhn, Latin American Program Coordinator, The Development GAP, 8/31/1998.
Stewart Hudson, formerly National Wildlife Fund, now Jane Goodall Institute, 10/22/1998.
Jules Katz, Deputy USTR under Carla Hills, 2/12/1998.
Jerome Levinson, Professor, Washington College of Law, 7/2/1996.
Victor Mennoti, International Forum on Globalization, 8/25/1998.
Mark Ritchie, President, Institute for Agriculture and Trade Policy, 4/17/1996, 3/23/1998, 10/13/1998; and series of interviews/E-mails throughout 1997–1998.
David Schorr, World Wildlife Fund (WWF) 11/18/1998 and 12/1/1998.
Alan Tonelson, U.S. Business and Industrial Council, 3/28/1997.
Justin Ward, NRDC (Natural Resources Defense Council), 11/18/1998.
Edie Wilson, Progressive Policy Institute, 1/14/1998.

On Economic Nationalism
John (Jock) Nash, Milliken and Company, 5/20/1998.

On Nationalist/Internationalist
Lori Wallach, Director, Global Trade Watch, 3/14/1995, 3/21/1995, and 4/5/1995; 7/2/1998; and 4/9/1999.

On the Advisory Committee Process and Trade Negotiations
Fred Montgomery, Assistant USTR for Policy, 9/10–11/1998.
Catherine Fields, Office of the General Counsel, USTR, 5/1/1994.

Regarding Canada

Steven Shrybman, Canadian Environmental Law Institute, 8/22/1998.
Daniel Schwanen, Senior Policy Analyst, C.D. Howe Institute, 6/9/1997.
Bruce Campbell, Canadian Centre for Policy Alternatives, 9/16/1998.
Sheila Katz, Canadian Labour Congress, 9/11/1998.

In England, on European Trade Critics

Guy de Jonquires, *London Financial Times,* 9/11/1998.
Colin Hines, independent author and Green Party, 9/23/1998.
Professor Tim Lang, Centre for Food Policy, Thames Valley University, 9/25/1998.
Kevin Watkins, Oxfam, 9/24/1998.
Leslie Sklair, London School of Economics, 9/25/1998.
James Cameron, Director, Foundation for International Environmental Law and Development (FIELD), 9/24/1998.

In Geneva

Andrew Crosby, Programmes Director, International Center for Trade and Sustainable Development (ICTSD), 5/27/1999.
Ricardo Melendez, Director, ICTSD, 5/27/1999.

In the Netherlands

Myriam Vander Stichele, SOMO (Centre for Research on Multinational Corporations), 5/29/1999.
Sabina Voogd, Environment and Trade, Greenpeace, 5/29/1999.

In Australia

Kate Gilmore, National Director, Amnesty International Australia, 6/16/1997.
Judy Henderson, Oxfam International, 6/16/1997.
Phyllis Campbell, Greenpeace, 6/16/1997.
Liam Phelen, Aidwatch, 6/16/1997.
Andre Fankovits, Human Rights Council of Australia, 6/16/1997.
Chris Sidoti, Human Rights Commissioner, 6/16/1998.

At the WTO

Mireille Cossy, Legal Affairs, Trade and Environment, WTO, 5/27/1999.
Richard Eglin, Director, WTO, 5/27/1999.
Alain Frank, Director, External Relations, WTO, 5/26/1999.
Keith Rockwell, Director, Public Affairs, WTO, 5/26/1999.
Gretchen Stanton, TBT/SPSS negotiator, 10/7/1998.

From the WTO

Tran Van Tinh, EU negotiator to the WTO, 10/16/1998.

Index

League of Nations, 45
Left-right coalition, of trade critics, 4–7, 109, 127, 179–80
Left wing: on economic internationalism, 108–9; movement away from internationalism, 106–9; trade agreement critics of, 177. *See also* Conservatives
Legislators. *See* Congress; *specific individuals*
Lend-lease agreements, 52, 183
Leonard, Rod, 149, 158–59, 177
Liberalization of trade, 56, 87, 100
Lind, Michael, 108, 166–67
Lipsey, Richard G., 114
Lobby: for competitiveness, 105; for protectionism, 42–43
Long, Jill, 167
Luc, Jean Marc, 160
Lyng, Richard, 149

Madison, James, 33
Mander, Jerry, 173
Manufacturing, 39, 48, 97–98; tariffs and, 34
Marine Mammal Protection Act (MMPA), 19–21
Markets: for agricultural products, 40–41; imports share of (1970), 73; tariff reform and, 50
Mason, George, 32
Matsui, Robert, 139
McKinley, William, 42, 47
Meany, George, 82, 180
Meat Inspection Act, 46
Mercantilism, 11
Merilees, Craig, 125
Mexican Network Against Free Trade, 127
Mexico: benefits of NAFTA negotiations, 127–28; corruption in, 119; fishing rights and, 19, 21; food safety standards and, 81; internationalism and, 178–79; NAFTA and, 3, 110–11, 116, 133; trade agreement with, 36. *See also* North American Free Trade Agreement (NAFTA)
Middle East, 75–76

Milliken, Roger, 5
Milliken and Company, 197 n105
Mills, Wilbur, 75
Minorities, trade and, 108
MODTLE (Mobilization on Development, Trade, Labor and the Environment), 124–25, 126, 127, 128, 161
Monetary system, 70. *See also* Bretton Woods; Dollar
Montreal Charter, 148
Moore, Michael, 2
Most favored nation status, 15
Motor Vehicle Manufacturers Association, 88
Multilateralism, 56, 100

Nader, Ralph, 4, 5, 13, 23, 58, 171, 179, 180, 186; food safety and, 146, 160; FTA and, 115; NAFTA and, 120–23; safety standards and, 63; tactics of, 69; trade activism of, 120–23; on trade and trade agreements, 121; *Unsafe at Any Speed* and, 58, 62; Web sites of, 203 n2
NAFTA. *See* North American Free Trade Agreement (NAFTA)
National Environmental Policy Act, 130
National Foreign Trade Council, 88
National governments, trade agreements as threats to, 3–4
Nationalism, 177; economic, 11–12, 56, 86, 93, 106; militance in, 166–67. *See also* Protectionism; *specific individuals*
National Toxics Campaign Fund, 152, 156
National treatment principle, 15
Neoclassical trade theory, 96
Nestlé; company, boycott of, 147
"New protectionists," 6
NGOs. *See* Nongovernmental organizations (NGOs)
Nixon, Richard, 184; dollar devaluation and, 73; inflation and, 74–75; labor and, 68; trade and, 75–79, 82; Williams Commission of, 71–72
Nongovernmental organizations (NGOs), 23, 31, 54; agricultural policy and, 148–49; international business

Trade (GATT); Nationalism; North
American Free Trade Agreement
(NAFTA); Protectionism; Protests;
Tokyo Round; Uruguay Round; World
Trade Organization (WTO)
Trade Agreements Act: of 1934, 26; of
1979, 90
Trade barriers. *See* Nontariff trade barri-
ers (NTBs); Protectionism; Regulation
Trade deficit, 73, 92, 98, 211 n29
Trade Expansion Act, 54
Trade policy: Congress and, 18–19, 66;
executive branch and, 51; free
trade/protectionist dialectic and, 9–11;
GATT and, 16–17; history in U.S., 2,
26–27; impact of critics on, 25–26; in
interwar period, 48; protests against, 1,
2, 3, 4. *See also* Congress; President
Trade regulation: and social regulation,
15–18; trade distortions through,
16–17, 175. *See also* Regulation
Traders, unfair. *See* Unfair traders
Trade sanctions, U.S. values and, 82
Trade surplus, 61
Trade talks: GATT-sponsored, 54. *See
also specific talks*
Trade wars, 19, 93
Trading partners, NTBs used by, 66
Traffic Safety Act (1966), 63
Tran Van Thinh, 148
Treaties: reciprocity, 46–47. *See also
specific treaties*
Truman, Harry S., 183
Tuna, dolphin protection and, 19–21,
122, 128
Tyson, Laura, 96

Ullman, Al, 76
Underwood Tariff, 47
Unfair traders, 10, 101; defined, xix. *See
also* Fair trade
Unilateral policy, 86
Unions: Canadian, 111–12; NAFTA and,
119, 137; Standards Code and, 89; Trade
Act of 1974 and, 81; trade policy and,
78. *See also* Labor
United Nations, hazardous materials
trade and, 107

United States: politics of trade in,
179–80; products of, 55; Standards
Code and, 88–89, 90; world status of,
91
U.S. Business and Industrial Council
(USBIC), 167
U.S./Canada Free Trade Agreement
(FTA), 27; Canada and, 110–16,
129–30
United States International Trade
Commission (ITC), 90
United We Stand, 136
Unsafe at Any Speed (Nader), 58, 62
Uruguay Round, 2, 3, 18, 28, 118, 119,
142, 158; agricultural and environmen-
tal safety standards under, 21–22,
142–63; Clinton and, 163–66; congres-
sional hearings on, 167–73; interna-
tional controversy over, 172; right-wing
critics of, 166–72. *See also* Food safety
standards; GATT/WTO system;
General Agreement on Tariffs and
Trade (GATT)
Uruguay Round Implementing Act, 172
USBIC. *See* U.S. Business and Industrial
Council (USBIC)
USTR. *See* Office of the United States
Trade Representative (USTR)

Vanik, Charles A., 69, 76, 77–78. *See
also* Jackson-Vanik amendment
Versailles Treaty, 44, 45
Viner, Jacob, 56
Vogel, David, 7, 176, 181

Waldman, Michael, 133
Wallach, Lori, 6, 120, 121, 122, 125, 139,
159, 171, 172, 173
Warnick, Bruce, 171
War of 1812, 34
Watergate scandal, Nixon trade policy
and, 75–76
Watkins, Kevin, 147
Waxman, Henry, 125
Wealth, mercantilism and, 11
Web sites, on trade policy-making, 176
Webster, Daniel, 37
Webster, Noah, 33